PANDEMIC COMMUNICATION

This book details how the processes of communication are affected by the presence of a pandemic and establishes a research agenda for those effects across the broad field of communication studies.

Through contributions from experts in communication subdisciplines such as crisis, organizational, interpersonal, health, intergroup, and intercultural, this book provides the reader with a comprehensive view of the emerging field of study "pandemic communication." Each chapter has four primary objectives to: (1) define critical issues for pandemic communication from its subdiscipline's perspective, (2) examine how communication varies during pandemic(s), (3) provide examples of how pandemic(s) have affected communication, and (4) propose a research agenda to build pandemic communication theory.

This book is suited to undergraduate or post-graduate courses or modules in communication studies across a variety of subdisciplines as well as a reference for researchers in the subject.

Stephen M. Croucher is Professor and Head of School in the School of Communication, Journalism and Marketing at Massey University, New Zealand.

Audra Diers-Lawson is Associate Professor in the School of Communication, Leadership, and Marketing at Kristiania University College, Norway.

PANDEMIC COMMUNICATION

Edited by
Stephen M. Croucher and
Audra Diers-Lawson

Routledge
Taylor & Francis Group

NEW YORK AND LONDON

Cover credit: © Getty Images

First published 2023
by Routledge
605 Third Avenue, New York, NY 10158

and by Routledge
4 Park Square, Milton Park, Abingdon, Oxon, OX14 4RN

Routledge is an imprint of the Taylor & Francis Group, an informa business

ISBN: 978-1-032-10264-1 (hbk)
ISBN: 978-1-032-07543-3 (pbk)
ISBN: 978-1-003-21449-6 (ebk)

DOI: 10.4324/9781003214496

Typeset in Bembo
by codeMantra

CONTENTS

FIGURES

TABLES

CONTRIBUTORS

Viktoria Adler is Senior Researcher at SYNYO Research, Austria.

Doug Ashwell is Senior Lecturer in School of Communication, Journalism and Marketing at Massey University, New Zealand.

Benjamin R. Bates is Barbara Geralds Schoonover Professor of Health Communication at School of Communication Studies, Ohio University, USA.

Diotima Bertel is Senior Researcher at SYNYO Research; Scientist, Austrian Institute of Technology, Austria.

Sandra Bustamante is Instructor at Universidad San Ignacio de Loyola, Peru.

Sofia E. Salazar Carballo is Graduate Teaching Associate in the Nicholson School of Communication and Media at the University of Central Florida, USA.

Stephen M. Croucher is Professor and Head of School of Communication, Journalism and Marketing at Massey University, New Zealand.

Joanna Cullinane is Deputy Pro Vice-Chancellor in Massey Business School at Massey University, New Zealand.

Audra Diers-Lawson is Associate Professor in the School of Communication, Leadership and Marketing at Kristiania University, Norway.

Mohan Dutta is Professor and Dean's Chair in the School of Communication, Journalism and Marketing at Massey University, New Zealand.

George Guoyu Ding is Assistant Lecturer in the School of Communication, Journalism and Marketing at Massey University, New Zealand.

Jason A. Edwards is Professor and Chair of the Department of Communication Studies at Bridgewater State University, USA.

Nadira Eskiçorapçı is Professor at the Department of Public Relations and Publicity, Yeditepe University, Turkey.

Davide Girardelli is Senior Lecturer at the Department of Applied IT, University of Gothenburg, Sweden.

Marina Ghersetti is Professor at the Department of Journalism Media and Communication, University of Gothenburg, Sweden.

Oscar Gomez is associated with West Michigan Academy of Environmental Sciences, MI, USA.

Bengt Johansson is Professor at the Department of Journalism Media and Communication, University of Gothenburg, Sweden.

Stephanie Kelly is Professor at the Department of Business Information Systems and Analytics, North Carolina A&T State University, USA.

Abbey Blake Levenshus is Associate Professor at Strategic Communication, Butler University, USA.

Brooke Fisher Liu is Professor at the Department of Communication, University of Maryland, USA.

Irina S. Morozova is Associate Professor at the Faculty of Computer Science, Economics and Social Sciences, National Research University, Higher School of Economics, Russia.

Nicola Murray is Senior Lecturer in the School of Communication, Journalism and Marketing at Massey University, New Zealand.

Thao Nguyen is Assistant Lecturer in the School of Communication, Journalism and Marketing at Massey University, New Zealand.

Tatiana M. Permyakova is Professor at the Faculty of Computer Science, Economics and Social Sciences, National Research University, Higher School of Economics, Russia.

Kenneth T. Rocker is Assistant Lecturer in the School of Communication, Journalism and Marketing at Massey University, New Zealand.

Matthew W. Seeger is Professor of Communication at the Department of Communication, Wayne State University, USA.

Henry S. Seeger is Post-doctoral Fellow at the Center for the Environment, Purdue University, USA.

Deanna D. Sellnow is Professor of Communication at the Nicholson School of Communication and Media, University of Central Florida, USA.

Timothy L. Sellnow is Pegasus Professor and Associate Director of Graduate Studies, Research and Creative Activity in the Nicholson School of Communication and Media at the University of Central Florida, USA.

Elena A. Smolianina is Lecturer at Foreign Languages National Research University, Higher School of Economics, Russia.

Anthony Spencer is Assistant Professor at School of Communications, Grand Valley State University, USA.

Maureen Taylor is Professor of Strategic Communication in the School of Communication, Arts and Social Sciences at the University of Technology Sydney, Australia.

Elira Turdubaeva is Professor at Online University, Kyrgyzstan.

Orla Vigsø is Professor at Journalism Media and Communication, University of Gothenburg, Sweden.

1

AN INTRODUCTION TO PANDEMIC COMMUNICATION

Stephen M. Croucher and Audra Diers-Lawson

An Introduction to Pandemic Communication

The COVID-19 pandemic is one of the greatest economic, political, social, mediated, and medical/health events in history. Since the start of the pandemic in November 2019, there have been more than 585 million confirmed cases, and more than 6.4 million deaths globally as of August 2022 (Johns Hopkins Coronavirus Resource Center, updated daily). During the pandemic, among many things, billions of people went into isolation as borders were closed; economies were strained (many are still not fully recovered); medical services have been put under immense pressure; increased attention has been put on the role of communication/digital media; and rapid initiatives were put in place to produce vaccines. Throughout the pandemic and then as the vaccine rollout commenced, the importance of communication during the pandemic became increasingly evident.

A Google Scholar search of the phrase 'COVID-19 and communication' showed more than 3.1 million results in August 2022, showing the scholarly significance of communication and the COVID-19 pandemic. There have been numerous calls for papers for conferences and special issues of many journals exploring the links between communication and the pandemic. In addition, various academic books have been published recently examining the links between communication and the COVID-19 pandemic (Koley & Dhole, 2021; Lewis et al., 2021; Lilleker et al., 2021; Lupton & Willis, 2021; O'Hair & O'Hair, 2021; Pollock & Vakoch, 2021; Price & Harbisher, 2021; Ryan, 2021). Each of these books, and countless journal publications and chapters have shed light on how communication facilitates understanding and impacts our understanding of the pandemic world.

DOI: 10.4324/9781003214496-1

The importance of communication in pandemics has not always been so explicitly stated. Academic research about pandemics has typically been discussed piecemeal, often as case studies applying traditional theories of communication to them to identify best practices to mitigate risk, share information, manage disinformation, or provide instructions to the public for protective behaviors. However, the MERS (Jang & Park, 2018; Lee & Jung, 2019; Yoo et al., 2016), SARS (Head et al., 2020; Lee, 2009; Ma, 2005), and Ebola pandemics (Guidry et al., 2017; Ratzan & Moritsugu, 2014; Toppenberg-Pejcic et al., 2019) offered clear and deadly evidence that piecemeal approaches to communication cost lives. Moreover, the fields of crisis and disaster communication have provided more than 20 years of evidence that the 'crisis context' is unique and that communication needs are fundamentally different compared to non-crisis contexts. Yet the lessons learned from research and practice during pandemics also suggest that while the pandemic context shares some common elements to crisis and disaster communication, it is also unique. As such, the COVID-19 pandemic has revealed that existing theories, models, and constructs may not adequately capture the relationship between a pandemic and communication processes.

Broadly, each of the chapters in this book on 'Pandemic Communication' addresses four questions that help define 'Pandemic Communication' as a distinctive sub-discipline of communication studies.

1   What has changed? Since the start of the COVID-19 pandemic, we cannot expect attitudes about politics, economics, health, work, organizations, interpersonal relationships, and other facets of life to be the same. The challenges these chapters have identified are that our perspectives on the world around us have changed. Are these changes short term or long term?

2   Do these changes fundamentally change our theorizing? If our perspectives on the world around us have changed, to what extent do these changes influence our existing theories? Croucher and colleagues have proposed that the presence of COVID-19 creates a contagion effect. When faced with fears such as that of a global pandemic/virus, individuals may be unable to separate their fear from communicative responses. Thus, our theorizing may need to be reconceptualized, taking into consideration our fight versus flight response (Izard, 1991).

3   How can we adequately reflect the global nature of the pandemic? Across the chapters, there is an acknowledgment that the research is often too US, Western, and North centric. While the volume actively incorporates research and considerations from around the globe, our authors still had to be conscious of perspective and voice across the chapters. Yet, one of the valuable aspects of this book is that we see the emergence of more genuinely cross-national, international, and cross-cultural perspectives, which represents the way forward in pandemic communication.

4   Finally, how can academic research balance the need for information
    with the rigors of the scientific process? Several chapters have pointed out
    that applied research needs to get to decision-makers and practitioners to
    inform policy and practice. However, there are two central challenges:
    (1) translating the science – especially in a rapidly changing context – can
    be difficult and (2) the rush to publish and be 'relevant' may also contrib-
    ute to the challenges of communicating in a pandemic. The uncertainty
    produced by the context means that while people may want certainty,
    certainty cannot be produced quickly. This represents a 'reputational'
    challenge for academia, practitioners, and governments but more impor-
    tantly represents a public health communication challenge in pandemics.

Constructing 'Pandemic Communication' through the Chapters

Our objective in putting together this book was to explore pandemic communication from across the field of communication with researchers from around
the world. In defining pandemic communication, these chapters explore different perspectives, ontologies, methodologies and critical reflections, and geographic perspectives.

Laying the Groundwork for Defining Pandemic Communication

Given the context was a pandemic, the book begins with Croucher et al.'s
chapter "Health Communication and Behaviors during the COVID-19
Pandemic: A 22-Nation Exploration of Mask Wearing". From a global perspective, this chapter represents an important contribution because it explored
attitudes about the self-protective behavior and accompanying mandates from
all continents, including regions that are chronically underrepresented like
South America, Central Asia, and Africa. Theoretically, the piece is a comparative analysis incorporating the theory of planned behavior, health belief model,
and patient self-advocacy, finding that the consistency in health message,
self-advocacy, and societal pressures are important contributors to attitudes
about mask wearing. The piece demonstrates that pandemic communication
represents the convergence of health, political, social, or interpersonal communication, as well as crisis communication.

Building on the convergence of these complex communication contexts,
Ashwell's chapter "Science Communication and Pandemics" provides a critical reflection with examples from around the world of the complications of
translating science in a pandemic. He points out that the political arena has
uniquely problematized the acceptance of scientific information as the basis
for decision-making, which has allowed for the growth of misinformation,
conspiracy theory, and 'infodemics'. Taking this as a starting point, the chapter focuses on how scientists and science communicators can manage the

convergence of actors and interests to ensure that the best information is used for decision-making. By exploring the history and politics of scientific communication, Ashwell suggests that a multi-actor, multi-platform effort is needed to combat misinformation and conspiracy theories.

In the health and science communication chapters, the book lays the groundwork for critical considerations and complexities in pandemic communication with the convergence of multiple arenas of communication. Then in Seeger and Seeger's crisis communication chapter, "Pandemic Communication: CDC and WHO Approaches to Emergency Risk Communication and Emerging Infectious Disease Crises", the authors provide a working definition of pandemic communication arguing that it '…not only involve[s] transmitting messages to diverse audiences, and *coordination* across different cultures, political systems, and approaches to both communication and health…' (p.). The authors take an applied approach that highlights three emergent applied crisis and risk communication frameworks – the Centers for Disease Control and Prevention's (CDC) principles of effective communication, the Crisis Emergency Risk Communication framework (CERC), and the World Health Organization's (WHO) guidelines for emergency risk communication (ERC). Like Croucher, et al.'s chapter, Seeger and Seeger identify points of convergence in these traditional frameworks. The authors suggest all emergency risk communication provides information to communities and promotes protective actions. To do so, they must be credible, timely, and manage uncertainty. Moreover, the authors suggest that capacity building and resource management enable more effective communication.

Institutional Perspectives on Pandemic Communication

With the explorations of health, science, and crisis communication establishing that pandemic communication necessarily requires a global, multi-disciplinary, and multi-platform communication approach and defining it as a unique communication environment, in the chapters on public relations and organizational communication, the book provides an institutional perspective on pandemic communication. Taylor's chapter, "Public Relations and Pandemics", identifies the uniqueness of the pandemic context for public relations (PR) and proposes a research agenda in PR that explores the influence of the pandemic to improve theory and practice for future pandemics. Taylor draws on systems theory and established research to address what industry-level change looks like and provide perspectives on disruptions in the field of public relations. Ultimately, she focuses on nine public relations pre-pandemic research themes to identify how the pandemic might affect them. In so doing, she argues that while the pandemic context requires innovation, reflection, and adaptation of current theory and practice, the core knowledge and research in the field provides a strong foundation for innovation. In short, her argument is there is no need to throw everything out and begin again.

In Diers-Lawson's organizational communication chapter, "The New Normal: Pandemic Communication and Sustainable Organizations", she argues the COVID-19 pandemic is a societal-level crisis and history suggests that such events typically usher in major evolutions in the ways we organize ourselves. In connecting the field's dominant research themes across time, she applies the stakeholder relationship management framework (SRM) to argue that the primary goal of organizational communication is to manage the inter-connected relationships between organizations, stakeholders (internal and external), and the issues that connect them. Diers-Lawson argues that while social responsibility is an inherent part of managing relationships between organizations and stakeholders the pandemic has intensified the pressure for all kinds of organizations to demonstrate better and more authentic commitments to social responsibility as a part of capacity building. She concludes that in a pandemic and post-pandemic context, organizational communication should focus on capacity building to reflect the organization's responsibilities to be stewards of stakeholder interests as the needs from the pandemic converge with sustainability needs highlighting the importance of strategic change commu-nication in coming years. In so doing, she suggests pandemic communication in organizations is essential not only for managing the present but also for how organizations define their own futures for stakeholders.

Pandemic Communication Applied across Diverse Communication Contexts

In the first two sections, we have argued the chapters have helped to define pandemic communication as a unique communication environment that requires: (1) a multi-disciplinary, multi-cultural, and multi-platform approach to communication; (2) convergence between political, health, socio-cultural, organizational, and crisis research; (3) theory development that does not aban-don previous knowledge but does not merely assume that past theories will predict future events in a pandemic or post-pandemic context; and (4) that the pandemic, placed in its historic context as a global societal-level event, requires a focus on communicating change. Across these first chapters, all of which were written independently and separately, the emergence of these themes provides a standard for exploring pandemic communication in future research as well as in the other major sub-fields of communication studies. The remaining chapters provide critical insights about the application of these characteristics of pan-demic communication across global research in communication.

For instance, the role of visual communication in our field is often ignored; however, Bertel et al.'s chapter "Meme-ing Accountability: Visual Communica-tion as Character Assassination of Austria and Swedish Politicians and Government Agencies during the COVID-19 Pandemic" highlights the power of citizens' use of multimodal (visual and textual) communication that demonstrates the intersection between current events – like the pandemic – popular culture, and politics. Conceptually, the authors argue that during the pandemic social media emerged as an indicator of the relative success or failure in the management of the disease pointing to examples of political leaders, health agencies, and well-known public figures who were all critiqued with highly critical memes circulating globally. In their analysis of emergent memes about Austrian and Swedish politicians, Bertel et al. create a framework for evaluating COVID-19 memes, suggesting 'templatability' and narrative functions help to explain why localized critiques tap into global themes, which create the power, shareability, and potential impact of memes and visual communication more broadly.

The evolution of visual communication and its impact that Bertel et al. demonstrate in their chapter highlights the need for thinking differently about pandemic communication and its implications. Similarly, in their applied communication chapter, "Applied Communication and Pandemics: Expanding the IDEA Model of Instructional Risk and Crisis Communication", Sellnow et al. argue pandemic communication requires applied communication theory – especially risk and crisis communication theory – to evolve to accommodate increasingly global and cross-cultural communication needs. Specifically, this chapter critiques the US CDC for its poor cultural communication with Hispanic communities regarding COVID-19 recommendations for holiday celebrations and small gatherings. Their findings suggest that as populations are increasingly diverse, theories and their application must evolve to be able to tailor messages to different social and cultural groups across and within borders. Specifically, they argue that in applied communication contexts one of the critical lessons from the COVID-19 pandemic is that theory must integrate cultural norms and practice that occur across time and space if those communication endeavors are to be successful.

While the importance of cultural adaptation and global communication emerges as consistent themes, unsurprisingly, in the context of pandemic communication, the need for integrating risk and crisis communication research emerges consistently. In Liu and Levenshus's interpersonal communication chapter, "Interpreting the Interpersonal: Crisis Communication Insights for Pandemics", the authors directly discuss the convergence of crisis and interpersonal communication. Their review of the state of theory and applied knowledge on interpersonal pandemic communication makes arguments that we have already discussed – the importance of conceptual convergence and the importance of using existing theory but developing and extending it based on the unique requirements of pandemic communication. Liu and Levenshus also argue one of the weaknesses of traditional interpersonal communication theory and research, using the field's handbooks, over the last 20 years is that it has failed to explicitly include or reference crisis communication research. Their chapter then identifies the core concepts developed across different interpersonal communication theories (e.g., subjective norms, corrective communication) and how crisis and pandemic communication research and theory would improve interpersonal communication theory. Thus, aside from offering valuable arguments about the importance of developing relevant pandemic interpersonal communication theory, this chapter underlines a weakness in communication research more generally – a failure to build, revise, and apply theory that reflects the multi-disciplinary nature of communication. In a pandemic and post-pandemic context, we argue this is a necessary evolution in the field of communication for theory to be relevant.

Beyond the convergence of concepts and the need for relevant theory building, the COVID-19 pandemic has also revealed global cracks in social cohesion. Croucher et al.'s chapter on intergroup communication, "Intergroup Communication during the COVID-19 Pandemic: A 20-Nation Analysis of Prejudice", demonstrates the combination of fear, isolation, economic vulnerabilities, and strains on health services has divided populations. In their application of integrated threat theory (ITT), Croucher et al. found ingroups not only use outgroups as scapegoats for their fear, but the uncertainty produced by the pandemic seems to produce heightened fear of the virus itself amongst ingroups. An important implication, however, is that the target of prejudice is not the same in every country because it is not about material questions or concerns regarding the virus's origin, transmission, or different groups willingness to comply with self-protective behavior recommendations. Instead, the conditions produced by the pandemic have revealed or heightened existing social divisions within countries; that is, the prejudices found in this study are not new – they are prejudices that already existed but were magnified by the pandemic. This chapter provides a global view of prejudice and the role of societal-level crises in shining a light on intergroup problems, underscoring the importance of culturally relevant communication.

As a societal-level crisis, the authors in this book argue that the pandemic has affected all aspects of our lives and communication. In many cases, the pandemic has revealed fundamental social, policy, health, and economic cracks. However, it has revealed both threats and opportunities for change. It is this balance between threat and opportunity that Kelly's chapter, "Instructional Communication during Pandemics", begins with the degree to which neither instructors nor students were prepared for the emergency move online. However, she develops a case for pandemic pedagogy being a complex concept distinctive from merely 'online education'. She argues the pandemic revealed fundamental gaps in faculty support, technology poverty amongst some faculty and many students, and support for mental health for both faculty and students. Yet in presenting these problems, she also identifies theories and models to help navigate pandemic learning, arguing not only that educators and educational institutions need to be prepared for future pandemics, but also that educators need to incorporate technology more actively into classrooms where it supports learning objectives. Therefore, within the context of instructional communication, Kelly underscores the arguments made in the institutional chapters – that COVID-19 has created a new normal and that the role of communication is to help support these changes.

The question of what our new normal is and will be in a post-COVID-19 context and the role of communication cannot be answered without considering the global impact and role(s) that social media plays. In his chapter "Pandemic Communication: International Communication" Anthony Spencer problematizes both the Western and heteronormative focus in international communication. He notes that one of the changes in international communication is the emergent centrality of social media as a tool to re-think how people communicate across borders. Therefore, he connects between language, migration, and work within the context of international social media engagement using the COVID-19 pandemic as a lens for evaluating the emergent changes in international communication across contexts. At the core, he argues pandemic communication, being highly mediated, has hastened a communication technological shift across different domains of our lives from the formation of micro-communities to the ways that we experience work. Like other authors, one of his core arguments is that the COVID-19 pandemic experience has irrevocably changed international communication and while the field remains dominated by the West and especially the US, there are now more effective spaces to consider inclusivity, equity, and access.

What many of our authors have discussed in their chapters is the influence and structure of pandemic communication across different arenas of interaction, from social to organizational settings with everything in between. If Spencer's argument is that the pandemic has more effectively opened the voices heard in international communication, then in his chapter, "Pandemic Rhetoric", Orla Vigsø argues we should view the pandemic as a multivocal and multifocal rhetorical arena. Drawing draws on Frandsen and Johansen's rhetorical arena theory Vigsø argues if we are to unpack the multiplicity of voices, issues, and questions surrounding the pandemic, we must consider that pandemics like COVID-19 are contexts in which there are scores of voices trying to make themselves heard. However, he argues that crises that are the scope of the COVID-19 pandemic cannot be viewed as a single arena of interaction; rather, he suggests that it is a multi-layered set of arenas where actors and issues are interconnected but have distinctive structures by themselves. In identifying several topics central to pandemic rhetoric like its origin, danger or risk, time, self-protective measures, national interests, economic impact, and personal freedoms, he suggests pandemic communication is an arena of 'conflict and cooperation' whether that is scientific discourse, politics, or social engagement. Across his chapter, Vigsø demonstrates a point that other chapters have likewise made – pandemic communication is complicated because of the topical convergence and to unpack the rhetorical implications, one must first understand the context or the rhetorical arenas in which people are arguing.

Ann Gill, a long-time department chair and Dean at Colorado State University, often said that we live *in* communication. This is the point that many of our chapters are making, but our last few chapters have suggested. Because of the importance of voice, being heard, being recognized, as Permyakova et al. argue in their chapter, "Language and Pandemic Communication", people respond to crises, disasters, and pandemics using culturally constructed language. Thus, their chapter focuses on the linguistics of pandemic communication as a vehicle for social change and new ways of socially constructing the world. As with Kelly's instructional communication and Spencer's international communication chapters, Permyakova et al. point out the importance of Internet technology as a part of pandemic communication. However, they also point out that with our highly mediated communication during the pandemic, new languages and new ways of socially constructing experiences like education have emerged. We have learned new concepts, new words, and new ways of categorizing this new language. In their comparison across languages, they identify the differences in which cultures have constructed the language of the pandemic based on cultural identity, priorities, and values. They suggest all this changes the lived experience. In tracking the linguistic changes that have occurred because of the pandemic, Permyakova et al.'s chapter strengthens the emergent argument across this book that as a global societal-level crisis, pandemic communication must be analyzed and evaluated as distinctive.

In the distinctive arena of the COVID-19 pandemic, however, one of the central themes that have emerged is the importance of politics. It has been one of the four or five core communication contexts that have been underscored as a vital part of pandemic communication across our chapters. We, therefore, conclude our exploration of pandemic communication across the field with Bates and Edwards' chapter "Political Communication and Pandemics". The authors argue that political communication in the COVID-19 context has challenged the field's established assumptions that political communication is a study of public messages delivered by leaders in a national context. Instead, they argue that the pandemic has broadened political communication beyond traditional understanding, beyond traditional speakers, and beyond the Western and Global Northern biases inherent in the field's study. In many cases, they – like other authors such as Vigsø or Spencer – suggest the broadening of voices heard through the pandemic may render traditional assumptions in political communication as less relevant, requiring new approaches and theories.

Toward Institutionalizing Pandemic Communication Research

By the end of the book, we hope readers – no matter their interests in the field of communication – have a clearer understanding of the emergent phenomenon of *pandemic communication* and its implications for theory and research across the field. In our last chapter in the book, "Reflecting on Theory and Research in Pandemic Communication", Diers-Lawson makes three arguments: (1) that internationalization in communication studies and especially pandemic communication is simply necessary; (2) that to consider the pandemic context, researchers in the field of communication need to more meaningfully engage with existing research in risk, crisis, and/or pandemic communication; and (3) that theory building in pandemic communication must be more than just applying the same theories to new pandemic contexts, but it should not throw out established concepts, suggesting a contingency approach to theory building may be a useful approach to re-building theory for pandemic communication.

These arguments align with those that have emerged in these chapters from communication scholars from across the field and around the world. In talking with our authors, we asked them to consider and from their own sub-disciplines and critically reflect on what pandemic communication is through four questions: (1) 'What has changed with the COVID-19 pandemic?'; (2) 'What are the implications of the pandemic on theory in communication?'; (3) 'What has the global nature of the COVID-19 pandemic revealed about communication studies?'; and (4) 'How do we produce rigorous and useful scholarship on the pandemic?'. In our view, what has emerged is a strong reflection of the diverse theoretical, ontological, and methodological perspectives in the field of communication but with a central set of principles and challenges unique to the pandemic context. Our intention with this book was to explore whether pandemic communication was conceptually distinctive enough to emerge as a sub-field. The findings, reflections, research agendas, and critical analyses in these chapters suggest it is distinctive and warrants institutionalization. We encourage the readers of these chapters to explore these questions and others as we consider the short- and long-term impacts of pandemics on the relationship between pandemics and communication.

References

Guidry, J. P. D., Jin, Y., Orr, C. A., Messner, M., & Meganck, S. (2017). Ebola on Instagram and Twitter: How health organizations address the health crisis in their social media engagement. *Public Relations Review, 43*(3), 477–486. https://doi.org/10.1016/j.pubrev.2017.04.009

Head, K., J., Kasting, M. L., Sturm, L. A., Harstock, J. A., & Zimet, G. D. (2020). A national survey assessing SARS-CoV-2 vaccination intentions: Implications for future public health communication efforts. *Science Communication, 42*(5), 698–723. https://doi.org/10.1177/1075547020960463.

Izard, C. E. (1991). *The psychology of emotions.* Plenum Press.

Jang, K., & Park, N. (2018). The effects of repetitive information communication through multiple channels on prevention behavior during the 2015 MERS outbreak in South Korea. *Journal of Health Communication, 23*(7), 670–678. https://doi.org/10.1080/10810730.2018.1501440

Johns Hopkins Coronavirus Resource Center. (Updated daily). Coronavirus Resource Center. https://coronavirus.jhu.edu/map.html

Koley, T. K., & Dhole, M. (2021). *The COVID-19 pandemic: The deadly corona-virus outbreak.* Routledge.

Lee, K. (2009). How the Hong Kong government lost the public trust in SARS: Insights for government communication in a health crisis. *Public Relations Review, 35*(1), 74–76. https://doi.org/10.1016/j.pubrev.2008.06.003

Lee, K.-M., & Jung, K. (2019). Factors influencing the responses to infectious diseases: Focusing on the case of SARS and MERS in South Korea. *International Journal of Environmental Research and Public Health, 16*(8), 1432. https://doi.org/10.3390/ijerph16081432

Lewis, M., Govender, E., & Holland, K. (Eds.). (2021). *Communicating COVID-19: Interdisciplinary perspectives.* Palgrave Macmillan.

Lilleker, D., Coman, I. A., Gregor, M., & Novelli, E. (2021). *Political communication and COVID-19 (Politics, media and political communication).* Routledge.

Lupton, D., & Willis, K. (Eds.). (2021). *The COVID-19 crisis: Social perspectives.* Routledge.

Ma, R. (2005). Media, crisis, and SARS: An introduction. *Asian Journal of Communication, 15*(3), 241–246. https://doi.org/10.1080/0129280500260656

O'Hair, H. D., & O'Hair, M. J. (2021). *Communicating science in times of crisis: COVID-19 pandemic.* Wiley Blackwell.

Pollock, J. C., & Vakoch, D. A. (2021). *COVID-19 in international media: Global pandemic perspectives (Routledge research in journalism).* Routledge.

Price, S., & Harbisher, B. (2021). *Power, media and the COVID-19 pandemic: Framing public discourse.* Routledge.

Ratzan, S. C., & Moritsugu, K. P. (2014). Ebola crisis – Communication chaos we can avoid. *Journal of Health Communication, 19*(11), 1213–1215. https://doi.org/10.1080/10810730.2014.977680

Ryan, J. M. (2021). *The COVID-19 pandemic series* (3 vols.). Routledge.

Toppenberg-Pejcic, D., Noyes, J., Allen, T., Alexander, N., Vanderford, M., & Gamhewage, G. (2019). Emergency risk communication: Lessons learned from a rapid review of recent gray literature on Ebola, Zika, and Yellow Fever. *Health Communication, 34*(4), 437–455. https://doi.org/10.1080.10410236.2017.1405488

Yoo, W., Choi, D.-H., & Park, K. (2016). The effects of SNS communication: How expressing and receiving information predict MERS-preventive behavioral intentions in South Korea. *Computers in Human Behavior, 62,* 34–43. https://doi.org/10.1016/j.chb.2016.03.058

2

HEALTH COMMUNICATION AND BEHAVIORS DURING THE COVID-19 PANDEMIC

A 22-Nation Exploration of Mask-Wearing

Stephen M. Croucher, Jo Cullinane, Nicola Murray, Kenneth T. Rocker, and Thao Nguyen

Since the start of the COVID-19 pandemic, there have been more than 550 million reported cases, and more than 6.3 million deaths globally (Johns Hopkins Coronavirus Resource Center, Updated daily; Worldometer 2022d). As the virus spread across the globe, nations imposed various forms of lock-downs and restrictions, and vaccinations ramped up globally. As of July 2022, more than 11.7 billion vaccines had been administered globally (Johns Hopkins Coronavirus Resource Center, n.d.). Along with vaccinations and lockdowns, a key preventative measure recommended in some, and mandated in many other, nations was mask-wearing. Various organizations, including the World Health Organization (WHO) and the Centers for Disease Control (CDC), advised mask-wearing in public to prevent the spread of the virus (WHO, 2020). With growing evidence showing mask-wearing reduces the spread of COVID-19, Canada, New Zealand, South Korea, the Czech Republic, and others have initiated mask-wearing mandates to varying degrees (Government of Canada, 2020; Lee, 2020). Even though evidence showed that mask-wearing reduced the spread of the virus, and that many governments initiated campaigns to encourage mask-wearing, mask-wearing remained a highly politicized health behavior, with many individuals refusing to wear masks (Clase et al., 2020; Croucher et al., 2021; Latkin et al., 2021; Liao et al., 2021). Thus, the purpose of this chapter is to explore mask-wearing during the COVID-19 pandemic. Specifically, this chapter examines the extent to which individuals in 22 nations supported mask-wearing mandates. The nations included in this analysis are Argentina, Brazil, Chile, China, England, France, India, Israel, Italy, Kenya, Kyrgyzstan, Mexico, New Zealand, Nigeria, Palestine, Peru, Russia, Singapore, South Africa, Spain, Turkey, and the United States. In the first section of this chapter, theoretical constructs that influence health and

DOI: 10.4324/9781003214496-2

health behaviors are outlined. In the second section, the COVID situation and responses to mask-wearing in each of the 22 nations are described. In the third section, the method and data are discussed. In the fourth section, results are presented. The final section provides implications from the study.

Key Theoretical Constructs

During the COVID-19 pandemic, governments and health professionals worked together globally to promote behaviors to prevent the spread of the COVID-19 virus. The importance of hand washing, mask-wearing, social distancing, and getting vaccinated were all identified as healthy behaviors to reduce the risk of contracting and/or spreading COVID-19. There is extensive literature in health communication exploring how to create effective health messages, how to motivate change, and how people respond to health needs. The theory of planned behavior (Ajzen, 1991), the health belief model (Janz & Becker, 1984; Johnson & Witte, 2003), and patient self-advocacy (Brashers, 2001; Brashers et al., 2000) provide three theoretical lenses for better under-standing support for mask-wearing mandates.

Theory of Planned Behavior

The Theory of Planned Behavior (TPB) developed out of the Theory of Rea-soned Action (TRA) (Ajzen & Fishbein, 1980). Ajzen and Fishbein proposed in the TRA that persuasive interventions intended to alter behaviors must focus on individual beliefs. Beliefs influence our expectations and attitudes. If a per-son believes an issue is false/untrue, they have an attitude about that issue. Those attitudes affect how an individual behaves toward actions linked with that issue. For example, during the COVID-19 pandemic, those individuals who perceived COVID-19 as a hoax were less likely to see vaccines or preven-tative measures as necessary, as their attitude was that the virus was a hoax. In revising TRA, to develop TPB, Ajzen (1991) added perceived behavioral con-trol. The TPB has three components (Croucher, 2016, p. 176):

1   Attitude toward the behavior – a cost-benefit analysis is performed regard-ing the behavioral choice
2   Subjective (societal) norms – pressure is felt regarding the behavior, for example from family, peers, media, etc.
3   Perceived behavioral control – the perception the person has about their ability to perform the behavior and their control over the behavior.

Critical to TPB is that the more open and positive a person is toward a pro-posed behavior, the more socially acceptable the behavior is, and the more perceived control they have over the behavior, the more likely they are to adopt the behavior. Thus, when designing persuasive messages, it is critical to address these elements of a proposed behavioral change. A significant body of research in persuasion, political communication, and health communication has explored the effectiveness of TPB in predicting behavioral change. For example, researchers have explored the links between TPB and organ donation (Bresnahan et al., 2007; Pauli et al., 2017), obesity (Andrews et al., 2010; Prapavessis et al., 2015), cigarette smoking (Brann & Sutton, 2009; Lee et al., 2018), bike sharing (Si et al., 2020), exercise (Norman & Conner, 2005), H1N1 and swine flu vaccinations (Myers & Goodwin, 2012; Yang, 2015), COVID-19 vaccinations (Shmueli, 2021), as well as numerous other issues. Relevance of the issue, perceived individual control over the issue and behavior, and societal norms have all been found to be significant predictors of behavioral adoption.

Health Belief Model

A theoretical model closely linked to the TPB is the Health Belief Model (HBM). Originally developed in the 1950s, the HBM explains how an individual's engagement (or lack of) in health-promoting actions and behaviors is explained by their perceived susceptibility, their perceived severity of the issue, their perceived benefits of taking the action(s), their perceived barriers to taking the action(s), the cues to action, and their overall motivation to take health actions (Bish et al., 2011; Janz & Becker, 1984; Johnson & Witte, 2003; Rosenstock, 1974; Rosenstock et al., 1988). Recognizing that adopting health behaviors and believing in the efficacy of such behaviors is influenced by numerous factors, researchers have widely used the HBM to explore individuals' willingness to engage in health behaviors: condom use (Volk & Koopman, 2001), HIV prevention and counseling (Buldeo & Gilbert, 2015; Mattson, 1999), mammograms (Menon et al., 2007), weight management (James et al., 2012), the human papillomavirus (HPV) (Mehta et al., 2013), influenza vaccine (Bish et al., 2011), the COVID-19 vaccine (Shmueli, 2021), and others. In most research looking at the HBM, researchers have found that there is no single reason why individuals fail to act on cues to action. In some cases, it is because barriers to action are perceived as too high, benefits seem too low, individuals do not perceive themselves as susceptible, there is too much uncertainty, people do not know how, or do not want to advocate for their health, etc., leading people to not act. Thus, it is difficult for health campaign message designers to effectively design messages to reach all audiences and effectively change or increase health engagement.

Patient Self-Advocacy

The notions of uncertainty and advocating for one's health are critical to behavioral change. Brashers (2001) argued uncertainty and anxiety are critical to understanding health decision making. When managing uncertainty, individuals gather and evaluate information to try to make health decisions. Patient self-advocacy (PSA) (Brashers et al., 2009) has been proposed as one method to understand this process of addressing uncertainty and making health-based decisions. When faced with cues to action, particularly those linked with uncertain health or life-threatening situations, individuals may become advocates for their health. There are three dimensions to PSA: increased information seeking, increased potential for non-adherence, and increased assertiveness in health interactions (Brashers et al., 2000).

When faced with a serious health situation, such as a pandemic, many individuals will seek out information to better understand the situation and how it relates to them personally. While by contrast, those who question the severity of the situation may be more likely to actively avoid information (Brashers et al., 2009). Mindful non-adherence is the second aspect of patient self-advocacy. Mindful non-adherence is when individuals reject or don't follow medical advice because they do not believe such advice will benefit them (Brashers et al., 2009). In terms of COVID-19, research has increasingly shown individuals actively non-adhere to medical advice, such as that to get vaccinated (Fedele et al., 2021). The final dimension is increased assertiveness in health interactions. When faced with a serious, often life-threatening situation, many individuals will have a heightened sense of autonomy in medical interactions. Thus, when faced with a threatening health situation, individuals will often ask more questions, and require more justification for medical decisions. It is critical for health practitioners and governments when responding to pandemics to recognize self-advocacy, as self-advocacy influences an individual's willingness to adopt behaviors.

During the COVID-19 pandemic, mask-wearing was identified to prevent the spread of COVID-19 (Clase et al., 2020). Hornik et al. (2021) found that the more an individual believed mask-wearing prevented the spread of COVID-19, the more likely the individual was to wear a mask. Increased fear of COVID-19 has also been found to be linked with higher levels of mask-wearing (Jørgensen et al., 2020; Rieger, 2020). However, mask-wearing has remained a controversial issue, with research in the United States showing more Republicans choosing to not mask after the 2020 election than before the election (Croucher et al., 2021). Mask-wearing has been proven to help prevent the spread of COVID-19, leading many nations to pass mandates on mask-wearing. However, many individuals during the pandemic questioned the effectiveness of this behavior, and the mandates globally. Thus, the following research question is posed to explore the level of support for mask-wearing and mandates:

RQ: To what extent does support for mask-wearing mandates differ among the 22 nations?

Contexts – 22 Nations

United States

The CDC confirmed the first case of COVID-19 in the United States on January 20, 2020. By the end of the month, travel to the United States was suspended by any foreign nationals who had traveled to China in the previous 14 days, excluding the immediate family members of American citizens or permanent residents. As hospitals began to become overwhelmed with the influx of cases, a lockdown officially went into effect on March 19, 2020. Following California's decision, 41 states followed by imposing their own lockdown restrictions which went into effect between the 19th of March and the 2nd of April. On April 3, 2020, public health officials suggested that all Americans should wear masks in public. This decision was beneficial in increasing the number of individuals who reported wearing masks; however, an increase in bullying was also reported during that time (Goldberg et al., 2020). Despite the increase in cases, a federal judge ruled on April 18, 2022, that the mask mandate was unlawful, which resulted in the masking requirement on airplanes, trains, buses, and other public transportation to no longer be enforced. It is estimated that by July 2022, the United States has experienced nearly 91 million COVID-19 cases and more than 1 million COVID-related deaths (Worldometers, 2022n). An estimated 67% of the population is fully vaccinated (Centers for Disease Control and Prevention, 2022).

Mexico

Mexico's COVID-19 numbers dramatically increased from its first case on the 27th of February 2020 to 19,224 confirmed cases and 1,859 deaths 64 days later (Suárez et al., 2020). Approximately one month after the first case was confirmed, in late March, community transmission was found and capacity limits began to be put in place alongside recommendations for vulnerable populations to isolate at home (Suárez et al., 2020). Following this, at the end of March through to the end of May 2020, all non-essential activities were suspended by the government, which was followed by a state-level alert system where the measures undertaken depended on the risk in that area (Sánchez-Talanquer et al., 2021). Also in May, an announcement was made for a "reopening plan" for a "new normal"; however, cases did not fall as expected but instead stabilized at high levels for three months before increasing again (Sánchez-Talanquer et al., 2021, p. 12). July 2022 figures show Mexico has had more than 6 million COVID-19 cases and 326,261 deaths (Worldometers, 2022h). Mask-wearing is not mandated in Mexico (Sánchez-Talanquer et al., 2021). Government officials, particularly in the first several months of the pandemic, "repeatedly objected to the use of face masks" and claimed the use of masks was not evidence-based (Sánchez-Talanquer et al., 2021, p. 57). A vaccination for COVID-19 is available in Mexico; however, health workers (one of the priority populations) have found it difficult to access, leading to protests (Sánchez-Talanquer et al., 2021). Further, vaccination access preference has been given by the President to certain communities that Sánchez-Talanquer et al. (2021) argue do not make epidemiological sense and appear to be prioritized for political reasons. In July 2022, Mexico's full vaccination rate sits at 63.10% (Our World in Data, 2022).

Argentina

The first confirmed case of COVID-19 in Argentina was reported to be that of a returning traveler in March 2020 (Lammertyn et al., 2020). By May 2020, Argentina was seeing community transmission of cases (WHO, 2020). According to a case study undertaken by the World Health Organization (2020), Argentina's government showed strong leadership and rapidly and effectively implemented WHO recommendations to flatten the growing number of cases. Lockdowns were implemented along with measures to mitigate the predicted socioeconomic consequences (WHO, 2020). Measures included mandatory face mask-wearing, social distancing practices, recommendations for regular hand washing, quarantine procedures for cases and in-bound travelers, and capacity limits on events (Decree 867, 2021). September 2021 saw the lifting of almost all restrictions due to COVID-19 as cases of the virus decreased (Goni, 2021). This announcement came ten days after a political shift in Argentina's open primaries with the ruling party, which enforced restrictions, gaining fewer votes than the coalition that strongly resisted restrictions (Goni, 2021). As of July 2022, more than 9 million cases of COVID-19 have been confirmed in Argentina alongside 129,145 deaths (Worldometers, 2022a). However, full vaccination numbers are high at 83.09% of the eligible population (Our World in Data, 2022).

Chile

The first case of COVID-19 was discovered in Chile in March 2020 (Tariq et al., 2021). In mid-March, the Chilean government responded to this and other cases by banning gatherings of more than 500 people at first, followed by closures of all educational facilities, closing the country's borders, introduction of a curfew, and localized lockdowns (Tariq et al., 2021). Relaxation of some restrictions occurred in April 2020; however, this led to an increase in infections, resulting in further lockdowns in some areas, and a plan for a gradual step-by-step relaxation of restrictions at a local level, once case numbers allowed (Tariq et al., 2021). In April 2022, a new impact-level system of restrictions was released with three levels (all of which included the continued mandatory use of masks): firstly the low impact level requires little restrictions apart from the use of a mobility card (a vaccine pass); the medium impact level requires the former, social distancing and capacity limitations; the high impact level requires all of the former with larger social distancing and smaller capacity limitation requirements (Government of Chile, 2022). Chile has to date reported more than 4 million cases and 58,884 deaths (Worldometers, 2022c) and 90.29% of the eligible population is fully vaccinated (Our World in Data, 2022).

Brazil

Brazil is the fifth largest country in the world and the largest in South America (World Population Review, 2022). The first COVID-19 case appeared in late February 2020 (Serdan et al., 2020). Unfortunately, the Brazilian federal government's approach to containment was marred by "conflicting and mismatching decisions", which was associated with the disease spreading (Serdan et al., 2021, p. 37). All of Brazil's 26 state governments were subject to a National Contingency Plan (NCP) which, among other things, required social distancing in the form of lockdowns, quarantine measures, and mandatory facemask use; however, only some states implemented this (Serdan et al., 2021). Further, the Brazilian President was investigated over a duration of six months via a senate inquiry as to, among other things, the accusation that the President committed crimes against humanity by spreading misinformation about preventive measures and encouraging gatherings of thousands at rallies, justified by his followers as encouraging herd immunity via contagion (Ventura et al., 2021). As of July 2022, Brazil reported more than 33 million COVID-19 cases and 674,554 deaths (Worldometers, 2022b). Currently, 79.09% of the eligible Brazilian population is fully vaccinated (Our World in Data, 2022).

Peru

Recent figures show Peru has had more than 3.6 million COVID-19 cases and 213,714 deaths (Worldometers, 2022j). Peru's journey with COVID-19 began in March 2020 (Reuters, 2020) and a week after the first case was detected the entire country went into lockdown (Beaubien, 2021). In May 2020, wearing KN95 masks or double masking became mandatory alongside wearing gloves in grocery stores, food markets, and banks (Global Monitoring, 2022). Over time, certain restrictions were relaxed and then reintroduced due to an upsurge in cases (Global Monitoring, 2022). In 2021, Peru's death rate was claimed to be the highest in the world, likely due to a combination of factors such as the relative low wealth of the country, underfunding of public health, an unstable political environment, overcrowded living conditions, the informal job market, and the dependence on imports including necessary medical supplies

(Beaubien, 2021). The Peruvian government introduced controls in December 2021 to further limit the spread of COVID-19, including showing proof of vaccination to enter most indoor spaces (US Mission Lima, 2022). Mask requirements were relaxed in May 2022; however, many Peruvians continued to wear masks due to fear of the high death rate (Buenos Aires Times, 2022; IHME, 2022), and in July 2022, the mask requirement was reintroduced and applied to both inside and outside contexts (Global Monitoring, 2022). As of June 6, 2022, 81% of Peruvians were fully vaccinated (IHME, 2022).

Spain

Spain's first case of COVID-19 was diagnosed on January 31, 2020, and by July 2022, Spain has had 12.8 million cases and more than 108,259 COVID-19–related deaths (Worldometers, 2022l). The Spanish public health responses included the use of national lockdown, and specific public sector and regional restrictions. Restrictions included aspects such as "States of Emergency" and a Halt to All Non-Essential Activity, quarantines and lockdowns, and travel restrictions. The response to COVID-19 is marked by criticism of slow and inadequate responses in the initial stages. In that initial stage of the pandemic there was a high national death rate, mostly due to low availability of Personal Protection Equipment (PPE) contributing to delays in effective mitigation. As Spain moved to de-escalate lockdown-type restrictions, strict requirements to wear masks inside were introduced by the National Spanish Cabinet on May 20, 2020. By the time they were suspended in April 2022, the strict and wide-ranging mandatory mask use rules had been in place for 699 days (Linde, 2022). Initially, these rules required masks be worn outside of the home; when these rules were changed in 2022, masks remained mandatory on public transport, taxis, healthcare settings, aged care facilities, and pharmacies. Paralleling the reliance on mask mandates, the Spanish public health response was supported by a strong vaccination push, and by July 2022 an estimated 86.1% of the Spanish population was fully vaccinated (Worldometers, 2022l).

Italy

Italy experienced its first confirmed cases of COVID-19 on January 31, 2020 and the virus rapidly spread across all its regions in February and March 2020. The Italian government relatively quickly imposed international border restrictions and a state of emergency, and as the virus continued to spread, regional quarantines were imposed. In March 2020, a national lockdown and a restriction of all non-essential commercial activity were imposed. The strict state of emergency and restrictions on movement and commercial activity started to be eased from May 2020 and a mask mandate was introduced to compensate for the easing of restrictions. However, in October 2020, the easing of the state

20 Stephen M. Croucher et al.

of emergency was postponed when a resurgence of the virus was experienced. Throughout this period and ongoing, Italy has had to reposition its primary and tertiary healthcare systems in response to the challenges of the virus, and public health initiatives have emphasized vaccinations as a means of mitigation. The majority of the mask mandates and most other restrictions were removed by the Italian government in June 2022. Between that first case in January 2020 and July 2022, Italy has had 19 million COVID-19 cases and more than 168,770 COVID-19–related deaths (Worldometers, 2022g). An estimated 79.6% of the population is fully vaccinated.

Russia

The Russian Deputy Prime Ministry Tatyana Golikova confirmed the first two COVID-19 cases in January 2020 (Sofiychuk, 2020). The government's first response to the virus was to restrict foreign visitors and produce imported from China (Sokhey, 2021). A month later after the WHO officially declared COVID-19 a global health pandemic, the government put the country into high alert (Sokhey, 2021). The government response was different in many regions, for example, Moscow had stricter restrictions than other places in the country (Sokhey, 2021). The restrictions included only leaving the house for a valid reason, banning all outdoor activities, requiring social distancing (at least 1.5 meters), and wearing a mask and gloves in public areas (Ausína et al., 2020). Even though wearing a mask in public was compulsory, Sokhey (2021) argued it was unclear how well Russians complied. As of early 2022, Russia only had one six-week lockdown from March 30 to May 12, 2020, and a one-week working from home requirement from the government; other than that, life remained largely normal in all regions, including easing most of the restrictions (RFE/RL, 2022). Russia was among the first countries in the world rolling out COVID-19 vaccination. As of July 2022, there have been nearly 18.2 million cases and almost 374,000 COVID-19–related deaths (Johns Hopkins Coronavirus Resource Center, n.d.).

England

We note that studies in the UK of COVID-19 require a separation of the four nations because health is devolved to England, Northern Ireland, Scotland, and Wales respectively. Importantly, these countries often had different policies and different health outcomes during the pandemic. England experienced its first COVID-19 Case in January 2020 and by July 2022, England has had 19.1 million cases and more than 157,037 COVID-19-–related deaths (Government of the United Kingdom, 2022), with an estimated 75.3% of the population being fully vaccinated. England's response to the pandemic has been complex and at times confusing. In March 2020, commercial activity was suspended and then a national lockdown was imposed, national restrictions were then eased from June in phases, and the potential for local regional restrictions was enabled. Mask mandates were imposed in July 2020. A series of local restrictions were imposed between June and October 2020 prior to another national lockdown being initiated but with schools and universities being excluded. The second lockdown was then ended in December but spikes in infection rates caused a third national lockdown to be imposed between January and March 2021. Restrictions and mask mandates have been eased, reimposed, and eased again according to national and regional infection rates.

France

As of July 2022, France has had 31.8 million COVID-19 cases and more than 149,854 COVID-19–related deaths (Worldometers, 2022e). The first COVID-19 Case may have reached France as early as December 2019, but the first case was officially diagnosed in late January 2020. By March 2020, the rates of infection were such that a national lockdown was determined to be necessary. The lockdown was extended repeatedly as infection rates increased. Mask mandates on public transport and in public spaces were introduced. Restrictions eventually began to ease in June and July 2020. The easing of personal restrictions was paralleled by mask mandates in public indoor spaces. The easing of restrictions caused a resurgence of infections in August and October 2020 and a second national lockdown was implemented with an expectation of that ending in December. The easing of restrictions when they came was limited as infection levels were still high. A third national lockdown was put in place in March and April 2021 with restrictions then easing in June and July. Further resurgences in infections related to variants in the virus brought further restrictions but these were matched to individual risk factors such as health and vaccination status. All restrictions including public mask mandates ended in February 2022. Throughout the pandemic, the French response to COVID-19 has been posited on restrictions being temporary while the public health mitigation through immunity arising from vaccinations was extended. By July 2022, an estimated 78.9% of the population has been fully vaccinated.

South Africa

The National Institute for Communicable Diseases of South Africa confirmed the first case of COVID-19 in March 2020 (Mkhize, 2020). The National Coronavirus Command Council of South Africa developed a five-level risk-adjusted strategy and throughout, five levels of lockdown, physical distancing, and face mask-wearing became mandatory in all public spaces (Moonasar et al., 2021). Twenty-two days after the first confirmed case, South Africa was put into a national lockdown (Moonasar et al., 2021). During the lockdown, educational institutions, public leisure activities, and non-essential businesses were completely shut down (Schröder et al., 2021). The government relaxed all restrictions in March 2022, including removing mask-wearing mandates outdoors, yet mandates remained compulsory inside public buildings and public transportation (Reuters, 2022). As of July 2022, there have been nearly 4 million reported cases and more than 101,000 deaths due to COVID-19 (Johns Hopkins Coronavirus Resource Center, n.d.). However, the actual number of fatalities could be three times the official number, since the outbreak, the South African Medical Research council has recorded over 300,000 deaths from natural causes (France-Presse, 2022). As of June 2022, the government lifted mask-wearing mandates (Vanek, 2022).

Kenya

In March 2020, the Ministry of Health in Kenya made an announcement on the first confirmed COVID-19 case in Nairobi (Aluga, 2020). Before the first confirmed case, the Kenyan government had already been preparing for the outbreak since February 2020 by encouraging the public to maintain personal hygiene, immediately go to the nearest health facility when having respiratory symptoms, and avoid direct contact with people with these symptoms (Aluga, 2020). After the first case was confirmed, the government implemented more measures, namely closing all schools, entertainment places, and social spaces based on a dawn to dusk curfew, practicing social distancing (of at least 1.5 meters), recommending people stay at home, and restricting inbound travelers (Brand et al., 2021). The country was put into lockdown in March 2020 leading to food supply struggles and energy consumption concerns, even though the government announced a stimulus package to address these difficulties (Aluga, 2020; The Conversation, 2021). In April 2020, mask-wearing in public places officially became mandatory (Chau, 2022). Chau (2022) argued that government efforts to combat the virus combined with responses to previous health crises was a reason why Kenya did not suffer catastrophically compared to other nations. As of July 2022, the government has reported nearly 336,000 cases and almost 5,700 deaths (Johns Hopkins Coronavirus Resource Center, n.d.).

Nigeria

The Federal Ministry of Health of Nigeria announced its first case of COVID-19 in sub-Saharan Africa in February 2020 (Burke, 2020). Even before COVID-19, Nigeria's healthcare system was not strong and faced many challenges with a large proportion of the population having underlying health conditions (The Conversation, 2022). Therefore, the Nigerian government immediately activated an Incident Control Centre, providing prompt report, routine surveillance, and quick diagnosis built on the previous successful response to Ebola

(The Conversation, 2022). Three weeks after the first confirmed case, the Nigerian government announced travel restrictions in March 2020. Interstate lockdown was implemented in Lagos, Kano, and the Federal Capital Territory in March 2020; but the 36 states of the country were not put into interstate travel restriction until late April 2020 (Jacobs & Okeke, 2022). Along with lockdown/travel restrictions, the government banned large gatherings; closed schools, churches, and markets; and issued a mandatory stay-at-home curfew from 8:00 pm to 6:00 am (Jacobs & Okeke, 2022). Wearing a face mask was mandatory in the public, the mask policies unfortunately led to a widespread misuse in Nigeria such as many people deliberately wearing masks incorrectly and using inappropriate cloth masks (Ongoina, 2020). This could be explained by a lack of effective communication strategies on when and why to use a face mask, and how to wear a face mask properly (Ongoina, 2020). Furthermore, the government lifted lockdown measures in May 2020 while the confirmed cases still increased (Jacobs & Okeke, 2022). As of July 2022, there have been nearly 260,000 reported cases and 3,144 COVID-19–related deaths (Johns Hopkins Coronavirus Resource Center, n.d.).

New Zealand

The first confirmed COVID-19 case was diagnosed in New Zealand in late February 2020. This first infection was experienced relatively late compared to many other countries and the delay gave the New Zealand government additional time to prepare its strategy, and a first step in that strategy was restrictions in movement through the national border in March 2020. However, infection rates necessitated a first national lockdown between late March and late May 2020. Targeted restrictions and lockdowns were then imposed regionally according to infection rates and risk factors. The response was effective compared to other nations' responses, meaning New Zealand only eventually re-entered a national lockdown in August 2021 when the delta variant escaped barriers and caused community transmission. Mask mandates were implemented at a similar time. The mandates permitted a comprehensive roll out of vaccinations (despite delays in accessing vaccines) and by July 2022, an estimated 82.7% of the population was fully vaccinated. New Zealand had 1.3 million cases and more than 1,534 COVID-19–related deaths by July 2022 (Worldometers, 2022i).

Singapore

The first imported case of COVID-19 in Singapore was recorded in January 2020, with the first locally transmitted case being confirmed on February 4, 2020. In comparison with the rest of the world, Singapore was viewed as firm and swift in creating measures that would promote virus tracing and mandated mask-wearing. Due to an increase in locally transmitted cases, the

Singaporean government decided to impose a national-wide lockdown in April 2022. In December 2020, Singapore was the first Asian country to approve Pfizer-BioNTech's coronavirus vaccine. By October 2021, the Singaporean Ministry of Health (MOH) reported that 82% of the country's population had been fully vaccinated, one of the highest vaccination rates in the world (MOH, 2022). With such a high vaccination rate, Singapore implemented a strategy that aimed to reopen the economy by using a "living with COVID" approach. This approach created strict barriers for unvaccinated individuals, such as public entry requirements, while also encouraging vaccinations in general by making them easily accessible. Singapore's Prime Minister announced that most COVID-19 restrictions would be eased in March 2022, resulting in increased capacity for social events, return to office spaces, and masks only being limited to indoor use. It is estimated that in July 2022, Singapore has had nearly 1.6 million cases and 1,440 deaths (Worldometers, 2022k). An estimated 92% of the population is fully vaccinated (MOH, 2022).

Kyrgyzstan

Kyrgyzstan officially reported its first case of COVID-19 in March 2020 (Tayfur, 2020). The Government of Kyrgyzstan immediately responded to the virus by establishing checkpoints in every city, closing entertainment places such as cafes, shopping malls, and non-essential services, and banning all large gatherings at mosques and churches on March 22, 2020 (Dzushupov et al., 2021). The government also closed country borders to foreigners, shut down schools and universities, and asked its citizens to work from home, maintain at least one-meter physical distance, refrain from handshaking, and wear a face mask while in the public areas (Larrea, 2021). The country was put into a state of emergency from March until May 2020, when locals were banned from going outside of their houses during curfew hours (Dzushupov et al., 2021). Most quarantine restrictions were lifted, and all businesses were resumed after June 1, 2020; as a result, not long after the relaxation announcement, the confirmed cases dramatically increased as of the end of June 2020 and the number of cases were almost three times higher than the start of the same month (Dzushupov et al., 2021). This led the Ministry of Health to develop a new action algorithm to provide guidelines as to whether patients with COVID-19 could be treated at home or not; by the end of 2021, the pandemic was partly under control (Dzushupov et al., 2021). Since March 2022, mask-wearing mandates have been removed from all educational institutions and entertainment places such as shopping centers, restaurants, and markets, but it is still mandatory to wear a mask in healthcare organizations and public transportation (Kabar News Agency, 2022). As of July 2022, there have been more than 201,000 cases and nearly 3,000 COVID-19–related deaths (Johns Hopkins Coronavirus Resource Center, n.d.).

Turkey

Turkey initially reacted quickly to the emergence of the virus by establishing a scientific advisory board and through the government issuing restrictions for businesses and imposing health checks in public spaces. The government also restricted international travel to delay the infections. The first COVID case in Turkey was confirmed in March 2020 and the government imposed significant restrictions on activity. Initially, restrictions applied to transport, indoor public gatherings, and business activity but extended to health status and then age-based curfews. Restrictions kept increasing but despite this, cases grew quickly, until April, when a national curfew was imposed and that, coupled with required mask use, caused a slowing of infection rates. In May 2020, the government then eased restrictions on public activity and movement. Infection and death rates then increased again and significant curfew restrictions were ordered in November 2020. Restrictions were eased and reimposed, but the situation was confused and worsening, culminating at a point in April 2021 where infection rates were among the highest in the world, and a national lockdown was imposed. The public health response in Turkey relied upon hygiene, temperature checks, masks, and vaccination but the response of the government was not as stringent as in other nations and by July 2022 there were 15 million confirmed COVID-19 cases and 99,057 deaths (Worldometers, 2022m).

Israel

Israel's first case of COVID-19 was reported in February 2020, leading within six weeks to government-imposed lockdowns (Last, 2020). This first lockdown required all non-essential businesses to shut, non-essential workers to stay home, and schools to move to distance learning (Kaim et al., 2021). Mask-wearing, restrictions on gathering numbers (before lockdown), and social distancing were also required in this, and future lockdowns (Staff, 2021). By May 2020, the first lockdown was eased; however, in the following months, cases began to increase again. Subsequently, short-period lockdowns were ordered in September and December 2020 after cases increased following declines; however, compliance among the public was not as supported as it had been previously, largely due to a desire for a normal routine and fears of economic loss (Kaim et al., 2021). A two-phase vaccination program was rolled out from December 2020, with more than half of the population fully vaccinated by April 2021 (Lesham & Wilder-Smith, 2021). As of July 2021, Israel offered the worldwide first booster shot against COVID-19 (Burki, 2022) but as of July 2022, Israel is continuing to struggle with the virus, reporting nearly 4.5 million cases alongside 11,101 deaths (Worldometers, 2022f).

Palestine

The COVID-19 pandemic reached Palestine in March 2020 (Abed et al., 2021). Understanding the COVID-19 situation in Palestine is complicated by complex status of the governance of the three main territories of the West Bank, East Jerusalem, and the Gaza Strip. Each territory was impacted differently due to different controls that were in effect (Abed et al., 2021). For these territories, a system of central national committees chaired by the Palestinian Minister of Health was supported by advisory committees from the West Bank and Gaza Strip, as well as WHO, UNICEF, and the National Institute of Public Health-supported Health Cluster Meetings. When COVID-19 was first noted in Palestine, at the start of the outbreak, the borders of the Gaza Strip were already closed. In response to the virus, any permitted travel into the area required the traveler to undertake a 21-day isolation period (Abed et al., 2021). However, in East Jerusalem and the West Bank, a 14-day quarantine period was imposed for travelers crossing the borders (Abed et al., 2021). The lockdowns ended at different times in each territory and were reinstated at different times as the virus spread (Abed et al., 2021). However, within the West Bank, lockdowns occurred in some areas but not in others, due to differing jurisdictions (Asi, 2020). COVID-19 infections in the Gaza Strip eventually led to a health-system crisis in late 2020, in part because medical supplies including personal protective equipment, ventilators, and medicines were in short supply and often blocked from import by Israeli limitations (Mahmoud, 2020). However, the situation was also exacerbated by mask-wearing, social distancing, and proper hygiene measures being ignored by many residents (Mahmoud, 2020). The West Bank and East Jerusalem saw similar non-compliance with social distancing due to population density and decreases in cases at times leading to a sense of security (Asi, 2020). When vaccines became available, high levels of vaccine hesitancy were reported by the public and health professionals (Mahmoud, 2020). Currently only 51.32% of the population has been fully vaccinated (WHO, 2022a). Overall, the WHO reports 662,600 cases and 5,700 deaths in Palestine (WHO, 2022b).

India

The Ministry of Health and Family Welfare (MoHFW) officially reported the first case of COVID-19 in India in January 2020 (Andrews et al., 2020). India has responded to the COVID-19 outbreak at national and state levels (Visaria & Dharamdasani, 2021). The Indian government enacted two laws, including the Epidemic Disease Act (EDA) of 1897 and the Disaster Management Act (DMA) of 2005, to respond to the outbreak (Gowd et al., 2021). The Indian government regularly updates guidelines on restrictions and clinical matters for both state and local authorities, and has recommended measures such as social distancing, mask-wearing, cough etiquette, and hand washing (Venkata-Subramani & Roman, 2020). In March 2020, the Indian government decided to implement a 21-day nationwide lockdown and closed its borders (Venkata-Subramani & Roman, 2020). A further series of lockdowns followed in 2020, but despite these, there were more than 640,000 confirmed cases and 18,000 deaths reported in India by June 2020 (Gowd et al., 2021). The lack of medical resources and relaxation of restrictions have contributed to a worsening of the pandemic (Yang et al., 2022). In April 2022, Maharashtra, Delhi, Telangana, and West Bengal authorities announced a complete relaxation of COVID-19 norms, and mask-wearing is no longer mandatory (Ghosh, 2022). As of July 2022, there have been more than 43.6 million cases and more than 525,000 COVID-19–related deaths (Johns Hopkins Coronavirus Resource Center, n.d.).

China

Despite China being one of the most populous countries in the world and the place where the virus emerged, by July 2022, a relatively small number of COVID-19 cases (227,030) and a very small number of deaths have been reported (5,226). COVID-19 is identified through retrospective analysis as likely to have been first discovered around mid-November 2019 in Wuhan, but not fully recognized as a significant threat until regional health authorities issued a public health alert on December 30, 2019. The provincial and national governments in China reacted swiftly to instances of infection with travel restrictions, public health requirements, lockdowns, and quarantines. The controls were sufficiently strong to reduce transmission in the community, but small outbreaks have persisted and where discovered these have been reacted to swiftly with strong restrictions. China has persisted with an elimination strategy. Many Chinese cities remain in differing levels of lockdown as of July 2022. As of July 2022, there have been nearly 2.2 million reported cases and almost 15,000 COVID-19–related deaths (Johns Hopkins Coronavirus Resource Center, n.d.).

Method and Analysis

After ethical approval, data were collected between November 2020 and June 2021 in Argentina ($n = 200$), Brazil ($n = 410$), Chile ($n = 367$), China ($n = 256$), England ($n = 364$), France ($n = 321$), India ($n = 402$), Israel ($n = 183$), Italy ($n = 311$), Kenya ($n = 226$), Kyrgyzstan ($n = 228$), Mexico ($n = 304$), New Zealand ($n = 650$), Nigeria ($n = 208$), Palestine ($n = 160$), Peru ($n = 251$), Russia ($n = 201$), Singapore ($n = 298$), South Africa ($n = 326$), Spain ($n = 298$), Turkey ($n = 217$), and the United States ($n = 681$). The total sample size is 6,882. Data were collected in two ways: via an online survey using Qualtrics or SurveyMonkey or via paper-based surveys. According to Troia and Graham (2017), online panels and face-to-face paper-based surveys are comparable in composition. It was necessary to use the combination of Qualtrics, SurveyMonkey, and paper-based surveys because participants could not be reached equally using one data collection approach. For example, in Nigeria, Russia, and Kenya, participants were more trusting of paper-based surveys than of online links to surveys. Thus, paper-based surveys were used in these nations. On the ground, contacts in Turkey found it easier to use SurveyMonkey, as participants were familiar with using it; thus, this method was employed. All surveys included demographic questions, a question asking participants the extent to which they support mask-wearing, and a question asking participants how often they wear a mask. Table 2.1 includes the demographic information for each nation.

TABLE 2.1 Participant Demographics by Nation

Nation	Sex (Female/Male)	Age (M; SD)
United States ($n = 681$)	354 females (52%) and 327 males (48%)	$M = 25.18$; $SD = 6.55$
New Zealand ($n = 650$)	325 females (50%) and 325 males (50%)	$M = 28.11$; $SD = 6.22$
Spain ($n = 298$)	134 females (45%) and 164 males (55%)	$M = 28.11$; $SD = 7.12$
Italy ($n = 311$)	145 females (46.6%) and 166 males (53.4%)	$M = 39.17$; $SD = 9.17$
Russia ($n = 201$)	96 females (47.8%) and 105 males (52.2%)	$M = 36.82$; $SD = 5.72$
South Africa ($n = 326$)	149 females (45.7%) and 177 males (54.3%)	$M = 38.16$; $SD = 9.98$
Mexico ($n = 304$)	156 females (51.3%) and 148 males (48.7%)	$M = 37.15$; $SD = 7.75$
India ($n = 402$)	286 females (71.1%) and 116 males (28.9%)	$M = 25.14$; $SD = 10.29$
Singapore ($n = 298$)	149 females (50%) and 149 males (50%)	$M = 26.98$; $SD = 11.25$
Brazil ($n = 410$)	197 females (48%) and 213 males (52%)	$M = 28.97$; $SD = 8.37$
Peru ($n = 251$)	97 females (38.6%) and 154 males (61.4%)	$M = 25.19$; $SD = 5.01$
Chile ($n = 367$)	173 females (47.1%) and 194 males (52.9%)	$M = 36.15$; $SD = 10.18$

Kyrgyzstan (n = 228)	144 females (63.2%) and 84 males (36.8%)	M = 34.79; SD = 9.24
Argentina (n = 220)	95 females (43.2%) and 125 males (56.8%)	M = 32.89; SD = 9.19
Turkey (n = 217)	99 females (43.2%) and 125 males (56.8%)	M = 34.67; SD = 7.89
England (n = 364)	134 females (36.8%) and 230 males (63.2%)	M = 32.45; SD = 6.79
France (n = 321)	160 females (49.8%) and 161 males (50.2%)	M = 30.50; SD = 11.15
Kenya (n = 226)	108 females (47.8%) and 118 males (52.2%)	M = 23.54; SD = 6.78
Nigeria (n = 208)	106 females (51%) and 102 males (49%)	M = 22.98; SD = 9.09
China (n = 256)	134 females (52.3%) and 122 males (47.7%)	M = 30.15; SD = 8.01
Israel (n = 183)	112 females (61.2%) and 71 males (38.8%)	M = 28.19; SD = 7.78
Palestine (n = 160)	70 females (43.8%) and 90 males (56.3%)	M = 26.14; SD = 5.89

Results

To answer the research question, two analysis of variance (ANOVAs) were conducted. The first ANOVA showed the effect of nation was significant on the extent to which participants "support" mask-wearing, $F(21,6642)$ = 68.65, p < .001. Post hoc analyses using the Games–Howell test indicated numerous differences between the nations (p < .01); these differences are shown in Table 2.2. Spain (M = 3.96), New Zealand (M = 3.28), and Kyrgyzstan (M = 3.06) scored the highest in support for mask-wearing, with Singapore (M = 1.97), the United States (M = 1.95), and Brazil (M = 1.82) scoring the lowest.

The second ANOVA showed the effect of nation was significant on the extent to which participants report "wearing" a mask, $F(21,6642)$ = 88.50, p < .001. Post hoc analyses using the Games–Howell test indicated numerous differences between the nations (p < .01); these differences are shown in Table 2.3. New Zealand (M = 3.45), Mexico (M = 3.19), and Spain (M = 2.85) scored the highest on reported mask-wearing. Brazil (M = 1.56), Russia (M = 1.51), and Palestine (M = 1.51) scored the lowest on reported mask-wearing.

TABLE 2.2 Means and Multiple Comparisons for Support for Mask-Wearing

Nation	(M; SD)	Nations with Sig. M Diff. (p < .001)
United States (USA)	M = 1.95; SD = 1.10	NZ, Spain, Italy, Russia, SA, Mexico, Kyrgyzstan, Argentina
New Zealand (NZ)	M = 3.28; SD = 1.43	USA, Spain, Italy, Russia, SA, India, Singapore, Brazil, Peru, Chile, Turkey, England, France, Kenya, Nigeria, China, Israel, Palestine
Spain	M = 3.96; SD = 1.16	USA, NZ, Italy, Russia, SA, Mexico, India, Singapore, Brazil, Peru, Chile, Kyrgyzstan, Argentina, Turkey, England, France, Kenya, Nigeria, China, Israel, Palestine
Italy	M = 2.73; SD = 1.25	USA, NZ, Spain, India, Singapore, Brazil, Peru, England, France, Kenya, Nigeria, China, Israel, Palestine
Russia	M = 2.58; SD = 1.27	USA, NZ, Spain, Singapore, Brazil, Peru, France
South Africa (SA)	M = 2.67; SD = 1.55	USA, NZ, Spain, India, Singapore, Brazil, Peru, England, France, Kenya, China
Mexico	M = 3.06; SD = 1.29	USA, Spain, India, Singapore, Brazil, Peru, Chile, Turkey, England, France, Kenya, Nigeria, China, Israel, Palestine
India	M = 2.10; SD = 1.08	NZ, Spain, Italy, SA, Mexico, Kyrgyzstan, Argentina
Singapore	M = 1.97; SD = .93	NZ, Spain, Italy, Russia, SA, Mexico, Kyrgyzstan, Argentina
Brazil	M = 1.82; SD = .94	NZ, Spain, Italy, Russia, SA, Mexico, Chile, Kyrgyzstan, Argentina, Turkey, England
Peru	M = 1.98; SD = .95	NZ, Spain, Italy, Russia, SA, Mexico, Kyrgyzstan, Argentina
Chile	M = 2.30; SD = 1.44	NZ, Spain, Mexico, Brazil, Kyrgyzstan
Kyrgyzstan	M = 3.00; SD = 1.09	US, Spain, India, Singapore, Brazil, Peru, Chile, Turkey, England, France, Kenya, Nigeria, China, Israel, Palestine
Argentina	M = 2.84; SD = 1.40	US, Spain, India, Singapore, Brazil, Peru, Turkey, England, France, Kenya, Nigeria, China, Israel, Palestine

Turkey	$M = 2.26; SD = 1.14$	NZ, Spain, Mexico, Brazil, Kyrgyzstan, Argentina
England	$M = 2.17; SD = 1.06$	NZ, Spain, Italy, SA, Mexico, Brazil, Kyrgyzstan, Argentina
France	$M = 2.06; SD = 1.09$	NZ, Spain, Italy, Russia, SA, Mexico, Kyrgyzstan, Argentina
Kenya	$M = 2.09; SD = .97$	NZ, Spain, Italy, SA Mexico, Kyrgyzstan, Argentina
Nigeria	$M = 2.21; SD = 1.06$	NZ, Spain, Italy, Mexico, Kyrgyzstan, Argentina
China	$M = 2.15; SD = .97$	NZ, Spain, Italy, SA, Mexico, Kyrgyzstan, Argentina
Israel	$M = 2.15; SD = 1.09$	NZ, Spain, Italy, Mexico, Kyrgyzstan, Argentina
Palestine	$M = 2.15; SD = 1.15$	NZ, Spain, Italy, Mexico, Kyrgyzstan, Argentina

TABLE 2.3 Means and Multiple Comparisons for Reported Mask-Wearing

Nation	(M; SD)	Nations with Sig. M Diff. (p < .001)
United States (USA)	$M = 1.72; SD = 1.03$	NZ, Spain, Italy, SA, Mexico, Argentina, England, Nigeria, China
New Zealand (NZ)	$M = 3.45; SD = 1.14$	USA, Spain, Italy, Russia, SA, India, Singapore, Brazil, Peru, Chile, Kyrgyzstan, Turkey, England, France, Kenya, Nigeria, China, Israel, Palestine
Spain	$M = 2.85; SD = 1.31$	USA, NZ, Russia, India, Singapore, Brazil, Peru, Chile, Kyrgyzstan, Turkey, England, France, Kenya, Nigeria, China, Israel, Palestine
Italy	$M = 2.52; SD = 1.16$	USA, NZ, Russia, Mexico, India, Singapore, Brazil, Peru, Chile, Kyrgyzstan, Turkey, France, Kenya, Palestine
Russia	$M = 1.51; SD = .62$	NZ, Spain, Italy, SA, Mexico, India, Peru, Chile, Argentina, England, France, Kenya, Nigeria, China, Israel
South Africa (SA)	$M = 2.40; SD = 1.44$	USA, NZ, Russia, Mexico, Singapore, Brazil, Kyrgyzstan, Turkey, France, Palestine

(Continued)

TABLE 2.3 (Continued)

Nation	(M; SD)	Nations with Sig. M Diff. (p < .001)
Mexico	M = 3.19; SD = 1.27	USA, Italy, Russia, SA, India, Singapore, Brazil, Peru, Chile, Kyrgyzstan, Turkey, England, France, Kenya, Nigeria, China, Israel, Palestine
India	M = 2.01; SD = 1.03	NZ, Spain, Italy, Russia, Mexico, Brazil, Argentina, Palestine
Singapore	M = 1.71; SD = .85	NZ, Spain, Italy, SA, Mexico, Argentina, England, Nigeria, China
Brazil	M = 1.56; SD = .79	NZ, Spain, Italy, SA, Mexico, India, Peru, Chile, Argentina, England, France, Kenya, Nigeria, China, Israel
Peru	M = 1.98; SD = .97	NZ, Spain, Italy, Russia, Mexico, Brazil, Argentina, Palestine
Chile	M = 2.07; SD = 1.39	NZ, Spain, Italy, Russia, Mexico, Brazil, Argentina, Palestine
Kyrgyzstan	M = 1.67; SD =.87	NZ Spain, Italy, SA, Mexico, Argentina, England, Nigeria, China, Israel
Argentina	M = 2.78; SD = 1.57	US, NZ, Russia, India, Singapore, Brazil, Peru, Chile, Kyrgyzstan, Turkey, England, France, Kenya, Israel, Palestine
Turkey	M = 1.76; SD = .99	NZ, Spain, Italy, SA, Mexico, Argentina, China
England	M = 2.15; SD = 1.05	US, NZ, Spain, Russia, Mexico, Singapore, Brazil, Kyrgyzstan, Argentina, Palestine
France	M = 1.91; SD = 1.01	NZ, Spain, Italy, Russia, SA, Mexico, Brazil, Argentina, Palestine
Kenya	M = 1.93; SD = .93	NZ, Spain, Italy, Russia, Mexico, Brazil, Argentina, Palestine
Nigeria	M = 2.22; SD = 1.19	US, NZ, Spain, Russia, Mexico, Singapore, Brazil, Kyrgyzstan, Palestine
China	M = 2.22; SD = 1.14	US, NZ, Spain, Russia, Mexico, Singapore, Brazil, Kyrgyzstan, Turkey, Palestine
Israel	M = 2.13; SD = 1.02	NZ, Spain, Russia, Mexico, Brazil, Kyrgyzstan, Argentina, Palestine
Palestine	M = 1.51; SD = .77	NZ, Spain, Italy, SA, Mexico, India, Peru, Chile, Argentina, England, France, Nigeria, China, Israel

Discussion

When considering the results of this study, three implications can be drawn. First, the importance of consistent health messaging cannot be understated. In nations such as New Zealand, Spain, and Kyrgystan, the governments were consistent in their messaging around mask-wearing. Each nation's government from the start of the pandemic consistently promoted the use of masks as a preventative measure. While in nations such as Brazil, Russia, and the United States, governments and political leaders either did not promote mask-wearing, or openly rejected COVID-19 as a public health crisis. In nations where mask-wearing was promoted, individuals were more likely to perceive the adoption of the behavior as achievable, thus meeting one of the critical criteria of the health belief model, and thus behavioral adoption (Johnson & Witte, 2003; Rosenstock, 1974).

Second, patient self-advocacy is a personal choice. Before the pandemic, it was more common in many Southeast nations for individuals to report wearing masks. Since the SARS outbreak in 2003, mask-wearing has become a more common occurrence in many Southeast Asian nations as way for individuals to advocate for their own health. However, it is possible that when a government mandates such a behavior, even when it is in the wake of a global pandemic, individuals may not be likely to see such a behavior favorably. Even in Singapore and China, both Southeast Asian nations, support for mask-wearing and reported mask-wearing were relatively low. Thus, future research should explore the relationship between patient self-advocacy as a choice and when such behavior is "forced" on an individual.

Third, societal pressures, particularly political influences, must be considered. A critical part of the TPB is societal pressures (Ajzen, 1991; Ajzen & Fishbein, 1980). In each of the nations within this study, politicians framed COVID-19, and related issues (such as masking) in different ways and this framing influenced the perception of making as a health behavior. In Brazil, Bolsonaro called COVID-19 a hoax (Brazil et al., 2021). The Turkish government has largely opposed preventative measures over economic gains (Gökay, 2020). Former U.S. President Donald Trump and many Republican leaders largely dismissed the severity of COVID-19 and preventative measures (Croucher et al., 2021). In New Zealand, the government quickly locked down the nation once the pandemic began and leaders overwhelmingly promoted preventative behaviors. In nations where political influence was used to promote preventative behaviors, uptake was higher.

While the results in this chapter offer areas for discussion and future research, there are a couple of limitations. First, the data for this study were collected between November 2020 and June 2021. This eight-month period does provide for variability in individual COVID-19 experiences. Second, Individuals were asked to self-report their mask-wearing. It is possible that there might be a social desirability bias in the results. We hope the results of this chapter and this review of some key health communication theories in the time of COVID-19 provide you with a greater understanding of health communication in the time of this pandemic.

References

Abed, Y., Shaheen, A., & Abedrabbo, A. (2021). Variations in COVID-19 spread and control measures in the Palestinian territories. *Frontiers in Public Health*. https://doi.org/10.3389/fpubh.2021.736005

Ajzen, I. (1991). The theory of planned behavior. *Organizational Behavior and Human Decision Processes, 50,* 179–211.

Ajzen, I., & Fishbein, M. (1980). *Attitudes, personality, and behavior* (2nd ed.). McGraw Hill.

Aluga, M. A. (2020). Coronavirus disease 2019 (COVID-19) in Kenya: Preparedness, response and transmissibility. *Journal of Microbiology, Immunology and Infection, 53*(5), 671–673. https://doi.org/10.1016/j.jmii.2020.04.011

Andrews, M. A., Areekal, B., Rajesh, K. R., Krishnan, J., Suryakala, R., Krishnan, B, Muraly, C. P., & Santhosh, P. V. (2020). First confirmed cases of COVID-19 infection in India: A case report. *Indian Journal of Medicine, 151*(5), 490–492. https://doi.org/10.4103/ijmr.IJMR_2131_20

Andrews, K. R., Silk, K. S., & Eneli, I. U. (2010). Parents as health promoters: A theory of planned behavior perspective on the prevention of childhood obesity. *Journal of Health Communication, 15,* 95–107.

Asi, Y. M. (2020). *Another test of Palestinian sumud: COVID-19 in the West Bank, Gaza Strip, and East Jerusalem.* Arab Center. https://arabcenterdc.org/resource/another-test-of-palestinian-sumud-covid-19-in-the-west-bank-gaza-strip-and-east-jerusalem/

Ausína, B., Castellanosb, M. A., González-Sanguinoa, C., Vakhantsevac, O. V., Almazovac, O. V., Shaigerovac, L. A., Dolgikhc, A. G., & Muñoz, A. G. (2020). The psychological impact of six weeks of lockdown as a consequence of COVID-19 and the importance of social support: A cross-cultural study comparing Spanish and Russian populations. *Psychology in Russia: State of the Art, 13*(4), 89–105.

Beaubien, J. (2021). *Peru has the world's highest COVID death rate. Here's why.* NPR. https://www.npr.org/sections/goatsandsoda/2021/11/27/1057387896/peru-has-the-worlds-highest-covid-death-rate-heres-why

Bish, A., Yardley, L., Nicoll, A., & Michie, S. (2011). Factors associated with uptake of vaccination against pandemic influenza: A systematic review. *Vaccine, 29*(38), 6472–6484. https://doi.org/10.1016/j.vaccine.2011.06.107

Brand, S. P. C., Ojal, J., Aziza, R., Were, V., Okiro, E. A., Kombe, I. K.,…, & Barasa, E. (2021). COVID-19 transmission dynamics underlying epidemic waves in Kenya. *Science, 374*(6570), 989–994. https://doi.org/10.1126/science.abk0414

Brann, M., & Sutton, M. L. (2009). The theory of planned behavior and college students' willingness to talk about smoking-related behavior. *Communication Research Reports, 26,* 198–207.

Brashers, D. E. (2001). Communication and uncertainty management. *Journal of Communication, 51,* 477–497. https://doi.org/10.1111/j.1460-2466.2001.tb02892.x

Brashers, D. E., Haas, S. M., & Neidig, J. L. (2009). The patient self advocacy scale: Measuring patient involvement in health care decision-making interactions. *Health Communication, 11,* 97–121. https://doi.org/10.1207/s15327027hc1102_1

Brashers, D. E., Neidig, J. L., Haas, S. M., Dobbs, L. K., Cardillo, L. W., & Russell, J. A. (2000). Communication in the management of uncertainty: The case of persons living with HIV or AIDS. *Communication Monographs, 67*(1), 63–84. https://doi. org/10.1080/03637750009376495

Bresnahan, M., Lee, S. Y., Smith, S. W., Shearman, S., Nebashi, R., Park, C. Y., & Yoo, J. (2007). A theory of planned behavior study of college students' intention to register as organ donors in Japan, Korea, and the United States. *Health Communication, 21,* 201–211.

Buenos Aires Times. (2022, May 2). Peruvians continue to wear masks, even though it's no longer mandatory. *Buenos Aires Times.* https://www.batimes.com.ar/news/latin-america/peruvians-continue-to-wear-masks-even-though-it-is-no-longer-mandatory.phtml

Buldeo, P., & Gilbert, L. (2015). Exploring the health belief model and first-year students' responses to HIV/AIDS and VCT at a South African university. *African Journal of AIDS Research, 14*(3), 209–218. https://doi.org/10.2989/16085906.2015.1052527

Burke, J. (2020, February 28). Nigeria confirms first coronavirus case in sub-Saharan Africa. *The Guardian.* https://www.theguardian.com/world/2020/feb/28/coronavirus-found-in-sub-saharan-africa-as-who-says-spread-could-get-out-of-control

Burki, T. K. (2022). Fourth dose of COVID-19 vaccines in Israel. *The Lancet Respiratory Medicine, 10*(2), E19. https://doi.org/10.1016/S2213-2600(22)00010-8

Centers for Disease Control and Prevention. (2022). *COVID Data Tracker.* Department of Health and Human Services. https://covid.cdc.gov/covid-data-tracker

Chau, D. C. (2022). The geography and politics of Kenya's response to COVID-19. *Prism, 9*(4), 213–222.

Clase, C. M., Fu, E. L., Joseph, M., Beale, R. C. L., Dolovich, M. B., Jardine, M., Mann, J. F. E., Pecoits-Filho, R., Winkelmayer, W. C., & Carrero, J. J. (2020). Cloth masks may prevent transmission of COVID-19: An evidence based, risk-based approach. *Annals of Internal Medicine.* https://doi.org/10.7326/M20-2567

Croucher, S. M. (2016). *Understanding communication theory: A beginner's guide.* Routledge.

Croucher, S. M., Ashwell, D., Murray, N., Condon, S. M., & Fletcher, P. (2021). A longitudinal analysis of handwashing and mask-wearing during COVID-19. *Frontiers in Health Communication.* https://doi.org/10.3389/fcomm.2021.689974

Dzushupov K., Lucero-Prisno D. E. III, Vishnyakov, D., Lin X., & Ahmadi A. (2021) COVID-19 in Kyrgyzstan: Navigating a way out. *Journal of Global Health, 11*(03020). https://doi.org/10.7189/jogh.11.03020

Fedele, F., Aria, M., Esposito, V., Micillo, M., Cecere, G., Spano, M., & De Marco, G. (2021). COVID-19 vaccine hesitancy: A survey in a population highly compliant to common vaccinations. *Human Vaccines & Immunotherapeutics, 17*(10), 3348–3354. https://doi.org/10.1080/21645515.2021.1928460

France-Presse, A. (2022, March 31). South Africa's Covid deaths could be 3 times the official count (100,000). *NDTV.* https://www.ndtv.com/world-news/covid-variant-in-south-africa-south-africa-coronavirus-variant-covid-variant-south-africas-covid-deaths-could-be-3-times-more-than-official-count-2853640

Ghosh, P. (2022, April 1). List of states where Covid-19 mask not mandatory anymore. Explained. *The Hindustan Times.* https://www.hindustantimes.com/india-news/list-of-states-where-covid-19-mask-not-mandatory-anymore-explained-101648789690816.html

Global Monitoring. (2022). *COVID-19 pandemic – Peru*. A3M Global Monitoring. https://global-monitoring.com/gm/page/events/epidemic-0002001.AodVzOVpSz03.html?lang=en

Gökay, B. (2020). Turkey tries to keep wheels of economy turning despite worsening coronavirus crisis. *The Conversation*. https://theconversation.com/turkey-tries-to-keep-wheels-of-economy-turning-despite-worsening-coronavirus-crisis-135370

Goldberg, M. H., Gustafson, A., Maibach, E. W., Ballew, M. T., Bergquist, P., Kotcher, J. E., Marlon, J. R., Rosenthal, S. A., & Leiserowitz, A. (2020). Mask-wearing increased after a government recommendation: A natural experiment in the U.S. during the COVID-19 Pandemic. *Frontiers in Communication, 5*, 1–23. https://doi.org/10.3389/fcomm.2020.00044

Goni, U. (2021, 20 May). 'People die in less than a week': Covid wave catches Argentina off-guard. *The Guardian*. https://www.theguardian.com/global-development/2021/may/20/argentina-covid-coronavirus-cases-deaths-hospitals

Government of Canada. (2020). Considerations in the use of homemade masks to protect against COVID-19. Notice to general public and healthcare professionals. https://www.canada.ca/en/health-canada/services/drugs-health-products/medical-devices/activities/announcements/covid19-notice-home-made-masks.html

Government of Chile. (2022). *Paso a paso*. Government of Chile. https://www.gob.cl/pasoapaso/

Government of the United Kingdom. (2022). Cases in England. https://coronavirus.data.gov.uk/details/cases?areaType=nation&areaName=England

Gowd, K. K., Veerababu, D., & Reddy, V. R. (2021). COVID-19 and the legislative response in India: The need for comprehensive health care law. *Journal of Public Affairs, 21*(4). https://doi.org/10.1002/pa.2669

Hornik, R., Kikut, A., Jesch, E., Woko, C., Siegel, L. & Kim, K. (2021). Association of COVID-19 misinformation with face mask wearing and social distancing in a nationally representative US sample. *Health Communication, 36*(1), 6–14. https://doi.org/10.1080/10410236.2020.1847437

Institute for Health Metrics and Evaluation (IHME). (2022). *COVID-19 results briefing – Peru*. IHME. https://www.healthdata.org/sites/default/files/covid_briefs/123_briefing_Peru.pdf

Jacobs, E. D., & Okeke, M. I. (2022). A critical evaluation of Nigeria's response to the first wave of COVID-19. *Bulletin of National Research Centre, 46*(44). https://doi.org/10.1186/s42269-022-00729-9

James, D. C. S., Pobee, J. W., Oxidine, D., Brown, L., & Joshi, G. (2012). Using the health belief model to develop culturally-appropriate weight-management materials for African-American women. *Journal of the Academy of Nutrition and Dietetics, 112*(5), 664–670. https://doi.org/10.1016/j.jand.20212.02.003

Janz, N. K., & Becker, M. H. (1984). The health belief model: A decade later. *Health Education Quarterly, 11*, 1–47.

Johns Hopkins Coronavirus Resource Center. (Updated daily). Covid-19 Dashboard to the Center for Systems for Science and Engineering (CSSE) at Johns Hopkins University. https://coronavirus.jhu.edu/map.html

Johnson, L. M., & Witte, K. (2003). Looking toward the future: Health massage design strategies. In Thompson, T., Dorsey, A. M., Miller, K. I., & Parrott, R. (Eds.), *Handbook of health communication*. (pp. 473–496). Lawrence Erlbaum.

Jørgensen, F., Bor, A., & Petersen, M.B. (2020). Compliance without fear: Predictors of protective behavior during the first wave of the COVID-19 pandemic. *PsychArXiv*, 1–61. https://doi.org/10.31234/osf.io/uzwgf.

Kabar News Agency. (2022, March 11). *Kyrgyzstan cancels mandatory wearing of masks.* http://en.kabar.kg/news/kyrgyzstan-cancels-mandatory-wearing-of-masks/

Kaim, A., Siman-Tov, M., Jaffe, E., & Adini, B. (2021). Factors that enhance or impede compliance of the public with governmental regulation of lockdown during COVID-19 in Israel. *International Journal of Disaster Risk Reduction, 66.* Article 102596. https://doi.org/10.1016/j.ijdrr.2021.102596

Lammertyn, M., Soria, H. & Otaola, J. (2020, October 20) World News. Argentina exceeds 1 million coronavirus cases as spike strains health system, 20202:48. *Reuters.* https://www.reuters.com/article/health-coronavirus-argentina-idINKBN275066

Larrea, A. (2021, June 29). COVID-19, life and death with the mobile brigade in Kyrgyzstan. *ReliefWeb.* https://reliefweb.int/report/kyrgyzstan/covid-19-life-and-death-mobile-brigade-kyrgyzstan

Last, M. (2020). The first wave of COVID-19 in Israel: Initial analysis of publicly available data. *PLoS One, 15*(10). Article e0240393. https://doi.org/ 10.1371/journal.pone.0240393

Latkin, C. A., Dayton, L., Moran, M., Strickland, J. C., & Collins, K. (2021). Behavioral and psychosocial factors associated with COVID-19 skepticism in the United States. *Current Psychology.* https://doi.org/10.1007/s12144-020-01211-3

Lee, H. K. (2020). South Korea takes new measures to have enough face masks domestically amid coronavirus. *ABC News.* https://abcnews.go.com/International/south-korea-takes-measures-face-masks-domestically-amid/story?id=69254114

Lee, H.-Y., Lin, H.-C., Seo, D-C., & Lohrmann, D. K. (2018). The effect of e-cigarette warning labels on college students' perception on e-cigarettes and intention to use e-cigarettes. *Addictive Behaviors, 76,* 106–112. https://doi.org/10.1016/j.addbeh.2017.07.033

Lesham, E., & Wilder-Smith, A. (2021). COVID-19 vaccine impact in Israel and a way out of the pandemic. *Lancet, 397,* 1783–1785. https://doi.org/10.1016/S0140-6736(21)01018-7

Liao, M., Liu, H., Wang, X., Hu, X., Huang, Y., Liu, X., Brenan, K., Mecha, J., Nirmalan, M., & Lu, J. R. (2021). A technical review of face mask wearing in preventing respiratory COVID-19 transmission. *Current Opinion in Colloid & Interface Science, 52.* https://doi.org/10.1016/j.cocis.2021.101417

Linde P. (2022, 20 April). After two years, Spain ends indoor face mask rule. *El País.* https://english.elpais.com/society/2022-04-20/after-two-years-spain-ends-indoor-face-mask-rule.html

Mahmoud, W. (2020, November 23). Gaza declares COVID-19 disaster with health system near collapse. *Aljazeera.* https://www.aljazeera.com/news/2020/11/23/gaza-declares-covid-19-disaster-with-health-system-near-collapse

Mattson, M. (1999). Toward a reconceputalisation of communication cues to action in the health belief model: HIV test counseling. *Communication Monographs, 66*(3), 240–265. https://doi.org/10.1080/03637759909376476.

Mehta, P., Sharma, M., & Lee, R. C. (2013). Designing and evaluating a health belief model-based intervention to increase HPV vaccination among college males. *Community Health Equity Research & Policy, 34*(1), 101–117. https://doi.org/10.2190/IQ.34.1.h

Menon, U., Champion, V., Monahan, P. O., Daggy, J., Hui, S., & Skinner, C. S. (2007). Health belief model variables as predictors of progression in stage of mammography adoption. *American Journal of Health Promotion, 21*(4), 255–261. https://doi.org/10.4278/0890-1171-21.4.255

Ministry of Health of Singapore. (2022). *News highlights.* Ministry of Health (MOH). https://www.moh.gov.sg/news-highlights/

Mkhize, Z. (2020, March 5). *First case of COVID-19 coronavirus reported in SA*. National Institute for Communicable Diseases. https://www.nicd.ac.za/first-case-of-covid-19-coronavirus-reported-in-sa/

Moonasar, D., Pillay, A., Leonard, E., Naidoo, R., Mngemane, S., Ramkrishna, W.,..., & Pillay, Y. (2021). COVID-19: Lessons and experiences from South Africa's first surge. *BMJ Global Health, 6*. https://doi.org/10.1136/bmjgh-2020-004393

Myers, L. B., & Goodwin, R. (2012). Using a theoretical framework to determine adults' intention to vaccinate against pandemic swine flu in priority groups in the UK. *Public Health, 126*, S53–S56. https://doi.org/10.1016/j.puhe.2012.05.024

Norman, P., & Conner, M. (2005). The Theory of Planned Behavior and exercise: Evidence for the mediating and moderating roles of planning on intention-behavior relationships. *Journal of Sport & Exercise Psychology, 27*(4), 488–504. https://doi.org/10.1123/jsep.27.4.488

Ongoina, D. (2020). COVID-19: The need for rational use of face masks in Nigeria. *The American Journal of Tropical Medicine and Hygiene, 103*(1), 33–34. https://doi.org/10.4269/ajtmh.20-0433

Our World in Data. (2022). *Coronavirus (COVID-19) vaccinations*. Global Change Data Lab. https://ourworldindata.org/covid-vaccinations?country=BRA

Pauli, J., Basso, K., & Ruffatto, J. (2017). The influence of beliefs on organ donation intention. *International Journal of Pharmaceutical and Healthcare Marketing, 11*(3), 291–308. https://doi.org/10.1108/IJPHM-08-2016-0040

Prapavessis, H., Gaston, A., & DeJesus, S. (2015). The theory of planned behavior as a model for understanding sedentary behavior. *Psychology of Sport and Exercise, 19*, 23–32. https://doi.org/10.1016/j.psychsport.2015.02.001

Reuters. (2020). *Peru records first confirmed case of coronavirus, President Vizcarra says*. Reuters. https://www.reuters.com/article/health-coronavirus-peru-idUSE6N29R02T

Reuters. (2022, March 23). *S. Africa's Ramaphosa eases COVID-19 restrictions to lift economy*. https://www.reuters.com/world/africa/safricas-ramaphosa-says-end-national-state-disaster-over-covid-19-soon-2022-03-22/

RFE/RL. (2022, February 9). *Russia's daily COVID-19 infection rate hits record again*. https://www.rferl.org/a/russia-covid-new-record/31694474.html

Rieger, M. O. (2020). To wear or not to wear? Factors influencing wearing face masks in Germany during the COVID-19 pandemic. *Social Health and Behavior, 3*(2), 50–54. https://doi.org/10.4103/SHB.SHB_23_20

Rosenstock, I. M. (1974). Historical origins of the health belief model. *Health Education Monographs, 2*(4), 328–335.

Rosenstock, I. M., Strecher, V. J., & Becker, M. H. (1988). Social learning theory and the health belief model. *Health Education & Behavior, 15*(2), 175–183. https://doi.org/10.1177/109019818801500203

Sánchez-Talanquer, M., González-Pier, E., Sepúlveda, J., Abascal-Miguel, L., Fieldhouse, J., Del Rio, C., & Gallalee, S. (2021). *Mexico's response to COVID-19: A case study*. UCSF Institute for Global Health Sciences. https://globalhealthsciences.ucsf.edu/sites/globalhealthsciences.ucsf.edu/files/mexico-covid-19-case-study-english.pdf

Schröder, M., Bossert, A., Kersting, M., Aeffner, S, Coetzee, J, Timme, M., & Schlüter, J. (2021). COVID-19 in South Africa: Outbreak despite interventions. *Scientific Reports, 11*(4956). https://doi.org/10.1038/s41598-021-84487-0

Serdan, T. D. A., Masi, L. N., Gorjao, R., Pithon-Curi, T. C., Curi, R., & Hirabara, S. M. (2020). COVID-19 in Brazil: Historical cases, disease milestones, and estimated outbreak peak. *Travel Medicine and Infectious Disease, 38*(November–December), Article 101733. https://doi.org/10.1016/j.tmaid.2020.101733

Serdan, T. D. A., Tang, Y., Lobato, T. B., da Silva, F. L. R., Tang, S., Masi, L. N., Gorjao, R., Palacios, R., Pithon-Curi, T. C., Curi, R., & Hirabara, S. M. (2021). COVID-19 pandemic in Brazil: History, characteristics, and evolution. In P. Guest (Ed.), *Identification of biomarkers, new treatments, and vaccines in COVID-19* (pp. 35–47). Springer.

Shmueli, L. (2021). Predicting intention to receive COVID-19 vaccine among the general population using the health belief model and the theory of planned behavior model. *BMC Public Health, 21,* 804. https://doi.org/10.1186/s12889-021-10816-7

Si, H., Shi, J.-G., Tang, D., Wu, G., & Lan, J. (2020). Understanding intention and behavior toward sustainable usage of bike sharing by extending the theory of planned behavior. *Resources, Conservation and Recycling, 152,* 104513. https://doi.org/10.1016/j.resconrec.2019.104513

Sofiychuk, E. (2020, February 1). *First two persons infected with coronavirus identified in Russia.* Tass. https://tass.com/society/1115101

Sokhey, S. W. (2021). Russia's response to COVID-19: Leveraging pre-pandemic data to theorize about public approval. *Problems of Post-Communism, 69*(1), 36–47. https://doi.org/10.1080/10758216.2021.1939717

Staff, T. (2021, August 15). Health Ministry unveils new caps on gatherings, mask mandate. *The Times of Israel.* https://www.timesofisrael.com/health-ministry-unveils-new-caps-on-gatherings-mask-mandate/

Suárez, V., Suarez Quezada, M., Oros Ruiz, S., & Ronquillo De Jesús, E. (2020). Epidemiology of COVID-19 in Mexico: From the 27th of February to the 30th of April 2020. Epidemiología de COVID-19 en México: Del 27 de febrero al 30 de abril de 2020. *Revista clinica espanola, 220*(8), 463–471. https://doi.org/10.1016/j.rce.2020.05.007

Tariq, A., Undurraga, E. A., Laborde, C. C., Vogt-Geisse, K., Luo, R., Rothenberg, R., & Chowell, G. (2021). Transmission dynamics and control of COVID-19 in Chile, March-October, 2020. *PLoS Neglected Tropical Diseases, 15*(1), Article e0009070. https://doi.org/10.1371/journal.pntd.0009070

Tayfur, N. A. (2020, March 18). *Kyrgyzstan reports 1st coronavirus cases.* Anadolu Agency. https://www.aa.com.tr/en/asia-pacific/kyrgyzstan-reports-1st-coronavirus-cases/1769954#The Conversation. (2021, April 20). *Kenya's COVID-19 lockdown is forcing people to make difficult food and household energy decisions.* https://theconversation.com/kenyas-covid-19-lockdown-is-forcing-people-to-make-difficult-food-and-household-energy-decisions-158449

The Conversation (2022, March 16). *The coronavirus in Nigeria has its own family history: Keeping track is vital.* https://theconversation.com/the-coronavirus-in-nigeria-has-its-own-family-history-keeping-track-is-vital-178912

Troia, G. A., & Graham, S. (2017). Use and acceptability of writing adaptations for students with disabilities: Survey of Grade 3–8 teachers. *Learning Disabilities Research & Practice*, 32, 257–269.

US Mission Lima. (2022). *COVID-19 information.* US Embassy in Peru. https://pe.usembassy.gov/covid-19-information/

Vanek, M. (2022, June 23). *South Africa ends Covid curbs including wearing of face masks.* Bloomberg. https://www.bloomberg.com/news/articles/2022-06-22/south-africa-ends-covid-curbs-including-wearing-of-face-masks

Venkata-Subramani, M., & Roman, J. (2020). The Coronavirus response in India – World' largest lockdown. *The American Journal of Medical Sciences, 360*(6), 742–748. https://doi.org/10.1016/j.amjms.2020.08.002

Ventura, D., Aith, F., & Reis, R. (2021). Crimes against humanity in Brazil's COVID-19 response – A lesson to us all. *BMJ, 375.* https://doi.org/10.1136/bmj.n2625

Visaria, A., & Dharamdasani, T. (2021). The complex causes of India's 2021 COVID-19 surge. *Correspondence, 397*(10293), 2464–2465. https://doi.org/10.1016/S0140-6736(21)01219-8.

Volk, J. E., & Koopman, C. (2001). Factors associated with condom use in Kenya: A test of the health belief model. *AIDS Education and Prevention, 13*(6), 495–508.

WHO. (2020). *Advice on the use of masks in the context of COVID-19: Interim guidance.* World Health Organization. https://www.who.int/publications-detail/advice-on-the-use-of-masks-in-the-community-during-home-care-and-in-healthcare-settings-in-the-context-of-the-novel-coronavirus-(2019-ncov)-outbreak.

WHO. (2020). *Argentina Covid-19 Case Study. COVID-19: WHO's action in countries.* May 2020. World Health Organization. https://www.who.int/docs/default-source/coronaviruse/country-case-studies/argentina-c19-case-study-20-may.pdf.

WHO. (2022a). *COVID-19 vaccination in the occupied Palestinian territory.* World Health Organization. https://app.powerbi.com/view?r=eyJrIjoiNTViN2Yx-NjItOTY0Ni00MTVhLTg1NzktYTIxNjRjYTIxODk3IiwidCI6ImY2MTB-jMGI3LWJkMjQtNGIzOS04MTBiLTNkYzI4MGFmYjU5MCIsImMiOjh9&pageName=ReportSection

WHO. (2022b). *Coronavirus disease 2019 (COVID-19) in the occupied Palestinian territory.* World Health Organization. https://app.powerbi.com/view?r=eyJrIjoiNTViN2YxNjItOTY0Ni00MTVhLTg1NzktYTIxNjRjYTIxODk3IiwidCI6ImY2MTBjMGI3LWJkMjQtNGIzOS04MTBiLTNkYzI4MGFmYjU5MCIsImMiOjh9&pageName=ReportSection

World Population Review. (2022). *Largest countries in South America 2022.* World Population Review. https://worldpopulationreview.com/country-rankings/largest-countries-in-south-america

Worldometers. (2022a). *Argentina COVID – Coronavirus statistics.* Worldometers. https://www.worldometers.info/coronavirus/country/argentina/

Worldometers. (2022b). *Brazil COVID – Coronavirus statistics.* Worldometers. https://www.worldometers.info/coronavirus/country/brazil/

Worldometers. (2022c). *Chile COVID – Coronavirus statistics.* Worldometers. https://www.worldometers.info/coronavirus/country/chile/

Worldometers. (2022d). *Coronavirus cases.* https://www.worldometers.info

Worldometers. (2022e). *France COVID – Coronavirus statistics.* Worldometers. https://www.worldometers.info/coronavirus/country/france/

Worldometers. (2022f). *Israel COVID – Coronavirus statistics.* Worldometers. https://www.worldometers.info/coronavirus/country/israel/

Worldometers. (2022g). *Italy COVID – Coronavirus statistics.* Worldometers. https://www.worldometers.info/coronavirus/country/italy/

Worldometers. (2022h). *Mexico COVID – Coronavirus statistics.* Worldometers. https://www.worldometers.info/coronavirus/country/mexico/

Worldometers. (2022i). *New Zealand COVID – Coronavirus statistics.* Worldometers. https://www.worldometers.info/coronavirus/country/new-zealand/

Worldometers. (2022j). *Peru COVID – Coronavirus statistics.* Worldometers. https://www.worldometers.info/coronavirus/country/peru/

Worldometers. (2022k). *Singapore COVID – Coronavirus statistics.* Worldometers. https://www.worldometers.info/coronavirus/country/singapore/

Worldometers. (2022l). *Spain COVID – Coronavirus statistics.* Worldometers. https://www.worldometers.info/coronavirus/country/spain/

Worldometers. (2022m). *Turkey COVID – Coronavirus statistics.* Worldometers. https://www.worldometers.info/coronavirus/country/turkey/

Worldometers. (2022n). *United States COVID – Coronavirus statistics.* Worldometers. https://www.worldometers.info/coronavirus/country/us/

Yang, J., Shi, L., Chen, H., Wang, X., Jiao, J., Yang, M., Liu, M., & Sun, G. (2022). Strategies comparison in response to the two waves of COVID-19 in the United States and India. *International Journal for Equity in Health, 21*(57). https://doi.org/10.1186/s12939-022-01666-9

Yang, Z. J. (2015). Predicting young adults' intentions to get the H1N1 vaccine: An integrated model. *Journal of Health Communication, 20*(1), 69–79. https://doi.org/10.1080/10810730.2014.90402

3

SCIENCE COMMUNICATION AND PANDEMICS

Doug Ashwell

To be truly successful any modern-day pandemic response must be supported by quality scientific advice. Science is seen as an integral and vital component in any modern-day society and the importance of good science communication during the current COVID-19 and any future pandemics cannot be overstated. Pandemics by their very nature create anxiety, uncertainty, confusion and a sense of urgency (Taylor, 2019). The ability of scientists to translate and provide accurate and timely scientific and health advice to policy makers and the public has the potential to eliminate or slow the spread of disease and prevent unnecessary deaths. This is especially the case when the pandemic is caused by an unknown virus, as governments and the public alike need to rely on experts to understand the disease (Battison et al., 2021). Throughout the COVID-19 pandemic, scientists have been at the forefront of advising governments on how to manage the virus and have been constantly quoted as local, national and international media sources to explain various aspects of the pandemic to the public. For example, scientists have explained the type of virus that causes COVID-19, its mode of transmission, possible consequences of uninhibited spread, and given advice on public health measures designed to prevent the spread of the virus. In addition, scientists have been instrumental in the development of vaccines to protect people from the virus.

Despite having and continuing to have access to quality science communication about the COVID-19 virus during the pandemic, the potential benefits of this scientific information to help limit the spread of the disease and reduce the mortality rate have been unevenly realized across the globe due to several challenges. This is because science and those who communicate it do not exist in a vacuum. As far back as the time of the ancient Greeks, science has had a relationship with politics, a relationship that has not always been positive. As

DOI: 10.4324/9781003214496-3

will be illustrated, depending on the country, the reception and utilization of the scientific information about COVID-19 has been either accepted, suppressed, ignored or, at times, dangerously distorted. An example of the latter by a leading political figure is the now infamous conference where then U.S. President Donald Trump, who was informed by one of his scientific advisors that disinfectants could kill the virus, appeared to go on to suggest people inject themselves with disinfectants to cure COVID-19. This was of course not the intended message of the scientific advisor, yet tragically after this press conference, some people did ingest disinfectants to combat COVID-19 with disastrous health consequences (Qamar, 2022).

The political arena is only one area where science communication about COVID-19 has struggled to be accepted. It has also had to compete against a small but strongly vocal minority who do not believe COVID-19 to be a serious disease or are distrusting of the newly developed COVID-19 vaccines, believing they have been developed too quickly and are therefore unsafe and/ or ineffective. Some in this group are likely to believe in and spread conspiracy theories and misinformation about COVID-19 and COVID-19 vaccines (Jolley & Douglas, 2017; Germani & Biller-Andorno, 2021). The explosion of false claims about COVID-19 following the announcement of the pandemic was labelled an infodemic by the World Health Organization (WHO) (BBC, 2020). According to the WHO, an infodemic "is too much information including false and misleading information in physical and digital environments during a disease outbreak" (WHO, 2022). Infodemics cause confusion, leaving some people to practise risk-taking behaviours and others unsure of how to protect themselves and others from the disease, resulting in an unnecessary lengthening of the outbreak (WHO, 2022). Infodemics are also a challenge to science communication as quality scientific information competes against false and misleading information circulating.

This chapter explores these issues and how scientists and science communicators might rise to these challenges. The chapter begins with a brief history of public understanding of science (PUS) and public engagement with science (PES) paradigms. This review illustrates the relationship science has always had, since ancient times, with politics – a relationship that has not always been positive. This relationship is then viewed in terms of the COVID-19 pandemic, examining the challenges posed by the differing political environments scientists and science communicators have operated in during the pandemic. Then the chapter moves to examine how some of the differing paradigms of PUS and PES apply in the case of COVID-19. Asking how scientists can positively communicate with the public to fill the deficit of knowledge they have about COVID-19 and pandemic responses while at the same time being ready to engage with the public by listening to and heeding the knowledge the public hold to deal with the COVID-19 response more effectively? Finally, the challenges posed for science communication by misinformation or disinformation during the pandemic are explored. Some possible remedies are considered for how scientists and science communicators can try and combat such information during a pandemic. The chapter concludes by examining what lessons can be learned from the pandemic for science communication with some suggestions made for science communication in future pandemics.

A Brief History of Science Communication

While the COVID-19 pandemic has highlighted the vital role science plays in society, it is hardly a new phenomenon. For example, Bucchi (1998) argued 20 years ago that the increasing importance of science in society has come at the price of an ever-widening gap between scientists and the more "generally educated" public (p. 1). Broks (2006) suggests this gap is the result of the professionalization of science beginning in the second half of the 19th century. A development resulting in the public being placed in the role of spectators and consumers of the utilitarian fruits of scientific progress, progress that, according to the popular press of the late 19th century, was destined to bring about a utopian future.

However, these utopian futures have been mainly unfulfilled. Rather, the conclusion of the Second World War revealed a more sinister side of scientific development in the form of the atomic bomb, raising fears of total annihilation, and in 1962, the publication of Rachel Carson's book *Silent Spring* raised public concerns over the potential for environmental damage caused by man-made chemicals (Broks, 2006). In the view of the UK Royal Society (Bodmer, 1985), these developments, and other incidents such as the deformities caused by the drug thalidomide, caused the public to become disillusioned and distrustful of science.

To combat this distrust the UK Royal Society commissioned the Public Understanding of Science Report in 1985. Commonly known as the Bodmer Report, after its chairman Walter Bodmer, the report argued the public understanding of science was:

> a major element in promoting national prosperity, in raising the quality of public and private decision-making and in enriching the life of the individual… Improving the public understanding of science is an investment in the future, not a luxury to be indulged in if and when resources allow.
>
> *Bodmer (1985, p. 9)*

The report argued it was the duty of scientists to communicate with the public about their research and the report's publication resulted in several initiatives, including the launch of *The Public Understanding of Science (PUS) Journal*. The report suggested increasing the public's understanding of science would see industries become more competitive by helping workers to become better at their jobs and enabling managers and policy makers to make better decisions.

Furthermore, individuals would be able to make better lifestyle choices, especially if they had a better understanding of risk (Jones, 2011).

However, the PUS model of science communication received criticism because it is based on a model of deficit (Irwin & Wynne, 1996; Ziman, 1991), where the public is assumed to lack a basic understanding of scientific facts, theories and methodologies and this lack causes public controversies over science (Irwin & Wynne, 1996). The deficit model conceptualized the public as a passive audience in their response to scientific information, and therefore, to overcome the distrust they held about science they just needed to be given the right information. This critique and the realization that many new advances in the biosciences, including genetically modified crops and cloning, raise several ethical issues for the public were recognized in the 2000 House of Lords Select Committee on Science and Technology report (House of Lords, Science and Technology Committee, 2000). According to the report, some of these issues saw strong opposition in Britain and parts of Europe against GM foods and a growing public distrust of science. This distrust was exacerbated by the BSE crisis when it was revealed the Government had been secretly deliberating about the issue for a decade before making the announcement about the safety of British beef consumption (Jacob & Hellstrom, 2000). This saw the House of Lords Select Committee on Science and Technology propose a move towards engaging the public in "dialogue about what science could and should be doing" (p. 13). This saw a shift from the PUS paradigm of science communication to the Science and Society paradigm (Bauer et al., 2007) with its attendant public engagement with science (PES) initiatives.

In accordance with the ideals of participatory democracy, the goal of PES is to "open up science governance to a more diverse range of perspectives, including those of politically and economically marginalized groups..." (Sturgis, 2014, p. 39) to decide which areas of science should or should not be pursued in the hope that science will "be shaped in more socially beneficial directions" (Sturgis, 2014, p. 39). Early public engagement with emerging technologies is designed to avoid future controversies and opposition by the public.

The involvement of the House of Lords in suggesting science policy illustrates the close link between science, science communication and politics. This link is nothing new as science's relation to politics can be traced back to the Ancient Greeks (Hannam, 2010). Hannam (2010) suggests Plato tried to communicate his ideas to a wide audience, both to earn a living and to influence policy makers of his time without having to enter politics himself. The relationship between science and politics has not always been easy with several historical examples where science and indeed scientists have come into conflict with the rulers or politicians of their time. For example, Grant (2011) argues "Arab science was the light of the world for the period roughly 750 and 1350 CE" (p. 11). However, a change in the political landscape accompanied by an increase in Islamic orthodoxy saw a crackdown on free will and reason, leading to the demise of science in the Arab world (Grant, 2011). In the 1600s, Galileo was brought before the ruling Catholic Church's Inquisition for supporting the Copernicium theory that the planets orbited the sun (Britannica, 2021). In more recent times, science and scientists have come under political pressure. For example, conservatives in several countries organized efforts to deny climate change science. This conservative ideology is particularly prevalent and influential in the U.S. where the science of climate change is more likely to be denied by Republicans than by Democrats (McCright et al., 2016). This divide deepened after the election of Republican President Donald Trump, whose views on climate change saw him remove the U.S. from the Paris Climate Agreement in 2017 (Dietz, 2020). Science has also faced political challenges during the COVID-19 pandemic.

The Politics of Science Communication during COVID-19

Despite the best efforts to educate the public about COVID-19 vaccines and other health responses, scientists have also operated in sometimes challenging political environments. The cultural authority of science has been built on the perception that the knowledge it produces is politically neutral and objective. Yet, as illustrated, science and politics have always had a close relationship and, Gauchat (2012) argues, science and science communication have always been politicized.

Certainly, the political communication chapter in this volume discusses this in more detail; however, this politization was clearly seen during the COVID-19 pandemic with some governments readily heeding scientific advice while others suppressed or ignored the scientific advice being given about COVID-19. For example, in India eight months before the second deadly wave of COVID-19 struck the country, a report by "government-appointed scientists downplayed the possibility of a new outbreak" (Singh, 2021). According to Singh (2021), this report fitted neatly into Prime Minister Narendra Modi's plans to restart the faltering Indian economy and kick off his new election campaign. Many Indian scientists who felt the risks of a second wave of COVID-19 were being downplayed were afraid of speaking out for fear of being passed over for promotion or missing out on other opportunities (Singh, 2021). Other examples of politicians or governments downplaying the COVID-19 pandemic were found in the U.S., where President Donald Trump publicly disagreed with top medical advisors and denied the seriousness of the pandemic to re-open the economy (Rutledge, 2020). In the UK, some alleged there was political interference with COVID-19 advice being supplied to the government by the Scientific Advisory Group for Emergencies (SAGE), because several meetings were attended by "Dominic Cummings, the Prime Minister's chief political advisor, and Ben Warner, his advisor on data science" (Scally et al., 2020, p. 2). A final example is Brazil's right-wing President Jair Bolsonaro who, supported by right-wing coalitions, downplayed the pandemic, spoke against mask wearing, lockdowns, and promoted unproven cures (Abers, 2021). Downplaying pandemics is nothing new with Taylor (2019) noting Russian authorities "denied the Bubonic plague in 1770, despite deaths that year, in an attempt to maintain foreign trade" (p. 21).

In contrast, other countries have taken approaches based on science and public health advice. For example, Brazil's neighbour Argentina, with its centre-left government, supported by progressive neo-developmentalists and leftist social movements, was able to instigate an inclusive health response based on scientific advice to deal with COVID-19. Other examples of scientifically informed positive responses to COVID-19 were to be found in South Korea, which having learned from Middle East Respiratory Syndrome (MERS) outbreaks adopted a well-financed and flexible response to the pandemic. Following communication guidelines from the Centre for Disease Control (CDC) and the WHO, South Korea's government held twice daily press briefings to inform the public about the pandemic. Reporters were allowed to ask questions of the Government at these briefings (You, 2020). This type of model was also successfully used in New Zealand with daily, televised, press briefings being held to inform the public about the pandemic. These briefings were often fronted by Prime Minister, Jacinda Adern, and Director General of Health, Dr Ashley Bloomfield, who both fielded questions from reporters present at the briefings.

South Korea and New Zealand are culturally distinct from one another. South Korea could be perceived as a "tight culture" where citizens have strong cultural norms and are willing to comply with government interventions (Yan et al., 2020). In contrast, New Zealand could be seen as a "loose culture" where individual choice and self-regulation are valued (Yan et al., 2020). However, while New Zealand is more individualistic in its cultural orientation, following scientific advice

> Prime Minister Jacinda Ardern provided empathic leadership and effectively communicated key messages to the public — framing combating the pandemic as the work of a unified "team of 5 million" — which resulted in high public confidence and adherence to a suite of relatively burdensome pandemic-control measures.
>
> *Baker et al. (2020)*

As both these positive and negative examples illustrate, scientists and their advice are at the mercy of political influence. Can scientists afford to be politically neutral when faced with politicians who deny or downplay the seriousness of the disease or ignore scientific advice? As already shown, scientists may face sanctions if they speak out; however, to not do so could cost lives. This is the moral challenge facing scientists and science communication. However, some scientists have already accepted this challenge, speaking out despite government pressure to the contrary. For example, Dr Anthony Fauci, who despite personal cost, believed he had to contradict false statements from the then President Donald Trump (McNeil Jnr, 2021). In India, some scientists openly challenged government reports that downplayed the virus, and in the UK, scientists tried to avoid political interference in the Scientific Advisory Group for Emergencies (SAGE). Sir David King, the UK's former chief science advisor, established an independent SAGE group to advise on the COVID-19 pandemic. While challenging the position taken by politicians, these scientists appeared to be able to maintain their political neutrality. Only time will tell whether or not these examples will be successful in encouraging future scientists to speak out against government inertia or unwillingness to follow scientific advice during future pandemics.

Political influence is not limited to central government. An individual's political ideology can also strongly shape their views about science and vaccination against COVID-19. For example, one U.S. study found those who supported political parties that "endorsed social health care" were more likely to be vaccinated (Mesch & Schwirian, 2015, p. 1164). In contrast, a number of other U.S. studies have found those with conservative views are more likely to believe that COVID-19 is not serious and are more likely to refuse vaccination (see, e.g., Callaghan et al., 2020; de Bruin et al., 2020; Malik et al., 2020). Similar trends have been found in Europe with those supporting typically right-leaning populist parties believing vaccines were not important and/or effective (Kennedy, 2019). Indeed conservatism has been linked to a distrust in science overall (Gauchat, 2012).

The challenge for science communicators in this case is to be prepared to enter dialogue with those holding such conservative views to understand why they hold such beliefs and take actions which appear to endanger their health. Only by reaching such an understanding may science communicators be able to understand the underlying assumptions held by this group and possibly adapt their messaging to challenge and inoculate people against such assumptions successfully and persuasively. More will be said about message inoculation later in the chapter. Dialogic attempts of persuasion are part of the PES approach to science communication and yet during a pandemic it can be argued that elements of both the PUS and PES science communication paradigms are required.

Science Communication Paradigms and COVID-19

Pandemics are very large-scale epidemics affecting millions of people, caused by viruses or bacteria that are easily transmitted and for which most people do not have immunity (Taylor, 2019). The COVID-19 pandemic fits this description well as it has been caused by a hitherto unknown virus that is very easily transmitted and that most people have no immunity to. While the assumption of a scientific knowledge deficit underlying the PUS paradigm has often been criticized, in this situation the assumption of deficit appears valid. Governments and the public alike had no real knowledge of the virus, the danger it posed, how it spread or what measures might be used to slow the spread or protect themselves or others against the virus. Therefore, the efforts of scientists to educate the public and governments about the virus and measures to stop its spread have been the correct approach.

However, the public are not a homogenous group or passive receivers of such information and therefore will react in differing ways to the information, and they also hold knowledge that is vital to the effectiveness of the scientific messages and advice being given. For example, Burningham et al. (2007) argue the "public" is a construction. While scientists and others in their study recognized the heterogeneity of the public, they still tended to act as if the public was unidimensional. In New Zealand, for example, it appears the original messaging concerning the need for COVID-19 vaccination from scientists and the New Zealand government treated the public as a homogenous group. However, some ethnic minorities, in particular Maori and Pasifika, may distrust and dismiss such messages due to the impacts of "racism, previous negative healthcare experiences and inequitably designed and delivered healthcare services" (Whitehead et al., 2021, p. 32). For these groups to adhere to the call to vaccinate against and follow other health advice regarding COVID-19, authorities must provide messages that are uniquely attuned to these groups ensuring they are clear and culturally safe (Whitehead et al., 2021).

Similarly, researchers in the Netherlands have also found it necessary to create uniquely crafted messages and interventions for ethnic minorities to encourage their uptake of COVID-19 vaccines (Antwi-Berko et al., 2021). To create these uniquely targeted and culturally safe messages, scientists and policy makers must also adopt a PES strategy to work with these diverse groups. While such groups may be deficient in their knowledge of the virus, they are experts in how to craft and deliver culturally appropriate health messages to these groups to improve health outcomes among them.

PES and Vaccines

In accordance with the swift spread and magnitude of the COVID-19 pandemic, governments globally instigated several strong measures to stop the spread of the virus. For example, governments introduced nationwide lockdowns and border closures, and strongly encouraged mask wearing and social distancing. As the pandemic progressed, some governments, for example, New Zealand, implemented vaccine mandates for employees working in particular industries and introduced vaccine passports for people to attend hospitality venues and sporting or large-scale events (e.g., concerts). Many of these measures have now been lifted as vaccination rates have risen and more efficacious treatments have become available. For example, in April 2022, the New Zealand government lifted most vaccine mandates apart from those working with people in aged care, and vaccine passes for hospitality venues were no longer required (Craymer, 2022). However, mask wearing in most retail outlets is still required.

Perhaps the most well-financed and urgent measure to combat COVID-19 was the development of vaccines. In comparison to previous vaccine developments, COVID-19 vaccines seemed to be made at a lightening pace (Ball, 2020). Before the development of the COVID-19 vaccine, the fastest development of a vaccine had taken four years in the 1960s (Ball, 2020). According to Han (2015), normal vaccine development goes through three stages and can typically take 10–15 years. In contrast, COVID-19 vaccines were developed, tested and approved by the Food and Drug Administration (FDA) in slightly less than 12 months (Solis-Moreira, 2021). There were several reasons for this. First, after years of advanced research, COVID-19 vaccine development did not just begin with the declaration of the pandemic. According to Ball (2020), before the COVID-19 pandemic, over two decades of research had already been conducted into DNA vaccines, and RNA vaccines have been researched for the past 10–15 years. Also, some scientists had been researching vaccines for other coronaviruses due to the SARS (severe acute respiratory syndrome) and MERS. Therefore, much of the research to develop COVID-19 vaccines had already been conducted. Second, the threat of COVID-19 meant vaccine manufacturers were given large sums of money allowing them to conduct trials in parallel rather sequentially without risk to safety. Finally, the urgency to bring efficacious vaccines to market to try and stem the spread of COVID-19 meant regulators expedited the process without any compromise to safety (Ball, 2020). Knowledge of these facts among the general public is not well known and a significant minority of people have refused the COVID-19 vaccination because they believe their development has been too fast and, therefore, they are unsafe (Ashwell et al., 2021). Concerns about vaccine safety are not new; for example, Bangerter et al. (2012) found a majority of respondents had safety concerns about H1N1 vaccines during the 2009 H1N1 outbreak in Switzerland. Given the recency of this example, concerns over COVID-19 vaccines should have been anticipated by scientists, policy makers and health authorities alike.

While vaccines have been in use since the 1800s and have been one of the most effective tools to protect people and societies from disease, some people have no understanding of how vaccines work (Diamond et al., 2016; Federman, 2014). This lack of understanding combined with a poor evaluation of risk of disease among the public can lead some to refuse vaccines for themselves and their children and these decisions are exacerbated by exposure to the large volume of misinformation available on the Internet (Diamond et al., 2016). As noted, concern and opposition to the newly developed COVID-19 vaccines should have been expected and communication strategies developed to meet such concerns head on. As Becker et al. (2016) argue, detecting public concern about a vaccine early is important to identify the issues with the vaccine or vaccination programme.

Understanding possible concerns that may have arisen regarding COVID-19 vaccine development should have been a priority for scientists and policy makers, followed by the development of PES initiatives that may have alleviated such concerns. As suggested, PES initiatives are in part designed to avoid controversy and future public opposition to new technologies including vaccines. The urgent need to develop vaccines against COVID-19 would make this difficult. However, the availability of an interactive and targeted education campaign, explaining how the COVID-19 vaccines were being developed so quickly and the precautions being taken to ensure safety, might have alleviated some of the concerns and opposition against them. Ideally the interactive component would allow the public to pose questions to experts so they could be further reassured. This may have removed uncertainty for some and possibly stopped them from turning to conspiracy theories or other misinformation to give themselves a sense of certainty and control.

Conspiracy Theories and Misinformation

Conspiracy theories and misinformation are not easy to combat. In her review of the literature, Douglas (2021) argues conspiracy theories are particularly difficult to disconfirm as they are often multi-layered, nebulous and strongly tied to an individual's political and social identities, groups ties which are difficult to break. Furthermore, there are a number of cognitive mechanisms which can also make exposure to misinformation resistant to change (Lewandowsky et al., 2012). Given conspiracy theories and misinformation can at times be resistant to change, the challenge for scientists and science communicators is how to rapidly counter such theories and other misinformation.

Research has found political extremism is often associated with beliefs in conspiracy theories (van Prooijen et al., 2015). Conspiracy theories and misinformation have been part of the landscape of the COVID-19 pandemic that scientists and science communicators have had to deal with. For example, rumours spread arguing there was a link between the rollout of 5G and the COVID-19 outbreak (Bruns et al., 2020). In some places, this led to cell phone masts being vandalized and engineers working on them to be attacked (Sherwood, 2020). Other conspiracy theories argued COVID-19 was a hoax, it was engineered as a bioweapon or the crisis was being used by governments to anti-democratically control people. Later conspiracy theories evolved asserting that testing for COVID-19 actually gave people the disease and another theory suggested COVID-19 vaccines were being used to inject a microchip into people to track them (Stein et al., 2021). Conspiracy theories about disease are nothing new. During the HIV/AIDS epidemic, conspiracy theories arose that the virus was man-made and/or it was designed to wipe out particular ethnic groups (Ross et al., 2006; Stein et al., 2021). It is argued the belief in conspiracy theories enables believers to make sense of threatening societal events and to avoid uncertainty (van Prooijen et al., 2015). Given the uncertainty and anxiety caused by the COVID-19 pandemic, it is no surprise then to see the emergence of such conspiracy theories.

Hardin (2002) argues those with beliefs contrary to mainstream society are more likely to associate with like-minded people, resulting in only being exposed to views and beliefs they already hold. Therefore, their views are consistently reinforced, leading them to have a "skewed ideology". While Hardin (2002) was discussing those with extreme political views, there are parallels with those who are strongly opposed to vaccination and who often appear to associate with like-minded individuals by making their own social media groups on platforms such as Facebook and Twitter where they share conspiracy theories and other misinformation. Cinelli et al. (2020) argue the reason individuals join such groups can be understood in terms of "confirmation bias" where members seek information already skewed towards their pre-existing opinions. In examining such groups, Cinelli et al. (2020) have found the news feed algorithms of Facebook and Twitter encourage the formation of social media echo chambers where members of the group have their particular viewpoint reinforced while becoming isolated from alternative viewpoints not unlike the extreme political groups described by Hardin (2002).

The Internet not only supplies these individuals with places where they can interact with like-minded individuals, it also enables them to spread conspiracy theories and other misinformation on the wider Internet where those who may be vulnerable to such beliefs or are vaccine hesitant may encounter and be influenced by them. The spread of misinformation on the Internet, such as the use of unproven cures, can have serious consequences. For example, in Nigeria a number of people were reported with overdoses of chloroquine, an anti-malaria drug, after media reported its supposed effectiveness in curing COVID-19 (Tasnim et al., 2020). In the U.S. one Arizona man died after ingesting chloroquine phosphate, believing it would prevent him from contracting COVID-19 (Edwards & Hillyard, 2020).

Previous research has suggested simply refuting misinformation or conspiracy theories can have the opposite effect with people becoming more entrenched in their beliefs about conspiracy theories or misinformation, the "backfire effect". A recent meta-analysis of the backfire research has found this not to be the case (see Swire-Thompson et al., 2020). This is good news for scientists and science communicators, as Swire-Thompson and her colleagues do have suggestions on the best ways to correct misinformation. First, fact checking has not been shown to cause a backfire effect and strategically targeting those most vulnerable to being misinformed is the best use of this strategy (Swire-Thompson et al., 2020). Second, the review of research suggests that merely repeating the misinformation without a correction can increase a person's belief in the misinformation, the illusory truth effect (Swire-Thompson et al., 2020). Therefore, Swire-Thompson et al. recommend that a clear correction be designed and then paired with the salient misinformation. Furthermore, in media corrections they suggest that the correction comes in the headline and the misinformation follows later in the article or story. The reason is that many people may only read or listen to headlines, rather than engage with news stories as a whole (Swire-Thompson et al., 2020).

Another way in which misinformation and conspiracy theories can be combatted is through inoculation. McGuire (1961) found people can be inoculated against the threat of misinformation and conspiracy theories by pre-exposing them to counterarguments against their beliefs. Inoculation theory has a great deal of support (Banas & Rains, 2010) and is another tool for scientists to prepare people to resist the misinformation and conspiracy theories that are bound to rise during any pandemic or crisis.

Misinformation and conspiracy theories during epidemics are nothing new. During the flu epidemics in Russia in 1890 and the Spanish flu epidemic of 1918, a large deal of misinformation and conspiracy theories also existed (Cohut, 2020; Knapp, 2020). However, without the Internet their ability to travel the globe was far slower than misinformation and conspiracy theories about COVID-19. The Internet and in particular social media allow such information to travel around the world instantly at the touch of a button. Some metrics even suggest websites that host sensationalist news and conspiracy theories generate more user engagement than more reputable sources such as the CDC or the WHO (Stein et al., 2021). Despite the ease with which misinformation and conspiracy theories travel on the Internet and on social media, there are ways that they can be controlled. For example, the WHO has developed relationships and reached agreement with a number of tech companies with social media platforms such as Facebook, LinkedIn, Google and others that they will stamp out fraud and misinformation on their platforms (Tasnim et al., 2020). Despite these agreements, misinformation and conspiracy theories are still widespread on the Internet and social media. Tasnim et al. (2020) suggest four additional strategies to try and control the spread of misinformation and conspiracy theories and these include:

1   Frontline medical staff should be armed with the most up-to-date medical information so they can provide robust information when dealing with patients
2   A coordinated effort between mass media, community groups and others is needed to ensure validated information is provided across all media platforms
3   Misinformation, conspiracy theories and hoaxes should be removed from the Internet. Data mining techniques might be useful in identifying information that has no basis in fact and

4   Those propagating such misinformation should face legal penalties for doing so

This latter goal may be difficult given the anonymity afforded by the Internet, making some perpetrators difficult to identify. And even when such people are identified, they may live outside the jurisdiction of the countries most affected. Furthermore, belief in conspiracy theories is not illegal and freedom of speech laws in many countries may prohibit any action being taken against those propagating such theories or misinformation

While some of the possibilities for combatting misinformation and conspiracy theories outlined above could see their impact lessened and more valid scientific information taking their place, there will always remain a minority who will not listen or be persuaded of the scientific facts. For example, since their inception there has always been a small percentage of the population who refuse any type of vaccine (Luyten et al., 2019). In the case of childhood vaccination in Australia, those who consciously object to vaccination have remained steady at around 2% (Trent et al., 2019), and in the U.S. this figure is estimated to be around 5% (Dube et al., 2015). It is unlikely that people in this group will ever be persuaded of the efficacy or need for vaccination and possibly other preventive measures. This being the case, it might be more useful for scientists and science communicators to identify and concentrate their communication efforts on those vaccine-hesitant individuals who are open to persuasion.

The COVID-19 pandemic has illustrated some of the challenges faced by scientists and science communication as a whole. Some of these challenges are not new; for example, navigating the political climate of the day or the fact that since their inception there has always been a small percentage of people who will refuse vaccines or indeed other medical advice. Again while misinformation and conspiracy theories during pandemics and epidemics are not new the Internet now gives a platform for such information to spread very rapidly. Inoculation and counterarguments against such theories and misinformation also need to be instigated rapidly. If there is a real lesson from the COVID-19 pandemic for scientists and science communication, it is that in any future pandemic misinformation and conspiracy theories will be part of the landscape. Scientists need to anticipate and be prepared to inoculate the population against such theories and also need be prepared to engage and combat misinformation quickly whenever it appears whether be at the level of central politics or social media. Pressure could also be brought to bear against social media companies to remove misinformation and conspiracy theories from their platforms when they appear. Finally, during the COVID-19 pandemic a number of strong scientists, including Anthony Fauci, Sir David King and others, have given examples of how scientists can speak out against misinformation and conspiracy theories without losing their scientific neutrality.

References

Abers, R. N. (2021). State–society relations in uncertain times: Social movement strategies, ideational contestation and the pandemic in Brazil and Argentina. *International Political Science Review, 42*(3), 333–349. https://doi.org/10.1177/0192512121993713

Antwi-Berko, D., Bakuri, A. Z., Otabil, K. B., & Kwarteng, A. (2021). Adherence to COVID-19 preventive measures among the Ghanaian-Dutch community in the Netherlands: A mixed method study in Amsterdam. *Frontiers in Public Health, 10*, 1–12. https://doi.org/10.3389/fpubh.2022.761987

Ashwell, D., Cullinane, J., & Croucher, S. M. (2021). Vaccine hesitancy and support for employer vaccine mandates. *Frontiers in Communication – Health Communication*, https://doi.org/10.3389/fcomm.2021.780415

Baker, M. G., Wilson, N., & Anglemyer, A. (2020). Successful elimination of Covid-19 transmission in New Zealand. *The New England Journal of Medicine, 383*(56) https://doi.org/10.1056/NEJMc2025203

Ball, P. (2020). The lightning-fast quest for COVID vaccines – and what it means for other diseases. *Nature, 589*, 16–18. https://doi.org/10.1038/d41586-020-03626-1

Banas, J. A., & Rains, S. A. (2010). A meta-analysis of research on inoculation theory. *Communication Monographs, 77*, 281–311. https://doi.org/10.1080/03637751003758193

Bangerter A., Krings F., Mouton A., Gilles I., Green E. G. T., & Clamaine, A. (2012). Longitudinal investigation of public trust in institutions relative to the 2009 H1N1 pandemic in Switzerland. *PLoS One, 7*(11), e49806. https://doi.org/10.1371/journal.pone.0049806

Battison, P., Kashyap, R., & Rotondi, V. (2021). Reliance on scientists and experts during an epidemic: Evidence from the COVID-19 outbreak in Italy. *SSM-Population Health, 13*, 100721.

Bauer, M. W., Allum, N., & Miller, S. (2007). What can we learn from 25 years of PUS Survey research? Liberating and expanding the agenda. *Public Understanding of Science, 16*, 79–95.

Becker, B. F. H., Larson, H. J., Bonhoeffer, J., van Mulligan, E. M., Kors, J. A., & Sturkenboom, M. C. J. M. (2016). Evaluation of a multinational, multilingual vaccine debate on Twitter. *Vaccine, 34*, 6166–6171. http://dx.doi.org/10.1016/j.vaccine.2016.11.007

Bodmer, W. (1985). *The public understanding of science.* The Royal Society.

Britannica. (2021). Galileo: Italian philosopher, astronomer and mathematician. https://www.britannica.com/biography/Galileo-Galilei

Broks, P. (2006). *Understanding popular science.* Open University Press.

Bruns, A., Harrington, S., & Hurcombe, E. (2020). 'Corona? 5G? or both?': The dynamics of COVID-19/5G conspiracy theories on Facebook. *Media International Australia, 177*(1), 12–29.

Bucchi, M. (1998). *Science and the media: Alternative routes in scientific communication.* Routledge Taylor & Francis Group.

Burningham, K., Barnett, J., Carr, A., Clift, R., & Wehrmeyer, W. (2007). Industrial constructions of publics and public knowledge: A qualitative investigation of practice in the UK chemicals industry. *Public Understanding of Science, 16*(1), 23–43. https://doi.org/10:1177/0963662506071285

Callaghan, T., Moghtaderi, A., Lueck, J. A., Hotez, P. J., Strych, U., Dor, A., Fowler, E. F., & Motta, M. (2020). Correlates and disparities of COVID-19 vaccine hesitancy. *Social science research network.* https://papers.ssrn.com/sol3/papers.cfm?abstract_id=3667971. https://doi.org/10.2139/ssrn.3667971

Cinelli, M., Morales, G. D. F., Galeazzi, A., Quattrociocchi, W., & Starnini, M. (2020). Echo chambers on social media: A comparative analysis. arXiv preprint arXiv:2004.09603.

Cohut, M. (2020). The flu pandemic of 1918 and early conspiracy theories. *Medical News Today*. https://www.medicalnewstoday.com/articles/the-flu-pandemic-of-1918-and-early-conspiracy-theories

Craymer, L. (2022, March 23) New Zealand lifts most vaccine mandates as Omicron outbreak nears peak. *Reuters*. https://www.reuters.com/world/asia-pacific/new-zealand-lifts-most-vaccine-mandates-omicron-outbreak-nears-peak-2022-03-23/

de Bruin, W. B., Saw, H., & Goldman, D. P. (2020) Political polarization in US residents' COVID-19 risk perceptions, policy preferences, and protective behaviors. *Journal of Risk and Uncertainty, 61*, 177–194. https://doi.org/10.1007/s11166-020-09336-3

Diamond, J., McQuillan, J., Spiegel, A. N., Hill, P. W., Smith, R., West, J., & Wood, C. (2016). Viruses, vaccines and the public. *Museums & Social Issues, 11*(1), 9–16. https://doi.org/10.1080/15596893.2016.1131099

Dietz, T. (2020). Political events and public views on climate change. *Climatic Change, 161*, 1–8. https://doi.org/10.1007/s10584-020-02791-6

Douglas, K. M. (2021). COVID-19 conspiracy theories. *Group Processes & Intergroup Relations, 24*(2), 270–275. https://doi.org/10.1177/1368430220982068

Dube, E., Vivion, M., & MacDonald, N. E. (2015). Vaccine hesitancy, vaccine refusal and the anti-vaccine movement: Influence, impact and implications. *Expert Reviews Vaccines, 14*(1), 99–117. https://doi.org/10.1586/14760584.2015.964212

Edwards, E. & Hillyard, V. (2020, March 24). Man dies after taking chloroquine in an attempt to prevent coronavirus. *NBC News*. https://www.nbcnews.com/health/health-news/man-dies-after-ingesting-chloroquine-attempt-prevent-coronavirus-n1167166

Federman, R. S. (2014). Understanding vaccines: A public imperative. *Yale Journal of Biology and Medicine, 87*(4), 417–422.

Gauchat, G. (2012). Politicization of science in the public sphere: A study of public trust in the United States, 1974 to 2010. *American Sociological Review, 77*(2), 167–187. https://doi.org/10.1177/0003122412438225

Germani F., & Biller-Andorno N. (2021). The anti-vaccination infodemic on social media: A behavioral analysis. *PLoS One, 16*(3), e0247642. https://doi.org/10.1371/journal.pone.0247642

Grant, J. (2011). *Denying science: Conspiracy theories, media distortions and the war against reality*. Prometheus Books.

Han, S. (2015). Clinical vaccine deployment. *Clinical and Experimental Vaccine Research, 4*(1), 46–53. https://doi.org/10.7774/cevr.2015.4.1.46

Hannam, J. (2010). Explaining the world: Communicating science through the ages. In *Successful science communication: Telling it like it is* (pp. 31–44). Cambridge.

Hardin, R. (2002). The crippled epistemology of extremism. In Breton, A., Galotti, G., Salmon, P., & Wintrobe, R. *Political extremism and rationality*. Cambridge.

House of Lords Science and Technology Committee. (2000). Third report. https://publications.parliament.uk/pa/ld199900/ldselect/ldsctech/38/3801.htm

Irwin, A., & Wynne, B. (1996). *Misunderstanding science?: The public reconstruction of science and technology*. Redwood Books.

Jacob, M., & Hellstrom, T. (2000). Policy understanding of science, public trust and the BSE-CJD crisis. *Journal of Hazardous Materials, 78*(1–3), 303–317. https://doi.org/10.1016/S0304-3894(00)00228-4

Jolley, D., & Douglas, K. M. (2017). Prevention is better than cure: Addressing anti-vaccine conspiracy theories. *Journal of Applied Psychology, 47*, 459–469. https://doi.org/10.1111/jasp.12453

Jones, R. A. L. (2011). Introduction: Public engagement in an evolving science policy landscape. In *Successful science communication: Telling it like it is* (pp. 1–13). Cambridge.

Kennedy, J. (2019). Populist politics and vaccine hesitancy in Western Europe: an analysis of national-level data. *European Journal of Public Health, 29*(3), 512–516.

Knapp, A. (2020). The original Plandemic: Unmasking the eerily familiar conspiracy theories behind the Russian flu of 1889. *Forbes*. https://www.forbes.com/sites/alex-knapp/2020/05/15/the-original-plandemic-unmasking-the-eerily-parallel-conspiracy-theories-behind-the-russian-flu-of-1889/?sh=1c443eae50d5

Lewandowsky, S., Ecker, U. K. H., Seifert, C. M., Schwarz, N., & Cook, J. (2012). Misinformation and its correction: Continued influence and successful debiasing. *Psychological Science in the Public Interest, 13*(3), 106–131. https://doi.org/10.1177/1529100612451018

Luyten, J., Bruyneel, L., & van Hoek A. J. (2019). Assessing vaccine hesitancy in the UK population using a generalized vaccine hesitancy survey instrument. *Vaccine, 37*, 2494–2501. https://doi.org/10.1016/j.vaccine.2019.03.041

McCright, A. M., Marquart-Pyatt, S. T., Shwom, R. L., Brechin, S. R., & Allen, S. (2016). Ideology, capitalism, and climate: Explaining public views about climate change in the United States. *Energy Research and Social Science, 21*, 180–189. https://doi.org/10.1016/j.erss.2016.08.003

McGuire, W. J. (1961). The effectiveness of supportive and refutational defenses in immunizing and restoring beliefs against persuasion. *Sociometry, 24*(2), 184–197.

McNeil Jnr, D. G. (2021, January 24). Fauci on what working for Trump was really like. *New York Times*. https://www.nytimes.com/2021/01/24/health/fauci-trump-covid.html

Malik, A. A., McFadden, S. M. Elharake, J., & Omer, S. B. (2020). Determinants of COVID-19 vaccine acceptance in the US. *eClinicalMedicine, 26*, 1–8. https://doi.org/10.1016/j.eclinm.2020.100495

Mesch, G. S., & Schwirian, K. P. (2015). Social and political determinants of vaccine hesitancy: Lessons learned from the H1N1 pandemic of 2009–2010. *American Journal of Infection Control, 43*, 1161–1165. http://dx.doi.org/10.1016/j.ajic.2015.06.031

Qamar, A. (2022). At least 5 states report an increase in calls to poison control after Trump's 'disinfectant' COVID-19 remarks. *Michigan poison and drug information center, Wayne State University*. https://www.poison.med.wayne.edu/updates-content/kstytapp2qfstf0pkacdxmz943u1hs

Ross, M. W., Essien, E. J., & Torres, I. (2006). Conspiracy beliefs about the origin of HIV/AIDS in four racial/ethnic groups. *Journal of Acquired Immune Deficiency Syndrome, 41*(3), 342–344.

Rutledge, P. E. (2020). Trump, COVID-19, and the war on expertise. *The American Review of Public Administration, 50*(6–7), 505–511. https://doi.org/1177/0275074020941683.

Scally, G., Jacobson, B., & Abbasi, K. (2020). The UK's public health response to covid-19. *British Medical Journal, 369*(m1932), 1–3. https://doi.org/10.1136/bmj.m1932

Sherwood, H. (2020, April 5). Call for social media platforms to act on 5G mast conspiracy theory. *The Guardian*. https://www.theguardian.com/technology/2020/apr/05/call-for-social-media-platforms-to-act-on-5g-mast-conspiracy-theory

Singh, K. D. (2021, September 14). As India's lethal Covid wave neared, politics overrode science. *The New York Times.* https://www.nytimes.com/2021/09/14/world/asia/india modi-science-icmr.html

Solis-Moreira, J. (2021). How did we develop a COVID-19 vaccine so quickly? *Medical News Today.* https://www.medicalnewstoday.com/articles/how-did-we-develop-a-covid-19-vaccine-so-quickly

Stein, R. A., Ometa, O., Shetty, S. P., Katz, A., Popitiu, M. I., & Brotherton, R. (2021). Conspiracy theories in the era of COVID-19: A tale of two pandemics. *Journal of International Clinical Practice, 75*(2), 1–5. https://doi.org/10.1111/ijcp.13778

Sturgis, P. (2014). On the limits of public engagement for the governance of emerging Technologies. *Public Understanding of Science, 23*(1), 38–42.

Swire-Thompson, B., DeGutis, J., & Lazer, D. (2020). Searching for the Backfire Effect: Measurement and design considerations. *Journal of Applied Research in Memory and Cognition, 9*(3), 286–299.

Tasnim, S., Mahbub, H., & Mazumder, H. (2020). Impact of rumours and misinformation on COVID-19 in social media. *Journal of Preventive Medicine and Public Health, 53,* 171–174. https://doi.org/10.3961/jpmph.20.094

Taylor, S. (2019). *The psychology of pandemics: Preparing for the next global outbreak of infectious disease.* Cambridge Scholars Publishing.

Trent, M. J., Zhang, E. J., Chughtai, A. A., & McIntyre, C. R. (2019). Parental opinions towards the "No Jab, No Pay" policy in Australia. *Vaccine, 37,* 5250–5256.

van Prooijen, J., Krouwel, A. P. M., & Pollet, T.V. (2015). Political extremism predicts beliefs in conspiracy theories. *Social Psychology and Personality Science, 6*(5), 570–578.

Whitehead, J., Scott, N., Carr, P. A., & Lawrenson, R. (2021). Will access to COVID-19 vaccine in Aotearoa be equitable for priority populations? *New Zealand Medical Journal, 134*(1535), 25–34.

World Health Organization. (2022). *Infodemic.* https://www.who.int/health-topics/infodemic#tab=tab_1

Yan, B., Zhang, X., Wu, L., Zhu, H., & Chen, B. (2020). Why do countries respond differently to COVID-19? A comparative study of Sweden, China, France, and Japan. *American Review of Public Administration, 50*(6–7), 762–769. https://doi.org/10.1177/0275074020942445

You, J. (2020). Lessons from South Korea's Covid-19 policy response. *American Review of Public Administration, 50,* 801–808. https://doi.org/10.1177/0275074020943708

Ziman, J. (1991). Public understanding of science. *Science, Technology, & Human Values, 16*(1), 99–105.

4

PANDEMIC COMMUNICATION

CDC and WHO Approaches to Emergency Risk Communication and Emerging Infectious Disease Crises

Matthew W. Seeger and Henry S. Seeger

The COVID-19 pandemic is the most significant infectious disease event since the 1918 Spanish flu, infecting over 540 million people worldwide and causing over 6.3 million deaths (WHO COVID Dashbaord, 2022). While the risk and impacts on public health are severe, they are compounded by inadequate, ineffective, and misleading crisis communication (Sauer et al., 2021). The World Health Organization (WHO) argued that the COVID-19 pandemic was also an *infodemic* wherein the rapid spread of misinformation directly caused deaths (WHO, 2020).

We describe the scope of the COVID-19 pandemic and the ways that emerging infectious disease outbreaks constitute crises. A working definition of pandemic crisis and emergency risk communication is offered. The crisis and emergency risk communication dimensions of the response to the disease are discussed. Several frameworks are utilized, including the Centers for Disease Control and Prevention's principles of effective communication, the Crisis and Emergency Risk Communication (CERC) framework, as well as the World Health Organization's guidelines for Emergency Risk Communication (ERC) in public health emergencies (Reynolds et al., 2002; WHO, 2017). CDC, CERC, and the WHO ERC guidelines are examined for areas of convergence. Finally, we offer a research agenda for further examination of pandemic crisis and emergency risk communication.

COVID-19

The emergence of a novel SARS virus in December of 2019 created a worldwide public health crisis and was eventually declared a pandemic by the World Health Organization on March 11, 2020. As of June 2022, the World Health

DOI: 10.4324/9781003214496-4

Organization reported 539,893,858 confirmed cases of COVID-19, including 6,324,112 deaths (WHO, 2022). These numbers are likely under-reported for a variety of reasons (Nowling & Seeger, 2021).

While the mortality rate varies significantly from country to country, Mexico reported the highest level of deaths per 100,000 at 5.5%, while Australia reported the lowest at .01%. The U.S. ranked fifth highest with 1.2 deaths per 100,000 cases (Johns Hopkins, 2022). These differences may be attributed to several factors: differences in the number of people tested, characteristics of the healthcare system, and population characteristics such as age and underlying health conditions. Observers also note that mortality rates are a function of the national response to the pandemic, including the communication processes used to inform and persuade the public. The *Lancet* argued that as much as 40% of the U.S. death rate can be attributed to a poorly executed national response (Woolhandler et al., 2021). The poorly executed national response includes ineffective communication from public health agencies such as the CDC.

COVID-19 as a Crisis

Crises are generally understood to be events or series of events that create severe disruption, harm or the potential for harm, produce high levels of uncertainty, and require a form of response to manage and contain harm (Sellnow & Seeger, 2021). These events are generally chronologically and geographically bounded – they occur at a particular time and within a particular location (Wombacher et al., 2018). Pandemics such as COVID-19 tend to transcend geographic boundaries, and thus require more coordination across countries and regions to manage. Pandemics may also extend over much longer time frames than most other crisis types, and may transition into endemic disease threats.

Crisis investigators have examined a wide range of crisis types, including hurricanes, floods, fires, terrorist events, transportation accidents, toxic spills, and infectious disease outbreaks (Sellnow & Seeger, 2021). Infectious disease outbreaks, such as pandemics, are often associated with high levels of mortality and morbidity, as well as significant and widespread social and economic disruption across wide geographic areas. The *Dictionary of Epidemiology* defines a pandemic as "an epidemic occurring worldwide, or over a very wide area, crossing international boundaries and usually affecting a large number of people" (Last, 2001). The definition suggests that a pandemic is a large or extended epidemic. It is unclear whether a disease outbreak must be "new, explosive, or severe" to be defined as a pandemic. Although there is some diversity in definitions, pandemics tend to severely impact large segments or entire populations over wide geographic areas (Morens et al., 2009).

Rapid disease movement, high attack rate, minimal population immunity, infectiousness, contagiousness, and severity are often identified as features of pandemics in addition to wide geographic distribution (Morens et al., 2009).

Because pandemics transcend geographic boundaries, they implicate diverse cultures, political systems, public health systems, and traditions and practices in response to disease management. Pandemics have the potential to create widespread mortality and morbidity as well as widespread social and economic disruption. Pandemics probably account for the highest levels of mortality of any crisis type as evidenced by the 1918 Spanish flu which is estimated to have claimed as many as 50 million lives worldwide.

Emerging diseases can be associated with high levels of uncertainty as novel patterns of infection, symptoms, and treatment present themselves. The Zika virus, an emerging disease associated with the 2015–2016 Zika virus epidemic, was a poorly understood and novel vector-borne disease that caused very severe birth defects. It was primarily spread by the *Aedis egipti* mosquito but could also be transmitted from men and women to their sexual partners, through vertical transmission during pregnancy or at delivery, or through blood transfusion. Emerging diseases often require periods of study by subject matter experts to reduce the uncertainty and inform the response. The origins of Middle Eastern Respiratory Syndrome (MERS) were initially unknown, and until such time as the host could be identified, it was difficult to control through public health intervention. Infectious diseases can be spread rapidly and require immediate response and sometimes intrusive measures to contain an outbreak. Measles is highly contagious and can spread very rapidly among unvaccinated communities such that control may require exclusion, isolation, and quarantine of unvaccinated individuals.

Pandemics impose a unique set of constraints and communication interventions. Because pandemics impact large groups across wide areas, they require interaction with diverse audiences who possess different needs, experiences, resources, values, beliefs, and languages. Often audiences are accessible through different channels, have varying capacities to process highly technical information, and have differing, sometimes distrustful, attitudes toward intervening agencies or organizations. Disease outbreaks often limit social interaction and impose financial and physical burdens on those impacted, restricting their capacity to be reached by communication interventions. Communication interventions need to take these burdens into account for messages to be heard, understood, believed, and put into practice. The challenges of science communication (i.e. to communicate highly complex expert information in ways that are understandable to a non-expert audience) are often especially salient during pandemics.

Communication during a pandemic does not only involve transmitting messages to diverse audiences and *coordination* across different cultures, political systems, and approaches to both communication and health. Communication coordination must account for different cultural experiences and norms toward disease, differing standards for transparency, inconsistent values, goals, and procedures, as well as diverse languages. International coordination such as those organized through the World Health Organization must achieve coordination between governments with highly divergent approaches to infection control policies, including quarantine, travel restrictions, public health care, social support programs, population monitoring, and public communication. Crisis and emergency risk communication during pandemics can be described as a program of information exchange among diverse communities, governments, and organizations, across geographic boundaries, toward the goals of reducing uncertainty, empowering and enabling rapid response, and limiting harm.

Principles of Crisis Communication and Pandemics

Two broad sets of guidelines and resources have been developed by public health agencies to inform communication during public health emergencies. The Crisis and Emergency Risk Communication framework was developed by the U.S. Centers for Disease Control and Prevention in 2002 and the World Health Organization developed the Guidelines for Emergency Risk Communication in 2017. A brief overview of these two frameworks is provided below.

CERC

The Crisis and Emergency Risk Communication (CERC) framework is an integrated conceptual, training, and application framework incorporating a wide range of risk and crisis communication principles (Miller et al., 2021; Reynolds & Seeger, 2006; Veil et al., 2008). The CERC framework was developed initially by the U.S. Centers for Disease Control and Prevention (CDC) and presented in a comprehensive manual and training program. CERC has subsequently been extended by a variety of research programs.

CERC was initially assembled by the communication office at the CDC following the 2001 Anthrax attacks, a prolonged crisis event wherein letters contaminated with anthrax spores were mailed through the U.S. postal system, killing five people and infecting 17 others (Clarke et al., 2006; Friemuth, 2006). The CDC was one of the lead agencies managing the crisis response. The crisis response necessitated sustained public communication that functioned to develop the public's understandings of the event as well as the risks involved. An effective communication-based response to the Anthrax attacks was made more difficult due to high uncertainty surrounding the event and the short response time available. Understandings of the risks and nature of the event changed drastically throughout the lifespan of the event, resulting in inconsistent messaging. The CDC's responses to the anthrax letter crisis were generally viewed by the public as inadequate, confusing, and ineffective.

While the public health community in the U.S. (including agencies such as the CDC) had developed significant capacity for health communication, risk communication, and health promotion, crisis communication was not generally seen as a core function of health communication. This need for a crisis communication capacity at the CDC remained largely unaddressed until the 2001 Anthrax attacks (Rubin, 2007, 2012). The communication failure during this event highlighted the need for an integrated approach to crisis, risk, and emergency response communication. CERC established principles of risk communication, crisis communication, and media relations that were applicable and accessible to the public health community. A subsequent version of CERC developed in 2006–2007 focused specifically on pandemic influenza, which at that time was generally seen as the primary pandemic threat.

The core principles of CERC were first presented in the CDC's 2002 Crisis and Emergency Risk Communication manual (Reynolds et al., 2002). The manual was used as a platform for training and as a guideline for responses. These principles have been applied in the context of many crisis events such as during the 2003 Severe Acute Respiratory Syndrome (SARS) outbreak, the 2009 H1N1 pandemic, the Zika outbreak, and various natural disasters, including hurricanes. CERC is based on a set of six core principles: Be Right, Be First, Be Credible, Express Empathy, Promote Action, and Show Respect (see Table 4.1).

The principle of "Be First" acknowledges the time-sensitive dimensions of crisis events, and the need for immediate responses to limit and contain harm. The first principle also seeks to position the CDC as the primary source for public health guidance during disasters. The longer the interval between the onset of an event and an organized response, the greater the probability of widespread harm. Infectious diseases can spread very quickly and, as a consequence, be difficult if not impossible to contain. Epidemiologists utilize the basic reproduction number, denoted R_0, to represent the level of contagion of a disease. R_0 is a calculation of the expected number of individuals within a given population who will contract a contagious disease from each infected person,

TABLE 4.1 Six Core Principles of CERC

1 Be First: Crises are time-sensitive. Communicating information quickly is crucial. For members of the public, the first source of information often becomes the preferred source.
2 Be Right: Accuracy establishes credibility. Information can include what is known, what is not known, and what is being done to fill in the gaps.
3 Be Credible: Honesty and truthfulness should not be compromised during crises.
4 Express Empathy: Crises create harm, and the suffering should be acknowledged in words. Addressing what people are feeling, and the challenges they face, builds trust and rapport.
5 Promote Action: Giving people meaningful things to do calms anxiety, helps restore order, and promotes some sense of control.
6 Show Respect: Respectful communication is particularly important when people feel vulnerable. Respectful communication promotes cooperation and rapport.

given that every individual within the population is susceptible. For example, the original COVID-19 virus had an R_0 of between 2 and 3, meaning that every person who has the disease will transmit it to an average of two to three others. Subsequent variants of COVID-19 had much higher R_0 factors. Thus, rapid response and public health intervention are important to limiting the spread and containing harm, especially when disease is especially contagious.

The first messages in response to any event establish the initial understanding of the event for the public and may designate a specific source as the primary or most trusted source for the public. CERC acknowledges the developmental feature of a crisis and the ways communication in early stages influences subsequent stages. Rapid response can also reduce the number of rumors by addressing initial uncertainty.

The second principle, "Being Right," refers to accuracy of information and is an essential element in effective response. Being Right may be especially challenging due to uncertain and changing conditions of a crisis. In general, public health has relied on subject matter experts and principles of effective science communication to disseminate accurate messages. One of the defining challenges in communicating during an emerging infectious disease outbreak is translating the science into messages that are accessible and understandable and yet retain accuracy. Messages that sacrifice accuracy to aid understandability will damage trust between the public and organizations, while messages that fail to simplify to maintain accuracy will not be understood by the public. Accuracy is made more difficult as the understanding of a crisis, including causes, risks, and effective mitigation strategies, will change drastically throughout the lifespan of the event, requiring messages to be changed and adapted. The early stages of most crises are characterized by information, and organizations frequently must communicate without necessary information for fully accurate messaging. As new information becomes available, messages will inevitably change. Changing messaging may be interpreted by publics as evidence that early messages were not accurate or not honest and may impact credibility, as was the case with evolving recommendations about wearing masks during COVID-19. To mitigate credibility damage from message changes, subject matter experts are often advised to issue caveats to their messages, such as "Based on what we currently know, this is our recommendation. As circumstances change, we will update our guidance." These provisional statements may help protect credibility when guidance will likely require future amendment.

"Credibility" and accuracy are closely interrelated. Credibility is the degree to which a message's source is regarded as believable based on reputations of honesty, truthfulness, and transparency. Sources viewed as credible are more likely to believed (Avery, 2010; Pornpitakpan, 2004). Credibility has been linked to two key perceptions of the source by the audience: expertise (or competence) and trustworthiness (or character). Credibility permeates the source, the channel, and the specific message (Hocevar et al., 2017). Source credibility is often established before the crisis event occurs and is based on the history of interactions between an organization or actor and key publics. Specific channels may have higher levels of credibility with particular audiences. Much attention, for example, has been focused on the credibility (or lack-there-of) of online information sources. Traditional or legacy media sources continue to be seen as more trustworthy. However, for particular audiences, certain online sources may have significantly higher credibility than traditional media. Credibility is also embedded within the message itself, through use of evidence, appeals, and argumentative structure. Credibility is especially important in high uncertainty conditions, when many messages are inaccurate or incomplete and when multiple sources of information, including both social and legacy media, are available. These are the conditions that often characterize a crisis (Endsley et al., 2014; van Zoonen & van der Meer, 2015).

The fourth core principle of CERC is "Empathy," denoting the degree of sympathy, understanding, and caring embedded in the message. Empathy functions primarily as a character appeal, supporting credibility and supporting the audience's understanding of the message; however, it also provides benefits in terms of social and personal resilience and recovery following the crisis event. Authentic expressions of empathy have been recognized as an important element of effective crisis communication, and are useful in acknowledging the emotional responses associated with crisis induced harm (Schoofs et al., 2022). Crises often elicit strong emotional responses, and empathy helps affected individuals process these emotional responses and respond to crises in rational ways (van der Meer & Verhoeven, 2014). Sandman noted that the emotional response to a risk, such as anger or fear, is sometimes disproportional to the actual risk, and argued that managing disproportional outrage-based responses was an essential challenge to effective crisis management (Sandman, 1988). Outraged individuals often do not respond to crises effectively. An initial expression of empathy shows that the sender cares, may increase the positive feelings audiences have toward the source of the message, and can enhance the degree to which audiences listen to and understand the message (De Waele et al., 2020).

An additional key element of the CDC's CERC framework is to "Promote Harm-Reducing Actions" among target audiences. Most crises require those impacted or potentially impacted to take actions or avoid actions to reduce or contain harm. Examples of harm-reducing actions include evacuation or sheltering in place, boiling water advisories, monitoring for symptoms, or seeking medical attention, depending on the specific form of the risk. As this list demonstrates, whether an action is harm-reducing is highly contingent on the nature of the crisis event. Many water-borne bacterial contaminations can be eliminated completely through boiling water; however, many toxic water contaminations are rendered more severe when water is boiled. The risk of contracting an infectious disease can be reduced by good hand hygiene, respiratory etiquette, and social distancing, including quarantine. The spread of viruses through aerosolization can be reduced by wearing appropriate masks. Vaccination, when available, is also a very effective strategy (Caeiro & Garzón, 2018; Handel et al., 2007). Regardless of the specific action necessary, widespread adoption of these actions requires coordinated, sustained, far-reaching, credible, and understandable messaging.

Communication to promote harm-reducing actions involves both informative and persuasive messages (Reynolds & Seeger, 2006). These messages should provide accurate information about target actions, including an explanation for why they are harm-reducing, instructions for adoption, and strategies to overcome any common obstacles to adoption of the action. If, for example, the target action is handwashing, messaging should include a technical explanation for why handwashing is effective as well as guidelines for how to wash hands correctly. Persuasive elements may include various appeals to social or personal values, such as *we need to do this to protect each other* or *this is the right thing to keep yourself safe*. Knowledge of the target audience is helpful in crafting persuasive appeals. Messages that enhance feelings of self-efficacy can be particularly effective in many crisis events, as many individuals feel a loss of control during a crisis.

The final of the CERC principles, "Showing Respect," is closely connected with empathy, credibility, and harm-reducing actions. A feeling of helplessness, of a loss of control or self-efficacy, is a common form of noise which interferes with audiences receiving communication messages during a crisis. These feelings may produce attitudes of distrust toward intervening organizations. Individuals may feel that *they know better* that organizations do not have their best interests at heart, and they are not being heard. Showing respect for audiences first and foremost combats these tendencies, helps build a sense of connection, and helps demonstrate a sense of control.

Summary of CERC

The six principles of CERC are operationalized through a broad set of recommended practices in risk and science communication, media relations, planning, coordinating, organizing response resources and capabilities, training, audience analysis, structures, and standard operating procedures. CERC functions as a framework for training, a foundation for a communication planning, and a set of principles for informing a response. It is not a standalone paradigm for crisis intervention and response; rather it is an integrated approach. As a resource and training framework, CERC is supported by a variety of resources including online training modules, videos, and presentations. CERC has been used extensively by the public health community and has contributed to a recognition that the communication is essential to public health responses to emergencies, including pandemics (see Miller et al., 2021). CERC has become an established and standard part of contemporary public health practice.

WHO Guidelines for Communicating Risk in Public Health Emergencies

In 2017, the World Health Organization began to develop guidelines for communicating risk during emergencies. These guidelines had some features in common with the CDC CERC guidelines, and like CERC, they came from a general recognition that communication is essential to an effective response to public health emergencies. As a global organization, WHO operates in a much more complex communication and political ecosystem than the CDC. Like the CDC, WHO has maintained a robust program of health and risk communication, but until recently neglected to develop a robust emergency and crisis program. A program of risk communication was one of the eight core functions that WHO Member States must fulfill according to the International Health Regulations treaty of 2005. Specifically, member states must "address risk, communications and community engagement challenges, proactively counter misinformation and disinformation."

WHO defines emergency risk communication as the:

> real-time exchange of information, advice and opinions between experts, community leaders, or officials and the people who are at risk. During epidemics and pandemics, and humanitarian crises and natural disasters, effective risk communication allows people most at risk to understand and adopt protective behaviours. It allows authorities and experts to listen to and address people's concerns and needs so that the advice they provide is relevant, trusted and acceptable.
>
> *WHO (2017, p. xi)*

WHO was criticized for its management of the 2013 Ebola outbreak in West Africa, including significant failures in communication resulting in damaged credibility with key publics. Failures in the Ebola response prompted WHO to recognize the need for greater emergency communication capacities. In 2017, WHO assembled a group of subject matter experts in risk communication, disaster preparedness, and response and health emergencies from diverse member countries in North America, Asia, Latin and South America, and Europe. This expert panel commissioned comprehensive summaries of published, peer-reviewed literature to inform the development of a set of emergency risk communication guidelines for member states (see Eckert et al., 2021; Sopory et al., 2009, 2021). The guidelines developed by this panel include policy recommendations, standards, and structures of an effective communication-based response to public health crises. These guidelines created a set of minimal capacities and standards of practice for all member states (see Eckert et al., 2021; Sopory et al., 2019, 2021). These standards facilitate coordination whenever more than one member state is involved in an emergency, such as a pandemic.

The WHO guidelines are organized around three general goals: building trust and engaging with affected populations; integrating ERC into health and emergency response systems; and effective emergency risk communication practice.

Building Trust

The first of these goals, building trust and engaging with affected populations, builds upon the same concepts of credibility highlighted in the CERC framework. The WHO guidelines emphasize that trust of a target population is a function of long-lasting relationships between communities and key stakeholders and WHO actors. Relationships formed pre-crisis provide a better foundation for response than relationships constituted once the crisis has manifest. The diversity of publics WHO interacts with creates additional challenges for crisis communication, and the development of trust-based relationships is an effective counter to many of these challenges. Trust from target publics is especially important to a multi-national organization that does not have the same legal nor cultural authority as a more local agency or government. WHO largely depends on the voluntary cooperation of member states in managing health crises. Trust is essential to eliciting voluntary cooperation. Trust is operationalized as follows:

> A.1. Trust. To build trust, risk communication interventions should be linked to functioning and accessible services, be transparent, timely, easy-to-understand, acknowledge uncertainty, address affected populations, link to self-efficacy, and be disseminated using multiple platforms, methods and channels.
>
> *WHO (2017, p. xiii)*

This articulation of trust largely mirrors the best practices of risk and crisis communication, such as transparency, timeliness, promoting self-efficacy, meeting audience needs, and broad dissemination to impacted audiences (Seeger, 2006; Seeger et al., 2018). Two activities are noteworthy. First, the guidelines suggest interventions should be linked to functioning and accessible services to build trust. WHO works in a variety of contexts, some of which are remote and most of which have limited resources for public health and emergency response. By foregrounding accessible and functioning services, the guidelines acknowledge the reality of many of its target contexts for intervention. A second novel element of these trust-building activities is the acknowledgment of the inherent uncertainty of an emerging infectious disease. Many crisis frameworks center uncertainty, but rarely is uncertainty discussed in terms of credibility with target audiences. This acknowledgment shows a nuanced understanding of the ways that uncertainty may modulate attitudes between stakeholders in a crisis event.

Communicating uncertainty plays an important role in WHO's approach to crisis communication. Uncertainty permeates all crisis events; however, the dynamic nature of many infectious disease crises is one of the essential complicating factors of emergency health communication. In many cases, these diseases are novel, or at least poorly understood, and it is an inescapable reality that any guidance issued by WHO will likely change as understandings and circumstances evolve. As this chapter highlighted with the CERC framework, agencies may undermine their credibility if they issue unequivocal statements and then are forced to modify or rescind their recommendations. WHO emphasizes that:

> Communication by authorities to the public should include explicit information about uncertainties associated with risks, events and interventions, and indicate what is known and not known at a given time.
>
> *WHO (2017, xiii)*

This explicit acknowledgment functions primarily as a form of reputational insurance – WHO is able to pivot its messaging to conform to new understandings without having to appear to have had incorrect information. However, acknowledgment of uncertainty has additional benefits beyond public communication. All organizations are subject to consensus seeking and overconfidence in their initial appraisals and decisions, and these phenomena can lead to flawed decision-making. By centralizing uncertainty in the communication process, the WHO guidelines create a psychological buffer against some of the more common pitfalls in organizational decision-making.

Community engagement is another important feature of building trust and has broader response functions related to the development of relational infrastructure within communities of focus. Effective response requires community leaders acting as cultural agents and sharing knowledge about effective channels of communication. These individuals have local knowledge about the communication ecosystems and can avoid mistakes and enhance the effectiveness of the messages. WHO advises:

> Identify people that the community trusts and build relationships with them. Involve them in decision-making to ensure interventions are collaborative, contextually appropriate and that communication is community-owned.
>
> *WHO (2017, xv)*

Notably, these community members are not conceptualized as mere channels of communication but are fully engaged as sources of information and decision makers. Community ownership requires a communication dynamic characterized by equity.

Integrating ERC

The second primary goal identified by the guidelines is integrating emergency risk communication into health and emergency response systems. Given the role and position of WHO as a multi-national public health agency, WHO advocates for standard best medical practices. This includes development and support of systems for promoting health and responding to health emergencies. WHO advocates for the integration of risk communication principles into the existing health infrastructure of governance and leadership, information systems, capacity building, and financial support. The guideline document notes:

> ERC should be a designated strategic role in global and national emergency preparedness and response leadership teams.
>
> *WHO (2017, xiv)*

Risk and crisis communication researchers have argued that communication should be treated as a strategic management function involved in decision-making rather than merely as a tactical function for the implementation of decisions and policies (Seeger, 2006). Involving the communication function in the process of strategic decision-making helps ensure audience perspectives, including informational needs, audience values, and communication capacity, are considered in decisions. In several cases, decisions in response to emergency situations have failed to fully consider larger circumstances, such as issuing boiling water advisories when there is no access to electricity or gas. While including the communication function will not ensure that all decisions are more effective, it will broaden the perspectives considered in those decisions.

Disaster researchers have often noted that coordination is one of the most difficult and common challenges in responding to emergencies. These challenges become even more critical when they require communication and coordination across multiple jurisdiction, regions, governments, and cultures. A number of factors can account for these challenges. Variable methods, channels, systems, structures, and cultures can impede the flow of information. Existing regional and national conflicts and competing interests may undermine cooperation. The WHO guideline acknowledges the need for coordination and advises member states to:

> Develop and build on agency and organizational networks across geographical, disciplinary and, where appropriate, national boundaries.
>
> *WHO (2017, xiv)*

In general, developing the agencies and structures of coordination is a pre-event activity when there is sufficient time to develop relationships and establish procedures. Regular interaction between geographic, disciplinary national boundaries can facilitate coordination during emergencies. To accommodate the diversity of audiences and reach the impacted audiences, networks and methods of coordination communication systems must extend to the local levels. In addition, WHO emphasizes tailoring information to meet the needs of users.

WHO member states represent highly variable levels, resources, and states of development. Some member states have robust disaster response capacity, highly trained medical professionals, and infrastructures to support the response. Others have limited capacity and resources, which may impede responses. WHO advocates, therefore, for programs of training, development, and capacity development not only in medical response but also in communication and coordination with stakeholders.

> Preparation and training of personnel for ERC should be organized regularly and focus on coordination across involved stakeholders.
>
> *WHO (2017, p. xv)*

A final element in WHO's guidance for integrating emergency risk communication into health and emergency response systems concerns funding. Capacity building and the development of coordinating systems require financial support. Both public health and emergency response capacity are chronically underfunded in many countries. Emergency response capacity is especially vulnerable to underfunding given that it is a capacity that is only utilized during emergencies. Maintaining the capacity is expensive, especially when there are significant competing demands for limited resources.

> ERC requires a defined and sustained budget that should be a part of core budgeting for emergency preparedness and response.
>
> *WHO (2017, p. xv)*

A defined and sustained budget can help ensure that an adequate response capacity exists when it is needed.

Effective Emergency Risk Communication Practice

The final goal articulated in the guidelines addresses basic standards for effective risk communication practice. Emergency risk communication principles are generally well developed and researched. This includes standards for best practice and principles for effectiveness across the emergency management life cycle (Seeger, 2006).

Risk communication practice should begin in the pre-crisis stage, before an emergency begins. Among the essential pre-crisis activities is the process of crisis planning. Planning is considered an overarching best practice necessary but not sufficient to an effective response. It is most effective when involving the range of stakeholders associated with a response and when it is framed as an ongoing activity rather than a one-time event.

> The WHO guidance defines pre-crisis planning as a strategic activity involving, the assessment of needs, setting of objectives, implementation of targeted interventions in a coordinated way, and monitoring and evaluation of intervention activities in order to improve public awareness and influence behaviour before, during and after a public health event or emergency.
>
> *WHO (2017, p. xvi)*

The guidance includes several specific recommendations about the planning process. These include creating collaboration among key constituent and stakeholder groups such as health and emergency response agencies and systems, public services, and community groups. Moreover, planning should involve representatives from potentially at-risk communities and populations. Planning processes can facilitate the development of the communication networks necessary for an effective response. Planning should also account for local conditions, community structures, cultures and lifestyles of stakeholder groups. WHO recommends that planning also accounts for educating communities about risk mitigation, disaster preparedness, response, and recovery. Crisis communication plans should include specific procedures for disseminating messages during an emergency through multiple channels. These channels as well as the basic structure of emergency messages should be specified in the plan. Finally, WHO recommends that planning includes mechanisms for receiving feedback about the effectiveness of emergency communication activities.

Despite the general recognition that monitoring and evaluation of emergency risk communication activities are essential, there have been comparatively few efforts to create a standard model, method, and set of criteria (see Seeger et al., 2018). WHO calls for research to develop methods that allow for rapidly evaluating the effectiveness of emergency risk communication activities, incorporating evaluation and feedback, and informing and improving subsequent response decisions.

The WHO's guidance acknowledges that social media has emerged as a power tool for direct communication in emergency situations. As a decentralized form of communication, social media can be used to reach audiences when other forms of communication may not be available. Communication channels may be disrupted by power outages, transportation problems, or loss of personnel. Social media may continue to be available in these contexts. Moreover, platforms such as Facebook, Twitter, WhatsApp, TikTok, and Instagram can create important peer-to-peer changes, provide real-time situational awareness, and help monitor public responses. While these channels may contribute to the propagation of rumors, they may also be useful in rumor control. The ability of social media systems to reach end users both directly and immediately without various levels of governmental or agency review may be especially valuable for a multi-national organization seeking to manage an emergency.

While social media has become an essential mean of emergency risk communication, legacy media remains important. As media convergence has accelerated, much of the content of social media comes legacy media sources. WHO's guidance suggests that both are important for disseminating timely and accurate information. The guidelines note:

> Social media and traditional media should be part of an integrated strategy with other forms of communication to achieve convergence of verified, accurate information.
> Member states and response partners are encouraged to develop capacity in social media to establish credibility and build trust with stakeholders.
> *WHO (2017, p. xvi)*

Emergency risk communication practice always implicates messages as a primary activity and substantial research has been conducted to inform the development and dissemination of effective messages. WHO emphasizes messaging as its final guiding principle. Risk messages, for example, should effectively translate technical guidance from subject matter experts into guidance for risk-mitigating behaviors that can be both understood and implemented by affected groups. This can be especially challenging with varying levels of health literacy among target audiences. Guidance should be consistent even when messages come from different sources. Consistency of messages is generally considered an essential element in effective risk and crisis communication. Messages should be time sensitive and be disseminated as early in an emergency situation as possible to establish credible sources for disaster-related information.

Summary of WHO ERC Guidelines

WHO developed a framework of research - informed and validated principles, and established standards and aspirational goals for member states. The guidelines are designed to accommodate a wide range of capabilities, resources, cultural contexts, communication infrastructure, and governmental systems. Establishing minimal standards facilitates a more effective response both in geographically bounded emergencies and in emergencies that transcend state borders, such as pandemics. The guidelines recognize the changing role of technology and the dynamic nature of emerging infectious disease. Diseases like Ebola, Zika, MERS, and COVID-19 vividly demonstrate the primacy of communication in an integrated global response.

Points of Convergence

The CDC's CERC and WHO's ERC guidelines seek to address very similar issues and needs, albeit from different standpoints. CDC developed CERC as a framework for the U.S. public health community while WHO sought to accommodate a much wider range of users. Accommodating a diverse global audience of member states requires a more general framework. CERC can assume a relatively high level of operations in both communication and public health. CERC functions primarily as a resource for training and practice while WHO offers more general guidelines to inform decisions and policy. Despite these differences, they share a number of commonalities.

In both cases, the impetus for development was an emergency response where the communication was judged as ineffective. Both approaches are the outcome of a learning process where systematic efforts were made to rectify deficiencies. Each effort drew heavily on published research and subject matter experts to translate principles to policy and practice. WHO instituted a rigorous process of systematic reviews guided by questions posed by a panel of subject matter experts. These helped ensure that the recommended practice was credible.

CERC drew on both subject matter experts and anecdotal experiences of the CDC communication staff to create an expansive and grounded framework for emergency communication practice.

Both approaches offer a strong acknowledgment of the essential role communication plays in response to public health emergencies. WHO states, "Risk communication is an integral part of any emergency response" while CERC suggests, "The right message at the right time from the right person can save lives." As noted, both CDC and WHO had well-established communication practices, but these focused primarily on health promotion and marketing and campaigns for risk communication. Events such as the Anthrax Letters in 2001, the West Africa Ebola virus outbreak in 2014–2015, and the emergence of the Zika virus in 2015–2016 illustrated the critical role communication can play in emergency response. Adding crisis and emergency risk communication capacity was necessary for comprehensive responses to these and similar disease emergencies.

Both frameworks suggest attending to the needs and perspectives of stakeholders through expressions of empathy, respectful communication, tailoring messages, and directly engaging with impacted communities. WHO, in particular, emphasizes working with established community structures and leaders and involving communities in decision-making. This is reflective of the diversity of contexts within which WHO operates. As essential goal of all emergency risk communication is to inform communities and promote protective actions. Doing so requires credible sources and messages, timely distribution, and sensitivity to the inherent uncertainty associated with crises.

Finally, both the CERC framework and the ERC guideline are important resources that significantly bolster capacity to manage and quickly respond to threatening and surprising disease threats. These resources do not ensure that the principles of effective emergency risk communication outlined by WHO and CERC will be applied.

Future Research Agenda

The application of principles of crisis and emergency risk communication to crises associated with public health is a relatively new development. In addition, research in risk and crisis communication has been centered primarily in North America and Europe (see Schwarz et al., 2016). There are several important areas for future research in risk and crisis communication, especially as applied to pandemics.

With few exceptions, emergency risk communication research has neglected the role culture plays in understanding risk and crisis. Other fields, including sociology, have placed culture at the center of theorizing about collective understanding and response to risks (see Douglas, 2013). Perceptions of risk and crisis response are collectively constructed and vary from context to context. Principles of intercultural communication are often used in programs of health communication, most often from what has been described as a culture sensitive perspective. Dutta (2007) argues for a culture-centered perspective which positions culture at the center of theory building and practice. This and similar approaches may be especially useful in understanding risks that extend beyond one national or cultural context.

In addition, most crisis communication theory and research views these events to have relatively short durations and crisis life cycles, in many cases a matter of days or perhaps weeks (see Sellnow & Seeger, 2021). This assumption likely comes from a focus on natural disasters. Infectious diseases, however, have a much longer life cycle. Factors such as risk fatigue, changing risk recommendations, evolving public perceptions, and understanding of risk become increasingly important when crisis conditions extend over months or even, in some cases, years. Pandemics, as illustrated by COVOD-19, do not follow a defined trajectory and have no clearly defined end date.

Future inquiry should also concern the ways in which crisis and disaster management can become politicized. While highly disruptive events have, for better or worse, impacted public perception of the effectiveness of political leaders, crisis response has not generally been driven by political agendas. The U.S. government's response to COVID-19 of withholding information, downplaying risk, shifting blame in ways that were described as racist, and undercutting international response efforts was antithetical to the very idea of crisis management. The intentional distribution of misinformation, often for economic or political gain, added to an epidemic of mistrust and confusion. Established principles of crisis and risk communication were simply inadequate to account for the ensuing chaos, and standards and practices for effective communication were often simply ignored.

A final area of future investigation should examine factors that may facilitate the application of principles of emergency risk communication. WHO emphasizes funding and training and key activities and these are necessary but may not be sufficient. Institutional impediments and factors of context may also limit communication effectiveness. In addition, disasters and crises are often seen as one-off events, and the opportunity to learn and enhance preparedness is, therefore, limited.

While COVID-19 was the most significant emerging infectious disease event since the 1918 Spanish flu, it was not the last. Most infectious disease researchers warn of more diseases as climate change continues to disrupt ecosystems, as human-animal interaction creates opportunities for zoonotic diseases, and as human population density and migration enhance transmission. Efforts such as the CDC's CERC and the WHO's ERC guidelines are essential tools and resources for facilitating a robust communicative response to pandemics.

References

Available: https://www.who.int/news/item/23-09-2020-managing-the-COVID-19-infodemic-promoting-healthy-behaviours-and-mitigating-the-harm-from-misinformation-and-disinformation

Avery, E. J. (2010). The role of source and the factors audiences rely on in evaluating credibility of health information. *Public Relations Review, 36*(1), 81–83. https://doi.org/10.1016/j.pubrev.2009.10.015

Caeiro, J. P., & Garzón, M. I. (2018). Controlling infectious disease outbreaks in low-income and middle-income countries. *Current Treatment Options in Infectious Diseases, 10*(1), 55–64. https://doi.org/10.1007/s40506-018-0154-z

Douglas, M. (2013). *Risk and blame: Essays in cultural theory.* Routledge.

Dutta, M. J. (2007). Communicating about culture and health: Theorizing culture-centered and cultural sensitivity approaches. *Communication Theory, 17*(3), 304–328. https://doi.org/10.1111/j.1468-2885.2007.00297.x

Eckert, S., Sopory, P., Day, A., Wilkins, L., Padgett, D., Novak, J.,... & Gamhewage, G. (2018). Health-related disaster communication and social media: mixed-method systematic review. *Health Communication, 33*(12), 1389–1400. https://doi.org/10.1080/10410236.2017.1351278

Endsley, T., Wu, Y., Reep, J., Eep, J., & Reep, J. (2014). The source of the story: Evaluating the credibility of crisis information sources. In *ISCRAM.*

Handel, A., Longini Jr, I. M., & Antia, R. (2007). What is the best control strategy for multiple infectious disease outbreaks?. *Proceedings of the Royal Society B: Biological Sciences, 274*(1611), 833–837.

Hocevar, K. P., Metzger, M., & Flanagin, A. J. (2017). Source credibility, expertise, and trust in health and risk messaging. In *Oxford Research Encyclopedia of Communication.*

Johns Hopkins University, (2022). Coronavirus Resource Center. Mortality Analysis. Available: https://coronavirus.jhu.edu/data/mortality

Last, J. M. (2001). Pandemic. *A Dictionary of Epidemiology.* 4th edition. Oxford University Press.

Miller, A. N., Collins, C., Neuberger, L., Todd, A., Sellnow, T. L., & Boutemen, L. (2021). Being first, being right, and being credible since 2002: A systematic review of Crisis and Emergency Risk Communication (CERC) research. *Journal of International Crisis and Risk Communication Research, 4*(1), 1–27.

Morens, D. M., Folkers, G. K., & Fauci, A. S. (2009). What is a pandemic?. *The Journal of Infectious Diseases, 200*(7), 1018–1021.

Nowling, W., & Seeger, M. M. (2021). Communicating Death and Dying in the COVID-19 Pandemic. *Communicating Science in Times of Crisis: COVID-19 Pandemic, 375.*

Pornpitakpan, C. (2004). The persuasiveness of source credibility: A critical review of five decades' evidence. *Journal of Applied Social Psychology, 34*(2), 243–281. https://doi.org/10.1111/j.1559-1816.2004.tb02547.x

Reynolds, B., Galdo, J. H., Sokler, L., & Freimuth, V. S. (2002). Crisis and emergency risk communication. *Centers for Disease Control and Prevention.*

Reynolds, B., & Seeger, M. W. (2005). Crisis and emergency risk communication as an integrative model. *Journal of Health Communication, 10*(1), 43–55.

Sandman, P. M. (1988). Risk communication: Facing public outrage. Management *Communication Quarterly, 2*(2), 235–238. https://doi.org/10.1080/10810730590904571

Sauer, M. A., Truelove, S., Gerste, A. K., & Limaye, R. J. (2021). A failure to communicate? How public messaging has strained the COVID-19 response in the United States. *Health Security, 19*(1), 65–74. https://doi.org/10.1089/hs.2020.1090

Schoofs, L., Fannes, G., & Claeys, A. S. (2022). Empathy as a main ingredient of impactful crisis communication: The perspectives of crisis communication practitioners. *Public Relations Review, 48*(1), 102150. https://doi.org/10.1016/j.pubrev.2022.102150

Schwarz, A., Seeger, M. W., & Auer, C. (Eds.). (2016). *The handbook of international crisis communication research.* John Wiley & Sons.

Seeger, M. W. (2006). Best practices in crisis communication: An expert panel process. *Journal of Applied Communication Research, 34*(3), 232–244. https://doi.org/10.1080/00909880600769944

Seeger, M. W., Pechta, L. E., Price, S. M., Lubell, K. M., Rose, D. A., Sapru, S.,... & Smith, B. J. (2018). A conceptual model for evaluating emergency risk communication in public health. *Health Security, 16*(3), 193–203. https://doi.org/10.1089/hs.2018.0020

Sellnow, T. L., & Seeger, M. W. (2021). *Theorizing crisis communication.* John Wiley & Sons.

Sopory, P., Novak, J. M., Day, A. M., Eckert, S., Wilkins, L., Padgett, D. R.,... & Gamhewage, G. M. (2021). Trust and public health emergency events: a mixed-methods systematic review. *Disaster medicine and public health preparedness,* 1–21.

Sopory, P., Day, A. M., Novak, J. M., Eckert, K., Wilkins, L., Padgett, D. R.,... & Gamhewage, G. M. (2019). Communicating uncertainty during public health emergency events: A systematic review. *Review of Communication Research,* 7, 67–108.

Trilla, A., Trilla, G., & Daer, C. (2008). The 1918 "spanish flu" in spain. *Clinical infectious diseases, 47*(5), 668–673.

Veil, S., Reynolds, B., Sellnow, T. L., & Seeger, M. W. (2008). CERC as a theoretical framework for research and practice. *Health promotion practice, 9*(4_suppl), 26S-34S.

Wombacher, K., Herovic, E., Sellnow, T. L., & Seeger, M. W. (2018). The complexities of place in crisis renewal discourse: A case study of the Sandy Hook Elementary School shooting. *Journal of Contingencies and Crisis Management, 26*(1), 164–172. https://doi.org/10.1111/1468-5973.12186

Woolhandler, S., Himmelstein, D. U., Ahmed, S., Bailey, Z., Bassett, M. T., Bird, M.,... & Venkataramani, A. (2021). Public policy and health in the Trump era. *The Lancet, 397*(10275), 705–753.

WHO (2017). *Communicating risk in public health emergencies: a WHO guideline for emergency risk communication (ERC) policy and practice.* https://www.who.int/emergencies/risk-communications/guidance

WHO (23, June 2022). WHO Coronavirus (COVID-19) Dashboard. Available: https://COVID19.who.int

Van der Meer, T. G., & Verhoeven, J. W. (2014). Emotional crisis communication. *Public Relations Review, 40*(3), 526–536.

van Zoonen, W., & van der Meer, T. (2015). The importance of source and credibility perception in times of crisis: Crisis communication in a socially mediated era. *Journal of Public Relations Research, 27*(5), 371–388. https://doi.org/10.1080/1062726X.2015.1062382

World Health Organization (23 September 2020). Joint statement by WHO, UN, UNICEF, UNDP, UNESCO, UNAIDS, ITU, UN Global Pulse, and IFRC.

5

PUBLIC RELATIONS AND PANDEMICS

Maureen Taylor

The COVID-19 pandemic had the potential to change everything. It changed how we greeted our friends, family, and colleagues. It changed how we worked and where we worked. It changed where we studied and how we learned. It also changed how we viewed organizations' role in society. Many people wanted to know what for-profit companies were doing to help their employees, customers, and communities survive the challenges of COVID-19. The COVID-19 pandemic made all of us realize that people across their home country and world were interconnected and that the actions of a few can affect the many. The pandemic also made us question some of our assumptions about relationships across society. In lockdowns and quarantine, we might have felt alone. But we also recognized our connectivity to others through communication technologies.

The pandemic created a whole new vocabulary and set of personal actions to help us both understand and cope with what was happening. We lived through "lockdowns", went into "quarantine", practiced "physical distancing", and thought carefully about who to interact with and who to keep at a distance. News media showed us infographics of what it might look like to "flatten the curve", virus "peaks", and virus "hot spots". Terms to describe the realities of COVID-19 for organizations and society alluded to "pivoting", "disruption", "endemics", "infodemics", and a host of scientific words that kept us updated on the scientific process of vaccine testing. From December 2019 to today, nothing is the same. Such changes have implications for all processes of communication.

The goals of this chapter are twofold. First, it seeks to explain the unique contexts of a pandemic from a public relations perspective. The pandemic was a good time to rethink the guiding assumptions of public relations and reimagine what public relations and relationships should and could be. Second, this chapter lays out a research

DOI: 10.4324/9781003214496-5

agenda in public relations that explores how the processes of communication are affected and can affect pandemics. The chapter proceeds from a realization that existing theories, models, and constructs may not adequately capture the effects of a pandemic on public relations and other communication processes. But, the best time to improve theory and practice for future pandemics is now.

The first part of the chapter provides a brief summary of the dominant theories and concepts in public relations. It summarizes a brief history of public relations theories and research topics through the lens of the functional theories that guided public relations past and then explains the co-creational turn that emerged in the last 20 years. The second section of the chapter takes nine current theories and topics and juxtaposes them in a consideration of the communication needs of society during a pandemic. The juxtaposition provides a way to "weigh" the value of the theories to guide relationship building and communication processes in a pandemic. The final section of the chapter identifies ways forward in public relations frameworks for communication and relationship building in the future so as to be prepared for future health crises like pandemics.

Dominant Approaches to Public Relations Theory and Practice

Public relations research has evolved over the last 40 years. Initially, it followed trends in media and agenda setting research, where scholars tried to identify the influence of publicity materials on news coverage (Botan & Taylor, 2004). Early public relations researchers studied organizational centric goals like agenda setting (McCombs & Shaw, 1972), information subsidies (Gandy, 1982), and persuasion (Pfau & Wan, 2006). Botan and Taylor defined public relations scholarship as the functional perspective, which "sees publics and communication as tools or means to achieve organizational ends" (p. 651).

By the 1990s, research in the functional approach moved to studying practitioners. There was interest in public relations as a management function, and excellence theory emerged as a dominant theme. Scholars sought out evidence that organizations were creating balanced, two-way symmetrical relationships with publics. Research on issues management (Heath & Cousino, 1990), the roles of research (Broom & Dozier, 1990), and corporate communication management (Vercic et al., 1996) showed that the field was focusing on the *internal management processes* of public relations.

Over time, however, the excellence theory was no longer a viable framework to answer questions about the evolving field because internationalization and technologies, like the internet, changed how organizations communicate with publics. By the late 1990s and early 2000s, the field was looking at *externally* focused research topics such as relationship management (Ledingham & Bruning, 1998), crisis management (Coombs, 1995), and dialogic communication (Kent & Taylor, 1998, 2002) as the lenses through which to focus theorizing about public relations. Botan and Taylor defined this as the cocreational perspective, which recognizes publics as "cocreators of meaning and communication as what makes it possible to agree to shared meanings, interpretations, and goals" (2004, p. 652), emerged. In contrast to focusing on only organizational goals, the cocreational perspective emphasizes the value of relationships and dialogue among individuals, groups, organizations, publics, and networks. By the mid-2010s, engagement (Johnston, 2014; Johnston & Taylor, 2018a,b) emerged to further move the field toward a cocreational, public-centered practice.

This brief history shows that over time public relations has moved away from more functional approaches to more cocreational approaches. There have been recent bibliometric studies that have examined theory formation and diffusion in public relations. Ki et al. (2019) examined influential authors and research topics to identify "four main areas—crisis communication, relationship management, new technologies, and dialogic communication—were at the center of the public relations scholarship" (p. 14). Morehouse and Saffer (2018) observed that research "has shifted from the once-dominant excellence theory to a more relationship-focused approach to public relations (cf. Botan & Taylor, 2004), the use of dialogue and digital dialogic communication have been starkly torn between differing philosophical, theoretical, and conceptual assumptions" (p. 79). Buhmann et al. (2019) identified "three main thematic research clusters on public relations and the public sphere, dialogic stakeholder relationships and engagement, as well as communication ethics – the latter of which can be shown to have both the strongest and most recent impact" (p. 455). The field of public relations has been evolving over the last 40 years and the recent conceptual developments have put it in a good place for being able to contribute to individuals, groups, organizations, and communities' communication processes during a pandemic.

The COVID-19 Pandemic Creates Challenges and Opportunities for Public Relations

It would not be an understatement to say that COVID-19 changed many industries, including the public relations industry. Pandemics, as life and community altering events, prompt changes across all sectors of society. Industries try to minimize change or at least work to influence the outcome of the change. Public relations is both an academic research area and a professional practice where each informs the other. The public relations industry has experienced many changes over the last 100 years and it is likely that the pandemic has already begun to change the industry.

What Does Industry-Level Change Look Like?

Change is a natural process in complex systems. Systems theory (Von Bertalanffy, 1950) provides a good framework for thinking about how systems and subsystems change and adapt to environmental changes. Public relations can be thought of as providing the *inputs* (research and environmental scanning), *throughputs* (flows of information in organizations from one unit to another), and *outputs* (public relations materials and relationships with publics) (Taylor & Grasso, 2000). The public relations industry is a large complex system of firms, relationships, and outcomes that is influenced by external factors like a pandemic. Change is a necessary part of a healthy system and organizations and industries that don't change will eventually die.

McGahan (2000, 2004) has studied industry evolution and change. McGahan (2004) identified four trajectories of industry change based on the level of threat to an industry's *core activities* or *core assets*. Core activities are considered to be the actions that attract and retain suppliers and buyers. Core assets are the tangible and intangible resources that make the organization efficient at performing its core activity.

The greatest risk to an industry occurs when both its core activities and core assets are threatened. It is at this time that radical change is needed. Radical change occurs when an industry's core assets and core activities are both threatened with obsolescence. For example, Netflix and other streaming services presented threats to Blockbuster Video's core asset and activities.

Intermediating change happens when core activities are threatened but core assets are not. McGahan notes that this type of industry change affects relationship-based industries where reputation and relationships are fragile. As an example, Sotheby's auction house was threatened by the rise of eBay and other online auctioneers. Companies can adapt to threats by finding "ways to preserve knowledge, brand capital, and other valuable assets while fundamentally changing relationships with customers and with supplier" (McGahan, 2004, p. 5). Creative changes occur when assets are threatened so the industry has to keep innovating and changing. Examples of creative industry change include the banking industry and the movie industry. Consider how the banking industry took advantage of the internet and mobile phone technology. There are now fully online banks with no branch locations. You can deposit a check with just a picture, and paying bills online through automatic debits has made it easier for people to manage their finances.

Progressive change occurs when neither core assets nor the core activities of an industry are threatened but the industry listens to, reacts to feedback, and then continually tests changes to improve operations and reduce costs. For example, McGahan noted that the budget airline is an example of a progressive change across an industry. When consumers were frustrated with high costs and poor service from the major airlines, smaller, more flexible airlines emerged to fill the "no frill gap". Budget airlines created a "pay for what you use" model that lowered the overall cost of a flight if a passenger did not want certain services. Today, the largest carriers have adapted some of the initiatives of the budget airlines such as charging passengers for bags and snacks, advance seat selection, and early priority boarding. The airline industry tries different tactics to increase revenue and then regularly evaluates the costs and benefits of the change. Such progressive change provides constant feedback and allows organizations to pilot test changes, keep the changes that are revenue positive, and eliminate changes that are unpopular.

Of the four types of industry change, McGahan (2004) noted that progressive change and intermediary change are the most common during normal economic conditions. However, during a chronic crisis like a pandemic, creative change and radical change may occur more frequently as pandemics disrupt industries and force changes to business models, relationships, or supply chains.

Disruption in the Public Relations

Gregory and Halff (2017) looked at the last major disruption in public relations due to the emergence and growth of the sharing economy. The sharing economy is considered to begin with eBay (1995), Airbnb (2008), and Uber (2009). In a sharing economy, the company does not have to make something or own in order to profit from it. eBay facilitates buyers while AirBnb and Uber only connect interested parties—they don't build or buy houses or cars. Gregory and Halff (2017) noted that the sharing economy puts "conceptual pressure on public relations" (p. 4) and the "public relations industry can be said to undergo intermediating change as a result of this conceptual pressure: Its core assets (skills, knowledge and abilities) retain their value, but some of its core activities are threatened with obsolescence" (p. 5).

The second major disruption to public relations is COVID. During COVID-19, the public relations industry no longer planned and held large-scale face-to-face events, meetings, or conferences. It rarely worked on experiential marketing or created public events to gain earned media. Public relations scholarship is also changing as the pandemic (and social events such as Black Lives Matter, climate change, elections of authoritarian leaders) prompted scholars to push public relations forward to even more social consciousness (Ciszek, 2020; Heath & Waymer, 2019; Waymer & Logan, 2021).

This chapter is an appropriate place to look critically at the past, current, and future questions and topics that drive public relations research and practice. Table 5.1 provides a summary of the nine pre-pandemic topics and identifies some possible changes to public relations in a pandemic and post-COVID-19 world.

As Table 5.1 shows, the pandemic has presented a disruption for individuals, organizations, and communities. Each of the nine topics will be discussed below.

TABLE 5.1 Topics, Themes, and Future Research in Public Relations

Public Relations Topics	Pre-Pandemic Themes	Pandemic and Post-Pandemic Themes
1 Crisis	• How organizations manage crisis • How publics respond to crisis messaging • How media cover crisis • Which channels do organizations use to communicate crisis response • Renewal	• How to avoid crises by open communication with publics • Engaging publics in crisis response • Listening • Communicating complex information in a low trust environment
2 Health communication	• One-way communication campaigns to target audiences	• Cocreating meaning around health contexts • Responding to mis- and disinformation • More tailored, inclusive health communication • Other groups join health agencies in creating communication outcomes
3 Corporate social responsibility	• How CSR effects purchase intention • Which CSR messages get the most social media engagement • How media cover CSR	• How organizations contribute to their communities (local and global) • How organizations respond to rapid and complex changes • Caring for employees
4 Employee communication	• Using communication to increase outputs and productivity • Leadership	• Employee well-being • Listening to employees • Facilitating flexible working arrangements
5 Communication engagement	• Lower tier engagement via social media • Engagement around brands	• Engagement for community benefits • Mid and higher tier engagement for social capital outcomes
6 Organization public relationships (OPR)	• Dyadic relationships between organizations and publics	• Multi-layered relationships in networks • Glocal resource dependency

7 Social capital	• What does public relations contribute to society	• Building micro, meso, and macro social capital from public relations • Leveraging social capital for health outcomes • Community health outcomes from relationships
8 Networks	• What relational networks look like	• How to leverage a network for information and behavior change • How to stop disinformation and misinformation • Building social capital outcomes
9 Socially mediated communication	• Describing social media uses by organizations and publics • Lower tier social media engagement	• Creating social capital by social media relationships and actions • Correcting misinformation and disinformation • Mid- and high-tier social media engagement

Topic 1: Changes in Crisis Communication

Traditional crisis communication research often put the organization at the center of research and practice. Studies have looked at how organizations have "managed" both acute (unexpected) and chronic (ongoing) crises through theories like situational crisis communication theory (SCCT) (Coombs, 2007) or image repair theory (IRT) (Benoit, 2014). COVID-19 first appeared as an acute crisis that required organizations, institutions, communities, and networks to abruptly change their behaviors. Public relations was used to help manage the acute crisis. Yet, by 2021, the pandemic had moved from being an acute crisis to a chronic crisis. The main difference is that acute crises are often a surprise and those responsible for responding have to move quickly to create messaging and policies. A chronic crisis, however, is ongoing and evolves over time. Public relations in the pandemic moved from acute, fast response crisis communication to more deliberate ongoing responses over time.

A good example of the movement from acute to chronic public relations in crisis response can be seen in how governments briefed citizens. At the beginning of the pandemic, high-ranking government leaders, including presidents and prime ministers, scheduled daily news conferences and briefings to announce the numbers of cases, hospitalizations, and deaths. Different government agencies had speaking roles to explain the steps that they had taken to stop the spread of COVID-19. These briefings occurred each day at a set time and dozens of media covered the conference live. These news conferences often preempted regular programming on television. But, over time, most national and state governments moved away from the large-scale, daily news briefing led by prominent leaders to smaller more focused updates from experts and health officials. The briefings changed from high-level *crisis* statements to more mundane, *chronic* health information exchange sessions.

Future crisis communication research will focus on how to avoid crises through open communication. There will be a recognition that trust is at the core of effective crisis communication. Both practitioners and scholars should be open to engaging the public before, during, and after crises.

Topic 2: Changes in Health Communication

Health communication also changed during the pandemic. Public health campaigns encompass public relations strategies and tactics. Health promotion draws upon and also informs public relations communication. During the pandemic, there was an acknowledgment that helping people to stay safe was more complicated than merely sending out one way messages. Second, data visualization emerged as important for communicating the spread of the virus and the uptake of vaccinations. National and local maps of cases, hospitalizations, and deaths provided quick summaries that captured the hardest hit areas. Third, we cannot underestimate the power that misinformation and disinformation had on health communication message design and patient outcomes. Finally, health communication about the virus acknowledged mental health. Indeed, the very public acknowledgment that community health outcomes are linked to individual mental health outcomes is a major change in thinking about health communication and public relations.

Future health communication will be based on the assumptions of co-created meaning and will be audience focused. There will need to be awareness of misinformation and disinformation. Effective health communication will need to address inclusiveness and diversity. Finally, future health communication should take a holistic approach that features partners such as community groups in health promotion.

Topic 3: The Story of Corporate Social Responsibility Changes

The need for companies to showcase their corporate social responsibility (CSR) efforts and respond to stakeholder demands may have been intensified by the ongoing COVID-19 pandemic. This pandemic has resulted in widespread socioeconomic disruptions for companies and consumers. It halted supply chains and global trades, creating scarcity and uncertainty. Additionally, the COVID-19 pandemic is a relational crisis as it has disrupted the ways businesses and organizations engage with their stakeholders (He & Harris, 2020). It is during this time of high uncertainty that stakeholders will scrutinize the CSR communications of profitable companies and beloved brands to ask "what have you done to contribute to COVID relief and keep their employees safe?" As such, companies across industries may have felt the need or experienced pressure to expand and communicate about their CSR efforts.

Corporations responded to the COVID-19 pandemic in a variety of ways. Some organizations announced donations community groups. Other CSR communication focused on employee and customer safety, financial assistance, home isolation, and mental health initiatives. The topic of remote working and employee welfare was a popular CSR topic at the beginning of the pandemic.

Topic 4: Changes in Employee Communication

Employee communication is an often overlooked area of public relations (Men & Yue, 2019). Research and practice have traditionally focused on how to improve productivity or create materials that support organizational leaders. One recurrent theme has been on CEO leadership and megaphoning to employees (Men, 2012). This also changed in the pandemic. While the world was "on hold", employee communication became more salient and meaningful and public relations was called upon to listen and speak to organizational members. Organizations created lots of content for employees around COVID-19. Messages ranged from how to stay healthy at the workplace, how to best work from home, suggestions on how to practice mindfulness, and mental health resources for employees (Li et al., 2021).

Future employee communication will need to move past studies of CEO leadership and megaphoning and really focus on employee health and wellness. Organizations will need to accept that how they treat their employees will influence decisions by some members of the public.

Topic 5: Changes in Communication Engagement

The pandemic kept us apart physically. Some people took advantage of the situation to promote divisiveness. Anti-vaxxers viewed government decisions to the pandemic as an infringement on their rights and reacted against mask mandates, vaccine passports, stay at home/lockdown orders, and other policies. With all of this divisiveness, there appears to be opportunities for communication engagement to help rebuild relationships fractured during the pandemic. Engagement as a theoretical perspective flows from the cocreational paradigm

(Botan & Taylor, 2004), arguing that public relations communication fosters interaction and exchanges to co-create meaning among organizations, groups, and networks.

Engagement is not a new term in public relations, and it has been used in many different ways to involve different types of actors, including organizations, stakeholders, consumers, employees, community, users, partners, parties, and social institutions (Johnston & Taylor, 2018a). It is conceptualized as an "iterative, dynamic process, where participation, experience and shared action emerge as central components of engagement" (Johnston & Taylor, 2018b, p. 3). Engagement can also be dialogic in that the orientation to the other proceeds from dialogic principles (Lane & Kent, 2018). Johnston and Taylor (2018b) identified three tiers of engagement. Tier 1 engagement is the low-level engagement where there is just interaction, usually one-way communication from an organization to its people on social media. Tier 2 engagement is mid-level interactions where the goal is building trust, reciprocity, credibility, legitimacy, openness, satisfaction, and understanding. Tier 3 engagement is the highest level where public relations creates social embeddedness, social awareness, and civic (greater good) indicators. There is recognition of diverse perspectives, and the outcomes are social capital for individuals and the community.

The opportunity for engagement is an important value in rebuilding relationships that may have been damaged during COVID-19. For example, a dialogic engagement orientation can help find common ground in communities that have experienced divisions around COVID-19 policies. Writing in the medical journal, *The Lancet*, Burgess et al. (2021) noted:

> In this new phase of the COVID-19 response, successful vaccine rollout will only be achieved by ensuring effective community engagement, building local vaccine acceptability and confidence, and overcoming cultural, socioeconomic, and political barriers that lead to mistrust and hinder uptake of vaccines.
>
> *(p. 8)*

Future engagement research and public relations practice should work toward tier 3. Burgess et al. encouraged policy makers to engage diversity and adopt comprehensive local approaches that give communities to ensure "diverse local voices are heard, map local concerns and alliances, and codesign programmes to maximise vaccine uptake from the ground up" (p. 9).

Topic 6: Changes in Organization-Public Relationships (OPRs)

At the core of a lot of COVID-19 responses is the interest in maintaining or even growing organization-public relationships (OPRs). Broom et al. (1997) explicated the concept of organizational-public relationships from research areas including interpersonal communication, psychotherapy, inter-organizational research, and systems theory. Ledingham and Bruning (1998, 2000) later extended Broom et al.'s work. They quantified measurements of dimensions of relationships which included openness, trust, involvement, investment, and commitment. Huang (2001) have further added to our understanding of OPR by identifying the antecedents to relationships, public relations strategies, and relationship outcomes. Ki and Hon (2007) linked OPRs to behavioral outcomes in public relations.

COVID-19 research that applied OPR has found that proactive relationships building between government and the public cultivate promoting pro-health and risk-reduction behavior (Liu & Huang, 2021). Additionally, public trust toward public agencies helps to predict how individuals assess the risk situation and make risk-mitigation decisions during health crises like pandemics (Liu & Huang, 2021).

In the future, organizations should also enhance their engagement with publics during COVID-19 if the followed OPR strategies (Huang et al., 2021) lead to positive outcomes like social capital. They will need to move past developing dyadic relationships and move toward network relationships.

Topic 7: Social Capital Outcomes

During COVID-19, arguments focused on the priority of the economy in discussions about response. National governments made decisions about life and death situations such as opening borders and schools based on *economic warrants*. The health of the economy became the rationale for all sorts of health decisions (Boettke & Powell, 2021)

However, another type of capital, social capital, may offer an alternative conceptual frame of reference for understanding how COVID-19 response and recovery programs could be implemented to draw on the power of communities and networks. An emergent stream in the public relations literature focuses on the social capital that is created by relationship building. Since the cocreational turn (Botan & Taylor, 2004), some public relations scholars have asked: "How can public relations contribute to making better societies and communities?" (Taylor, 2010).

Future public relations research and practice should work toward building community level society capital. This means that public relations will need to engage publics and help all types of organizations respond to public feedback.

Topic 8: Evolving Network Relationships

Networks matter in the age of COVID as both potential sources of the virus and potential solutions. We are living in a networked age (Castells, 2011). Networks comprise "a set of actors or nodes along with a set of ties of a specified type that link them" (Borgatti & Halgin, 2011, p. 1169). Today, all individuals, groups, organizations, and communities exist in networks. People and organizations are tied together through communication into social networks. Social ties connect people and communication provides one of the most powerful connections. This line of research has established that public relations can create all kinds of public goods through its communicative and relational functions within inter-organizational networks. In COVID-19, studying networks helps us to trace the spread of the virus and can help up to identify ways to leverage networks to promote protective behaviors and vaccine uptake.

Public relations scholars can study the network structures of relationships to look for ways to address vaccine hesitance. As Yang and Saffer (2019) suggest:

> By focusing on structures and relationships that were previously invisible to social scientists, the network perspective is a major shift from the traditional attribute-based worldview. Traditional approaches to key performance indicators for an organization's public relations efforts often are explained by organizational resources, values and culture, and communication strategies and tactics. A study adopting a network perspective would instead focus on the communication networks in which the organization, its messages, and its stakeholders are embedded within.
>
> *(p. 3)*

In the future, the main concepts underlying a public relations application of network theory in pandemics should include centrality (a node, or individual/ organization, interacting with others in the network), density (how closely nodes are linked together), bridging and bonding (network roles that link others), weak ties (diversity of heterophilous, or unrelated, relationships), and strong ties (deeply trusted and usually homophilous, or related, ties). Public relations can be used to forge, maintain, and change network dynamics in a world still struggling with pandemics.

Topic 9: Socially Mediated Communication Holds Us Together and Breaks Us Apart

One way to leverage the previous eight public relations topics is through social media. Social media communication is discussed last in this chapter because social media reflect and amplify all of the previous public relations topics that have been changed through the COVID-19 pandemic. Cinelli et al. (2020) were the first to trace social media in the COVID-19 pandemic, showing the diffusion of information. They concluded that social media can strongly influence people's behavior and alter the effectiveness of the countermeasures deployed by governments. Research in 2021 confirmed their findings and raised red flags about who is spreading misinformation and how it affects COVID-19 behaviors (Volkner, 2021).

Public relations was an early adapter of social media to spread information, build relationships, and help organizations to listen to publics. During COVID-19, social media moved from being considered a marketing and relationship-building platform to being considered a social lifeline to also being considered a tool that fragmented relationships, families, and communities. On the positive side, social media brought people together during periods of isolation. They provided outlets for creativity and interaction. Organizations used social media to communicate their COVID-19 response and to listen to stakeholders.

On the negative side, social media created unfiltered channels for misinformation and disinformation to spread. Social media platforms were bombarded with misleading information that had the potential to harm users.

In the future, regardless of the outcome, public relations emerged as a way for people, organizations, health experts, and governments to communicate directly with others. Social media is one way that civil society organizations and social movements can amplify their activism.

Toward a Public Relations Research Agenda for Pandemic Communication

McGahan's (2004) work describing the trajectories of industry change based on the level of threat to an industry's core activities or core assets suggests that the public relations industry and functions will always be changing. The one thing that we have learned during COVID-19 is that there are very few absolutes. New variants have emerged and the pandemic will probably not end in 2022. Making predictions about the end of the virus has proven futile. But, we can make some predictions about the field of public relations in a post-pandemic (or pre-pandemic) world.

First, I believe that we now realize the pro-social value of using strategic communication to combat misinformation or disinformation. This is a job for public relations because public relations communication cocreates meaning. Public relations will help organizations listen (see Macnamara, 2016) to and respond to whatever the pandemic brings next. Public relations from a cocreational perspective will allow all types of organizations to be more attuned to what is happening in society. Public relations will help organizations achieve their objectives in a complex and uncertain world. There seems to be some consensus that public relations is not just about communicating about a topic but there is interest in having public relations help organizations to listen to public expectations and needs.

Second, there is an acknowledgment of the power of a persuasive message delivered in the right medium, at the right time, directed to the target audience. Governments and health agencies spent millions (if not billions) of dollars to communicate messages about COVID-19. They hired public relations agencies to help them develop, tailor, disseminate, and evaluate communication outcomes. Public relations can contribute to enhanced health outcomes by helping health organizations, government agencies, and companies better target communication messages, select the most appropriate channels, and evaluate communication outcomes. Pandemic public relations will become integral to future health communication campaigns and initiatives.

Third, we see that members of the public are interested in how organizations are keeping them and their employees safe in a pandemic. The traditional public relations function of informing people continues and is strengthened under a pandemic research agenda. People across the world visited websites and social media accounts in record numbers to learn how organizations were changing their actions during COVID-19. Organizations will need to continue to keep up two-way communication with consumers, media, and government in the post-pandemic world. Public relations channels such as social media, websites, annual reports, sustainability reporting, and C-suite communication will help people understand which organizations share their values and which ones do not. This knowledge will be used by consumers and investors who care about CSR.

Fourth, even though we don't know when this pandemic will end and when the next one will begin, we do know that pandemics heighten public awareness of social issues beyond the pandemic. For example, topics such as climate change, increasing levels of economic disparities, systemic racism, violations of privacy, and policies of authoritarian governments provided a context for COVID-19. People began to see the convergence of these topics with the pandemic, and public awareness and demands for social and political change occurred. Pandemics show the interconnections among systems and people. They have the potential to heighten our awareness and foment demands for social change. Public relations is one way that civil society organizations and social movements can amplify their activism.

Finally, the world has seen firsthand how much networks of relationships matter. COVID-19 was a social virus. It spread through human contact and it was often isolation from social networks that broke the chain of the virus. Vaccines were most effective when entire networks of people were fully immunized. Public relations is a network building function. If networks were one of the entry points to the pandemic, then networks can be the solution as well. Public relations can help build stronger, more resilient social and community networks in the post-pandemic world.

Conclusions

The creation of a formalized pandemic research topic in communication is a timely and much-needed innovation. Pandemic communication research should draw upon and extend the traditional areas of communication research, including public relations. By drawing upon public relations theories and practices, pandemic communication will be able to reflect and extend our understanding of the social and meaning-making processes that guide human interactions during times of threat and uncertainty. Such a line of research would have both theoretical and practical value.

References

Benoit, W. L. (2014). *Accounts, excuses, and apologies: Image repair theory and research.* SUNY Press.

Boettke, P., & Powell, B. (2021). The political economy of the COVID-19 pandemic. *Southern Economic Journal, 87*(4), 1090–1106.

Borgatti, S. P., & Halgin, D. S. (2011). On network theory. *Organization Science, 22*(5), 1168–1181.

Botan, C., & Taylor M. (2004). Public relations: State of the field. *Journal of Communication, 54*(4), 645–661. http://doi.org/10.1111/j.1460-2466.2004.tb02649.

Broom, G. M., Casey, S., & Ritchey, J. (1997). Toward a concept and theory of organization–public relationships. *Journal of Public Relations Research, 9*, 83–98. https://doi.org/10.1207/s1532754xjprr0902_01

Broom, G. M., & Dozier, D. M. (1990). *Using research in public relations: Applications to program management.* Prentice Hall.

Buhmann, A., Ihlen, Ø., & Aaen-Stockdale, C. (2019). Connecting the dots: A bibliometric review of Habermasian theory in public relations research. *Journal of Communication Management, 23*, 444–467.

Burgess, R. A., Osborne, R. H., Yongabi, K. A., Greenhalgh, T., Gurdasani, D., Kang, G., Falade, A. G., Odone, A., Busse, R., Martin-Moreno, J. M., Reicher, S., & McKee, M. (2021). The COVID-19 vaccines rush: Participatory community engagement matters more than ever. *Lancet* (London, England), *397*(10268), 8–10. https://doi.org/10.1016/S0140-6736(20)32642-8

Castells, M. (2011). *The rise of the network society (Vol. 12).* John Wiley Sons.

Cinelli, M., Quattrociocchi, W., Galeazzi, A., et al. (2020). The COVID-19 social media infodemic. *Scientific Reports* 10, 16598. https://doi.org/10.1038/s41598-020-73510-5

Ciszek, E. (2020). "We are people, not transactions": Trust as a precursor to dialogue with LGBTQ publics. *Public Relations Review, 46*(1), 101759.

Coombs, W. T. (1995). Choosing the right words: The development of guidelines for the selection of the "appropriate" crisis-response strategies. *Management Communication Quarterly, 8*(4), 447–476.

Coombs, W. T. (2007). Attribution theory as a guide for post-crisis communication research. *Public Relations Review, 33*(2), 135–139. Huang, Q., Jin, J., Lynn, B. J., & Men, L. R. (2021). Relationship cultivation and public engagement via social media during the covid-19 pandemic in China. *Public Relations Review, 47*(4), 102064.

Huang, Y. H. (2001). OPRA: A cross-cultural, multiple-item scale for measuring organization-public relationships. *Journal of Public Relations Research, 13*(1), 61–90.

Gandy, O. H. (1982). *Beyond agenda setting: Information subsidies and public policy.* Ablex.

Gregory, A., & Halff, G. (2017). Understanding public relations in the 'sharing economy'. *Public Relations Review, 43*(1), 4–13.

He, H., & Harris, L. (2020). The impact of Covid-19 pandemic on corporate social responsibility and marketing philosophy. *Journal of Business Research, 116*, 176–182. https://doi.org/10.1016/j.jbusres.2020.05.030.

Heath, R. L., & Cousino, K. R. (1990). Issues management: End of first decade progress report. *Public Relations Review, 16*(1), 6–18.

Heath, R. L., & Waymer, D. (2019). Public relations intersections: Statues, monuments, and narrative continuity. *Public Relations Review, 45*(5), 101766.

Johnston, K. A. (2014). Public relations and engagement: Theoretical imperatives of a multidimensional concept. *Journal of Public Relations Research, 26*(5), 381–383.

Johnston, K. A., & Taylor, M. (2018a). *The handbook of communication engagement.* Wiley Blackwell.

Johnston, K. A., & Taylor, M. (2018b). Engagement as communication: Pathways, possibilities and future directions. In K. Johnston & M. Taylor (Eds.), *Handbook of communication engagement* (pp. 1–16). Wiley-Blackwell.

Kent, M. L., & Taylor, M. (1998). Building dialogic relationships through the World Wide Web. *Public Relations Review, 24*(3), 321–334.

Kent, M. L., & Taylor, M. (2002). Toward a dialogic theory of public relations. *Public Relations Review, 28*, 21–37.

Ki, E. J., & Hon, L. C. (2007). Testing the linkages among the organization–public relationship and attitude and behavioral intentions. *Journal of Public Relations Research, 19*(1), 1–23.

Ki, E. J., Pasadeos, Y., & Ertem-Eray, T. (2019). Growth of public relations research networks: A bibliometric analysis. *Journal of Public Relations Research, 31*(1–2), 5–31.

Lane, A., & Kent, M. L. (2018). Dialogic engagement. In K. Johnston & M. Taylor (Eds.), *Handbook of communication engagement* (pp. 61–72). Wiley-Blackwell.

Ledingham, J., & Bruning, S. (2000). (Eds.). *Public relations as relationship management: A relational approach to the study and practice of public relations.* Lawrence Erlbaum Associates.

Ledingham, J. A., & Bruning, S. D. (1998). Relationship management in public relations: Dimensions of an organization–public relationship. *Public Relations Review, 24*, 55–65.

Liu, W., & Huang, Y. (2021). Does relationship matter during a health crisis: Examining the role of local government-public relationship in the public acceptance of COVID-19 vaccines. *Health Communication*, 1–11. https://www.tandfonline.com/doi/full/10.1080/10410236.2021.1993586

Macnamara, J. R. (2016). *Organizational listening: The missing essential in public communication.* Peter Lang Publishing.

McCombs, M. E., & Shaw, D. L. (1972). The agenda-setting function of mass media. *Public Opinion Quarterly, 36*(2), 176–187.

McGahan, A. M. (2000). How industries evolve. *Business Strategy Review, 11*(3), 1–16.

McGahan, A. M. (2004). How industries change. *Harvard Business Review, 82*(10), 86–94.

Men, L. R. (2012). CEO credibility, perceived organizational reputation, and employee engagement. *Public Relations Review, 38*(1), 171–173.

Men, L. R., & Yue, C. A. (2019). Creating a positive emotional culture: Effect of internal communication and impact on employee supportive behaviors. *Public Relations Review, 45*(3), 101764.

Morehouse, J., & Saffer, A. J. (2018). A bibliometric analysis of dialogue and digital dialogic research: Mapping the knowledge construction and invisible colleges in public relations research. *Journal of Public Relations Research, 30*(3), 65–82.

Pfau, M., & Wan, H.-H. (2006). Persuasion: An intrinsic function of public relations. In C. H. Botan & V. Hazleton (Eds.), *Public relations theory II* (pp. 101–136). Lawrence Erlbaum Associates Publishers.

Taylor, M. (2010). Public relations in the enactment of civil society. In R. L. Heath (Ed.), *Handbook of public relations II* (pp. 5–12). Thousand Oaks, CA: Sage.

Taylor, M., & Grasso, J. A. (2000). Public relations: The alignment of communication theory and practice. In L. Lederman, & D. Gibson (Eds.), *Communication theory: A case study approach* (2nd ed.) (pp. 203–207). Dubuque, IA: Kendall Hunt Publishers.

Vercic, D., Grunig, L. A., & Grunig, J. E. (1996). Global and specific principles of public relations: Evidence from Slovenia. In N. Chen & H. Culbertson (Eds.), *International public relations: A comparative analysis* (pp. 31–65). Lawrence Erlbaum.

Volkner, I. (2021). Social media and COVID-19: A global study of digital crisis interaction among Gen Z and millennials. *WHO Report.* https://www.who.int/news-room/feature-stories/detail/social-media-covid-19-a-global-study-of-digital-crisis-interaction-among-gen-z-and-millennials

Von Bertalanffy, L. (1950). An outline of general system theory. *British Journal for the Philosophy of Science, 1*, 134–165. https://doi.org/10.1093/bjps/I.2.134

Waymer, D., & Logan, N. (2021). Corporate social advocacy as engagement: Nike's social justice communication. *Public Relations Review, 47*(1), 102005.

Yang, A., & Saffer, A. J. (2019). Embracing a network perspective in the network society: The dawn of a new paradigm in strategic public relations. *Public Relations Review, 45*(4), 101843. doi:10.1016/j.pubrev.2019.101843

6

THE NEW NORMAL

Pandemic Communication and Sustainable Organizations

Audra Diers-Lawson

Broadly speaking, this book asks the question 'what is pandemic communication?' We are asking this question from the viewpoints of many of the different theoretical, evidential, and ontological perspectives in the field of communication. Yet, to answer this from the organizational perspective, we need to better understand the implications of a global pandemic. Of course, each of us probably has our own idea of what a pandemic is and means, because we have all been living with this experience since early 2020. However, from a more generalizable perspective, a pandemic represents a deep global societal crisis. Reeves et al. (2020) argue that because societal level crises disrupt all aspects of our lives, they can fundamentally reshape our beliefs and our behaviors across multiple domains.

From an historic organizational perspective, Reeves et al. (2020) suggest many of the major 'organizational' changes in the West have been a result of societal level crises. For example, the Bubonic plague, which killed more than 20 million people in 14th century Europe, is largely credited for ending feudalism and serfdom, as labor resources were increasingly scarce, which ushered in the Enlightenment. They also discuss World War II's contribution to enabling women's entry into the workforce by reducing both social and legal barriers to entry. Of course, this was attributable to a labor shortage during the war, but afterward the workforce was irrevocably changed, driving women's growing participation in the workforce. In a COVID-19 context, there is already evidence of changes in people's attitudes toward work in industries like hospitality (Bajrami et al., 2021) and there are ongoing discussions globally about how organizational and work life have to change after the pandemic – driven in no small part because workers have now experienced different ways to do their jobs (Arneson, 2021; Davis, 2021; Mass, 2021; Williams, 2021).

DOI: 10.4324/9781003214496-6

Also affecting organizations is evidence of changing patterns of consumption when societal level changes happen. For example, the SARS pandemic encouraged people in China to change their attitudes about online shopping to reduce their risk of catching the disease in public (Reeves et al., 2020). In many places throughout North and South America, as well as Europe, there is already evidence of the same transformation for retail as a result of the COVID-19 pandemic (Sayyida et al., 2021). In fact, the pandemic has forced a transformation of the food retail industry because consumers now demand more in-store safety, expect more online shopping options, and have changed many of their shopping habits (Wang et al., 2020).

Based on historic experience with societal level crises, change is occurring – that is a genie that is not going to be put back in its bottle. Reeves et al. (2020) argue these types of crises spark attitudinal shifts – some of which remain, some do not – but they result in new policies, new ways of working, and new consumer behaviors. Along with these kinds of organizational and consumer changes, the COVID-19 pandemic has also become linked with climate change and sustainability because: (1) it can provide a model for how societal level change can be initiated; (2) addressing the climate change crisis will require substantial organizational and consumer change; and (3) there is already evidence of joint issues of public health, social justice, education, and advocacy being explored in organizational, political, and social contexts (Manzanedo & Manning, 2020; Zang et al., 2021). More than that, during the lockdowns, we could all visibly see the difference in basic air quality when commuter traffic was significantly reduced in our own communities and with broadcast images from cities around the world like Beijing, Delhi, Paris, and New York City. There are also meaningful environmental links between some of the potential enduring changes in work environments, like home working and more online retail.

Therefore, what is a pandemic? From the organizational perspective, it is not only a societal level crisis, but it presents both the need and opportunity for organizations to re-examine their relationships with issues confronting both the organization and their critical stakeholders – internal and external alike. In this chapter, I argue organizational communication is an essential tool to help organizations not only maneuver the new reality of a world with COVID-19 but also help organizations become more sustainable. In short, this chapter explores the role of organizational communication in creating and maintaining more sustainable organizations. Sustainable organizations should be thought of as not only those that are crisis resilient and better at anticipatory risk management, but also ones that improve citizenship behaviors (Diers-Lawson, 2020a,b). I do so by exploring the foundations of the field of organizational communication and pressures on organizations to be more sustainable, and then applying a case study of an English university's post-COVID development of a sustainability agenda to demonstrate the intersection of pandemic, risk, crisis, and organizational communication. In short, my main aim is to suggest how more authentic organizations are likely to be more effective at meeting both modern employee and consumer expectations. In so doing, this chapter takes a stakeholder-centered approach to organizational communication in the pandemic era.

Evolution of Organizational Communication

In their review of the development of the field of organizational communication, Tompkins and Wanca-Thibault (2001) identify that the earliest studies of the field emerged in the 1930s and 1940s, but it was not until the mid-1960s that we began to see theoretical constructs begin to emerge. From there, in the 1970s, the field focused on internal communication, but typically from a positivistic and managerial biased perspective. In the early 1980s, the focus on internal communication and a managerial bias began to change with greater consideration that organizational communication involves stakeholders inside and outside the organization. At the same time, work began that challenged the idea of what counted as 'knowledge' in organizations to focus more on the interactions between people associated with organizations, opening studies of channels, climate, networks, and superior-subordinate relationships. These approaches validated different ontological perspectives and different foci of study in organizational communication. This creates a challenge in defining organizational communication because it surely must be more than just 'communicating in the context of an organization'. In his seminal work to define organizational communication, as a field of study, Deetz (2001) suggests there are typically three ways organizational communication is conceptualized:

1 *The Sociological Approach* conceptualizing it as a field defined by the work published in the field.
2 *The Phenomenological Approach* conceptualizing it as a field inclusive of all things organizational.
3 *The Communication Approach* conceptualizing it as a distinctive way to think about the process of organizing through symbolic interaction with the duality of 'studying human interaction in a specific location and... that human interaction is a core formative feature' (p. 6).

Deetz (2001) also argued one of the most important potential contributions from the field of organizational communication is to focus on the stakeholder voice. This is one of the ways organizational communication may differ from related fields, like public relations, which focuses more exclusively on organizational voice. As Volk (2016) points out in her systematic review of public relations research, the field's focus is on demonstrating the value of communication for businesses and organizations and not to represent the stakeholder voice. That is not to say there is no overlap or mutual interest in concepts and theories used in fields such as public relations and organizational communication, but it is to say the objectives and priorities in organizational communication research are more aligned with stakeholder concerns rather than purely organizational interests.

In the same book that Deetz's essay appears in – Jablin and Putnam's *New Handbook of Organizational Communication: Advances in Theory, Research, and Methods* – foundational organizational communication scholars endeavored to codify the core constructs in the field as inclusive of all ontological perspectives (Conrad & Haynes, 2001) but focusing on a range of topics including both internal and external stakeholders that were relevant more than 20 years ago and are still relevant in organizational communication today. These include organizational identity (Cheney & Christensen, 2001; Rains & Scott, 2022; Scott, 2019), organizational culture (Eisenberg & Riley, 2001; Thelen & Formanchuk, 2022), socio-political environments and issues (Finet, 2001; Fröhlich & Knobloch, 2021), communication competence (Claeys & Cauberghe, 2014; He et al., 2021; Jablin & Sias, 2001), communication networks (Coleman, 2013; Monge & Contractor, 2001; Zito et al., 2021), new media (Rice & Gattiker, 2001; Waters & D'Urso, 2021), and organizational communication in a global context (Cruz & Sodeke, 2021; Stohl, 2001). Additionally, the book included topics that focused on internal stakeholders like organizational entry, assimilation, and disengagement (Jablin, 2001; Scott et al., 2021), the influence of organizational structure on communication (Lambert et al., 2021; McPhee & Poole, 2001), power and politics within organizations (Buzzanell, 2021; Mumby, 2001; Stensaker et al., 2021), participation and decision-making (Li et al., 2021; Seibold & Shea, 2001), and organizational sensemaking and learning (Awoonor-Williams & Phillips, 2022; Weick, 2021; Weick & Ashford, 2001).

Stakeholder Relationship Management: An Organizational Communication Framework

It is clear from these topics that the relationship between organizations and stakeholders is of vital importance in the modern field of organizational communication. Aligned with Deetz's perspective that it is a study of communication in particular locations, this definition does not consider the reasons for organizations and stakeholders to interact. Some of the topics commonly explored in organizational communication do – for example, analyses of socio-political environments and issues, assimilation, power, participation, and change all provide a context for these interactions, but most organizational frameworks fail to consider that organizations and stakeholders will have relationships with these issues, challenges, and topics (Chen et al., 2001; Diers-Lawson, 2020a,b; Haley, 1996; Kim, 2013). Yet, when organizations and their stakeholders communicate, it is always going to be 'about something'. Whereas the organizational context differentiates organizational communication from other communication contexts, what organizations and stakeholders communicate about will also influence those relationships and interactions (Diers-Lawson, 2021; Diers-Lawson & Collins, 2022). The stakeholder relationship management (SRM) framework provides a straightforward heuristic for exploring the intersection of organizations, stakeholders, and the issues affecting them. Previous research establishes that stakeholders evaluate organizations based on their perception of three interconnected relationships – between themselves and the organization, between themselves and the issues (or stakes) of the relationship, and between the organization and the stakes (Diers-Lawson, 2020b). Within a crisis context – including the COVID-19 pandemic – I have found that considering these three factors together produces significant predictability in outcomes like perceptions of organizational stability, organizational disengagement, and organizational satisfaction among both internal and external stakeholders (Diers, 2012; Diers-Lawson & Collins, 2022; Diers-Lawson et al., 2021).

Social Responsibility and Stakeholder Relationship Management

Relational factors also become important when we consider stakeholders are now increasingly linking organizational performance and broad concepts of social responsibility like climate change, employee satisfaction, and community engagement in a post-COVID context (Manzanedo & Manning, 2020; Zang et al., 2021). From an organizational perspective, these are becoming issues that organizations must manage to various stakeholders' satisfaction to achieve their strategic objectives. From the stakeholder perspective, these are issues aligned with political, social, and personal values they expect to see organizations enact more consistently (Diers-Lawson et al., 2020; Hamby et al., 2019; Yagnik, 2020).

While the pandemic has amplified the importance of these issues for many stakeholders, it did not 'cause' them. In fact, the pressure for increased social responsibility as a part organizational capacity building has been building over the last decade because stakeholders are interested in organizations that care about the broader societal good (Erdiaw-Kwasie, 2018; Graafland & Smid, 2019; Kurucz et al., 2008). The pressure has been driven from consumer interests, increased competition, fear of scrutiny, and a growing number of employees and potential employees wanting to be associated with *good* organizations (Lacey et al., 2015; Manimegalai & Baral, 2018). The challenge is that social responsibility is often discussed in terms of 'corporate social responsibility' (CSR) programs where there are mixed results on their positive impact on relationships with stakeholders, with increasingly cynical stakeholder reactions that the CSR programs are purely about an organization's blatant self-promotion (Abraham et al., 2018; Ahmad et al., 2020). Motivation hygiene theory helps to explain this phenomenon because when stakeholders judge the relationship between the organization and the CSR program as being authentic – or a motivation factor – tied to the organization's core mission, then it will improve the relationship between stakeholders and the organization (Ahmad et al., 2020; Diers-Lawson et al., 2020; Erdiaw-Kwasie, 2018; Islam et al., 2016; Lacey et al., 2015). However, if it is judged as a hygiene factor – actions seen as mere lip service – then it can be counterproductive (Lacey et al., 2015; Lee & Yoon, 2018).

Building Crisis Capacity and Goodwill

The concept of social responsibility and its potential contribution to an organization's core value proposition aligns with Heath's (2002) argument that organizations are obligated to be stewards of their stakeholders' interests. He suggests it is both ethically and strategically important for organizations to manage critical issues affecting stakeholders to manage and build relationships with them. He argues successful issues management: improves the organization's ability to develop strategic plans; encourages organizations to behave in ethically and socially responsible ways as simply a part of daily activities; enhances the organization's ability to monitor its environment; and most importantly enhances the organization's ability to develop strategic dialogue with internal and external stakeholders. As such, issues or risk management is not a matter of a hygiene CSR program, it is built into the organization's daily activities and routines, resulting in increased crisis capacity (Diers-Lawson, 2020b). Research finds organizations taking this long-term approach to building crisis capacity demonstrate goodwill and trustworthiness in ways that not only help the organizations respond more effectively when crises emerge, but also mean stakeholders can be activated as a part of crisis response and mitigation (Bae et al., 2020; Kim & Lee, 2015; Tao & Song, 2020; Zhou & Ki, 2018). However, these kinds of shifts in an organization's modus operandi require change initiatives that *should be* communication-intensive events between organizations and their stakeholders (Lewis, 2011).

Pandemic Organizational Change and Communication: A Case Study

In the introduction, I argued that from an organizational standpoint, the COVID-19 pandemic has opened a Pandora's box for change in organizations and suggested increased interest in sustainability, changes in people's attitudes toward work, desire for more work-life balance, and how/where employees can work across industries have changed (Arneson, 2021; Davis, 2021; Mass, 2021; Williams, 2021). Globally, education is an industry that often represents the stalwart of the 'bricks and mortar' approach to work. One of the common assumptions is people learn best, and the institutions operate best in face-to-face environments. The reality, however, is quite different, with a growing body of data suggesting online education is not only rapidly growing but there is no meaningful difference in learning outcomes or satisfaction when comparing online to traditional modes of delivery (Bailey, 2020), that blending learning environments often enhances learning outcomes (Daskan & Yildiz, 2020; Lin et al., 2019), and that online learning environments may make education more accessible.

In the highly disruptive contexts of the escalating environmental crisis and the COVID-19 pandemic, institutions of higher education have the opportunity to be examples of social and economic change with research finding that there is a clear trend for universities to adopt sustainable development goals in the post-COVID context (Vogel & Breßler, 2022). However, the question is: how can institutions of higher education build the internal support necessary to successfully implement this kind of change? Lewis (2011) argues effective organizational communication is key to implementing change by evaluating existing message effectiveness, establishing the institutional credibility of the issue, and better understanding the factors driving attitudes about change.

Evaluating Post-Pandemic Sustainability in English Higher Education

This case study applies the SRM framework as a model for approaching pandemic communication in complex issue environments by exploring the Sustainability Advisory Group (SAG) at one English institution work to position itself as a 'sustainable university'. Though the early planning for the sustainability initiatives began at the university before the pandemic, most of SAG's work and consideration has been during the pandemic and the pandemic changed the nature and approach to the conversations. The SAG initiative is part of a broader sustainability approach in higher education in England where the university decided to adopt the Association of University Directors of Estates (AUDE) Sustainability Leadership Scorecard, which has been adopted by several universities as a framework for assessing and improving sustainability. The AUDE scorecard identifies communication as a critical determinant of the institution's success in achieving its sustainability goals across each of its four priorities areas: leadership and governance; partnerships and engagement; learning, teaching, and research; and estates operations. Despite the importance of communication in implementing planned change, especially in a post-pandemic context (Lewis, 2011; Mehta & Xavier, 2012; van Zoonen et al., 2021; Yue, 2021), the communication sub-group for SAG identified that no systematic evaluations of the university's communication and engagement about sustainability had been taken, the university community had never been asked what they believe it means to have a sustainable university, nor had any sense of the commitment from staff and students about sustainability ever been evaluated. Strategically, this limited the potential success of the initiative and risked relegating the initiative to the hygiene bin by the university's key internal stakeholders.

In an initial analysis of the relationships between the university, internal stakeholders, and the issue of sustainability in a post-pandemic environment, members of staff were surveyed in late 2021 and early 2022 within two schools (Business School and School of Public Health) and two professional services (External Relations and University Recruitment). Participants included faculty and staff. Across the four groups surveyed, 117 academic faculty and staff participated. Most of the employees in the Business School ($N = 48$), External Relations group ($N = 23$), University Recruitment ($N = 26$), and School of Health also participating ($N = 20$) responded to the online questionnaire; therefore, there was no self-selection bias.

Of these, there was a mix between academics (i.e., lectures, senior lecturers, readers, and professors) as well as professional services and other support staff. Colleagues ranged in length of service, from newcomers with less than one year of service to those who had been at LBU for more than 20 years. Taken together, there was a broad representation of both the different areas surveyed as well as distinct roles and years of service within those areas.

Demographics (i.e., age, type of role, and school or service) were collected. Then in alignment with the SRM framework (see Appendix A) university employees were asked about: (1) their knowledge of university sustainability actions and information satisfaction (White et al., 2010) with sustainability (organization to issue); (2) their evaluation of the university's sustainability reputation and trustworthiness (stakeholder to organization) (Diers-Lawson, 2020b); and (3) their identification with the university's sustainability mission and personal commitment to the university's sustainability mission (Boydell et al., 2007).

Staff Knowledge of Sustainability Objectives and Activities

Staff were randomly assigned to read *either* a summary of the university's sustainability policy and the key parts of the university's objectives *or* information about the university's activities regarding its implemented sustainability initiatives over the last several years as a part of the university's strategic plan. They were asked if they were familiar with the initiatives as well as the source(s) of information about the initiatives. These data suggest there is a significantly higher level of knowledge among all faculty and staff about the specific sustainability activities ($M = 1.36$) connected with the strategic plan than the university's sustainability policy ($M = 1.17$) (t (116) = 3.48, $p < .01$). However, these data also suggest that while there is some knowledge about specific sustainability activities the university has adopted, there is a limited amount of knowledge about the sum of the university's work for sustainability as well as its approach or broad sustainability objectives. In fact, knowledge of overall sustainability activities (χ^2 (5) = 62.05; $p < .01$) and policy (χ^2 (9) = 484.45; $p < .01$) are significantly lower than expected. These data suggest that while faculty and staff have good knowledge about some of the specific sustainability initiatives, they will likely lack the context to connect these initiatives to the larger work the university is doing to become a sustainable university.

These data also suggest that while email updates from the Vice Chancellor were the single most important source of information about sustainable policy and initiatives (63.25%), there is a broad spectrum of cross-platform sources where colleagues receive information about sustainability, including interpersonal channels such as team meetings (23%) and conversations with colleagues (34%). These data also suggest there is little earned media coverage of the sustainability agenda (1.71%), which also represents an important gap in gaining broad support for institutional change, successes, and connection with the local community.

Communication Satisfaction about Sustainability and Implications

There was low knowledge among academic and professional staff at the university about the university's objective to be a 'sustainable university', which may have potential implications on initiatives routine work, travel, and life at the university as it implements 'sustainable university' policies. This section addresses the findings indicating why the lack of staff knowledge creates a risk to the sustainability agenda's success in the long term. The bottom line is that only 25.64% of the staff are satisfied with the amount of information that they have about sustainability at the university – and they were not even aware of what they did not know.

Communication satisfaction has long been established as a critical predictor of the quality of relationships between organizations and their employees (Kumar et al., 2014; Men & Sung, 2019; Sass & Canary, 1991). It is often tied to risk management (Kim, 2020), success in managing organizational change (Miller & Monge, 1985), and fosters a climate ready for improving organizational citizenship behaviors (Ahmad et al., 2020; Boukis et al., 2014; Dutton et al., 1994) and employee identification (Dutton et al., 1994; Lohndorf & Diamantopoulos, 2014; Sass & Canary, 1991). Similarly, there are strong links between attitudes about the organization and employee job outcomes (Islam et al., 2016; Manimegalai & Baral, 2018).

These data found there were significant connections between principal factors like staff demographics, their role at the university, their attitudes about the university, their knowledge of the university's sustainability actions with mediating factors like sustainability information satisfaction, and their identification with the university's sustainability mission. In combination, these factors influenced employee commitment to the university's sustainability mission (see Figure 6.1). Of course, because the questionnaire only included four groups and a relatively low overall number, this would make insignificant findings more likely because of a lack of predictive power in the calculations.

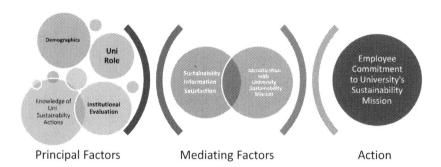

Principal Factors   Mediating Factors   Action

FIGURE 6.1 Summary of Factors Influencing Employee Commitment to the University's Sustainability Mission.

Correlations between the principal, mediating, and action factors were identified and then hierarchical regressions run to evaluate the causal relationships between these variables (see Figure 6.2 for the summary results). These data demonstrate that while demographics and university role(s) significantly influence sustainability information satisfaction and participants' identification with the university's sustainability mission, knowledge of the university's actions and institutional factors like the university's sustainability reputation and trustworthiness among its staff not only drive attitudes of sustainability information satisfaction but also meaningfully influence their identification with the university's sustainability mission, and their personal commitment to the university's sustainability mission. These factors account for not only statistically significant levels of change in these three outcomes but also demonstrate meaningful impact, opportunity, and risk for the success of SAG's objectives.

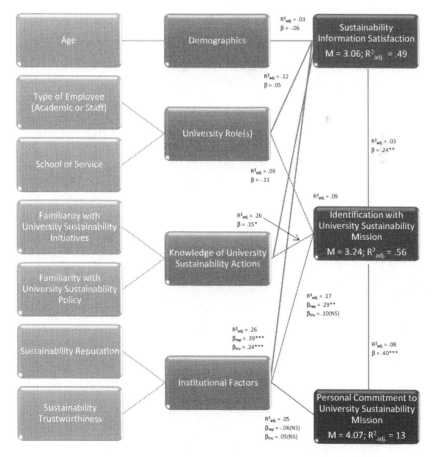

FIGURE 6.2 Summary of Key Findings Connecting Principal, Mediating, and Action Factors for University and Sustainability.

Each of these factors has clear strategic communication implications – small things that the university could do to better support its own sustainability mission by more effectively communicating about it with all staff.

Organizational Communication for Sustainability and Change Post-Pandemic

These data suggest there is an information deficit regarding the university's sustainability objectives and actions. In an era where organizations are trying to rapidly change to react to the pandemic and also meet increasing sustainability demands (Bodenheimer & Leidenberger, 2020; Zang et al., 2021), this case study seems to reflect a common theme of organizations failing to effectively communicate about change when what is needed is clear transparent communication and employee support (Li et al., 2021; Yue, 2021). These communication failures create credible risks for organizations to foster, maintain, or create a healthy set of relationships between employees and their organizations (Diers-Lawson & Collins, 2022; Li et al., 2021). This is particularly true given that sustainability is a social responsibility endeavor and generally research suggests the positive outcomes for all social responsibility initiatives are mixed at best (see, e.g., Diers-Lawson et al., 2020 for a more thorough literature review on this). This means an investment of time, resources, and multi-platform engagement about sustainability and the changes that the organization is making is essential for organizations to make post-COVID changes, especially regarding sustainability and crisis readiness. More specifically, these data suggest that knowledge, information satisfaction, identification with the sustainability mission, and colleagues' personal commitment to sustainability would all be improved with consistent and cross-platform communication that:

- Provides periodic background information about the organization's sustainability objectives
- Celebrates sustainability successes
- Provides updates on ongoing initiatives
- Calls for organization-wide and group-specific participation in initiatives
- Incentivizes participation – this should not be viewed as 'extra work'
- Always provides links to additional information for colleague follow-up
- Develops consistent media engagement across influencers, print, radio, and television media about what the university is doing – including local access programming.

More than just meeting information expectations, organizations should ensure that they are authentic in communicating about post-COVID sustainability agendas – sustainability cannot simply be seen as a gimmick or a way to achieve cost savings. These data also suggest that the institution's reputation and trustworthiness about sustainability is critical to the success of engagement with staff and ultimately persuading staff to be committed to the organization's sustainability agenda. There was a communicated willingness and interest among staff to be more sustainable with colleagues commenting on their interest in the subject on the questionnaire. However, one of the critical challenges identified both in the quantitative findings and in short-answer qualitative responses was ensuring that colleagues believe the institution is authentically motivated to be more sustainable and not simply using sustainability to make itself look good. Therefore, based on research (see Bodenheimer & Leidenberger, 2020; Diers-Lawson et al., 2020; Li et al., 2021), to ensure a sustainability agenda is viewed by staff as authentic it should:

1   **Focus on the organization's overall reputation among staff** because it directly influences whether social responsibility initiatives, like sustainability initiatives, are viewed as motivated by interest in sustainability or broadly dismissed as an effort to make the institution look good (Lacey et al., 2015). Fortunately, the university has an annual staff survey that provides some insights into diagnosing reputational threats, opportunities, strengths, and weaknesses across the university. This is a best practice that can be adapted into different organizations (Diers-Lawson & Collins, 2022).
2   **Demonstrate localized sustainability impact** by showing staff how initiatives are influencing the campus and local communities on a routine basis; it is likely to support a view of the university's sustainability effort as authentic and therefore improve identification and commitment to the effort. This has the added value of being a community engagement opportunity (Lim et al., 2016).
3   **Empower more staff to take part in sustainability efforts** because the literature basis on employee ownership of organizational action is decades old. Findings related to social responsibility suggest that the more staff are actively included in the dialogue, decision-making, and program participation relating to sustainability, the more they will own it, affecting perceptions of sustainability activities inside and outside the organization (Almeida & Coelho, 2019). However, it must be voluntary for it to feel empowering and therefore authentic.

There are also pitfalls to avoid or risks that can derail the communication and overall sustainability effort for organizations (see Diers-Lawson et al., 2020) and those include:

1   Leaving colleagues feeling like they cannot be a part of the sustainability strategy implementation and/or development.
2   Focusing too 'big' (i.e., on national or global sustainability objectives, instead of local initiatives).

3 Using the sustainability initiative as a promotional effort (i.e., paid communication). Instead, it is more effective to focus on earned and owned media coverage of sustainability. Particularly with 'green' initiatives, it can feel like green washing the university instead of the university making it a priority. This effect can be reduced if sustained and clear communication is developed about why the commitment to sustainability has emerged and to demonstrate a strong history of action.

4 Ignoring any institutional reputation problems among staff.

Conclusions

This book project has broadly asked the question, 'what is pandemic communication?' across the broad field of communication. In this chapter, I have argued pandemic communication in the organizational context is characterized by the profound impact of the pandemic as a global societal level crisis. Therefore, in organizations, pandemic communication is a natural extension of organizational communication in that it focuses on stakeholders and organizations interacting within the context of mutual interest. However, in a 'post'-COVID context, it asks the question of how organizations can be more sustainable. I would suggest that pandemic organizational communication *reflects organizations' responsibilities to be stewards of stakeholder interests in the convergence of the pandemic and sustainability needs and can therefore be considered as strategic change communication.* For pandemic communication to be successful, organizations must understand the complex relationships between organizations, issues, and stakeholders and therefore it should blend the best practices emerging from decades of research in change communication with capacity building, anticipatory issues management, stakeholder communication, social responsibility, and crisis response. The findings from the case study exploring the convergence of pandemic and sustainability issues in higher education were consistent with this convergence but also produced actionable recommendations for moving forward with theory development and practice.

Based on historic precedence, we can expect the global disruption people have experienced from the pandemic to result in the next great evolution of organizations. While I argue the indicators suggest there is a convergence of interests between post-pandemic recovery and sustainability, these issues are far from settled. What our new normal will look like remains to be seen; however, the foundations of organizational communication provide a clear path for organizations and stakeholders to engage on the issues that matter to them in the years to come.

References

Abraham, E. M., Asor, V., Torviawu, F., Yeboah, H., & Laryea, F. (2018). Public perception of corporate social responsibility of AngloGold Ashanti in Obuasi Municipality, Ghana. *Social Responsibility Journal, 14*(3), 485–500. https://doi.org/10.1108/SRJ-08-2016-0149.

Ahmad, R., Ahmad, S., Islam, T., & Kaleem, A. (2020). The nexus of corporate social responsibility (CSR), affective commitment and organisational citizenship behaviour in academia: A model of trust. *Employee Relations, 42*(1), 232–247. https://doi.org/10.1108/ER-04-2018-0105.

Almeida, M. d. G. M. C., & Coelho, A. F. M. (2019). The antecedents of corporate reputation and image and their impacts on employee commitment and performance: The moderating role of CSR. *Corporate Reputation Review, 22*(1), 10–25. https://doi.org/10.1057/s41299-018-0053-8.

Arneson, K. (2021). How companies around the world are shifting the way they work. *BBC News: Worklife*. Retrieved 29 June 2022, from https://www.bbc.com/worklife/article/20210915-how-companies-around-the-world-are-shifting-the-way-they-work.

Awoonor-Williams, J. K., & Phillips, J. F. (2022). Developing organizational learning for scaling-up community-based primary health care in Ghana. *Learning Health Systems, 6*(1), e10282. https://doi.org/10.1002/lrh2.10282.

Bae, J., Choi, W., & Lim, J. (2020). Corporate social responsibility: An umbrella or a puddle on a rainy day? Evidence surrounding corporate financial misconduct. *European Financial Management, 26*(1), 77–117. https://doi.org/10.1111/eufm.12235.

Bailey, L. M. (2020). *Comparing students' learning outcomes and satisfaction in online, hybrid and face-to-face education courses.* Temple University.

Bajrami, D. D., Terzić, A., Petrović, M. D., Radovanović, M., Tretiakova, T. N., & Hadoud, A. (2021). Will we have the same employees in hospitality after all? The impact of COVID-19 on employees' work attitudes and turnover intentions. *International Journal of Hospitality Management, 94*, 102754. https://doi.org/10.1016/j.ijhm.2020.102754.

Bodenheimer, M., & Leidenberger, J. (2020). COVID-19 as a window of opportunity for sustainability transitions? Narratives and communication strategies beyond the pandemic. *Sustainability: Science, Practice and Policy, 16*(1), 61–66. https://doi.org/10.1080/15487733.2020.1766318.

Boukis, A., Kostopoulos, G., & Katsaridou, I. (2014). IMO and different fit types as key enablers of employee brand-supporting behaviour. *Journal of Strategic Marketing, 22*(2), 117–134. https://doi.org/10.1080/0965254X.2013.876066.

Boydell, L., Rugkasa, J., Hoggett, P., & Cummins, A. (2007). *Partnerships: The benefits.* Institute of Public Health in Ireland. Retrieved November 15, 2014 from http://www.partnershiptool.ie/.

Buzzanell, P. M. (2021). Reflections on Feminist Organizational Communication. *Management Communication Quarterly, 35*(1), 127–141. https://doi.org/10.1177%2F0893318920975211.

Chen, G., Gully, S. M., & Eden, D. (2001). Validation of a new general self-efficacy scale. *Organizational Research Methods, 4*(1), 62–83.

Cheney, G., & Christensen, L. T. (2001). Organizational identity: Linkages between internal and external communication. In F. M. Jablin & L. L. Putnam (Eds.), *The new handbook of organizational communication: Advances in theory, research, and methods* (pp. 231–269). Sage.

Claeys, A. S., & Cauberghe, V. (2014). Keeping control: The importance of nonverbal expressions of power by organizational spokespersons in times of crisis. *Journal of Communication, 64*(6), 1160–1180. https://doi.org/10.1111/jcom.12122.

Coleman, A. (2013). Managing a crisis in the era of social communication: How Greater Manchester Police is developing community engagement and communication. *Journal of Brand Strategy, 2*(2), 128–133.

Conrad, C., & Haynes, J. (2001). Development of key constructs. In F. M. Jablin & L. L. Putnam (Eds.), *The new handbook of organizational communication: Advances in theory, research, and methods* (pp. 47–77). Sage.

Cruz, J. M., & Sodeke, C. U. (2021). Debunking eurocentrism in organizational communication theory: Marginality and liquidities in postcolonial contexts. *Communication Theory, 31*(3), 528–548. https://doi.org/10.1093/ct/qtz038

Daskan, A., & Yildiz, Y. (2020). Blended learning: A potential approach to promote learning outcomes. *International Journal of Social Sciences & Educational Studies, 7*(4), 103–108.

Davis, D. (2021). 5 Models for the post-pandemic workplace. *Harvard Business Review.* Retrieved 29 June, 2022, from https://hbr.org/2021/06/5-models-for-the-post-pandemic-workplace

Deetz, S. (2001). Conceptual foundations. In F. M. Jablin & L. L. Putnam (Eds.), *The new handbook of organizational communication: Advances in theory, research, and methods* (pp. 3–46). Sage.

Diers-Lawson, A. (2020a). Applying the stakeholder relationship model as an issue management and risk communication Tool. In B. S. Peksevgen (Ed.), *Themes in issues, risk, and crisis communication: A multi-dimensional perspective.* Peter Lang. https://doi.org/10.3726/b17931

Diers-Lawson, A. (2020b). *Crisis communication: Managing stakeholder relationships.* Routledge.

Diers-Lawson, A. (2021). Norsk Tipping's lonliest stakeholder: Crisis, issues, and the stakeholder voice. In J.-O. S. Peer Jacob Svenkerud, & Larry Browning (Ed.), *Whistleblowing, communication and consequences: Lessons from The Norwegian National Lottery* (pp. 164–182). Routledge.

Diers-Lawson, A., & Collins, L. (2022). Taking off the rose-colored glasses: The influence of crises on employee relationship management. *Employee Relations: The International Journal, 44*(4), 833–849. https://doi.org/10.1108/ER-03-2021-0115

Diers-Lawson, A., Coope, K., & Tench, R. (2020). Why can CSR seem like putting lipstick on a pig? Evaluating CSR authenticity by comparing practitioner and consumer perspectives. *Journal of Global Responsibility, 11*(4), 329–346. https://doi.org/10.1108/JGR-02-2020-0033

Diers-Lawson, A., Symons, A., & Zeng, C. (2021). Building crisis capacity with data breaches: The role of stakeholder relationship management and strategic communication. *Corporate Communications: An International Journal, 26*(4), 675–699. https://doi.org/10.1108/CCIJ-02-2021-0024

Diers, A. R. (2012). Reconstructing stakeholder relationships using 'corporate social responsibility' as a response strategy to cases of corporate irresponsibility: The case of the 2010 BP spill in the Gulf of Mexico. In R. Tench, W. Sun, & B. Jones (Eds.), *Corporate social irresponsibility: A challenging concept* (Vol. 4, pp. 177–206). Emerald. https://doi.org/10.1108/S2043-9059(2012)0000004017

Dutton, J. E., Dukerich, J. M., & Harquail, C. V. (1994). Organizational images and member identification. *Administrative Science Quarterly, 39*(2), 239–264.

Eisenberg, E. M., & Riley, P. (2001). Organizational culture. In F. M. Jablin & L. L. Putnam (Eds.), *The new handbook of organizational communication: Advances in theory, research, and methods* (pp. 291–322). Sage.

Erdiaw-Kwasie, M. O. (2018). Does pressure-induced partnership really matter? Empirical modelling of stakeholder pressure and firms' CSR attitude. *Social Responsibility Journal, 14*(3), 685–698.

Finet, D. (2001). Sociopolitical environments and issues. In F. M. Jablin & L. L. Putnam (Eds.), *The new handbook of organizational communication: Advances in theory, research, and methods* (pp. 270–290). Sage.

Fröhlich, R., & Knobloch, A. S. (2021). "Are they allowed to do that?" Content and typology of corporate socio-political positioning on TWITTER. A study of DAX-30 companies in Germany. *Public Relations Review, 47*(5), 102113. https://doi.org/10.1016/j.pubrev.2021.102113

Graafland, J., & Smid, H. (2019). Decoupling among CSR policies, programs, and impacts: An empirical study. *Business & Society, 58*(2), 231–267.

Haley, E. (1996). Exploring the construct of organization as source: Consumers' understandings of organizational sponsorship of advocacy advertising. *Journal of Advertising, 25*, 19–36.

Hamby, A., Brinberg, D., & Daniloski, K. (2019). It's about our values: How founder's stories influence brand authenticity. *Psychology & Marketing, 36*(11), 1014–1026. https://doi.org/10.1002/mar.21252

He, C., Jia, G., McCabe, B., & Sun, J. (2021). Relationship between leader–member exchange and construction worker safety behavior: The mediating role of communication competence. *International Journal of Occupational Safety and Ergonomics, 27*(2), 371–383. https://doi.org/10.1080/10803548.2019.1579484

Heath, R. L. (2002). Issues management: Its past, present, and future. *Journal of Public Affairs, 2*(2), 209–214.

Islam, T., Ahmed, I., Ali, G., & Sadiq, T. (2016). Behavioral and psychological consequences of corporate social responsibility: Need of the time. *Social Responsibility Journal, 12*(2), 307–320. https://doi.org/10.1108/SRJ-04-2015-0053

Jablin, F. M. (2001). Organizational entry, assimilation, and disengagement/exit. In F. M. Jablin & L. L. Putnam (Eds.), *The new handbook of organizational communication: Advances in theory, research, and methods* (pp. 732–818). Sage.

Jablin, F. M., & Sias, P. M. (2001). Communication competence. In F. M. Jablin & L. L. Putnam (Eds.), *The new handbook of organizational communication: Advances in theory, research, and methods* (pp. 819–864). Sage.

Kim, H.-S., & Lee, S. Y. (2015). Testing the buffering and boomerang effects of CSR practices on consumers' perception of a corporation during a crisis. *Corporate Reputation Review, 18*(4), 277–293. https://doi.org/10.1057/crr.2015.18

Kim, S. (2013). Corporate ability or virtue? Relative effectivenss of prior corporate associations in times of crisis. *International Journal of Strategic Communication, 7*(4), 241–256. https://doi.org/10.1080/1553118X.2013.824886

Kim, Y. (2020). Organizational resilience and employee work-role performance after a crisis situation: Exploring the effects of organizational resilience on internal crisis communication. *Journal of Public Relations Research, 32*(1–2), 47–75. https://doi.org/10.1080/1062726X.2020.1765368

Kumar, P., Dass, M., & Topaloglu, O. (2014). Understanding the drivers of job satisfaction of frontline service employees: Learning from "lost employees". *Journal of Service Research, 17*(4), 367–380. https://doi.org/10.1177/1094670514540981

Kurucz, E. C., Colbert, B. A., & Wheeler, D. (2008). The business case for corporate social responsibility. In A. Crane, A. McWilliams, D. Matten, J. Moon, & D. S. Siegel (Eds.), *The Oxford handbook of corporate social responsibility* (pp. 83–112). Oxford University Press.

Lacey, R., Kennett-Hensel, P. A., & Manolis, C. (2015). Is corporate social responsibility a motivator or hygiene factor? Insights into its bivalent nature. *Journal of the Academy of Marketing Science, 42*(3). https://doi.org/10.1007/s11747-014-0390-9

Lambert, E. G., Berthelot, E., Morrow, W., Block, L., & Hogan, N. (2021). Exploring the effects of organizational structure variables on the organizational justice perceptions of correctional staff. *The Prison Journal, 101*(5), 553–574. https://doi.org/10.1177%2F00328855211048173

Lee, E.-M., & Yoon, S.-J. (2018). The effect of customer citizenship in corporate social responsibility (CSR) activities on purchase intention: The important role of the CSR image. *Social Responsibility Journal, 14*(4), 753–763.

Lewis, L. K. (2011). *Organizational change: Creating change through strategy communication.* Wiley-Blackwell.

Li, J.-Y., Sun, R., Tao, W., & Lee, Y. (2021). Employee coping with organizational change in the face of a pandemic: The role of transparent internal communication. *Public Relations Review, 47*(1), 101984. https://doi.org/10.1016/j.pubrev.2020.101984

Lim, J. S., Greenwood, C. A., & Jiang, H. (2016). The situational public engagement model in a municipal watershed protection program: Information seeking, information sharing, and the use of organizational and social media. *Journal of Public Affairs, 16*(3), 231–244. https://doi.org/10.1002/pa.1583

Lin, L.-C., Hung, I.-C., & Chen, N.-S. (2019). The impact of student engagement on learning outcomes in a cyber-flipped course. *Educational Technology Research and Development, 67*(6), 1573–1591.

Lohndorf, B., & Diamantopoulos, A. (2014). Internal branding: Social identity and social exchange perspectives on turning employees into brand champions. *Journal of Service Research, 17*(3), 310–325. https://doi.org/10.1177/1094670514522098

Manimegalai, S., & Baral, R. (2018). Examining the mediating role of organizational trust in the relationship between CSR practices and job outcomes. *Social Responsibility Journal, 14*(3), 433–447.

Manzanedo, R. D., & Manning, P. (2020). COVID-19: Lessons for the climate change emergency. *Science of the Total Environment, 742*, 140563. https://doi.org/10.1016/j.scitotenv.2020.140563

Mass, S. (2021). Work from home likely to remain elevated post pandemic. *The Digest, 6*. Retrieved 29 June, 2022, from https://www.nber.org/digest-202106/work-home-likely-remain-elevated-post-pandemic.

McPhee, R. D., & Poole, M. S. (2001). Organizational structures and configurations. In F. M. Jablin & L. L. Putnam (Eds.), *The new handbook of organizational communication: Advances in theory, research, and methods* (pp. 503–435). Sage.

Mehta, A., & Xavier, R. (2012). Tracking the defining moments in crisis process and practice. *Public Relations Review, 38*, 376–382. https://doi.org/10.1016/j.pubrev.2011.12.009

Men, L. R., & Sung, Y. (2019). Shaping corporate character through symmetrical communication: The effects on employee-organization relationships. *International Journal of Business Communication*, 1–23. https://doi.org/10.1177/2329488418824989

Miller, K. I., & Monge, P. R. (1985). Social information and employee anxiety about organizational change. *Human Communication Research, 11*(3), 365–386.

Monge, P. R., & Contractor, N. S. (2001). Emergence of communication networks. In F. M. Jablin & L. L. Putnam (Eds.), *The new handbook of organizational communication: Advances in theory, research, and methods* (pp. 440–502). Sage.

Mumby, D. K. (2001). Power and politics. In F. M. Jablin & L. L. Putnam (Eds.), *The new handbook of organizational communication: Advances in theory, research, and methods* (pp. 585–623). Sage.

Rains, S. A., & Scott, C. R. (2022). To Identify or Not to identify? That… depends on the context: testing a model of receiver responses to anonymous communication. *Communication Reports*, 1–14. https://doi.org/10.1080/08934215.2022.2037676

Reeves, M., Carlsson-Szlezak, P., Whitaker, K., & Abraham, M. (2020). *Sensing and shaping the post-COVID era*. T. B. H. Institute. https://web-assets.bcg.com/img-src/BCG-Sensing-and-Shaping-the-Post-COVID-Era-Apr-2020-rev_tcm9-244426.pdf

Rice, R. E., & Gattiker, U. E. (2001). New media and organizational structuring. In F. M. Jablin & L. L. Putnam (Eds.), *The new handbook of organizational communication: Advances in theory, research, and methods* (pp. 544–581). Sage.

Sass, J. S., & Canary, D. J. (1991). Organizational commitment and identification: An examination of conceptual and operational convergence. *Western Journal of Communication*, *55*, 275–293.

Sayyida, S., Hartini, S., Gunawan, S., & Husin, S. N. (2021). The impact of the COVID-19 pandemic on retail consumer behavior. *Aptisi Transactions on Management (ATM)*, *5*(1), 79–88. https://doi.org/10.33050/atm.v5i1.1497

Scott, C., Dieguez, T., Deepak, P., Gu, S., & Wildman, J. (2021). Onboarding during COVID-19: Create structure, connect people, and continue adapting. *Organizational Dynamics*, *51*(2), 100828–100828. https://doi.org/https://dx.doi.org/10.1016%2Fj.orgdyn.2021.100828.

Scott, C. R. (2019). Identity and identification. In A. M. Nicotera (Ed.), *Origins and traditions of organizational communication* (pp. 207–227). Routledge.

Seibold, D. R., & Shea, B. C. (2001). Participation and decision making. In F. M. Jablin & L. L. Putnam (Eds.), *The new handbook of organizational communication: Advances in theory, research, and methods* (pp. 664–703). Sage.

Stensaker, I. G., Balogun, J., & Langley, A. (2021). The power of the platform: Place and employee responses to organizational change. *The Journal of Applied Behavioral Science*, *57*(2), 174–203. https://doi.org/10.1177%2F0021886320933736.

Stohl, C. (2001). Globalizing organizational communication. In F. M. Jablin & L. L. Putnam (Eds.), *The new handbook of organizational communication: Advances in theory, research, and methods* (pp. 323–375). Sage.

Tao, W., & Song, B. (2020). The interplay between post-crisis response strategy and pre-crisis corporate associations in the context of CSR crises. *Public Relations Review*, *46*(2), 101883. https://doi.org/10.1016/j.pubrev.2020.101883

Thelen, P. D., & Formanchuk, A. (2022). Culture and internal communication in Chile: Linking ethical organizational culture, transparent communication, and employee advocacy. *Public Relations Review*, *48*(1), 102137. https://doi.org/10.1016/j.pubrev.2021.102137

Tompkins, P. K., & Wanca-Thibault, M. (2001). Organizational communication: Prelude and prospects. In F. M. Jablin & L. L. Putnam (Eds.), *The new handbook of organizational communication: Advances in theory, research, and methods* (pp. xvii–xxix). Sage.

van Zoonen, W., Sivunen, A., Blomqvist, K., Olsson, T., Ropponen, A., Henttonen, K., & Vartiainen, M. (2021). Factors influencing adjustment to remote work: Employees' initial responses to the COVID-19 pandemic. *International Journal of Environmental Research and Public Health*, *18*(13), 6966. https://doi.org/10.3390/ijerph18136966

Vogel, A., & Breßler, J. (2022). The implementation of sustainability at universities: A study based on sustainable development goals. *International Journal of Innovation and Sustainable Development*, *16*(3–4), 461–489. https://doi.org/10.1504/IJISD.2022.123906

Volk, S. C. (2016). A systematic review of 40 years of public relations evaluation and measurement research: Looking into the past, the present, and future. *Public Relations Review, 42*(5), 962–977. https://doi.org/10.1016/j.pubrev.2016.07.003

Wang, Y., Xu, R., Schwartz, M., Ghosh, D., & Chen, X. (2020). COVID-19 and retail grocery management: Insights from a broad-based consumer survey. *IEEE Engineering Management Review, 48*(3), 202–211. https://doi.org/10.1109/EMR.2020.3011054

Waters, E. D., & D'Urso, S. C. (2021). Commentary—Space is hard: Using social media for selective investigative disclosure as a multi-faceted crisis communication strategy to achieve technical transparency. *International Journal of Business Communication,* 2329488420978607. https://doi.org/10.1177%2F2329488420978607

Weick, K. E. (2021). Sensemaking and whistleblowing. In P. J. Svenkerud, J.-O. Sørnes, & L. D. Browning (Eds.), *Whistleblowing, Communication and Consequences* (pp. 81–92). Routledge.

Weick, K. E., & Ashford, S. J. (2001). Learning in Organizations. In F. M. Jablin & L. L. Putnam (Eds.), *The new handbook of organizational communication: Advances in theory, research, and methods* (pp. 704–731). Sage.

White, C., Vanc, A., & Stafford, G. (2010). Internal communication, information satisfaction, and sense of community: The effect of personal influence. *Journal of Public Relations, 22*(1), 65–84.

Williams, C. (2021). The future of work. *The Economist.* Retrieved 29 June, 2022, from https://www.economist.com/special-report/2021-04-10?utm_source=google&utm_medium=cpc&utm_campaign=a_21futurework&utm_content=work&gclid=CjwKCAiAhreNBhAYEiwAFGGKPGsvl6UrTQWn8nNDEuSIm8UiJO-VZ73UjcHBOEbja3ovjkEesvA0SsxoCGb4QAvD_BwE&gclsrc=aw.ds

Yagnik, A. T. (2020). Corporate social responsibility and corporate sustainability as forces of change. In A. A. Vertès, N. Qureshi, H. P. Blaschek, & H. Yukawa (Eds.), *Green energy to sustainability: Strategies for global industries* (pp. 587–611). Wiley. https://doi.org/10.1002/9781119152057.ch24

Yue, C. A. (2021). Navigating change in the era of COVID-19: The role of top leaders' charismatic rhetoric and employees' organizational identification. *Public Relations Review, 47*(5), 1–12. https://doi.org/10.1016/j.pubrev.2021.102118

Zang, S. M., Benjenk, I., Breakey, S., Pusey-Reid, E., & Nicholas, P. K. (2021). The intersection of climate change with the era of COVID-19. *Public Health Nursing, 38*(2), 321–335. https://doi.org/10.1111/phn.12866

Zhou, Z., & Ki, E.-J. (2018). Exploring the role of CSR fit and the length of CSR involvement in routine business and corporate crises settings. *Public Relations Review, 44*(1), 75–83. https://doi.org/10.1016/j.pubrev.2017.11.004

Zito, M., Ingusci, E., Cortese, C. G., Giancaspro, M. L., Manuti, A., Molino, M., Signore, F., & Russo, V. (2021). Does the end justify the means? The role of organizational communication among work-from-home employees during the COVID-19 pandemic. *International Journal of Environmental Research and Public Health, 18*(8), 3933. https://doi.org/10.3390/ijerph18083933

APPENDIX A

OPERATIONALIZATION OF STUDY VARIABLES

Variable	Questions	Eigen-Value	Variance Explained	Factor Loading	Alpha
Information satisfaction	How satisfied are you with the information received about sustainability	3.68	61.40	.62	.87
	...I feel the right amount of information on sustainability is shared			.83	
	...the information I receive about sustainability gives me a clear understanding of what the university is doing			.84 .68	
	...the information I receive is accurate			.86	
	...the information I receive is timely			.83	
	...the information I receive is relevant to my needs				
Institution's sustainability reputation	...cares about being sustainable	3.89	77.87	.87	.93
	...demonstrates a commitment to sustainability			.92	
	...objectives represent sustainability			.89	
	...competent record for sustainability			.88	
	...sets a good example for sustainability in HE			.85	

(Continued)

(Continued)

Variable	Questions	Eigen-Value	Variance Explained	Factor Loading	Alpha
Institution's trustworthy source of information on sustainability	...the information gives me a trustworthy impression	2.46	82.09	.91	.89
	...I believe the information is truthful			.88	
	...it gives me a feeling of trust in the university			.93	
identification with the sustainability mission	Purpose of creating a more sustainably university is clear to me.	3.29	54.79	.60	.83
	...goals are clearly defined			.81	
	...members of my school/ unit broadly agree with sustainability objectives			.80	
	...has a shared vision of what we would like to accomplish with sustainability			.86	
	...my ideas about sustainability are the same as my colleagues'			.76	
	...regarding sustainability objectives, the university is unique among universities in England			.61	
Personal commitment to sustainability	I am committed to improving sustainability at work.	2.82	70.39	.89	.86
	I feel I can meaningfully contribute to improving the university's sustainability.			.85	
	I feel a sense of pride in creating a more sustainable university.			.87	
	I care about the future of sustainability at my university.			.74	

7

MEME-ING ACCOUNTABILITY

Visual Communication as Character Assassination of Austrian and Swedish Politicians and Government Agencies during the COVID-19 Pandemic

Diotima Bertel, Bengt Johansson, Viktoria Adler, and Marina Ghersetti

Politicians and other people in power have always been objects of parody and satire. From the medieval court jester and carnival to the political cartoon and satire in newspapers, magazines, and TV shows, humour has been a method for ridiculing both people and institutions at the highest levels of power (Hodgart & Connery, 2017). The concept of character assassination has been proposed as an analytical tool to understand different aspects of how power holders are targeted to undermine their credibility in accountability work (Samoilenko et al., 2018).

A newer form of contesting power is the use and spread of political memes as a viral, multimodal (visual and text) genre in the intersection between popular culture and politics (Miltner, 2018). They spread following social media logics, such as programmability and popularity, depending on algorithms, commercial interests, and human agency (van Dijck & Poell, 2013). When memes appear outside the electoral cycle in democratic countries, they can be viewed as an indicator of how politics are discussed and analysed by social media-literate, politically engaged citizens. As 'vessels for public sharing' (Dynel, 2021, p. 176), memes can provide insights into social and political issues which are relevant to the public. As such, memes can be understood as a medium for character assassination. Indeed, politicians and public officials are often the targets of memes. This is particularly the case since the personalization of politics reduces major political and societal challenges to the level of individual actors and their interplay instead of focusing on more abstract social/political structures and interests (Bennett, 2012; Hjarvard, 2013). This personalization of politics fits well into the meme culture, where humour, emotions, morality, and immediate reactions are essential parts (Kristensen & Mortensen, 2021).

DOI: 10.4324/9781003214496-7

Concerns about responsibility and accountability are central to risk communication; the ongoing COVID-19 pandemic is no exception. As during other crises, there were debates about mistakes in handling the pandemic and who is to blame for failing strategies to mitigate the disease around the world. These concerns were central in the public discourse about the COVID-19 pandemic (Coman et al., 2021; Garland & Lilleker, 2022). Quite naturally, political leaders and other actors responsible for crisis management were at the centre of this debate, not at least since the news media has been occupied with the (mis) management of how to defeat the global pandemic (Yang & Bennet, 2022). Just like in other contemporary issues, memes of success and failures in the management of the COVID-19 have gone viral on social media. Politicians, like the UK Prime Minister, Boris Johnson, and the former President of the US, Donald Trump, became targets of numerous memes challenging their leadership, where accusations of hypocrisy and incompetence were central themes (e.g., Kristensen & Mortensen 2021). Even so, COVID-19 is a global pandemic and the public discourse about responsibility and accountability is not limited to one or two countries (see, e.g., Davis, 2022). Further, crisis management was not just a responsibility of politicians. In many countries, also in the US and the UK, other representatives of government agencies were well-known public figures and targets for accountability claims, both in mainstream and social media (Lilleker et al., 2021).

Against this background, this chapter seeks to analyse memes in social media about political leaders and other actors responsible for crisis management during the COVID-19 pandemic. More precisely, we explore emergent themes in the memes to understand how they work in contesting power and holding responsible actors accountable. Our research question is how character assassination of leading politicians and other power holders was articulated in political memes during COVID-19 in Austria and Sweden.

The analysis builds on memes collected in Austria and Sweden during the first 16 months of the pandemic (March 2020–June 2021). By doing so, we aspire for a deeper understanding of how the mechanism of public accountability works during a crisis (Boin et al., 2017; Djerf-Pierre et al., 2013). Further, the comparative perspective gives opportunities to discuss to what extent public accountability in social media was related to country-specific experiences of the pandemic, death tolls, crisis management, and political culture. Austria and Sweden are two countries with two quite different experiences of the pandemic, which might be visible in how accountability was thematized during the pandemic in political memes.

COVID-19 Experiences in Austria and Sweden

In Austria, the pandemic management and its communication were the responsibility of the government, in particular, the chancellor, the Ministry of Health, and the Ministry of Interior. Several COVID-19 laws and extensions to the already existing epidemic law were passed, giving the Minister of Health and his department power and authority to manage the coronavirus pandemic. Measures included lockdowns in spring and autumn/winter of 2020, curfews, wearing of masks, home schooling, and recommendations for home office.

During the first lockdown, the Austrian government held almost daily press conferences. Present were the then Chancellor Sebastian Kurz, Minister of Health Rudolf Anschober, and Minister of Interior Karl Nehammer. This was the beginning of a tight-knit schedule of COVID-19–related press conferences in which the government presented the current state of the pandemic, new measures, or other important announcements related to the pandemic. In the following weeks, Kurz, Anschober, and Nehammer were often joined by Vice-chancellor Werner Kogler, a constellation Austrians casually referred to as the 'Corona Quartett' or 'Virologisches Quartett' (virological quartet). Overall, Sebastian Kurz, and at times Werner Kogler, announced the latest measures or addressed the public with general comments aimed to increase morale, using fear to increase compliance of his audience. Rudolf Anschober and Karl Nehammer, as well as other ministers occasionally joining the press conferences, talked about matters specific to their departments. Regular press conferences were held until May 2020. June, July, and August were a phase of less communication, with reduced measures and the announcement of the 'new normal'. In September and October, with the beginning of the second wave, infections and the number of press conferences started to rise again. The Austrian government received positive feedback for their crisis communication during the initial phase of the pandemic. However, the straightforward style of crisis communication quickly changed. In the subsequent months, the government received a lot of criticism for its 'message control', information overload, contradictions, and confusion, as well as for repeatedly announcing prematurely that the pandemic was over.

The Swedish government declared the COVID-19 as being publicly disseminated in Sweden on 11 March 2020, and several measures were taken to mitigate the spread of the virus. However, Sweden became somewhat of an outlier compared to other countries, in not declaring a strict lockdown, generally imposing fewer restrictions, and relying on 'nudges' rather than prohibition (Pierre, 2020). One explanation for this strategy was Swedes' high trust in public authorities and a general high interpersonal trust in society which gave a prerequisite for more voluntary and sustainable strategies (Johansson & Vigsø, 2021). This 'soft strategy' was communicated by the experts, especially the chief epidemiologist Anders Tegnell at the PHA (Public Health Agency) who gave his updates at a 2 p.m. daily broadcasted press conference. The strategy was said to build on previous experiences of how to handle pandemics and, most important, on scientific evidence (Andersson & Aylott, 2020). This is the core argument why Sweden for example chose to decline a general use of facemasks. PHA argued that public health should not only be about saving lives but should instead be addressed from a more holistic approach, taking into consideration mental health. The argument was that since the virus could not be eliminated, the spread of infection should be kept on a level where it could be handled, and at the same time society should be kept as open as possible. This strategy was heavily criticized by other EU countries. In Spring 2020, as the death toll increased in Sweden, domestic critique became more prevalent (Johansson et al., 2021). Further, the choice to make the PHA the 'communicator-in-chief' was also questioned, as the prime minister and the government were not perceived as taking the lead in the crisis management. Instead, they were accused of being backseat drivers in the fight against COVID-19. This said, levels of political polarization have been rather low in Sweden during the pandemic. The government has been criticized from time to time, but due to the multi-level political system, where healthcare is a regional responsibility and elderly care is handled on the municipal level, accountability was to some extent unclear. Especially since the government was led by the Social Democratic Party and most regions by centre/right-wing parties. When comparing death tolls in May 2022, Sweden was one of the least affected in Europe. However, it was many times more affected than the neighbouring Nordic countries. In consequence, evaluations of the Swedish strategy by the official Corona Commission delivered severe critique against different aspects of the crisis management, such as being too slow in imposing measures to stop the spread of the virus, relying too much on the PHA, and not being able to protect the elderly in care homes (SOU 2022, p. 10).

Political Memes: Harmless Amusement or Societal Critique?

The concept of 'memes' originally stems from evolutionary biology. In his book *The Selfish Gene* (1976), Richard Dawkins uses the concept as a cultural analogy for the biological transmission of genetic information. However, in the last decades, the cultural phenomenon of 'memes' along with its concept came to great fame within the disciplines of communication and cultural studies. In this setting, memes can be defined as a message spreading by imitation from person to person, often carrying symbolic meanings, transmittable through any act of communication (words, images, gestures, rituals, etc.) (Miltner, 2018). In contemporary society, memes are closely related to digital culture, where humorous combinations of text and visuals are the key components that help them gain traction among online audiences. In combination with the speed of the internet, the growing importance of social media, and the lack of gatekeeping, memes can also spread from the outskirts of society to its centre. One of the main characteristics of memes is that their content changes while being disseminated. This change relates to three dimensions of the meme: the content (ideas and ideologies), its form, and its stance (Shifman, 2013b). Memes are also intertextual by nature, by including parodies of tributes to or quotations from pre-existing texts. Thus, they create a 'web of meanings', leveraging social memory and a sense of belonging (Murru, & Vicari, 2021, p. 2424).

In the literature, memes are often framed as having two oppositional meanings or functions in society. Shifman describes memes as, on the one hand, 'trivial pieces of pop culture', and, on the other, as 'an integral part in some of the defining events of the twenty-first century' (2013a, p. 4). Denisova defines memes as the 'fast food' of social media. Still, she argues that they represent significant means of information, interaction, and political deliberation (2019, p. 2). Sebba-Elran discusses memes between the poles of popular culture and folklore, which may explain their 'contradictory roles as both a reinforcement and subversion of hegemonic discourse' (2021, p. 231). Finally, Kristensen and Mortensen point out that political memes 'simultaneously circumvent and reaffirm populist logics' (2021, p. 2444). This framing between meaningless entertainment and cultural criticism highlights how contested memes and their role in society are.

Regardless of critique, memes can articulate and spread critique of political power. As a cheap and accessible means for personal expression, and as a strategy to persuade and summon publics, memes can contribute to political participation (Murru & Vicari, 2021). In this process, they might also contribute to political mobilization. Further, memes are an important channel for expressing political dissent in authoritarian regimes (e.g., Al Zidjaly, 2017). However, memes are also used as means of oppression, to undermine the credibility of political opposition, by regimes (Pearce, 2015 p. 1165). Similarly, memes are also used for indoctrination, e.g., by alt-right movements such as 'the Proud Boys' (Murru & Vicari, 2021). Their lack of attribution – they are mostly anonymous, where metadata about who produced them, when, and where is not available – works both ways. Dissidents can hide their identity when criticizing the regime, but authoritarian regimes (and politicians in democratic systems) might also use this lack of attribution in campaigns against political opponents.

Meme-ing COVID-19

There is a growing body of literature studying internet memes about COVID-19. Most of them are exploratively trying to map out the meme culture related to the pandemic. Other studies investigate the effects of COVID-19 memes on their audiences, particularly their use as a coping mechanism (e.g., Torres-Marín et al., 2022; Akram et al., 2021; Flecha Ortiz, 2020; Hussein & Aljamili, 2020), as well as users' motivations for creating and sharing memes (Jensen et al., 2020), and the reasons for their credibility and persuasiveness (Wasike, 2022).

Through their 'templatability' (Murru & Vicari, 2021, p. 2425), memes provide the possibility to create new meanings by replacing and recombining pre-existing elements. This way, they allow a collective narration of challenging events (ibid.). Further, memes often bridge the global with the local (see, e.g., Cancelas-Ouviña, 2021). Through social media, they discuss a global event, the pandemic, embedded in a local context. As a specific form of 'disaster jokes', memes contribute to narratives about the pandemic within a given cultural context, as Sebba-Elran (2021) reports in an analysis of Israeli meme responses to the pandemic. Vicari and Murru (2020) show how COVID-19 memes often hinted at local political values and identities while addressing 'global' narratives such as 'we are all in this together'. Norstrom and Sarna (2021) explore how the COVID-19 pandemic in Poland was narrated through internet memes in the form of a commentary on measures, citizens, and the incompetence of those in charge to fight the pandemic. Chlopicki and Brzozowska (2021) analyse Polish memes which embrace memories of the history of the country (the socialist times) and call on references to movies and well-known characters in order to illustrate the re-discovered absurdity of life during a pandemic.

Memes can also function as an expression of counterculture and/or narratives, as Ponton and Mantello's (2021) analysis of COVID-19 memes found. Here, online community members can express their critique by highlighting the incompetence of people in charge of managing the pandemic by using satire. The authors also highlight the social catharsis function of memes, showing the absurdity of daily life during the pandemic: memes were playing a crucial role in visualizing, amplifying, and alleviating public fears and anxieties over the dangers of contagion. During COVID-19 politicians were often the themes of critical COVID-19 memes (see, e.g., Cancelas-Ouviña, 2021). For example, Nørgaard Kristensen and Mortensen (2021) analyse COVID-19 memes of populist politicians, namely Boris Johnson and Donald Trump, showing how memes point at contradictions and hypocrisy of these populist politicians and reveal their simplistic and inconsistent communicative strategies. The authors show how memes are challenging these politicians' body appearances, including their 'counter-establishment staging, i.e., unorthodox or overtly expressive and masculine body language' (p. 2453). Further, Murru and Vicari (2021) found anti-elitist narratives in their analysis of early Italian pandemic memes, targeting well-known political leaders and experts. Cancelas-Ouviña (2021) found in her analysis of Spanish COVID-19 memes that the category most represented within the analysed sample was memes targeting political leaders involved in crisis management; she also found that most of the memes, while addressing global themes, were set within a specific local context.

Character Assassination

Memes can also be seen as a means of negative campaigning, or character assassination. Samoilenko et al. (2018) define character assassination as a 'deliberate and sustained effort to damage the reputation or credibility of an individual'

(p. 441). The concept can refer to both the effect of the process (damaged reputation) and the process itself (the campaign and its content). Similarly, negative campaigning focuses on the shortcomings of the policies/ideologies or the ethics of political opponent(s) to undermine them (Johansson & Holtz-Bacha, 2019).

Drawing on this literature, we distinguish between three different dimensions of character assassination/negative campaigning for our analysis. The first one relates to the *ethics* of the target and focuses on personal characteristics (such as honesty, benevolence, issue stance/consistency, and similar traits). The memes referring to *ethics* can insinuate distrust in the intentions and goals of the politician. Is she/he telling the truth? Does she/he have a hidden agenda? Does she/he have questionable group affiliations? The second dimension focuses on the (lack of) *competence* of the targeted politician or expert. Are qualifications being questioned? Did she/he perform poorly before being in office? Does the target of the attack have the ability/power to handle the upcoming situation? The third and last dimension is about the (physical) *appearance* of the politician or expert. Humour and satire often focus on the looks of an object to ridicule him or her, and political memes also use everything from looks to how they dress to damage reputation.

In our analysis, we use these three dimensions of character assassination and see to what extent they are applicable to COVID-19 memes focusing on political leaders and other persons responsible for the crisis management in Austria and Sweden. The ways in which these leading public health authorities, who were meant to guide their citizens through the COVID-19 pandemic, were assassinated through memes will also shed light on how people dealt with a challenging event of global scale as well as some of the collective fears and anxieties triggered by it (Murru & Vicari, 2021; Ponton & Mantello, 2021).

Methods

Studying memes can be challenging due to the difficulties of collecting data. The meme culture, as described above, is viral in its nature and almost always lacks attribution about who created the meme, when it was created, and where it was published. Previous research has used different strategies to collect memes, such as relying on an archive (e.g., Chłopicki & Brzozowska, 2021), using automated collection via keywords or hashtags from social media channels (e.g., Dynel, 2021), or following an explorative approach via search engines (e.g., Kristensen & Mortensen, 2021).

For our analysis, we have focused on memes produced and shared within two countries: Austria and Sweden. Besides the interesting differences in the strategies to handle the pandemic, which sparked memetic reactions within the public, there are two main reasons for focusing on these countries. First, we have not found any substantial research for these contexts and hope to contribute to filling this gap. Second, to analyse memes, a profound understanding of cultural and social contexts is necessary. Previous research (e.g., Cancelas-Ouviña, 2021) has shown that while COVID-19 memes touch upon global topics (e.g., hoarding of toilet paper), they are situated in and need to be interpreted within a specific context. Because of the research team's social and cultural knowledge of the countries, it also made sense to select them for a sufficiently authentic interpretation.

Our search strategy has been to use search strings such as 'COVID-19', 'memes', and 'Austria'/'Sweden', in combination with the identification of relevant channels such as Reddit, Imgur, 9gag, Facebook, Instagram, and Twitter; and relevant profiles sharing memes within these channels. Our collection is neither representative nor comprehensive; following a qualitative approach, our goal was to explore COVID-19 memes shared during the first 16 months of the pandemic. We have not included any alt-right channels into our collection; as such, there is a certain political bias or focus on the collected memes. From the corpus of collected memes, we have selected the ones where a politician or other person responsible for crisis management is the target of character assassination. We focused on a time span from March 2020 to June 2021. Based on the above outlined attributes of character assassination, i.e., *ethics, competence,* and *appearance*, we selected memes as illustrative examples of these attributes and analysed them in depth to compare how this form of negative campaigning was carried out during the COVID-19 pandemic. We strived in our sample to find memes illustrating different dimensions of character assassination to give a broad picture of the phenomenon.

Results: Character Assassination through Memes

In this section, we present eight memes: four from Austria and four from Sweden. We focus on character assassination of the chancellor/prime minister in both countries, as well as on another important public figure during the pandemic. In Austria, this is the Minister of Health Rudolf Anschober. In Sweden, the memes focus on the Chief Epidemiologist Anders Tegnell. We seek to illustrate how COVID-19 memes use aspects of character assassination – targeting *ethics, competence,* and *appearance* – in their critique and commentary of COVID-19 measures. We also consider both explicit and implicit references to popular culture, situating these memes within their cultural, societal, and political context.

Sebastian Kurz – Hypocritical, Young and Incompetent, Untrustworthy and Cold-Hearted

The meme uses a picture from Sebastian Kurz's election campaign in 2010. The slogan of his campaign was 'Schwarz macht geil' (Black makes hot). This is a word play as the conservative's party's visual identity was using the colour black until May 2017, when Sebastin Kurz himself changed the colour to turquoise.[1] The meme/campaign picture shows an image of a young Sebastian Kurz and two young women in tight, black clothing sitting on a black Hummer in front of a Viennese nightclub called 'Moulin Rouge'. Kurz looks dapper but casual while sitting at the bonnet of the black car. Next to him is a blond woman. The other woman is standing at the back of the car. All three are smiling into the camera. Above the photo, there is a text that says 'Sebastian Kurz: "The virus comes with the car". Also Sebastian Kurz' (Figure 7.1).

The meme plays on a statement the chancellor made in Summer 2020. He urged Austrians to be cautious of the COVID-19 even though case numbers were relatively low but slowly back on the rise. Kurz announced: 'Das Virus kommt mit dem Auto nach Österreich'. (The virus comes by car to Austria.) He was commenting on Austrians who were coming back from holidays in Croatia and other Balkan countries. This also included Austrians of migrant backgrounds visiting families in Balkan countries. Here, he stated 'that people who spent the summer in their countries of origin, have dragged the infections back into the country'[2] (Spieß, 2021). With such statements, Kurz justified an increase of controls at Austrian borders.[3]

In terms of *appearance*, the meme plays on his young age as the picture was taken when he was in his early twenties. His young age was often used to

Sebastian Kurz: "Das Virus kommt mit dem Auto." Auch Sebastian Kurz:

FIGURE 7.1 The Virus Comes with the Car. Meme of Austrian Chancellor Sebastian Kurz, 17 August 2020.

portray him as an inexperienced politician. It also draws a picture of him being a cold-hearted person with little moral by engaging with his harsh and hard-liner migration policy and ideology that he publicly stands for. Kurz became (in)famous for the closure of the so-called Balkan route during the 2015 "refugee crisis". Kurz took a strong stance against open and welcoming refugee policies. He positioned himself as an opponent of Merkel and her rather welcoming refugee politics. Finally, the central theme of the car in this meme discursively portrays him as a hypocrite, using whatever he can (women or refugees) for his purposes without moral integrity or continuity. His change of rhetoric could be interpreted as not trustworthy and opportunistic.

The second meme shows chancellor Sebastian Kurz together with Austrian entrepreneur Martin Ho. Kurz has a black book in his hand with the inscription 'Top Secret. Secret lockdown plans'. Both Kurz and Ho are smiling smugly into the camera. Above the image is a text that reads 'When the opening hours of Martin Ho provide you with more information than the federal government' (Figure 7.2).

Sebastian Kurz and Martin Ho are known to be good friends. Ho owns multiple restaurants and nightclubs in Vienna. Sebastian Kurz was a regular guest at his events prior to the COVID-19 pandemic.[4] During the multiple

FIGURE 7.2 Opening Hours. Meme of Austrian Chancellor Sebastian Kurz, 13 January 2021.

lockdowns, there were rumours that Martin Ho was informed prior to the public about upcoming lockdowns. The reason for this rumour was that Martin Ho posted on 30 October 2020 on his restaurant's website that his restaurant would be closed from 2 November 2020 onwards (which was a day prior to the start of the lockdown). At this point in time, this information was not yet publicly available. The lockdown was only announced a day later.[5] In subsequent lockdowns, the word creation 'Horakel' (Ho+Orakel, which means oracle in German) turned into a running gag.[6] Ho already received bad press when it became public that there was an illegal party at one of his restaurants during the first lockdown in May 2020. The police reported that 21 people celebrated at one of Ho's Sushi restaurants. Small amounts of drugs were also found at the venue.

The character assassination of Kurz in this meme comments on his morality and *ethics*: it plays on allegations of nepotism, which in Austria is often trivialized as 'Freundlwirschaft' (Friendship business). His competence is challenged too as it is also a criticism about his confusing and untransparent crisis communication during COVID-19.

Stefan Lövfen – Naive, Blaming China, Incompetent, Cold-Hearted, Cynical

Stefan Löfven of the Social Democratic Party was Swedish prime minister between 2014 and 2021. During this time, he led a minority government with the Green party. As described earlier, Löfven was not the most visible public figure, not even the most visible politician during the pandemic. Instead, ministers from the health and social affairs department and the financial department were more active in communicating issues under their responsibilities. However, Löfven gave a few televised public speeches during the pandemic and the meme (Figure 7.3) is taken from the one given on 22 March 2020. The Swedish flag in the background gives his appearance official weight and underlines the gravity of the moment. The Prime Minister very rarely makes this type of speech to the nation, and it only happened twice during the pandemic. The subtitle in the meme says, 'Stop eating bats, and that's all for now'. At the beginning of the pandemic, there was a well-known theory claiming that the origin of the pandemic was the spread of the SARS-CoV-2 virus from bats to humans. The market in Wuhan where live animals were sold was suspected to be the source of the COVID-19 outbreak.[7] The meme including the Swedish prime minister's 'quote' is open for several interpretations and is not necessarily ridiculing Löfven. One way of perceiving it is as a humorous critique of the cultural custom of eating bats which is common in parts of Asia. Another is as an attack on the government for lacking a credible strategy on how to manage the pandemic and for trying to avoid responsibility by blaming someone else. This interpretation can be considered as a character assassination in that the prime minister lacks the *competence* to handle the outbreak of COVID-19 and has no other advice to residents who need information about protective actions than to stop eating bats, an advice which apparently has no impact whatsoever on mitigating the outbreak.

The second meme is from the beginning of December 2020, when the first vaccinations of particularly vulnerable groups had just started. An information campaign was launched to promote the COVID-19 vaccine and the Social Democratic Party published an ad where Prime Minister Löfven declared that 'The vaccine will be free of charge'. In the meme, an additional text is put on the top saying that 'the morphine was also free of charge'. In this way, the meme takes the opportunity to bash the government for its failure to protect the elderly. By December 2020, several thousand persons in elderly care or with home care had died. Reports claimed that older people in care homes did not receive medical treatment, only morphine as palliative care. The failure to protect the elderly was a common critique regarding the Swedish strategy, articulated by the political opposition, by affected relatives, and later also by the appointed Corona Commission.

By contrasting the positive message of free vaccines to the morphine given to elderly persons in the final stage of life, the meme can be interpreted as a character assassination related to Löfvens *ethics*, in that he did not care if the elderly lived or died. The Prime Minister is stamped as being cold-hearted. Yet, another interpretation builds on the meme criticizing the effectiveness of the vaccine. From this perspective, the vaccine is as useless and ineffective to protect against COVID-19 as is morphine, and the character assassination suggests a lack of *competence*. The meme implies that the government has no cure for the disease and that it puts its hope in dangerous or ineffective measures (Figure 7.4).

FIGURE 7.3 Stop Eating Bats! Meme of the Swedish Prime Minister Stefan Löfven, from March 2020.

FIGURE 7.4 The Morphine Was Free of Charge! Meme of the Swedish Prime Minister Stefan Löfven, from November 2020.

Rudolf Anschober – Out of Touch with the Real World, Not Understandable, Too Complicated

The meme uses a screenshot of the US-American TV show 'It's always sunny in Philadelphia', with text added on top of it. The face of Minister of Health Rudolf Anschober is photoshopped into the picture. He is shown standing in front of an 'investigation board'. Usually used as an illustrative element in TV shows to visualize either criminal investigations or obsessive interests, the 'investigation board' in this meme indicates some kind of manic energy, trying to explain something overly complicated. The text above the image says 'Rudi Anschober: "The rules for Christmas should be clear and understandable"'. Also Rudi Anschober:'. The black box under the picture says (Figure 7.5):

> Six grown-ups and five children from two households are allowed to meet, but if another child joins, everyone needs to wear a mask, but if grandma also joins, one grown-up has to leave again and watch from outside, if grandma is from a third household, then everyone needs to go outside and only she is allowed to open the presents after she has disinfected her hands three times.

RUDI ANSCHOBER: „DIE REGELN FÜR WEIHNACHTEN SOLLEN
KLAR UND VERSTÄNDLICH SEIN."

AUCH RUDI ANSCHOBER:

MEME_Minister.gv

„ES KÖNNEN SICH 6 ERWACHSENE UND 5 KINDER AUS ZWEI
HAUSHALTEN TREFFEN, KOMMT ABER NOCH EIN KIND HINZU
MÜSSEN ALLE EINE MASKE TRAGEN, KOMMT JEDOCH DIE OMA
HINZU MUSS EIN ERWACHSENER WIEDER RAUS UND VON
DRAUßEN AUS ZUSEHEN, IST DIE OMA AUS EINEM DRITTEN
HAUSHALT, DANN MÜSSEN ALLE RAUS UND NUR SIE DARF ALLE
GESCHENKE ÖFFNEN NACHDEM SIE SICH 3X DIE HÄNDE
DESINFIZIERT HAT."

FIGURE 7.5   The Rules for Christmas Should Be Clear and Understandable. Meme
of Austrian Minister of Health Rudolf Anschober, 15 December 2020.

Posted mid-December 2020, the meme references several changes and updates
to COVID-19 regulations in Autumn and Winter 2020, resulting in confusion in the public. This development started with the beginning of the second
wave in October 2020; Austria's second lockdown started on 3 November
2020, after the government announced on 27 October that a lockdown was
not foreseen. This was coined a 'lockdown light' that introduced a curfew,
yet shops were allowed to stay open. This was replaced by a 'hard lockdown' on 17 November, returning to a 'light lockdown' on 7 December, and
another return to a 'hard lockdown' on 26 December. During the Christmas
holidays, from 24 to 25 December, rules were relaxed: visits in care homes
were allowed and up to ten people from up to ten households were allowed
to meet; the regulation before allowed six persons of up to two households
to meet. The third 'hard lockdown' was supposed to last until 24 January but
was subsequently extended until 7 February 2021, with a return to another
'light lockdown' (Pollark et al., 2021).

The meme references this chaos of regulations, as well as the lack of clear
crisis communication by the Minister of Health and the many contradictions,
updates, and changes. As such, this meme attacks Anschober's *competencies* as
the main responsible person during this health crisis. Like other members of

the Green party, Anschober is portrayed as out of touch with the real world; his regulations are not understandable and too complicated.

However, the meme needs to be understood in a wider context. In autumn and early winter 2020, conflicts within the government could be observed. For example, in mid-November 2020, chancellor Kurz announced mass testing of the Austrian population without informing the Ministry of Health.[8] This wider context is also important for the second meme, which consists of several elements: at the top is a screenshot of a news headline, published online by the Austrian Public Broadcaster ORF, stating: 'Kurz in favour of more speed in the vaccination process'. Below, there is a text box stating 'Rudi Anschober:', which is placed above a screenshot of the popular TV show 'The Simpsons'. This includes the subtitles 'My goodness, what an idea! Why didn't I think of that' (Figure 7.6).

The meme refers to a practice – increasingly over the course of the pandemic – of both coalition parties to publicly debate inner-governmental conflicts via the media. As such, these address – at least to some degree – the *competencies* of both Kurz and Anschober. However, while putting Anschober in the centre, the meme is a character assassination of chancellor Kurz: his *ethics* are attacked through this practice of providing obvious suggestions and, through

FIGURE 7.6 My Goodness, What an Idea! Meme of Austrian Minister of Health Rudolf Anschober, 2 March 2021.

this, making the other person appear in a bad light. This reflects on Kurz's strategy throughout the pandemic management: he announced the pandemic to be a 'matter for the boss' (Chefsache). His role within the above-mentioned 'virological quartett' was to announce trends and numbers; details were provided by the ministers.[9] This was interpreted to position himself in a good light, thus improving polls for himself, and assign blame to the Ministry of Health, which is led by the coalition partner. Indeed, many Austrian newspapers[10] reported on power struggles between Kurz and Anschober. Within this context, the meme can be seen as an attack on Kurz's *ethics*, as someone who only looks out for himself, who makes himself look better at the cost of others, and who has a willingness to lie for his own advantage.

Anders Tegnell – The (Failed) Communicator-in-Chief

As mentioned earlier, the PHA and especially their chief epidemiologist Anders Tegnell became 'communicator-in-chief' for the pandemic communication in Sweden. He was assigned a key role as he presented daily analyses and recommendations by the PHA, and gradually gained iconic status for his calm communicative style and steady appeal to react according to 'what we know in the scientific community'. In so doing, he also underlined his belonging to the (limited) group of experts relying only on scientific evidence. This said, he still became a target of critique, since those questioning the Swedish strategy consequently also attacked Anders Tegnell and his recommendations and predictions of how the pandemic would evolve.

This meme from early March 2020 borrows another well-known character to undermine the credibility of the chief epidemiologist. Mohammed Saeed al-Sahhaf (Baghdad Bob) functioned as spokesperson for the Saddam Hussein government during the 2003 Iraq War. He became famous worldwide for making apparently false claims about the development of the war and became a symbol of presenting inaccurate facts when being interviewed by US media. During the interviews, one could spot US tanks in the background when he on live camera claimed US soldiers died at the gates of Bagdad. In the meme, Baghdad Bob's face is replaced by the face of chief epidemiologist Anders Tegnell. The Baghdad Bob meme can be found all over social media, maybe even more today since fake news is in the centre of the public discourse. Baghdad Bob has apparently become a symbol of misinformation, for spreading propaganda and false news. In the background of the meme, like a halo around his head, is an image of the COVID-19 virus, and Tegeell simultaneously raises his hands in a deprecating gesture as if to underline his sincerity and his innocence. Hence, Tegnell's *ethics* are called into question by the dual messages of the meme; his seeming sincerity (saintly glory) is contrasted with Baghdad Bob, the iconic liar (Figure 7.7).

By portraying Tegnell this way his *ethics*, *competence*, and *appearance* are assassinated. The subtext of the meme is that Tegnell is not telling the truth (the association with Baghdah-Bob) but that he is still trying to appear sincere and truthful. In fact, the meme conveys the image of chief epidemiologist and communication commander Tegnell as false and unreliable. The meme should be seen in the context of Sweden's soft strategy, which was criticized by those claiming that a stricter strategy and more efficient protective measures were needed.

Meme number eight is from the same period and portrays Tegnell as the evil dictator Tengil in the children's fantasy novel The *Brothers Lionheart* by the famous Swedish author Astrid Lindgren. In the meme, the chief epidemiologist is wearing the outfit of the dictator Tengil from the movie which is based on the above-mentioned novel. Associating Tegnell with Tengil is also a play on words since both names are spelled and pronounced similarly (Figure 7.8).

FIGURE 7.7 The COVID-19 'Baghdad Bob'. Meme of the Swedish Chief Epidemiologist Anders Tegnell, from March 2020.

FIGURE 7.8 Tegnell as Tengil. Meme of the Swedish Chief Epidemiologist Anders Tegnell, from March 2020.

The meme focuses on Tegnell's appearance, but it does not target his physical looks. Instead, it deals with his appearance in a symbolic way. By putting him in Tengil's battle helmet, the image of Tegnell is charged with a different meaning. The association with a cruel dictator implies that the chief epidemiologist has evil intentions, and that he is not acting in a benevolent spirit. His appearance in the meme also connotes his presence at the press conferences as very serious, stern, and almost emotionless. He never threw a joke, laughed, or smiled even. In the meme, he is associated with a figure that is obsessed with his power. One can, of course, wonder how the image of Tegnell as a dictator relates to the Swedish soft strategy mentioned earlier. The meme might be interpreted as focusing the power Tegnell has been assigned in managing the outbreak of the pandemic. As the most visible communicator during the pandemic, daily informing the Swedes about what was happening on and guiding them on what to do, he was perceived as the person leading the country. The connection to Tengil the dictator may also mirror a recurring critique of him not changing his mind when being questioned. It is however important to point out that for the meme to be interpreted in the intended way, both the sender and the receiver of the meme must share the same cultural preconception of its symbolic content.

Discussion and Conclusions

The aim of our analysis was to understand how character assassination as a form of pandemic communication is used in memes targeted at political leaders and other actors responsible for crisis management. Exploring character assassination in COVID-19 memes, we have identified attacks on *ethics* and *competence*, and, to some degree, on the *appearance* of politicians and other actors involved in COVID-19 crisis management. In the following, we want to discuss how these categories are interwoven, what parallels and differences we have found between Austria and Sweden, how these memes are an expression of the collective fears accompanying the pandemic, and what differences we observed in the character assassinations of different actors.

First, we want to discuss the connections between the categories of character assassination. On the one hand, we have found connections between attacks on *appearance* and *competence*, particularly in the case of Austrian Chancellor Kurz. His young appearance was used as a proxy for his young age, which was then equated with a lack of competence in general; and in particular in managing the health crisis. In selecting a photo from his 2010 election campaign, i.e., a 10-year-old photo, his youth is used to underline his perceived incompetence and lack of experience. More generally, and in line with what Samoilenko et al. (2018) call *visual distortion*, we can observe that the memes pick unflattering pictures of their targets. On the other hand, we can observe an intertwinement between *ethics* and *competence*. This can be illustrated by one of the memes targeting the Swedish Prime Minister Löfven: his competence is questioned by addressing the Swedish government's crisis management, implying that due to the 'soft' Swedish strategy older people died. At the same time, Löfven is portrayed as heartless ('the morphine was also free of charge'). Similarly, Austrian Chancellor Sebastian Kurz's morality has been attacked by implying nepotism in the meme showing him and his friend Martin Ho. Simultaneously, his competence is attacked through the accusation of a lack of transparency in crisis communication (i.e., the announcement of lockdown). Interestingly, we have not found any connection between attacks on *appearance* and *ethics*. While this analysis is explorative in nature and we cannot provide any conclusive answers, we argue that attacks on appearance are socially and culturally contested in Austria and even more so in Sweden. However, they are a reoccurring topic in character assassination (e.g., Kristensen & Mette Mortensen, 2021; Seiffert-Brockmann, 2019) as an effective way to communicate ideas. As Jens Seiffert-Brockmann (2019, p. 406) points out, the visual nature of internet memes 'makes them the perfect media for conveying simple but powerful ideas'. We can observe this in the combination of *appearance* and *competence* (young age and incompetence) and *competence* and *ethics* (cold-heartedness and incompetence). The link between *ethics* and *appearance* seems a less obvious, and thus less simply and intuitively communicable one. Second, we found an interesting parallel between the analysed memes in Austria and Sweden questioning the politicians' – in this case, the Austrian chancellors' and Swedish prime minister's – values and integrity, yet on different levels. Austrian Chancellor Sebastian Kurz's values are questioned by accusing him of being cold-hearted (harsh anti-migration and refugee discourse and policies), of nepotism (i.e., of looking out for his friend's success rather than the Austrian population), and by calling out his practice of publicly attacking his coalition partner. Thus, his priorities in crisis management are questioned and other goals – those of making himself look better, and of profiting from the crisis – are implied. Swedish Prime Minister Stefan Löfven, however, is attacked for the 'soft' Swedish strategy: his priorities – as portrayed through the memes under analysis – are not with the elderly; rather, he chose a strategy that allowed the Swedish public more freedom yet endangered the older population.

In the case of Sebastian Kurz, the character assassinations summarized above are not new nor specific to the COVID-19 setting. Even prior to the pandemic, he was ridiculed for his young age as well as his antiquated and conservative political discourse. This is interesting, as he was accused of being too young for his political position due to a lack of experience. Simultaneously, he was attacked for being too conservative for a young politician.

Third, even if we find similarities in the use of memes between Austria and Sweden, there is an important difference. The attribute of *appearance* seems to be less prominent in the Swedish context. This might reflect a more sensitive public sphere for uncivic behaviour in the Swedish political culture, where attacking physical appearance is considered being very impolite, distasteful even, and – as it seems – also less successful when trying to make a meme going viral. So, even when shielded by anonymity, attacking physical appearance seems to be less adaptive to a contextualized social media logic. This said, we saw examples of *appearance* assassination in Sweden, but these were limited to parodying by putting the face of the person in another setting (Bhagdad-Bob or Tengil) as a kind of symbolic appearance. This distinction between physical and symbolic appearance might be important in further research on character assassination, to make the aspect more nuanced.

Fourth, through our analysis, we wanted to understand the ways in which memes are used to deal with a global event that has been accompanied by collective fears. It is important to contextualize these character assassinations on politicians and other actors. In the context of COVID-19, these memes arose in an environment of uncertainty and unpredictability. These attacks on people in charge of crisis management may reflect feelings of powerlessness and helplessness that may be evoked by a lack of understandability and/or transparency of the decisions taken. Indeed, several studies (e.g., Torres-Marín et al., 2022; Akram et al., 2021; Flecha Ortiz et al., 2021; Hussein & Aljamili, 2020) have hinted at how humour can be a coping strategy for dealing with the pandemic situation. In times of crisis, accusations of incompetence may also reflect fear and express a lack of trust. However, trust is crucial in crisis management. In unprecedented and unpredictable times, how do we proceed and how do we overcome the crisis if we cannot trust those who are in charge of leading us? Furthermore, the meme portraying Rudolf Anschober (see Figure 7.5) points at the absurdity of (some of the) measures and the impossibility to understand them.

Comparing the memes of the two Austrian politicians shows how both politicians are assassinated in different ways even in terms of their incompetence. Whereas Kurz is portrayed as cold-hearted, opportunistic, hypocritical, and untrustworthy, Anschober is ridiculed as overly complicated, impractical, not 'down-to-earth' and, to some extent, weak. This weakness speaks directly to the portrayal of Sebastian Kurz as the stronger coalition partner who used every opportunity to betray his weaker coalition partner, the Green party. As such, the memes tell a story that goes beyond an individual picture.

At last, pandemic communication have many aspects and accountability and blame is a central one to understand the public discourse surrounding a pandemic. Political memes fulfil this function, and by using popular culture and humour with a negative twist, they make critiques against power holders become a viral phenomenon.

There are clear differences in cultural context and connotations how character assassination is used in pandemic communication. It would therefore be interesting in future studies to extend the comparison to countries with different media systems (Hallin & Mancini, 2004) and different risk and crisis cultures (Cornia et al., 2016) in order to broaden our knowledge of how memes are used in pandemic communication to comment on and relate to periods of national uncertainty and collective fears. Furthermore, our focus was limited on mainstream memes; particularly when investigating character assassination targeting appearance, we may find different results when extending this scope.

Funding

This chapter is based on research conducted in the context of the COVINFORM project, which has received funding from the European Union's H2020 research and innovation programme under Grant Agreement No. 101016247.

Notes

1 https://www.derstandard.at/story/1302745628398/mit-dem-geilomobil-ins-staatssekretariat.
2 Original in German: 'Sehr geehrte Damen und Herren. Wir hatten im Sommer sehr, sehr niedrige Ansteckungszahlen nach dem Lockdown und haben dann durch Reiserückkehrer und insbesondere auch durch Menschen, die in ihren Herkunftsländern den Sommer verbracht haben, uns Ansteckungen wieder ins Land herein geschleppt. Daher ist es notwendig, dass wir diesmal auf ein sehr konsequentes Grenzregime setzen, das verhindern soll, dass wir in Österreich zwar mit den Zahlen nach unten kommen uns aber dann durch Auslandsreisen in der Weihnachtszeit das Virus wieder ins Land schleppen' (Kurz,Pressekonferenz vom 2.12.2020).
3 https://www.sueddeutsche.de/politik/kurz-oesterreich-corona-auto-1.5006720.
4 https://www.meinbezirk.at/wien/c-leute/wiens-society-stoesst-mit-martin-ho-auf-zehn-jahre-dots-experimental-sushi-an_a1545236.
5 https://www.parlament.gv.at/PAKT/VHG/XXVII/J/J_03993/index.shtml.
6 https://www.derstandard.at/story/2000131269396/kommt-der-lockdown-martin-ho-kuendigt-wieder-lokalschliessungen-an.
7 https://www.nature.com/articles/d41586-022-00584-8.
8 https://orf.at/stories/3189878/.
9 https://www.zeit.de/politik/ausland/2020–04/sebastian-kurz-coronavirus-krisenmanagement-strategie.
10 See, e.g., https://www.wienerzeitung.at/nachrichten/politik/oesterreich/2082601-Corona-Das-Suendenregister-der-Regierung.html.

References

Akram, U., Irvine, K., Allen, S. F., Stevenson, J. C., Ellis, J. G., & Drabble, J. (2021). Internet memes related to the COVID-19 pandemic as a potential coping mechanism for anxiety. *Scientific Reports, 11*(1), 1–8.

Al Zidjaly, N. (2017). Memes as reasonably hostile laments: A discourse analysis of political dissent in Oman. *Discourse & Society, 28*(6), 573–594. https://doi.org/10.1177%2F0957926517721083.

Andersson, S., & Aylott, N. (2020). Sweden and coronavirus: Unexceptional exceptionalism *Social Sciences, 9*(12), 232. https://doi.org/10.3390/socsci9120232.

Bennett, L. W. (2012 [2007]). *News: The politics of illusion.* Pearson Education.

Boin, A., t'Hart, P., Stern, E. and Sundelius, B. E. (2017). *The politics of crisis management: Public leadership under pressure.* Cambridge University Press.

Cancelas-Ouviña, L. P. (2021). Humor in times of COVID-19 in Spain: Viewing coronavirus through memes disseminated via WhatsApp. *Frontiers in Psychology, 12,* 1075. https://doi.org/10.3389/fpsyg.2021.611788.

Chłopicki, W., & Brzozowska, D. (2021). Sophisticated humor against COVID-19: The Polish case. *HUMOR, 34*(2): 201–227. https://doi.org/10.1515/humor-2021-0015.

Coman, I.A., Elsheik, D, Gregor, M., Lilleker, D., & Novelli, E. (2021). Introduction. In D. Lilleker, I. A. Coman, M. Gregor, & E. Novelli (Eds.), *Political communication and COVID-19: Governance and rhetoric in times of crisis* (pp. 1–15). Routledge.

Cornia, A., Dressel, K., & Pfeil, P. (2016). Risk cultures and dominant approaches towards disasters in seven European countries. *Journal of Risk Research, 19*(3), 288–304. https://doi.org/10.1080/13669877.2014.961520

Davis, S. (2022). More than "a Little Flu": Alternative digital journalism and the struggle to re-frame the Brazilian government's response to the COVID-19 outbreak. In P. Van Aelst & J. Blumler (Eds.), *Political communication in the time of coronavirus* (pp. 120–135). Routledge.

Dawkins, R. (1976). *The selfish gene.* Oxford University Press.

Denisova, A. (2019). *Internet memes and society: Social, cultural, and political contexts.* Routledge.

Djerf-Pierre, M., Ekström, M., & Johansson, B. (2013). Policy failure or moral scandal? Political accountability, journalism and new public management. *Media, Culture & Society, 35*(8), 960–976.

Dynel, M. (2021). COVID-19 memes going viral: On the multiple multimodal voices behind face masks. *Discourse & Society, 32*(2), 175–195. https://doi.org/10.1177%2F0957926520970385.

Flecha Ortiz, J. A., Santos Corrada, M. A., Lopez, E., & Dones, V. (2021). Analysis of the use of memes as an exponent of collective coping during COVID-19 in Puerto Rico. *Media International Australia, 178*(1), 168–181.

Garland, R., & Lilleker, D. (2022). From consensus to dissensus: The UK's management of a pandemic in a divided nation. In P. Van Aelst & J. Blumler (Eds.), *Political communication in the time of coronavirus* (pp. 17–32). Routledge.

Hallin, D. C., & Mancini, P. (2004). *Comparing media systems: Three models of media and politics.* Cambridge University Press.

Hjarvard, S. (2013). *The mediatization of culture and society.* Routledge.

Hodgart, M., & Connery, B.A. (2017). *Satire. Origins and principles.* Routledge.

Hussein, A. T., & Aljamili, L. N. (2020). COVID-19 humor in Jordanian social media: A socio-semiotic approach. *Heliyon, 6*(12), e05696. https://doi.org/10.1016/j.heliyon.2020.e05696.

Jensen, M. S., Neumayer, C., & Rossi, L. (2020). 'Brussels will land on its feet like a cat': Motivations for memefying# Brusselslockdown. *Information, Communication & Society, 23*(1), 59–75.

Johansson, B., & Holtz-Bacha, C. (2019). From Analogue to Digital Negativity: Attacks and Counterattacks, Satire, and Absurdism on Election Posters Offline and Online. In A. Veneti, D. Jackson & D. G. Lilleker, (Eds). *Visual Political Communication,* (pp. 99–118). Palgrave Macmillan.

Johansson, B., & Vigsø, O. (2021). Sweden: Lone hero of stubborn outlier? In D. Lilleker, I. A. Coman, M. Gregor, & E. Novelli (Eds.), *Political communication and COVID-19: Governance and rhetoric in times of crisis* (pp. 155–164). Routledge.

Johansson, B., Hopmann, D. N., & Shehata, A. (2021). When the rally-around-the-flag effect disappears, or: When the COVID-19 pandemic becomes "normalized". *Journal of Elections, Public Opinion and Parties, 31*(sup1), 321–334. https://doi.org/10.1 080/17457289.2021.1924742.

Lilleker, D., Coman, I. A., Gregor, M., & Novelli, E. (2021). Political communication and COVID-19: Governance and rhetoric in global comparative perspective. In Darren Lilleker, Joana A. Coman, Miloš Gregor, and Edoardo Novelli (Eds.) *Political Communication and COVID-19* (pp. 333–350). Routledge.

Miltner, K. (2018). Internet memes. In J. Burgess, A. Marwick, & T. Poell (Eds.), *The Sage handbook of social media* (pp. 412–428). SAGE Publications Ltd, https://dx.doi.org/10.4135/9781473984066.n23.

Murru, M. F., & Vicari, S. (2021). Memetising the pandemic: Memes, covid-19 mundanity, and political cultures. *Information, Communication & Society, 24*(16), 2422–2441.

Nørgaard Kristensen, N., & Mortensen, M. (2021). 'Don't panic people! Trump will tweet the virus away': memes contesting and confirming populist political leaders during the COVID-19 crisis. *Information, Communication & Society, 24*(16), 2442–2458.

Norstrom, R., & Sarna, P. (2021). Internet memes in Covid-19 lockdown times in Poland. *Comunicar, 29*(67). https://doi.org/10.3916/C67-2021-06.

Pearce, K. E. (2015). Democratizing kompromat: the affordances of social media for state-sponsored harassment. *Information, Communication & Society, 18*(10), 1158–1174.

Pierre, J. (2020). Nudges against pandemics: Sweden's COVID-19 containment strategy in perspective. *Policy and Society, 39*(3), 478–493. https://doi.org/10.1080/1449 4035.2020.1783787.

Ponton, D. M., & Mantello, P. (2021). Virality, contagion and public discourse. The role of memes as prophylaxis and catharsis in an age of crisis. *Rhetoric and Communications, 46*, 44–63.

Pollark, M., Kowarz, N. & Parthemüller, J. (2021). Chronologie zur Corona-Krise in Österreich – Teil 4: Erneute Lockdowns, Massentests und der Beginn der Impfkampagne. *Austria Corona Panel Project.* Available at https://viecer.univie.ac.at/ corona-blog/corona-blog-beitraege/blog100/ (25.05.2022).

Samoilenko, S. A., Shiraev, E., Keohane, J., & Icks, M. (2016). Character assassination. *The SAGE Encyclopedia of Corporate Reputation, 1*, 115–118.

Seiffert-Brockmann, J. (2019). Character assassination by memes: Mosquitos versus elephants. In S. A. Samoilenko, M. Icks, J. Keohane, & E. Shiraev (Eds.), *Routledge handbook of character assassination and reputation management* (pp. 402–421). Routledge.

Shifman, L. (2013a). Memes in a digital world: Reconciling with a conceptual troublemaker. *Journal of Computer-Mediated Communication, 18*(3), 362–377.

Shifman, L. (2013b). *Memes in digital culture.* MIT Press.

Sebba-Elran, T. (2021). A pandemic of jokes? The Israeli COVID-19 meme and the construction of a collective response to risk. *HUMOR, 34*(2), 229–257. https://doi.org/10.1515/humor-2021-0012.

SOU 2022:10. (2022). *Sweden during the pandemic [Sverige under pandemin].* https:// coronakommissionen.com/wp-content/uploads/2022/02/sverige-under-pande-min-volym-1_webb-slutbetankande.pdf.

Torres-Marín, J., Navarro-Carrillo, G., Eid, M., & Carretero-Dios, H. (2022). Humor styles, perceived threat, funniness of COVID-19 memes, and affective mood in the early stages of COVID-19 lockdown. *Journal of Happiness Studies, 1*–21.

van Dijck, J., & Poell, T. (2013). Understanding social media logic. *Media and Communication, 1*(1), 2–14. https://doi.org/10.17645/mac.v1i1.70.

Vicari, S., & Murru, M. F. (2020). One platform, a thousand worlds: On Twitter irony in the early response to the COVID-19 pandemic in Italy. *Social Media+ Society, 6*(3), 2056305120948254.

Wasike, B. (2022). Memes, memes, everywhere, nor any meme to trust: Examining the credibility and persuasiveness of COVID-19-related memes. *Journal of Computer-Mediated Communication, 27*(2), zmab024. https://doi.org/10.1093/jcmc/zmab024.

Yang, Y., & Bennet, L.W. (2022). Interactive propaganda. How Fox News and Donald Trump co-produced false narratives about the COVID-19 crisis. In P. Van Aelst & J. Blumler (Eds.), *Political communication in the time of coronavirus* (pp. 84–100). Routledge.

8

APPLIED COMMUNICATION AND PANDEMICS

Expanding the IDEA Model of Instructional Risk and Crisis Communication

Deanna D. Sellnow, Sofia E. Salazar Carballo, and Timothy L. Sellnow

On March 11, 2020, the World Health Organization (WHO) declared the novel coronavirus (COVID-19) outbreak a global pandemic (Cucinotta & Vanelli, 2020). At that time, few fathomed that the world would still be dealing with its ramifications more than two years later. Moreover, its unprecedented and far-reaching consequences impacted sectors ranging from business and industry to public health and education, to personal well-being and financial solvency; as well as across international borders and among co-cultural groups within them (Center on Budget and Policy Priority, 2022). In essence, the pandemic triggered what Helsloot et al. (2012) define as a mega-crisis that "def[ies] boundaries, limits, neat demarcations, patterned connections and linear consequences" (p. 5). Thus, we argue that applied risk and crisis communication theory and research must be contextualized globally when examining pandemic communication.

In this chapter, we illustrate why and how applied crisis and risk communication theory and practice must evolve to accommodate cross-cultural and transnational interactions and implications as they evolve over time. We clarify our argument through the theoretical lens of the IDEA model for effective instructional risk and crisis communication as applied to the Spanish version of COVID-19 guidelines distributed by the United States Centers for Disease Control and Prevention (CDC). Ultimately, we propose suggestions for future research that embrace an emerging field of study characterized herein as pandemic communication.

To clarify, most of the applied communication research focused on risk and crisis published to date tends to be both temporally and spatially bound. By temporally bound, we mean that existing crisis life-cycle theories point to a clear beginning, middle, and end (e.g., pre-crisis, crisis, post-crisis) (Millar &

DOI: 10.4324/9781003214496-8

Heath, 2004; Sellnow & Seeger, 2020). In terms of being spatially bound, most studies identify clear geographic parameters where an "event" is occurring or did occur (Ulmer et al., 2019). Moreover, these parameters tend to ignore the role cultural norms and values necessarily play in effective decision-making message design and engaged learning among diverse people and groups. As Sellnow et al. (2020) discovered, such communication gaps can have deadly consequences.

While conclusions drawn from such studies delimited by time and space (and sometimes overlooking cultural norms) are valuable, pandemic communication in risk and crisis does not fit neatly within these parameters. COVID-19 emerged and evolved over time and across space as disease outbreaks spiked in different locations around the world and new variants emerged frequently over time. Although the WHO officially declared the pandemic on March 11, 2020, outbreaks had already been occurring in China and spreading rapidly across national borders (Taylor, 2021). For this reason, it is impossible to identify a precise starting point. Also, contrary to prevailing assumptions at that time, the ongoing rise and fall of outbreaks and deaths in various locations around the world would continue not just for months but for years. In fact, as of May 1, 2022, the WHO confirmed over 500 million cases reported worldwide, had reported over 6 million deaths globally, and had still not declared an end of the pandemic (World Health Organization, 2022). Moreover, weekly cases reported in the African Region had risen by 31% and by 13% in the Region of the Americas. Hence, the parameters of pandemic communication in the context of mega-crises must be broadly defined in terms of time and space.

The IDEA Model

The IDEA model for effective instructional risk and crisis communication has demonstrated utility for communicating across myriad risk situations and crisis events, as well as among diverse people and groups. It is essentially a framework for communicating in ways that effectively prompts receivers to pay attention to, as well as comprehend and take appropriate actions during times of crisis (Sellnow et al., 2017). *IDEA* is an acronym for the four fundamental elements of effective instructional risk and crisis communication (Sellnow & Sellnow, 2019).

"I" stands for internalization. To be effective, receivers must be compelled to pay attention. This can be achieved by indicating the relevance of the event to and potential impact on them and their livelihood or those they care about. In terms of the COVID-19 pandemic, this was achieved by clarifying how contagious the virus is, where it is spreading most quickly, as well as implications (illness, hospitalization, death) for those that contract it.

Unlike many risk situations and crisis events (for example, those triggered by natural disasters such as hurricanes, tornadoes, fires, mudslides, and tsunamis—that can be isolated to a particular geographical region and demarcated by time), however, the novel coronavirus knows no geographical boundaries and has no clear beginning or end. To be effective, risks must be monitored continuously, and messages tailored accordingly as the events fluctuate for those living in different parts of the world over the duration of the pandemic. Regarding internalization, this means adjusting messages to account for ebb and flow of disease outbreaks, spread, and severity based on where target audiences and those they care about reside.

"D" stands for distribution. To be effective, communication must take place via channels that are likely to reach intended audiences (Sellnow & Sellnow, 2019). In other words, the selected communication channels must be both accessible to them and ones that they typically look to when seeking information. It follows that multiple channels ought to be used when addressing diverse publics (Petrun et al., 2019). In the case of pandemic communication, doing so requires coordination among spokespersons and agencies to manage the master narrative, competing narratives, as well as mis-, dis-, and mal-information. In many ways, spokespersons in the United States failed to do so as evidenced by the fact that government officials, public health experts, and epidemiologists very often conveyed different and even contradictory information and advice simultaneously (Sullum, 2020). Thus, critical to effective distribution of messages in pandemic communication is the ability to manage competing narratives—some of them spreading mis-, dis-, and mal-information—that can so quickly go viral across media and over social networks (Vijaykumar et al., 2021).

We argue that one way to manage competing narratives within the context of pandemic communication is to form strategic alliances among key agencies in the form of global communities of practice (CoPs). These CoPs may then collaboratively assess events as they unfold and craft messages that convey them accurately across regions, countries, and continues over time (Edwards et al., 2021). Finally, these CoPs ought to include social media influencers (SMIs) who can help spread accurate information based on scientific evidence to niche populations comprised of followers that are likely to trust them over other spokespersons. Although SMIs have traditionally been examined for their role in marketing, we argue that they may play a vital role in strategic communication, particularly during mega-crises and risk situations (Enke & Borchers, 2019).

"E" stands for explanation. To be effective, receivers must ultimately understand what is happening and why, as well as what is being done to deal with it. According to the model, explanations must be accurate, transparent, and translated intelligibly (Sellnow & Sellnow, 2019). In other words, spokespersons need to be honest about what they know and what they do not yet know, what they are doing to learn more, and how often they will update receivers. In the case of COVID-19, experts made a misstep when they claimed to know more about the novel coronavirus than they did. When they proposed that the virus spread via touching infected surfaces (fomite) and probably not through the air (breathing, coughing, sneezing), they set themselves up to be wrong when they learned more about it. Being perceived as wrong rather than as unsure but seeking additional information and answers erodes trust (Balog-Way & McComas, 2020).

Transparency about what is known and not yet known has long been lauded as a best practice for risk and crisis communication (Sellnow & Seeger, 2020). When dealing with high-impact and high-uncertainty risk situations, transparency may be even more critical to effective communication. This contention was confirmed by Lee and Li (2021) in their analysis of state government transparency and public trust during COVID-19. In terms of explanation, transparency plays a vital role in effective pandemic communication.

In addition to accuracy and transparency, explanations must be translated intelligibly for intended audiences. Even the most precise explanations communicated ever so transparently are doomed to fail if receivers are not able to interpret them correctly. Laid bare during COVID-19 is the fact that, regarding pandemic communication that crosses national and international boundaries, multilingual communication is clearly one daunting challenge (Piller et al., 2020). Moreover, intelligible translation of explanations in global pandemic communication must also reach people whose primary language is indigenous to a culture, community, or region (Ahmad & Hillman, 2021; Ortega et al., 2020).

Intelligible explanations must also be translated based on literacy level of intended receivers. In the case of COVID-19, medical science needed to be explained in ways that non-medical experts could understand. Cook et al. (2021) clarify, for instance, how COVID-19 information was translated intelligibly for preschool and primary school children in the "meet the helpers" campaign on public television in the United States. Literacy levels may also vary according to numeracy (i.e., the ability to comprehend numerical concepts). Sellnow et al. (2019b), for example, discovered that earthquake early warnings (EEW) garnered better behavioral responses when intensity levels were reported with words and sounds rather than numbers. One means by which to overcome translation challenges in pandemic communication may be found in the use of exemplars (Zillmann, 1999). In terms of global mega-crises and pandemic communication, exemplars include any short words, phrases, visual images, or sounds that both get attention and represent a larger phenomenon. Emergency sirens are one common example and color-coded warning labels are another. Unfortunately, however, different countries may use different sounds and colors to mean the same thing. A challenge for pandemic communication going forward may be to encourage collaboration among countries regarding interpretation of exemplars in risk situations and crisis events.

"A" stands for action. Effective instructional communication in applied crisis and risk contexts must be specific in terms of what receivers are being asked to do and, sometimes, what not to do to protect themselves and loved ones, as well as to reduce risks and mitigate harms. This differs from explaining what officials and agencies are doing to address specifically what individuals can do themselves. Regarding COVID-19, what the pharmaceutical companies were doing to develop vaccines serves as explanation in that it provides information about the situation to receivers. Appeals to wear a mask, practice social distancing, wash hands thoroughly, and, eventually, get vaccinated, however, are specific actions receivers can take to protect themselves and others. Exemplars (e.g., visual images and diagrams) may perhaps be even most important for actionable compliance across national and international boundaries. For example, wearing a mask will not protect anyone if it does not cover both the nose and the mouth (Tso & Cowling, 2020). Visual messages may garner better results in terms of overcoming translational barriers.

In terms of behavioral compliance, being specific about what to do or not to do will not necessarily suffice, however, if doing so is not feasible. If masks are not available, for instance, people cannot comply with instructions about when, how, and where to wear them (Hakim et al., 2021). During COVID-19, many people also necessarily failed to comply with protective action instructions due to overcrowded living conditions, as well as inadequate hygiene and sanitation facilities (Lancet, 2020). Moreover, many vulnerable populations (e.g., migrant field workers) that live at the bottom of the income distribution and have non-tele-workable jobs could not comply with social distancing or self-quarantine actions and still feed their families (Fasani & Mazza, 2020). The fact that essential workers who could not comply with protective measures reported disproportionate cases and deaths from COVID-19 speaks to this challenge in pandemic communication going forward (Rogers et al., 2020).

People may also not comply with instructions if doing so violates cultural norms. Ma and Zhan (2022) discovered, for example, that people may choose *not* to comply to avoid being stigmatized or ostracized by significant others in their community. Moreover, in their examination of COVID-19 behavioral compliance across 111 countries, Chen et al. (2021) confirmed that cultural norms did in fact play a significant role in compliance regarding lockdown rules imposed by their governments. Their comprehensive examination points to the fact that cultural norms must be integrated into pandemic communication if it is to be effective across national and international borders, as well as among cultural and co-cultural groups.

Application

To illustrate how expanding the theoretical constructs in the IDEA model may account for the complexities of pandemic communication, this section offers a thematic analysis of COVID-19 messages provided on the United States Centers for Disease Control and Prevention (CDC) website. More specifically, we examine the Spanish version of the "Celebraciones y pequeñas reuniones por las fiestas" [Holiday Celebrations and Small Gatherings] guidelines as posted on November 27, 2020. We take an etic approach to conduct the thematic analysis using IDEA model elements as "conceptual categories" (Lindlof & Taylor, 2011, p. 95). Since 16,000,000 Hispanics living in the United States rate their ability to speak English as "less than very well" (Krogstad et al., 2015) and about 74% choose to seek news information from the Internet (Flores & Lopez, 2018), we believe the CDC website was a viable information source for them during the COVID-19 pandemic.

For purposes of this analysis, we coded each sentence as one unit of analysis (N = 138) and coded each sentence only once based on its primary focus. Of the 138 sentences, 27 (19.57%) focused primarily on internalization, 9 (6.52%) on distribution, 17 (12.31%) on explanation, and 85 (61.60%) on action (see Figure 8.1). Since the goal of the U.S. CDC in posting the website information was to provide behavioral guidance, it is heartening to see that most items address action.

Regarding internalization, the website focused primarily on potential impact (harms) to older people that become infected and, to a lesser degree, proximity and timeliness. For example, sentences pointing to potential impact included "Si es adulto mayor o tiene ciertas afecciones que suponen mayor riesgo de enfermarse gravemente a causa del COVID-19 o vive o trabaja con una persona con mayor riesgo…" [If you are an older adult or person with certain medical conditions who is at increased risk of severe illness from COVID-19, or live or work with someone at increased risk…] (CDC, 2020) and "las personas que no respetaron de manera consistente las normas de distanciamiento social, uso de mascarillas, lavado de manos y otras medidas de prevención aumentan el riesgo de propagación…" [Individuals who did not consistently adhere to social distancing, mask wearing, handwashing, and other prevention behaviors pose more risk…] (CDC, 2020).

In terms of proximity, some of the questions included were "¿Los casos en su comunidad o en su lugar de destino son muchos o están aumentando?" [Are cases high or increasing in your community or your destination?] (CDC, 2020)

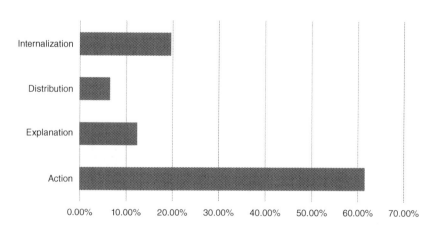

FIGURE 8.1 IDEA Model Distribution.

and "¿El lugar donde vive o su lugar de destino tienen requisitos o restricciones para viajeros?" [Does your home or destination have requirements or restrictions for travelers?] (CDC, 2020). Finally, some sentences focused on timeliness, such as "En esta temporada festiva" [This holiday season] and "El Día de Acción de Gracias es un momento" [Thanksgiving is a time]. Expressions like this provide relevance to the messages shared in this space. The CDC also included some messages that involved compassion but to a lesser extent. For instance, "La pandemia del COVID-19 ha sido motivo de estrés y aislamiento para muchas personas. Las reuniones para las próximas fiestas pueden ser una oportunidad de volver a conectarse con familiares y amigos." [The COVID-19 pandemic has been stressful and isolating for many people. Gatherings during the upcoming holidays can be an opportunity to reconnect with family and friends.] (CDC, 2020).

In terms of distribution, at the macro-level, the only communication channel used was the website. However, nine sentences (of $N = 138$) did encourage readers to continue checking the CDC website and other government organization's websites for updates on COVID-19. For example, "Visite la página de los CDC" [Visit the CDC's website] and "…los sitios web de los departamentos de salud locales suelen publicar información." […check state and local public health department websites.] (CDC, 2020).

A total of 17 (of $N = 138$) sentences were coded as explanation. These items focused on statistical updates and information about progress being made to bring an end to the pandemic. For example, "Se notificaron más de 1 millón de casos de COVID-19 en los Estados Unidos en los últimos 7 días." [More than 1 million COVID-19 cases were reported in the United States over the last 7 days.], and "El consumo de alcohol o drogas puede afectar el criterio y dificultar más la puesta en práctica de las medidas de seguridad contra el COVID-19." [Use of alcohol or drugs may alter judgment and make it more difficult to practice COVID-19 safety measures.] (CDC, 2020). Explanations were translated intelligibly not only in terms of being in Spanish but also in terms of accuracy and simplicity as illustrated in this sentence about ventilation during cold winter months, "En invierno puede hacer frío, haber humedad o el clima puede ser impredecible. Las inclemencias del tiempo dificultan la posibilidad de aumentar la ventilación abriendo ventanas o de organizar un evento al aire libre" [Winter weather can be cold, wet, and unpredictable. Inclement weather makes it difficult to increase ventilation by opening windows or to hold an event outdoors.] (CDC, 2020).

Most sentences coded in this analysis (85 of 138; 61.60%) focused on action steps to take or not to take regarding COVID-19. In fact, nearly all of these action statements used action verbs (e.g., "provide," "clean," "limit," "use," "plan," "limit," "wear," "wash," "avoid"). Many of these action steps focused on how to stay during the holidays and when attending small gatherings. For example, "Los familiares y amigos deben evaluar la cantidad de casos de

COVID-19 en sus comunidades y en la comunidad donde tienen previsto celebrar a la hora de decidir si van a organizar una reunión o asistir a un encuentro" [Family and friends should consider the number of COVID-19 cases in their community and in the community where they plan to celebrate when deciding whether to host or attend a gathering.] (CDC, 2020) and "Monitoree a los anfitriones e invitados para detectar síntomas de COVID-19 como fiebre, tos o dificultad para respirar." [Monitor hosts and guests for symptoms of COVID-19 such as fever, cough, or shortness of breath.] (CDC, 2020). In addition, the CDC included action steps regarding pets. For instance, "Trate a las mascotas como trataría a otros familiares humanos: no deje que las mascotas interactúen con personas fuera de su hogar." [Treat pets as you would other human family members – do not let pets interact with people outside the household.] (CDC, 2020). Finally, although the CDC offered strategies to stay safe when attending small gatherings or holiday parties, they also never stopped encouraging audiences to stay home and avoid such gatherings altogether.

The results of this thematic analysis illustrate that the Spanish version of the U.S. CDC website did address all elements of the IDEA model. Moreover, the website content emphasized specific actionable instructions for protection of self and loved ones during the holidays and small gatherings. As such, it appears to be an appropriate resource for Hispanic people and groups regarding what to do and not to do for health and safety regarding COVID-19 during the holidays and small gatherings.

Discussion

Fundamentally, the fact that the CDC website content for "Celebraciones y pequeñas reuniones por las fiestas" [Holiday Celebrations and Small Gatherings] did not privilege explanation over action or internalization is encouraging. The content focused instead primarily on specific actionable instructions, which signals improvement since their 2014 communication on Ebola that was largely focused on explanation (Sellnow-Richmond et al., 2018). In terms of instructional communication in times of risk and crisis, explanations offered without actionable instructions will not evoke desired behavioral outcomes for compliance (Merrill et al., 2019). This is not to dismiss the role of explanation and internalization in achieving compliance, however, as actionable instructions without them are also doomed to fail (Sellnow et al., 2019c).

Although the U.S. CDC did incorporate all elements of the IDEA model in the "Celebraciones y pequeñas reuniones por las fiestas" [Holiday Celebrations and Small Gatherings] section of the website, the information provided was time-bound and merely a word-for-word translation of the English version.

By time-bound we mean that the message implies a singularity to the upcoming holiday season. In other words, getting through the holiday season assumes there is a beginning, middle, and end, which clearly was not the case for the COVID-19–induced mega-crisis. Given its prolonged nature, the more accurate and effective approach would be to propose these actions as a new normal to be followed for an extended period (with an end point not yet known). The holiday message would have served the audience better if it had portrayed the season as a reminder to remain vigilant in all aspects of interpersonal and small group gatherings now and in the future. A time-bound message implies one can return to engaging in routine, habitual, less protective behaviors once the holidays were over, which was clearly not the intent of the U.S. CDC.

A second concern is that the messages were not tailored strategically to appeal to Hispanic cultural norms even though the CDC acknowledges the importance of doing so. In its "Cultural Insights" (n.d.) publication, the CDC advises readers to:

> Emphasize cultural diversity within the Hispanic population when conducting health assessments and promotion activities. Subgroups of the Hispanic population such as Mexicans, Puerto Ricans, and Cubans differ in their lifestyles, health beliefs, and health practices.
>
> *(p. 4)*

Thus, in the "Celebraciones y pequeñas reuniones por las fiestas" [Holiday Celebrations and Small Gatherings] section, the CDC did not follow its own advice. Crisis and risk communication research confirms that merely translating English messages into Spanish is not sufficient to achieve affective, cognitive, and behavioral learning outcomes (e.g., Johansson et al., 2021; Petrun et al., 2019; Sellnow et al., 2019a; Spence et al., 2007, 2011). When it comes to pandemic communication, crisis and risk spokespersons must resist the temptation to merely translate messages without tailoring them to address relevant cultural norms and values.

The absence of message tailoring implies that repeating a narrative via mere language translation across cultural and co-cultural groups is sufficient. This assumption is perhaps most problematic in the action phase of the IDEA model. Actions befitting one segment of a population may be impossible for another to perform. Behavioral outcome achievement may not rest with motivation but, rather, with efficacy. Maintaining social distance may, for instance, necessitate strategies for those living in multi-generational homes that are distinct from those living in single-family dwellings. Also, cultural traditions may create higher risks during holidays than a single message can accommodate. Simply put, best practices of risk and crisis communication do not advocate a single message approach (Sellnow & Seeger, 2020). Unfortunately, repeating content with no tailoring other than that of language translation is using an ineffective single message approach.

To be most effective, some research suggests further that messages should be co-created with these cultural groups prior to distribution. Dutta et al. (2012), for example, contend that vulnerable populations should be involved in both the decision-making process and solution development of issues that impact them. Sellnow et al. (2020) point out that doing so can avert life-threatening consequences arising from competing narratives rooted in cultural norms. Finally, Pyrko et al. (2019) suggest forming diverse communities of practice (CoPs) that create spaces for "triple – legitimatization of situated learning" (p. 482).

Regarding the IDEA model for effective instructional risk and crisis communication, several points for expansion are required to account for the nuances of pandemic communication. In terms of internalization, for example, unique cultural norms that influence interactions during various points of the year ought to be acknowledged and honored. To clarify, the website did offer content focused on potential impact (harms), proximity (where the disease was spreading), and timeliness (during holidays).

To be more effective, however, internalization ought to be tailored in ways that acknowledge Hispanic cultural norms about holiday celebrations that are distinct from dominant American culture. Rather than merely translating information provided in English, Hispanic people and groups may have been more inclined to pay attention to and follow instructions that begin with compassionate empathy about the sacrifices being asked of them during the holidays (Salazar, 2021). Moreover, had the website tailored its content about gatherings over time (e.g., small gatherings in general versus small gatherings during the holidays), Hispanic readers may have felt seen/heard/valued and more likely to comply.

Regarding distribution, the website did encourage viewers to visit it regularly for updates, as well as to review other pertinent government publications. Although research suggests that Hispanic populations living in the United States do seek information via the Internet, research confirms that people seek convergence among a variety of sources, particularly during risk and crisis events. For pandemic communication to be effective across diverse cultural groups, convergent messages must be conveyed across multiple communication channels and by various spokespersons/opinion leaders (e.g., Robinson, 2021; Sellnow & Sellnow, 2019). Moreover, these messages must be monitored and updated over time as details of a mega-crisis such as the COVID-19 pandemic change, as well as across space as details erupt uniquely in different sectors around the world. Finally, the fact that a high percentage of Hispanic people living in the United States also encounter language and literacy barriers—particularly in terms of health literacy—speaks to a need for providing information via multiple channels (e.g., oral, written, visual) (Jacobs et al., 2017).

Explanation about COVID-19 was addressed in the website content. Moreover, it was accurately translated into Spanish. What was missing, however, was clear explanation about what was being done to address disease spread for those living in close proximity (e.g., multi-family dwellings) and for Hispanic ethnicities (e.g., Elkafrawi et al., 2022; Goldfarb et al., 2020; Levorson et al., 2021). Again, mere translation of the generic English message failed to account for unique constraints for Hispanic populations as the situation unfolded over time and across locations.

Although it is promising to see how much attention the U.S. CDC gave to specific actionable instructions, the instructions were generic word-for-word translations of the English version for holidays and small gatherings. Again, telling readers to consider the number of COVID-19 cases in their community when deciding whether to host or attend a gathering and to monitor hosts and guests for symptoms does not speak to the unique norms of Hispanic cultures regarding the importance of such gatherings in holiday celebrations. Perhaps, for example, action steps that provide specific guidelines regarding how to modify those gatherings in ways that reduce risk rather than simply suggesting not having them at all would have been more effective. Doing so would honor family cohesion as a core value that is prioritized and celebrated in holiday gatherings (Gonzalez & Méndez-Pounds, 2018).

Conclusion

Applied communication in the context of mega-crises such as the COVID-19 pandemic exposes a need to integrate cultural norms and practices as they occur across time and space. Whereas risk situations and crisis events have been explained within clearly demarcated time parameters marked as pre-crisis, crisis, and post-crisis, the COVID-19 pandemic has illuminated limitations of doing so. Pandemics do not necessarily have a clear beginning, middle, and end. As such, our theoretical models and research methods must be expanded to account for why and how communication must adapt over time. Similarly, risk situations and crisis events have been described traditionally as they impact people in a particular geographic location. Again, pandemic communication reveals that doing so is inadequate for informing our understanding and proffering adequate instructional communication. Finally, effective pandemic communication must not only consider changes over time and space, but also tailoring (beyond mere translation) to be effective across cultural and co-cultural people and groups. Clearly, the time has come to expand our research in ways that involve diverse people and groups in decision-making, message design, and engaged dialogue in the form of global communities of practice. If our goal is to use communication to reduce harms and safe lives, doing so is not an option. It is a must.

References

Ahmad, R., & Hillman, S. (2021). Laboring to communicate: Use of migrant languages in COVID-19 awareness campaign in Qatar. *Multilingua, 40*(3), 303–337. https://doi.org/10.1515/multi-2020-0119

Balog-Way, D. H., & McComas, K. A. (2020). COVID-19: Reflections on trust, tradeoffs, and preparedness. *Journal of Risk Research, 23*(7–8), 838–848. https://doi.org/10.1080/13669877.2020.1758192

Center on Budget and Policy Priority. (2022, February 10). *Tracking the COVID-19 economy's effects on food, housing, and employment hardships.* Center on Budget and Policy Priority. https://www.cbpp.org/research/poverty-and-inequality/tracking-the-covid-economys-effects-on-food-housing-and

Center for Disease Control and Prevention. (2020, November 27). *Celebraciones y pequeñas reuniones por las fiestas* [Holiday Celebrations and Small Gatherings]. https://espanol.cdc.gov/coronavirus/2019-ncov/daily-lifecoping/holidays.html

Chen, C., Frey, C. B., & Presidente, G. (2021). Culture and contagion: Individualism and compliance with COVID-19 policy. *Journal of Economic Behavior & Organization, 190,* 191–200.

Cook, J., Sellnow, T. L., Sellnow, D. D., Parrish, A. J., & Soares, R. (2021). Communicating the science of COVID-19 to children: Meet the helpers. In H. D. O'Hair & M. J. O'Hair (Eds.). *Communicating science in times of crisis: The COVID-19 pandemic* (pp. 172–188). John Wiley & Sons.

Cucinotta, D., & Vanelli, M. (2020). WHO declares COVID-19 a pandemic. *Acta Bio-Medica: Atenei Parmensis, 91*(1), 157–160. https://doi.org/10.23750/abm.v91i1.9397

Dutta, M. J., Ban, Z., & Mahuya, P. (2012). Engaging worldviews, cultures, and structures through dialogue: The culture-centred approach to public relations. *Prism, 9*(2), http://www.prismjournal.org/homepage.html

Edwards, A. L., Sellnow, T. L., Sellnow, D. D., Iverson, J., Parrish, A., & Dritz, S. (2021). Communities of practice as purveyors of instructional communication during crises. *Communication Education, 70*(1), 49–70. https://doi.org/10.1080/03634523.2020.1802053

Elkafrawi, D., Sisti, G., Mercado, F., Rodriguez, B., Joseph, J., Jones, C.,... & Upadhyay, R. (2022). Hispanic race is a risk factor for COVID-19 during pregnancy: Data from an urban New York City hospital. *Journal of Obstetrics and Gynaecology,* 1–4. https://doi.org/10.1080/01443615.2021.1998890

Enke, N., & Borchers, N. S. (2019). Social media influencers in strategic communication: A conceptual framework for strategic social media influencer communication. *International Journal of Strategic Communication, 13*(4), 261–277. https://doi.org/10.1080/1553118X.2019.1620234

Fasani, F., & Mazza, J. (2020). *A vulnerable workforce: Migrant workers in the COVID-19 pandemic.* Publications Office of the European Union.

Flores, A., & Lopez, M. (2018, January 11). Among U.S. Latinos, the internet now rivals television as a source for news. *Pew Research Center.* https://www.pewresearch.org/fact-tank/2018/01/11/among-u-s-latinos-the-internet-now-rivals-television-as-a-source-for-news/

Goldfarb, I. T., Clapp, M. A., Soffer, M. D., Shook, L. L., Rushfirth, K., Edlow, A. G.,... & Bryant, A. S. (2020). Prevalence and severity of coronavirus disease 2019 (COVID-19) illness in symptomatic pregnant and postpartum women stratified by Hispanic ethnicity. *Obstetrics and Gynecology, 136*(2), 300. https://doi.org/10.1097/AOG.0000000000004005

Gonzalez, N., & Méndez-Pounds, J. (2018). The impact of acculturation and cultural values on Hispanic immigrants' parenting. *Contemporary Family Therapy, 40*(1), 56–67. https://doi-org/10.1007/s10591-017-9428-8

Hakim, M., Khattak, F. A., Muhammad, S., Ismail, M., Ullah, N., Atiq Orakzai, M.,... & Ul-Haq, Z. (2021). Access and use experience of personal protective equipment among frontline healthcare workers in Pakistan during the COVID-19 emergency: A cross-sectional study. *Health Security, 19*(2), 140–149. https://doi.org/10.1089/hs.2020.0142

Helsloot, I., Boin, A., Jacobs, B., & Comfort, L. K. (2012). *Mega-crises: Understanding the prospects, nature, characteristics, and the effects of cataclysmic events.* Charles C. Thomas Publisher.

Jacobs, R. J., Ownby, R. L., Acevedo, A., Waldrop-Valverde, D. (2017). A qualitative study examining health literacy and chronic illness self-management in Hispanic and non-Hispanic older adults. *Journal of Multidisciplinary Healthcare, 2017*(10), 167–177. https://doi.org/10.2147/JMDH.S135370

Johansson, B., Lane, D. R., Sellnow, D. D., & Sellnow, T. L. (2021). No heat, no electricity, no water, oh no!: An IDEA model experiment in instructional risk communication. *Journal of Risk Research, 24*(12), 1576–1588. https://doi.org/10.1080/13669877.2021.1894468

Krogstad, M., Stepler, R., & Lopez, M. (2015, May 12). English proficiency on the rise among latinos. *Pew Research Center.* https://www.pewresearch.org/hispanic/2015/05/12/english-proficiency-on-the-rise-among-latinos/

Lancet, T. (2020). India under COVID-19 lockdown. *Lancet (London, England), 395*(10233), 1315.

Lee, Y., & Li, J. Y. Q. (2021). The role of communication transparency and organizational trust in publics' perceptions, attitudes and social distancing behaviour: A case study of the COVID-19 outbreak. *Journal of Contingencies and Crisis Management, 29*(4), 368–384. https://doi.org/10.1111/1468-5973.12354

Levorson, R. E., Christian, E., Hunter, B., Sayal, J., Sun, J., Bruce, S. A.,... & Hourigan, S. K. (2021). A cross-sectional investigation of SARS-CoV-2 seroprevalence and associated risk factors in children and adolescents in the United States. *PLoS One, 16*(11), e0259823. https://doi.org/10.1371/journal.pone.0259823

Lindlof, T. R., & Taylor, B. C. (2011). *Qualitative communication research methods* (3rd ed.). Sage.

Ma, Y., & Zhan, N. (2022). To mask or not to mask amid the COVID-19 pandemic: How Chinese students in America experience and cope with stigma. *Chinese Sociological Review, 54*(1), 1–26. https://doi.org/10.1080/21620555.2020.1833712

Merrill, S. C., Moegenburg, S., Koliba, C. J., Zia, A., Trinity, L., Clark, E.,... & Smith, J. M. (2019). Willingness to comply with biosecurity in livestock facilities: Evidence from experimental simulations. *Frontiers in Veterinary Science, 6,* 156. https://doi.org/10.3389/fvets.2019.00156

Millar, D. P., & Heath, R. L. (2004). *Responding to crisis: A rhetorical approach to crisis communication.* Routledge.

Ortega, P., Martínez, G., & Diamond, L. (2020). Language and health equity during COVID-19: Lessons and opportunities. *Journal of Health Care for the Poor and Underserved, 31*(4), 1530–1535. https://doi.org/10.1353/hpu.2020.0114

Petrun, E. L., Parker, A. M., Ramchand, R., Finucane, M. L., Parks, V., & Seelam, R. (2019). Reaching vulnerable populations in the disaster-prone US Gulf Coast: Communicating across the crisis lifecycle. *Journal of Emergency Management, 17*(4), 271–286. https://doi.org/10.5055/jem.2019.0426

Piller, I., Zhang, J., & Li, J. (2020). Linguistic diversity in a time of crisis: Language challenges of the COVID-19 pandemic. *Multilingua, 39*(5), 503–515. https://doi.org/10.1515/multi-2020-0136.

Pyrko, I., Dörfler, V., & Eden, C. (2019). Communities of practice in landscapes of practice. *Management Learning, 50*(4), 482–499. https://doi.org/10.1177/1350507619860854

Robinson, H. (2021). *Community ambassador real equality–Developing Spanish bilingual, bicultural COVID-19 health ambassadors in rural Western North Carolina: A case study.* https://doi.org/10.17615/brq6-9h57

Rogers, T. N., Rogers, C. R., VanSant-Webb, E., Gu, L. Y., Yan, B., & Qeadan, F. (2020). Racial disparities in COVID-19 mortality among essential workers in the United States. *World Medical & Health Policy, 12*(3), 311–327. https://doi.org/10.1002/wmh3.358.

Salazar, S. E. (2021). *The IDEA Model as an effective instructional crisis and risk communication framework to analyze the CDC's messages aimed at Hispanics in the COVID-19 era.* https://doi.org/10.30658/icrcc.2021.11

Sellnow, T. L., & Seeger, M. W. (2020). *Theorizing crisis communication* (2nd ed.). Wiley.

Sellnow, D. D., Johansson, B., Sellnow, T. L., & Lane, D. R. (2019a). Toward a global understanding of the effects of the IDEA model for designing instructional risk and crisis messages: A food contamination experiment in Sweden. *Contingencies and Crisis Management, 9*(27), 102–115. https://doi/org/10.1111/1468-5973.12234

Sellnow, T. L., Parker, J. S., Sellnow, D. D., Littlefield, R. R., Helsel, E. M., Getchell, M. C., Smith, J. M., & Merrill, S. C. (2017). Improving biosecurity through instructional crisis communication: Lessons learned from the PEDv outbreak. *Journal of Applied Communications, 101*(4). COVC+. https://link.gale.com/apps/doc/A568258225/AONE?u=anon~10762218&sid=googleScholar&xid=06b4e1d4

Sellnow, D. D., Jones, L. M., Sellnow, T. L., Spence, P., Lane, D. R., & Haarstad, N. (2019b). The IDEA model as a conceptual framework for designing earthquake early warning (EEW) messages distributed via mobile phone apps. In J. Santos-Reyes (Ed.). *Earthquakes – Impact, Community Vulnerability and Resilience* (pp. 11–20). InTechOpen. doi: 10.5772/intechopen.85557

Sellnow-Richmond, D., George, A., & Sellnow, D. (2018). An IDEA model analysis of instructional risk communication messages in the time of Ebola. *Journal of International Crisis and Risk Communication Research, 1*(1), 135–165. Doi: 10.30658/jicrcr.1.1.7

Sellnow, D. D., & Sellnow, T. L. (2019). The IDEA model for effective instructional risk and crisis communication by emergency managers and other key spokespersons. *Journal of Emergency Management, 17*(1), 67–78.

Sellnow, D. D., Sellnow, T. L., & Martin, J. M. (2019c). Strategic message convergence in communicating biosecurity: The case of the 2013 porcine epidemic diarrhea virus. *Communication Reports, 32*(3), 125–136. https://doi.org/10.1080/13669877.2017.1422787.

Sellnow, T. L., Sellnow, D. D., & Reis, C. D. (2021). Calming giants in the earth: The internalization, distribution, explanation, and action (IDEA) model as strategic communication in crises with competing narratives. In Y. Jin, B. H. Re3ber, & G. J. Nowak (Eds.), *Advancing Crisis Communication Effectiveness* (pp. 198–213). Routledge.

Spence, P. R., Lachlan, K. A., & Griffin, D. R. (2007). Crisis communication, race, and natural disasters. *Journal of Black Studies, 37*(4), 539–554. https://doi.org/10.1177/0021934706296192

Spence, P. R., Lachlan, K. A., & Burke, J. A. (2011). Differences in crisis knowledge across age, race, and socioeconomic status during Hurricane Ike: A field test and extension of the knowledge gap hypothesis. *Communication Theory, 21*(3), 261–278. https://doi.org/10.1111/j.1468-2885.2011.01385.x

Sullum, J. (2020, April 1). What's up with all the contradictory advice about COVID-19 and face masks? *Reason.* https://reason.com/2020/04/01/whats-up-with-all-the-contradictory-advice-about-covid-19-and-face-masks

Taylor, D. B. (2021, March 17). A timeline of the coronavirus pandemic. *The New York Times.* https://www.nytimes.com/article/coronavirus-timeline.html

Tso, R. V., & Cowling, B. J. (2020). Importance of face masks for COVID-19: A call for effective public education. *Clinical Infectious Diseases, 71*(16), 2195–2198. https://doi.org/10.1093/cid/ciaa593

Ulmer, R. R., Sellnow, R. L., & Seeger, M. W. (2019). *Effective crisis communication: Moving from crisis to opportunity* (4th ed.). Sage.

Vijaykumar, S., Jin, Y., Rogerson, D., Lu, X., Sharma, S., Maughan, A.,... & Morris, D. (2021). How shades of truth and age affect responses to COVID-19 (Mis) information: Randomized survey experiment among WhatsApp users in UK and Brazil. *Humanities and Social Sciences Communications, 8*(1), 1–12. https://doi.org/10.1057/s41599-021-00752-7

World Health Organization. (2022, May 1). *Weekly epidemiological update on COVID-19-4-May-2022.* https://www.who.int/publicaions/m/item/weekly-epidemiological-update-on-covid-19-4-may-2022

Zillmann, D. (1999). Exemplification theory: Judging the whole by some of its parts. *Media Psychology, 1*, 69–94. https://doi.org/10.1207/s1532785xmep0101_5

9

INTERPRETING THE INTERPERSONAL

Crisis Communication Insights for Pandemics

Brooke Fisher Liu and Abbey Blake Levenshus

Pandemics, like other mega-crises, are highly disruptive events that jeopardize communities' well-being and safety. They can be long-lasting, deadly, and traverse the globe. For instance, estimates indicate that the COVID-19 pandemic has taken more than 5 million lives (World Health Organization, 2022). The pandemic has caused deep recessions, which will "leave lasting scars through lower investment, an erosion in human capital through lost work and schooling, and fragmentation of global trade and supply linkages" (World Bank, 2021, p. 3).

With this devastation come opportunities for renewal. Crises offer opportunities for communities to become more resilient, in part because individuals reconnect with family and friends (Dutta-Bergman, 2004b; Houston et al., 2017; Houston & Franken, 2015). Such interpersonal communication often plays an essential role in spreading helpful crisis information and supporting protective action decision-making (Ahn et al., 2020; Cho et al., 2021; Clarke & McComas, 2012; Liu et al., 2016). Despite the recognized importance of interpersonal communication in crises, few studies have focused on theorizing the central role of interpersonal crisis communication (Liu & Viens, 2020). Likewise, the broader field of interpersonal communication has not emphasized connections with crisis communication as evidenced by the scant references to risk, crisis, and disaster in interpersonal communication handbooks (e.g., Antos et al., 2008; Berger, 2014; Berger & Roloff, 2019; Knapp & Daly, 2010b).

In this chapter, we review the state of theory and applied knowledge on interpersonal crisis communication with a focus on pandemics. In brief, interpersonal communication is the "study of social interaction between people" (Berger & Roloff, 2019, p. 277). Scholars have found it difficult to define interpersonal communication because it constantly changes (Knapp & Daly, 2010a). For example, Berger and Roloff (2019) noted that interpersonal

DOI: 10.4324/9781003214496-9

communication research and theory have evolved from a focus on a face-to-face communication process toward a more comprehensive view of social interaction that can be mediated through communication technologies such as computers, social media, and mobile phones. The rising use of interactive online communication tools has led to mass communication and interpersonal communication "rapidly converging" and increasing research attention on the "generation-old call to integrate mass and interpersonal perspectives on communication" (Flanagin, 2017, p. 450).

In addition to research on new and social media, health communication has emerged over the past 30 years of interpersonal communication research as one of the "most rapidly growing and interesting topics in the field," typically emphasizing the provider-patient relationship and communication dyad (Thompson et al., 2010, p. 633). This expansion of scope and potential for overlaps with other fields and disciplines provides more opportunities for pandemic communication researchers and practitioners to learn from and contribute to interpersonal communication research. In that vein, we conclude the chapter with recommendations for filling critical knowledge gaps. In the next section, we review the state of theory on connecting interpersonal and crisis communication.

Emerging Theoretical Approaches Connecting Interpersonal and Crisis Communication

The existing theoretical landscape of interpersonal crisis communication is largely uncharted. After reviewing interpersonal communication handbooks over the last 20 years (e.g., Antos et al., 2008; Berger, 2014; Berger & Roloff, 2019; Knapp & Daly, 2010a), crisis communication, generally, and pandemics, specifically, were not explicitly included or referenced. Tangential concepts were present, and useful connections can certainly be made. In fact, our exploration reveals a great deal of promise exists for harnessing interpersonal communication knowledge and bringing it into conversation with pandemic communicators and scholars. As scholars have noted, more work needs to focus on practical applications so that risk and crisis theorizing can truly benefit society (Balog-Way et al., 2020; Liu & Viens, 2020). In answer to those calls, we first summarize three major implications from interpersonal crisis communication theory and research that is applicable to pandemics. Specifically, we focus on interpersonal communication implications for crisis message design, crisis information seeking and processing, and community resilience.

Message Design

Researchers have just begun to examine the roles of interpersonal communication in crisis message design. This work focuses on three areas: subjective norms, corrective communication, and fear appeals. While formal theories have yet to be developed, the research findings and related concepts summarized below present promising areas for future theorizing about the role of interpersonal communication in pandemic (and other crisis) contexts.

Subjective Norms

Expectations from others (i.e., subjective norms) can motivate risk information seeking and sharing for members of the public and medical professionals (Ahn et al., 2020; Cho et al., 2021; Clarke & McComas, 2012), especially when risk information is sparse and/or conflicting (Hu & Zhang, 2014). For both the MERS-CoV outbreak and the COVID-19 pandemic, expectations from close interpersonal connections were predictive of South Korean adults' risk information seeking and sharing (Ahn et al., 2020; Kim & Hong, 2021). In the case of US healthcare providers, perceived social pressure from co-workers and colleagues to remain informed about influenza vaccination was a strong predictor of physicians' and nurses' information seeking and systematic processing of vaccination information (Clarke & McComas, 2012).

Expectations from others can also influence adoption of protective actions. In the case of the COVID-19 pandemic in the United States, social norms negatively moderated the relationship between perceived effectiveness and social distancing behavior, with this relationship strongest for students with social networks that expressed uncertainty about social distancing (Jiang et al., 2021). Relatedly, messages that emphasize benefits to others, rather than individual benefits, can positively influence protective actions. For the avian flu pandemic, messages that centered vaccination benefits on loved ones (compared to individuals) were more successful at increasing US adults' intentions to seek more information and obtain the vaccine (Kelly & Hornik, 2016).

Given these findings, messages should emphasize that "there is an expectation within families and social groups that individuals will do their part to keep the group healthy and that sharing helpful information about health risks is an expected way to do that" (Ahn et al., 2020, p. 957). Motivating productive information seeking and sharing during pandemics can help combat misinformation, as further discussed below.

Corrective Communication

Given the prevalence of misinformation during pandemics, researchers have begun to investigate how interpersonal communication can combat misinformation through the lens of corrective communication. Emerging research finds members of social networks can employ corrective communication to refute false or misleading health information with appropriate sources. Such corrective communication can limit misperceptions for both high and low conspiracy belief individuals (Bode & Vraga, 2018) and provide support for organizational responses (Jin et al., 2020). Corrections can also come from journalists and other expert sources on social media during pandemics (Bode & Vraga, 2018). When public health authorities include other expert sources in their corrective messages, these messages are more effective at correcting misperceptions and motivating appropriate public protective action taking (van der Meer & Jin, 2020). We next turn to a discussion of fear appeals.

Fear Appeals

Fear appeals are controversial in that there are some ethical concerns about the appropriateness of amplifying fear as a persuasive strategy for government communicators. Consequently, fact-based educational approaches are considered less controversial and risky (Liu et al., 2020). Fear appeals can also generate narratives of panic, which can detract from public health goals. Such was the case for the redistribution of media panic narratives about the Ebola pandemic on Reddit (Kilgo et al., 2019). Nevertheless, there are some benefits to fear appeals in terms of motivating appropriate behavioral responses to risky situations, especially when fear appeals are combined with efficacy statements (Tannenbaum et al., 2015).

In the context of the Zika pandemic, messages that arouse moderate and high levels of fear through sensationalism (e.g., use of phrases like killer virus and close-up images of blood-filled mosquitos) increased public engagement with English-language Facebook messages (Ali et al., 2019). Fear appeals have also motivated US adults to acquire and transmit information about infectious disease outbreaks to their social networks (Chon & Park, 2021; Li, 2021). In turn, fear appeals, coupled with strong organizational-public relationships, predicted US adults' willingness to follow instructions from public health authorities during an infectious disease outbreak (Chon & Park, 2021). Unfortunately, messages in online social networks about pandemics often do not include efficacy information to help individuals understand how to protect themselves and loved ones (Ali et al., 2019), presenting an opportunity for future public health interventions.

Information Seeking and Processing

Given that interpersonal communication focuses on social interactions, researchers have examined the effects of such interactions on people's information seeking and processing, including in crisis situations. Three relevant areas related to this research include the influences of prior expectations, the desire to reduce or manage uncertainty, and the role and use of different media types. In these areas researchers have developed and tested theories that apply to interpersonal communication about pandemics and other crisis contexts.

Influences of Prior Expectations

Expectations can influence interactions between organizations and their publics during crises. Organizations must gauge their publics' expectations of them and then meet those expectations as part of their efforts to manage their organization-public relationships and reputation (Cho et al., 2021). As noted in the earlier section focused on message design, others' expectations can also motivate risk information seeking and sharing. Expectancy Violations Theory (EVT), rooted in interpersonal communication, originated as an attempt to understand what happens when an individual's nonverbal behaviors violate proxemic expectations (individual use of personal space) (Burgoon et al., 2011). Over time the theory expanded to include other nonverbal behaviors (Burgoon, 1991) and eventually online mediated communication contexts (Ramirez & Wang, 2008). Expectancies are defined as "enduring patterns of anticipated nonverbal (and verbal) behavior – about others' communication" that are typically rooted in social norms and prior knowledge of the other entity's typical behavior (Burgoon et al., 2022, p. 280). EVT holds that in any interaction, both parties hold and bring to the interaction those prior-held expectancies.

Crisis researchers have applied EVT to study how expectations can be violated or confirmed in positive or negative ways along a continuum, which has implications for crisis audiences' perceptions of the organization (e.g., Lee et al., 2018; Sohn & Lariscy, 2015; Tao, 2018), online social media communication about and interaction with organizations (Bogomoletc & Lee, 2021), and relational outcomes (e.g., Kim, 2014). EVT provides a framework for examining the critical, but under-studied pre-crisis phase (Lee et al., 2018). Corporate social responsibility crises can backfire on organizations with strong prior reputations (Cho et al., 2021; Kim, 2014; Sohn & Lariscy, 2015; Tao, 2018). When stakeholders come in with higher expectations based on an accrued perception of positive reputation, a CSR crisis can draw outsized attention to these negative cues – above and beyond what stakeholders might perceive related to a crisis in an organization for which they previously held neutral or negative reputational perceptions (Lee et al., 2018; Sohn & Lariscy, 2015). Strong organization-public relationships could help temper such impacts. For example, an experimental study in the context of the 2010 BP Oil Spill crisis found pre-existing strong organization-public relationships between stakeholders and BP reduced expectancy violations (Kim, 2014). Organizations should focus on "increasing relational satisfaction through substantial commitments rather than raising unrealistic expectations with empty promotions" that could be easily violated in a crisis (Kim, 2014, p. 152). In an unpredictable and long-lasting pandemic, setting realistic expectations may be especially critical.

Expectancy violations can also work the other way – with positive violations drawing increased attention from publics and generating positive reevaluations. A case study of Steak-Umms, a producer of frozen sliced beef, used EVT to help explain why the company's unexpected tweets about COVID-19 and information literacy earned widespread positive attention from online audiences and substantial news media coverage (Bogomoletc & Lee, 2021). On April 6, 2020, the Steak-Umms Twitter account shared a thread about credible data and how to tell the difference between truth and misinformation about COVID-19. It continued to share such posts, and tweets about the company expressed praise and pleasant surprise as well as comments about the company's unexpected leader and expressions of purchase intentions.

In sum, EVT offers cautionary tales for crisis communicators that strong prior reputations can backfire should a crisis violate stakeholder expectations (Lee et al., 2018; Sohn & Lariscy, 2015; Tao, 2018). It also provides evidence that crisis communicators may want to consider including communication partners that would trigger positive expectancy violations and arouse more attention to pandemic messaging (Bogomoletc & Lee, 2021). And as Lee et al. (2018) noted, organizations must work to ascertain in ongoing ways what their publics' expectations are for them, so they can gauge whether their actions and messages will be congruent or in violation of those expectations.

Desire to Reduce or Manage Uncertainty

Multiple scholars have applied Uncertainty Reduction Theory (URT) to organizational settings to better understand information-seeking behaviors following a crisis (e.g., Boyle et al., 2004; Grace & Tham, 2021; Kubey & Peluso, 1990; Procopio & Procopio, 2007). This interpersonal-based theory initially focused on explaining strangers' interpersonal interactions and their desire to seek information that would reduce uncomfortable uncertainty between individuals in an initial encounter (Berger & Calabrese, 1975).

The theory expanded to apply its underlying principles to mass communication where such information sources serve to reduce post-crisis uncertainty. In a study of information seeking following the terrorist attacks of September 11, 2001, Boyle et al. (2004) did indeed find that individuals with high amounts of negative affect worked harder to reduce uncertainty (and perhaps negative feelings) by seeking information about the terrorist attacks. More recently, Grace and Tham (2021) applied the theory to COVID-19, analyzing pandemic communication from the City of Lubbock, Texas. The three stages of URT – entry, personal, and exit – were observed with corresponding messages, frequency, and information-seeking behaviors from their residents. COVID crisis communicators were urged to adopt URT-centered user design approaches for communicating with citizens trying to mitigate their uncertainty and risk.

Given criticism that uncertainty may not always be desirable or possible to reduce, Uncertainty Management Theory (UMT) was developed to broaden the concept of uncertainty to a state of mind in which people do not feel secure in their circumstances regardless of the information they have received (Brashers, 2001). UMT holds that uncertainty itself is neither inherently good nor bad, and people's perception of uncertainty can change over time based on the circumstances (Brashers, 2001; Bylund et al., 2012). In a study of undergraduate university student parents' uncertainty management strategies, Scharp et al. (2021) identified the concept of "uncertainty flooding" that can overwhelm people who find themselves in complex or long-term situations where uncertainty becomes the "new normal" and cannot be easily resolved (p. 1078). Pandemics and mega-crises could result in uncertainty flooding. For the university student parents, instead of always seeking to reduce uncertainty, they sought to manage it in healthy ways such as normalizing the uncertainty and taking a break from it (Scharp et al., 2021). The authors noted these strategies align with Buzzanell's (2010) community theory of resilience discussed later in this chapter.

Role and Use of Different Media Types

Today's information seekers have access to more ways to gather information than perhaps in any time in history (Rains & Ruppel, 2016). Interpersonal communication research can also provide helpful insights into how and why crisis stakeholders seek and process information. In the wake of the September 11, 2001 terrorist attacks, Americans sought sources that complemented and satisfied their needs for information and social support (Dutta-Bergman, 2004b). Those findings prompted the development of the Theory of Channel Complementarity (TCC), which posited that individuals would seek out any sources that fulfill their content needs (Dutta-Bergman, 2004a,b). That theory, however, was limited in its application or predictive ability (Ruppel & Rains, 2012). In a health context, information seeking is more likely to be systematic and based on four complementary source characteristics: access to medical expertise, tailorability (to the specific context or situation), anonymity (ability to seek information without revealing one's identity), and convenience (Rains & Ruppel, 2016; Ruppel & Rains, 2012). When participants in the survey were exposed to relatively greater threats, they were more likely to prioritize sources high in access to medical expertise complementarity and anonymity complementarity than participants exposed to lower threats (Rains & Ruppel, 2016). Beyond message design, crisis communicators in a pandemic or health-related crisis could use these source characteristics to guide media planning decisions. Threat level has frequently been identified as a factor driving media source selection in pandemic scenarios. In the worst phase of the 2009 Chinese H1N1 outbreak, people's interpersonal network dependency dropped to its lowest level with very low overall use compared to other channels such as television, print media, and the Internet (Hu & Zhang, 2014).

Community Resilience

Buzzanell (2010, p. 1) was the first to define resilience for the communication discipline, noting human resilience is "the ability to bounce back or reintegrate after difficult life experiences" through communicative processes such as crafting normalcy and maintaining networks. In the crisis context, Houston (2018) defined a resilient community as "not simply a grouping of resilient individuals or organizations, but a collection of people and groups who are able to interact successfully to facilitate adoption as a whole" (Houston, 2018, p. 19). In particular, conversations among friends, family, and neighbors can foster community resilience, a sense of neighborhood belonging after crises, and correct rumors (Houston et al., 2017; Spialek & Houston, 2019). Storytelling among friends, family, and neighbors similarly contributes to resilience and perceptions of neighborhood belonging after US natural disasters (Spialek & Houston, 2019). In the context of the COVID-19 pandemic, higher levels of social resources, including conversations with friends and family, are associated with lower levels of physical and mental distress among South Korean adults (Ihm & Lee, 2021).

Interpersonal crisis communication can also have a dark side when it comes to resilience. In the U.S. tornado context, Houston and Franken (2015) found those with post-traumatic stress syndrome were more likely to have talked with neighbors and attended community meetings about a deadly tornado. In the case of the Fukushima nuclear disaster, interpersonal communication had benefits and drawbacks for Japanese survivors. On the negative side, interpersonal communication stigmatized survivors, leading to extreme social isolation and other dire consequences (Kwesell & Jung, 2019). On the plus side, interpersonal communication contributed to stronger relationships with supportive friends and family (Kwesell & Jung, 2019).

Clearly, interpersonal communication can have positive and negative effects when it comes to resilience. More research is needed to unpack these findings, especially outside of the natural disaster context. It may be that providing community members with resources to form their own messages could contribute to community pandemic resilience, as Spialek and Houston (2019) recommended for the natural disaster context. Some research supports this hypothesis, as discussed earlier.

Discussion and Future Research Directions

Effective communication is essential for saving lives during public health crises like pandemics (Reynolds & Seeger, 2005). To date, the majority of crisis communication theorizing has focused on organizational rather than interpersonal communication (Liu & Viens, 2020; Manias-Muñoz et al., 2019). However, research clearly shows the central role of interpersonal communication in processing crisis information, especially when there is low trust in authorities, high crisis uncertainty, and/or official information is sparse (Jang & Baek, 2019; Meadows et al., 2019). Here we offer our recommendations for future research in order to harness the potential power of peer-to-peer crisis communication for community resilience.

More Theory on Interpersonal Crisis Communication

As this chapter has indicated, the interpersonal crisis communication landscape has not been well charted from an organizational or community crisis perspective. As such, more application of interpersonal communication theories would be welcome. This section urges such exploration based on three key reasons.

Inter-Audience Interpersonal Communication

Theories like URT (e.g., Boyle et al., 2004; Grace & Tham, 2021) and EVT (e.g., Bogomoletc & Lee, 2021; Kim, 2014; Lee et al., 2018) originated in interpersonal communication and were later applied to crisis communication. These theories made the jump from person to person to person to organization. Clearly, there are blurred lines and levels between individual, group, team, family, neighbors, organizations, institutions, communities, and societies. Pandemics challenge these levels given that they represent a public health crisis with far-reaching impacts at all levels. Understanding more clearly the role of interpersonal communication at each of these levels can make pandemic communication more effective. Crisis communication is often focused on the audience, public or stakeholder group. However, each of these groupings is made up of individuals and dyads. Similarly, individuals are typically part of larger groups that bring their own norms and expectations. Future research should investigate inter-audience interpersonal communication to further tease out the various interpersonal communication interactions that occur before, during, and after pandemics with a goal of harnessing the positive power of interpersonal communication for community resilience.

Interpersonal Intersections within the Digital Media Landscape

Interpersonal communication's disciplinary boundaries have expanded as more communication among individuals has moved to digital channels – including social media. Scholars have emphasized that fragmentation of the media landscape has increased the need to examine interpersonal communication (e.g., Ali et al., 2019; Liu & Viens, 2020; Park et al., 2019). Future theoretical research could benefit both increased integration of interpersonal communication related to information sources and information seeking – including why individuals may seek and process risk information differently via different interpersonal networks. Park et al. (2019) encouraged crisis messaging to emphasize interpersonal networks' importance for helping individuals prepare for a crisis as well as how friends and family can encourage others to prepare and help them to do so. Starting with the natural overlap of social media and offline interpersonal communication could allow researchers to better understand the importance of messages that include supportive communication, nonverbal expressions, and appropriate emotions during pandemics and other large-scale crises.

Widening the Emotional Spectrum

While crisis communicators have increasingly emphasized the role of emotion (e.g., Jin et al., 2016; Kim & Hong, 2021), interpersonal communication researchers have a longer history of studying emotions like shame, jealousy, sadness, guilt, and anger. As such, interpersonal crisis communication theory development could pull in a wider range of emotions beyond fear. This emphasis on emotion could be useful for pandemics that can result in loss of life and trigger myriad emotions. Various communities or sociodemographic groups can be disproportionately impacted and may experience different emotions or severity of feelings (Philibin et al., 2019). Understanding such inequalities and post-traumatic stress's influence on interpersonal communication behaviors could be instructive for predicting and explaining pandemic communication (Houston & Franken, 2015).

More Longitudinal Research

The vast majority of the current research provides a snapshot rather than an understanding of longitudinal effects of interpersonal crisis communication. A lack of longitudinal research is a well-recognized gap in the broader crisis communication literature (Liu & Viens, 2020). In the context of pandemics, this gap is especially noteworthy given that many pandemics last months and even years. As such, there is ample opportunity to conduct longitudinal research to better understand how interpersonal communication can help communities survive future long-term crises. While communication campaigns often have fixed beginnings, designated insertion orders of messages, and scheduled targeted messages, interpersonal communication among friends and family can happen in a more natural, ongoing way. Such longitudinal research work could take a variety of methodological approaches including surveys, ethnography, and in-depth interviews.

More Health Disparities Research

Minimal empirical research focuses on the roles of interpersonal communication in overcoming health disparities, despite the well-known disproportionate impacts of crises like the COVID-19 pandemic on disadvantaged populations (Hull et al., 2020). In a rare exception to this research gap, Day et al. (2019) found that African American residents favored interpersonal networks for information and resources during the Flint, Michigan clean water crisis. Furthermore, African Americans had higher information needs than their White counterparts. This knowledge can help guide crisis communication strategy to reach disadvantaged populations. Currently, some researchers are taking creative approaches to deploying interpersonal crisis communication interventions in response to the COVID-19 pandemic. For instance, the "shots at the shop" intervention harnesses conversations between barbers/stylists and their clients in communities of color to stay safe against COVID-19 (University of Maryland, 2021). Additional research innovation is needed to understand how to best support those who are most vulnerable during pandemics.

More Research on Expert Populations

Only a handful of studies have examined interpersonal crisis communication among experts such as journalists, emergency managers, scientists, and health-care providers (Liu & Atwell Seate, 2021; Liu et al., 2018; McLean & Power, 2014). This research reveals traditional theorizing might not be the best fit for all organizational contexts. Clearly more research is needed to understand the role of interpersonal crisis communication among experts. Future research could explore topics such as how these experts build and sustain relationships. Other promising avenues for future research are how to navigate interpersonal conflict when experts disagree on the best public guidance, and the effects of mixed guidance on publics' responses to pandemics.

More Research on the Dark Side of Interpersonal Communication

Researchers have begun to unpack the benefits of interpersonal crisis communication. These benefits include increasing community resilience and neighborhood belonging after natural disasters (Houston et al., 2017; Spialek & Houston, 2019) and reducing social isolationism and fatalism during pandemics (Ngien & Jiang, 2021). In their review of interpersonal communication, Berger and Roloff (2019) discussed ten fundamental interpersonal communication processes, including deception, bargaining and negotiation, conflict management, and conversation management. Each of these processes has the potential for negative or harmful behaviors and outcomes. Yet, much less research has investigated the potential dark side of interpersonal communication such as spreading harmful rumors, stigmatizing crisis survivors, and contributing to crisis burnout (Kwesell & Jung, 2019; Tang & Zou, 2021). We call for researchers to consider both the prosocial and detrimental impacts of interpersonal crisis communication in future work.

More Message Testing

Scholars have just begun to integrate interpersonal factors like subjective norms into crisis message research (e.g., Clarke & McComas, 2012; Kelly & Hornik, 2016). We echo the call to design and test messages that emphasize the importance of friends and family helping each other to prepare for health crises (Park et al., 2019). We also call for research that integrates interpersonal factors into crisis response and recovery message testing. Importantly, such research needs to consider the cultural context given that collectivistic cultures may be more open to this messaging approach than individualistic cultures, as suggested in prior COVID-19 research (Kim & Hong, 2021). Future research also should consider whether messages that integrate interpersonal factors perform differently for lay audiences (e.g., members of the public) and experts (e.g., healthcare providers). Equally important is to consider how other demographic differences influence message effects such as information seeking/sharing, attitudes, and behaviors. Additionally, research should examine message sources. For instance, do messages that integrate interpersonal factors perform better when they come from friends and family members than when they come from public health authorities?

More Global Research

As noted above, pandemics are dynamic and traverse countries and continents. Yet studies on interpersonal crisis communication tend to focus on a single country and cultural context. Social media and other channels can facilitate interpersonal communication with global friends and family during pandemics. Clearly, there is a need for more cross-national and cross-cultural pandemic research, reflecting a pervasive research gap in the broader risk and crisis communication literature (Diers-Lawson & Meissner, 2021; Liu & Viens, 2020). We also echo the need for more research that simultaneously examines multiple infectious disease outbreak types across a variety of cultural contexts (Jin et al., 2021). Specifically, we call for more research to understand how global interpersonal communication can provide social support, as well as the potential for misinformation spread, stigma, and other negative outcomes.

Conclusion

The COVID-19 pandemic reminded the world that crises are unpredictable. This unpredictable nature, coupled with the fact that no two events are the same, challenges theorizing and generating applicable insights for practice. As we have seen with COVID-19, the megaphones and mass efforts to persuade Americans to get vaccinated worked for some and not for others. A July 19, 2021 *New York Times* article described three themes found in Kaiser Family Foundation poll data about why initially skeptical Americans had decided to get vaccinated. One of three reasons was hearing directly from people they knew like doctors, friends, and relatives. As the article noted, "continued grassroots campaigns may have a bigger effect at this stage than public-service ad campaigns" (Leonhardt, 2021).

Winning the war on COVID-19, or any global pandemic, requires reaching these individuals, and interpersonal communication knowledge may be a critical key to understanding that process. In this chapter, we have centered the role of interpersonal communication with an emphasis on pandemics and other mega-crises. Our goal has been to shed light on trends at the intersection of interpersonal and crisis communication research in order to inform future theorizing and practice. A long-tailed and wide-armed pandemic like COVID-19 is a formidable opponent requiring all of the communication weapons we can amass. Walther (2017) said, "If new media bring together processes that were formerly ascribed to mass or interpersonal domains, theoretical integration requires us to recognize those essential processes now co-occur, manifest, emerge, interact, and affect one another in any particular setting" (p. 559). To that end, we must continue to bring crisis communication scholars into conversation with interpersonal communication research so that, with additional work, we can help individuals and the global community be better prepared for the next pandemic.

References

Ahn, J., Kahlor, L. A., & Noh, G-Y. (2020). Outbreak! Socio-cognitive motivators of risk information sharing during the 2018 South Korea MERS-CoV epidemic. *Journal of Risk Research*, *23*(7–8), 945–961. https://doi.org/10.1080/13669877.2020.1800065

Ali, K., Zain-ul-abdin, K., Li, C., Johns, L., Ali, A. A., & Carcioppolo, N. (2019). Viruses going viral: Impact of fear-arousing sensationalist social media messages under user engagement. *Science Communication*, *4*(3), 314–338. https://doi.org/10.1177%2F1075547019846124

Antos, G., Ventola, E., & Weber, T. (2008). *Handbook of interpersonal communication*. Walter de Gruyter. https://doi.org/10.1515/9783110211399

Balog-Way, D., McComas, K., & Besley, J. (2020). The evolving field of risk communication. *Risk Analysis*, *40*(S1), 2240–2262. https://doi.org/10.1111/risa.13615

Berger, C. R. (Ed.). (2014). *Interpersonal communication* (Ser. *Handbooks of Communication Science*, v. 6). De Gruyter Mouton. https://doi.org/10.1515/9783110276794

Berger, C. R., & Calabrese, R. J. (1975). Some explorations in initial interaction and beyond: Toward a developmental theory of interpersonal communication. *Human Communication Research*, *1*(2), 99–112. https://doi.org/10.1111/j.1468-2958.1975.tb00258.x

Berger, C. R., & Roloff, M. E. (2019). Interpersonal communication. In D. W. Stacks, M. B. Salwen, & K. C. Eichhorn (Eds.), *An integrated approach to communication theory and research* (3rd ed., pp. 277–291). Routledge. https://doi.org/10.4324/9780203710753-24

Bode, L., & Vraga, E. K. (2018). See something, say something: Correction of global health misinformation on social media. *Health Communication*, *33*(9), 1131–1140. https://doi.org/10.1080/10410236.2017.1331312

Bogomoletc, E., & Lee, N. M. (2021). Frozen meat against COVID-19 misinformation: An analysis of Steak-Umm and positive expectancy violations. *Journal of Business & Technical Communication*, *35*(1), 118–125. https://doi.org/10.1177/1050651920959187

Boyle, M. P., Schmierbach, M., Armstrong, C. L., McLeod, D. M., Shah, D. V., & Pan, Z. (2004). Information seeking and emotional reactions to the September 11 terrorist attacks. *Journalism & Mass Communication Quarterly*, *81*(1), 155–167. https://doi.org/10.1177/107769900408100111

Brashers, D. E. (2001). Communication and uncertainty management. *Journal of Communication, 51*(3), 477–497. https://doi.org/10.1111/j.1460-2466.2001.tb02892.x

Burgoon, J. K. (1991). Relational message interpretations of touch, conversational distance, and posture. *Journal of Nonverbal Behavior, 15*(4), 233–259. https://doi.org/10.1007/BF00986924

Burgoon, J. K., Guerrero, L. K., & Manusov, V. (2011). Nonverbal signals. In M. L. Knapp & J. A. Daly (Eds.), *The Sage handbook of interpersonal communication* (4th ed., pp. 239–280). Sage.

Burgoon, J. K., Manusov, V., & Guerrero, L. K. (2022). *Nonverbal communication* (2nd ed.). Routledge.

Buzzanell, P. M. (2010). Resilience: Talking, resisting, and imagining new normalcies into being. *Journal of Communication, 60*(1), 1. https://doi.org/10.1111/j.1460-2466.2009.01469.x

Bylund, C. L., Peterson, E. B., & Cameron, K. A. (2012). A practitioner's guide to interpersonal communication theory: An overview and exploration of selected theories. *Patient Education and Counseling, 87*(3), 261–267. https://doi.org/10.1016/j.pec.2011.10.006

Cho, M., Park, S.-Y., & Kim, S. (2021). When an organization violates public expectations: A comparative analysis of sustainability communication for corporate and nonprofit organizations. *Public Relations Review, 47*(1), 1–9. https://doi.org/10.1016/j.pubrev.2020.101928

Chon, M-G., & Park, H. (2021). Predicting public support for government actions in public health crises: Testing fear, organization-public relationship, and behavioral intention in the framework of the situational theory of problem solving. *Health Communication, 36*(4), 476–486. https://doi.org/10.1080/10410236.2019.1700439

Clarke, C. E., & McComas, K. (2012). Seeking and processing influenza vaccine information: A study of health care workers at a large urban hospital. *Health Communication, 27*(3), 244–256. https://doi.org/10.1080/10410236.2011.578332

Day, A. M., O'Shay-Wallae, S., Seeger, M. W., & McElmurry, S. P. (2019). Informational sources, social media use, and race in the Flint, Michigan, water crisis. *Communication Studies, 70*(3), 352–376. https://doi.org/10.1080/10510974.2019.1567566

Diers-Lawson, A., & Meissner, F. (2021). Editor's essay: Moving beyond Western corporate perspectives: On the need to increase the diversity of risk and crisis communication research. *Journal of International Crisis and Risk Communication Research, 4*(1), 165–176. https://doi.org/10.30658/jicrcr.4.1.6

Dutta-Bergman, M. J. (2004a). Complementarity in consumption of news types across traditional and new media. *Journal of Broadcasting & Electronic Media, 48*(1), 41–60. https://doi.org/10.1207/s15506878jobem4801_3

Dutta-Bergman, M. J. (2004b). Interpersonal communication after 9/11 via telephone and internet: A theory of channel complementarity. *New Media & Society, 6*(5), 659–673. https://doi.org/10.1177%2F146144804047086

Flanagin, A. J. (2017). Online social influence and the convergence of mass and interpersonal communication. *Human Communication Research, 43*(4), 450–463. https://doi.org/10.1111/hcre.12116

Grace, R., & Tham, J. C. K. (2021). Adapting uncertainty reduction theory for crisis communication: Guidelines for technical communicators. *Journal of Business and Technical Communication, 35*(1), 110–117. https://doi.org/10.1177%2F1050651920959188

Houston, J. B. (2018). Community resilience and communication: Dynamic interconnections between and among individuals, families, and organizations. *Journal of Applied Communication Research, 46*(1), 19–22. https://doi.org/10.1080/00909882.2018.1426704

Houston, J. B., & Franken, N. J. (2015). Disaster interpersonal communication and posttraumatic stress following the 2011 Joplin, Missouri, Tornado. *Journal of Loss and Trauma, 20*(3), 195–206. https://doi.org/10.1080/15325024.2013.848614

Houston, J. B., Spialek, M. L., First, J., Stevens, J., & First, N. L. (2017). Individual perceptions of community resilience following the 2011 Joplin Tornado. *Journal of Contingencies and Crisis Management, 25*(4), 354–363. https://doi.org/10.1111/1468-5973.12171

Hu, B., & Zhang, D. (2014). Channel selection and knowledge acquisition during the 2009 Beijing H1N1 flu crisis: A media system dependency theory perspective. *Chinese Journal of Communication, 7*(3), 299–318. http://doi.org/10.1080/17544750.2014.926951

Hull, S., Stevens, R., & Cobb, J. (2020). Masks are the new condoms: Health communication, intersectionality and racial equity in COVID-times. *Health Communication, 35*(14), 1740–1742. https://doi.org/10.1080/10410236.2020.1838095

Ihm, J., & Lee, C.-J. (2021). Toward more effective public health interventions during the COVID-19 pandemic: Suggesting audience segmentation based on social and media resources. *Health Communication, 36*(1), 98–108. https://doi.org/10.1080/10410236.2020.1847450

Jang, K., & Baek, Y. M. (2019). When information from public health officials is untrustworthy: The use of online news, interpersonal networks, and social media during the MERS outbreak in South Korea. *Health Communication, 34*(9), 991–998. https://doi.org/10.1080/10410236.2018.1449552

Jiang, X., Hwang, J., Shah, D. V., Ghosh, S., & Brauer, M. (2021). News attention and social distancing behavior amid COVID-19: How media trust and social norms moderate a mediated relationship. *Health Communication, 37*(6), 768–777. https://doi.org/10.1080/10410236.2020.1868064

Jin, Y., Fraustino, J. D., & Liu, B. F. (2016). The scared, the outraged, and the anxious: How crisis emotions, involvement, and demographics predict publics' conative coping. *International Journal of Strategic Communication, 10*(4), 289–308. https://doi.org/10.1080/1553118X.2016.1160401

Jin, Y., Lee, Y-I, Liu, B. F., Austin, L., & Kim, S. (2021). How college students assess the threat of infectious diseases: Implications for university leaders and health communicators. *Journal of International Crisis and Risk Communication Research, 4*(1), 129–164. https://doi.org/10.30658/jicrcr.4.1.5

Jin, Y., van der Meer, T. G. L. A., Lee, Y.-I., & Lu, X. (2020). The effect of corrective communication and employee backup on the effectiveness of fighting crisis misinformation. *Public Relations Review, 46*(3), 101910. http://doi.org/10.1016/j.pubrev.2020.101910

Kelly, B. J., & Hornik, R. C. (2016). Effects of framing health messages in terms of benefits to loved ones or others: An experimental study. *Health Communication, 31*(10), 1284–1290. http://doi.org/10.1080/10410236.2015.1062976

Kilgo, D. K., Yoo, J., & Johnson, T. J. (2019). Spreading Ebola panic: Newspaper and social media coverage of the 2014 Ebola health crisis. *Health Communication, 34*(8), 811–817. https://doi.org/10.1080/10410236.2018.1437524

Kim, S. (2014). The role of prior expectancies and relational satisfaction in crisis. *Journalism & Mass Communication Quarterly, 91*(1), 139–158. https://doi.org/10.1177/1077699013514413

Kim, H. J., & Hong, H. (2021). Predicting information behaviors in the COVID-19 pandemic: Integrating the role of emotions and subjective norms into the situational theory of problem solving (STOPS) framework. *Health Communication, 37*(6), 768–777. https://doi.org/10.1080/10410236.2021.1911399

Knapp, M. L., & Daly, J. A. (2010a). Background and current trends in the study of interpersonal communication. In M. L. Knapp, & J. A., Daly (Eds.), *The Sage handbook of interpersonal communication.* (4th ed., pp. 3–22). Sage. https://doi. org/10.4135/9781446262238

Knapp, M. L., & Daly, J. A. (2010b). *The Sage handbook of interpersonal communication.* Sage. (4th ed.). http://dx.doi.org/10.4135/9781446262238

Kubey, R. W., & Peluso, T. (1990). Emotional response as a cause of interpersonal news diffusion: The case of the space shuttle tragedy. *Journal of Broadcasting & Electronic Media, 34*(1), 69–76. https://doi.org/10.1080/08838159009386726

Kwesell, A., & Joo-Young Jung. (2019). A multidimensional analysis of stigma: Findings from a qualitative study of Fukushima residents following Japan's 2011 nuclear disaster. *Journal of International Crisis and Risk Communication Research, 2*(2), 233–258. https://doi.org/10.30658/jicrcr.2.2.4

Lee, S. Y., Lim, E. R., & Drumwright, M. E. (2018). Hybrid happening: Organizational reputations in corporate crises. *Public Relations Review, 44*(4), 598–609. https://doi.org/10.1016/j.pubrev.2018.05.008

Leonhardt, D. (2021, July). Vaccine persuasion: Many vaccine skeptics have changed their minds. *New York Times.* https://www.nytimes.com/2021/07/19/briefing/vaccine-skepticism-vaccination-drive.html

Li, R. (2021). Fear of COVID-19: What causes fear and how individuals cope with it. *Health Communication.* Advance online publication. https://doi.org/10.1080/104102 36.2021.1901423

Liu, B. F., & Atwell Seate, A. (2021). The evolving Weather Service: Forecasters' perceptions of their relationships with core partners. *Weather, Climate & Society, 13*(3), 437–448. https://doi.org/10.1175/WCAS-D-20-0097.1

Liu, B. F., Fraustino, J. D., & Jin, Y. (2016). Social media use during disasters: How information form and source influence intended behavioral responses. *Communication Research, 43*(5), 626–646. https://doi.org/10.1177%2F0093650214565917

Liu, B. F., Fowler, B. M., Roberts, H. A., & Herovic, E. (2018). Keeping hospitals operating during disasters through crisis communication preparedness. *Public Relations Review, 44*(4), 85–597. https://doi.org/10.1016/j.pubrev.2018.06.002

Liu, B. F., & Viens, J. L. (2020). Crisis and risk communication scholarship of the future: Reflections on research gaps. *Journal of International Crisis and Risk Communication Research, 3*(1), 7–13. https://doi.org/10.30658/jicrcr.3.1.1

Liu, R., Wang, L., Lei, J., Wang, Q., & Ren, Y. (2020). Effects of an immersive virtual reality-based classroom on students' learning performance in science lessons. *British Journal of Educational Technology, 51*(6), 2034–2049. https://doi.org/10.1111/bjet.13028

Manias-Muñoz, I., Jin, Y., & Reber, B. H. (2019). The state of crisis communication research and education through the lens of crisis scholars: An international Delphi study. *Public Relations Review, 45*(4), 101797. https://doi.org/10.1016/j.pubrev.2019.101797

Meadows, C. W., Meadows, C. Z., Tang, L., & Liu, W. (2019). Unraveling public health crises across stages: Understanding Twitter emotions and message types during the California measles outbreak. *Communication Studies, 70*(4), 453–469. https://doi.org/10.1080/10510974.2019.1582546

McLean, H., & Power, M. R. (2014). When minutes count: Tension and trust in the relationship between emergency managers and the media. *Journalism, 15*(3), 307–325. https://doi.org/10.1177%2F1464884913480873

Ngien, A., & Jiang, S. (2021). The effect of social media on stress among young adults during COVID-19 pandemic: Taking into account fatalism and social media exhaustion. *Health Communication.* Advance online publication. https://doi.org/10.1080/10410236.2021.1888438

Park, S., Boatwright, B., & Avery, E. J. (2019). Information channel preference in health crisis: Exploring the roles of perceived risk, preparedness, knowledge, and intent to follow directives. *Public Relations Review, 45*(5), 101794. https://doi.org/10.1016/j.pubrev.2019.05.015

Philibin, M. M., Parish, C., Pereyra, M., Feaster, D. J., Cohen, M., Wingood, G., Konkle-Parker, D., Adedimeji, A., Wilson, T. E., Cohen, J., Goparaju, L., Adimora, A. A., Golub, E. T., & Metsch, L. R. (2019). Health disparities and the digital divide: The relationship between communication inequalities and quality of life among women in a nationwide prospective cohort study in the United States. *Journal of Health Communication, 24*(4), 405–412. https://doi.org/10.1080/10810730.2019.1630524

Procopio, C., & Procopio, S. (2007). Do you know what it means to miss New Orleans? Internet communication, geographic community, and social capital in crisis. *Journal of Applied Communication Research, 35*(1), 67–87. https://doi.org/10.1080/00909880601065722

Rains, S. A., & Ruppel, E. K. (2016). Channel complementarity theory and the health information-seeking process: Further investigating the implications of source characteristic complementarity. *Communication Research, 43*(2), 232–252. https://doi.org/10.1177/0093650213510939

Ramirez, A., & Wang, Z. (2008). When online meets offline: An expectancy violations theory perspective on modality switching. *Journal of Communication, 58*(1), 20–39. https://doi.org/10.1111/j.1460-2466.2007.00372.x

Reynolds, B., & Seeger, M. W. (2005). Crisis and emergency risk communication as an integrative model. *Journal of Health Communication 10*(1), 43–55. https://doi.org/10.1080/10810730590904571

Ruppel, E. K., & Rains, S. A. (2012). Information sources and the health information-seeking process: An application and extension of channel complementarity theory. *Communication Monographs, 79*(3), 385–405. https://doi.org/10.1080/03637751.2012.697627

Scharp, K. M., Cooper, R. A., Worwood, J. V., & Dorrance Hall, E. (2021). "There's always going to be uncertainty": Exploring undergraduate student parents' sources of uncertainty and related management practices. *Communication Research, 48*(7), 1059–1084. https://doi.org/10.1177/0093650220903872

Sohn, Y., & Lariscy, R. W. (2015). A "buffer" or "boomerang?" – The role of corporate reputation in bad times. *Communication Research, 42*(2), 237–259. https://doi.org/10.1177/0093650212466891

Spialek, M. L., & Houston, J. B. (2019). The influence of citizen disaster communication on perceptions of neighborhood belonging and community resilience. *Journal of Applied Communication Research, 47*(1), 1–23. https://doi.org/10.1080/00909882.2018.1544718

Tannenbaum, M. B., Helper, J., Zimmerman, R. S., Saul, L., Jacobs, S., Wilson, K., & Albarracin, D. (2015). Appealing to fear: A meta-analysis of fear appeal effectiveness and theories. *Psychological Bulletin, 141*(6), 1178–1204. https://content.apa.org/doi/10.1037/a0039729

Tang, L., & Zou, W. (2021). Health information consumption under COVID-19 lockdown: An interview study with residents of Hubei Province, China. *Health Communication*, *36*(1), 74–80. https://doi.org/10.1080/10410236.2020.1847447

Tao, W. (2018). How consumers' pre-crisis associations and attitude certainty impact their responses to different crises. *Communication Research*, *45*(6), 815–839. https://doi.org/10.1177/0093650217733361

Thompson, T. L., & Robinson, J. D., & Brashers, D. E. (2010). Interpersonal communication and health care. In M. L. Knapp, & J. A., Daly (Eds.), *The Sage handbook of interpersonal communication*. (4th ed., pp. 633–677). Sage.

University of Maryland. (2021). Shots at the shop. https://sph.umd.edu/shotsattheshop

van der Meer, T. G. L. A., & Jin, Y. (2020). Seeking formula for misinformation treatment in public health crises: The effects of corrective information type and source. *Health Communication*, *35*(5), 560–575. https://doi.org/10.1080/10410236.2019.1573295

Walther, J. B. (2017). The merger of mass and interpersonal communication via new media: Integrating metaconstructs. *Human Communication Research*, *43*(4), 559–572. https://doi.org/10.1111/hcre.12122

World Bank. (2021, July). The global economic outlook during the COVID-19 pandemic: A changed world. https://www.worldbank.org/en/news/feature/2020/06/08/the-global-economic-outlook-during-the-covid-19-pandemic-a-changed-world

World Health Organization. (2022, May). WHO coronavirus (COVID-19) dashboard. https://covid19.who.int/

10

INTERGROUP COMMUNICATION DURING THE COVID-19 PANDEMIC

A 20-Nation Analysis of Prejudice

Stephen M. Croucher, Thao Nguyen, George Guoyu Ding, Audra Diers-Lawson, Anthony Spencer, Nadira Eskiçorapçı, Davide Girardelli, Tatiana M. Permyakova, Mohan Dutta, Elira Turdubaeva, Doug Ashwell, Sandra Bustamante, and Oscar Gomez

Since the start of the COVID-19 pandemic, there have been more than 506 million cases and more than 6 million deaths globally from the COVID-19 virus (Johns Hopkins Coronavirus Resource Center, Updated daily). Throughout the pandemic, millions of people went through isolation, economies were affected, health services were strained, and populations were divided. During the pandemic, discriminatory and racist acts toward minorities often blamed for the spread of the virus increased globally. The United Nations Educational, Scientific and Cultural Organization (UNESCO) reported an increase in discriminatory acts toward minority groups during the COVID-19 pandemic (COVID-19–related discrimination and stigma: A global phenomenon, 2020). Scholarly research has shown prejudice, racism, and discrimination toward minorities blamed for the COVID-19 pandemic have been a significant concern (e.g., Choi, 2021; Clissold et al., 2020; Croucher et al., 2020, 2021a,b, 2022; Girardelli et al., 2021; Mandalaywala et al., 2021; Nguyen et al., 2021; Roberto et al., 2020; Sorokowski et al., 2020; Tan et al., 2021).

To clarify the global prejudice toward minorities blamed for the COVID-19 pandemic, and its influence on intergroup communication, this chapter examines COVID-19 prejudice during the COVID-19 pandemic cross-culturally. Specifically, this chapter examines COVID-19 prejudice, and intergroup contact in 20 nations, which each experienced the COVID-19 pandemic differently: Argentina, Brazil, Chile, China, England, France, India, Italy, Kenya, Kyrgyzstan, Mexico, New Zealand, Nigeria, Peru, Russia, Singapore, South Africa, Spain, Turkey, and the United States. These nations represent a geographic, political, cultural, and economic cross section of the COVID-19 pandemic. In the first

DOI: 10.4324/9781003214496-10

section of this chapter, COVID-19 prejudice and intergroup contact are defined as theoretical constructs. For this chapter, prejudice will be conceptualized and operationalized as integrated threat. In the second section, prejudice and intergroup contact in each nation during COVID-19 are discussed. In the third section, the method and data analysis are described. In the fourth section, the results are presented. The fifth and final section is the discussion.

Theoretical Constructs: Prejudice and Intergroup Contact

Prejudice is a "negative attitude toward a socially defined group and toward any person perceived to be a member of that group" (Ashmore, 1970, p. 253). While numerous theories have been developed to understand and study prejudice, for the purposes of this chapter, prejudice is conceptualized using integrated threat theory (ITT) (Stephan et al., 2015; Stephan & Stephan, 1996, 2000). The original ITT described how an ingroup will perceive an outgroup as posing threats to an ingroup and its position in society. There are four kinds of threats an ingroup may perceive an outgroup as posing, and it is critical to note these threats do not have to be real, but only need to be perceived. These threats are symbolic threats, realistic threats, intergroup anxiety, and negative stereotypes (Croucher, 2017; Stephan & Stephan, 2000). Realistic threats are those fears an ingroup perceives from an outgroup toward their economic, political, and/or physical well-being. Symbolic threats are the beliefs or perceptions the dominant group/ culture has about the outgroup because of perceived differences in attitudes, beliefs, morals, values, standards, etc. (Stephan & Stephan, 2000). Essentially, these are threats the dominant group/culture sees to their culture or way of life. Intergroup anxiety is the fear or anxiety individuals experience when they interact with outgroup members. This anxiety can be heighted when individuals have an intergroup history of conflict, misunderstanding, or lack of contact with one another. Negative stereotypes are common and negative assumptions an ingroup has about an outgroup. When these assumptions guide behaviors and decision-making, prejudice is increased (Croucher, 2017).

Stephan et al. (2015) later revised ITT and condensed the four threats into only realistic and symbolic. Intergroup anxiety and negative stereotypes were determined to be more suited as antecedent factors and not threats. The revised version of ITT, known as intergroup threat theory (ITT), identifies two kinds of threat, realistic and symbolic threats. These two threats are preceded by antecedent factors, such as intergroup anxiety, negative stereotypes, intergroup conflict, intergroup contact, status inequities, and strength of ingroup identification (Croucher, 2017; González et al., 2008). Such factors either heighten or diminish the extent to which the ingroup perceives the outgroup as a threat.

An extensive body of research has explored ITT in various contexts. Most research into ITT (whether the original or revised concept) has focused on religion, race, and/or ethnicity as critical cultural or political issues (e.g., Atwell

Seate et al., 2018; Atwell Seate & Mastro, 2016; Banas et al., 2020; Croucher, 2013; González, et al., 2008; Ramsay & Pang, 2017; Stephan & Stephan, 1996, 2000; Tausch et al., 2008). This line of research has overwhelmingly shown ingroup perception of threat from a variety of outgroups. Increasingly, researchers have applied ITT to outgroups that are not religiously, racially, or ethnically identified, such as those differentiated by a health condition such as cancer, HIV/AIDS, or drug users (Berrenberg et al., 2007; Bowles et al., 2020; Faulkner et al., 2004; Navarrete & Fessler, 2006; Schaller & Neuberg, 2012). Similarly, this line of work has found those who identify as "healthy" prejudice those they identify as "not healthy."

Combining these threads of research and considering the impact of the COVID-19 pandemic, we (see Croucher et al., 2020; Croucher et al., 2021a,b, 2022; Girardelli et al., 2021; Nguyen et al., 2021) have explored ITT when the ingroup perceives the outgroup as spreading/causing a virus. In this line of research, we have found that like an identified ethnic, racial, political, or cultural group outgroup, an ingroup perceives similar threats to an outgroup that it perceives as presenting a health threat. In the case of the COVID-19 pandemic; however, the primary threat is realistic and not symbolic, as ingroups more fear the contagion (the virus) and less the outgroup changing their way of life. However, realistic threat is related to perceived anxiety and anger (Stephan & Stephan, 1996). Recent research has indicated minority groups, targeted by the dominant culture groups based on their existing stigma and prejudice, have been verbally and physically attacked in both online and offline contexts during COVID-19 pandemic (Kim et al., 2021).

In the original conceptualization of the intergroup contact hypothesis, Allport (1954) asserted increased intergroup contact decreases prejudice. However, it is not that simple. Research has increasingly shown that the intergroup contact needs to be positive, where the groups are cooperative and share some semblance of common goals (Pettigrew & Tropp, 2008). While González et al.'s (2008) research showed a negative relationship between intergroup contact and threat (realistic and symbolic), Croucher's (2013) research among Muslims in Western Europe and Croucher et al.'s (2021b) research exploring the COVID-19 pandemic in Russia and Kyrgyzstan showed a positive relationship between intergroup contact and threat (realistic and symbolic). Thus, along with considering the political, economic, cultural, and physical history of groups (Croucher, 2016), it is essential to consider if an imminent danger faces the ingroup, such as a pandemic. In such cases, negative factors might override positive intergroup contact factors.

Contextual: Prejudice and Intergroup Contact during COVID-19

During the COVID-19 pandemic, nations and publics responded in different ways. The 20 nations included in this analysis represent a cross section of how the global community responded to the pandemic. Additionally, these nations demonstrate how ingroups (dominant cultures) responded to outgroups during the pandemic. In this section, we briefly review how ingroups in each of the 20 nations prejudiced and blamed outgroups for the COVID-19 pandemic. The ingroups within the 20 nations can be separated into four categories, depending on the outgroup they blamed and/or identified as being responsible for the spread of COVID-19 in their nation: Asians/Chinese (12), foreigners who are not Asian/Chinese (3), workers returning to the nation (2), and miscellaneous (3).

There has been an alarming increase in the level of racism, discrimination, prejudice, and violence toward Asians since the start of the COVID-19 pandemic (Cowan, 2021; Croucher et al., 2020; Young & Cho, 2021; Rzymski & Nowicki, 2020; Ziems et al., 2020), the full extent to which is impossible to determine (Lu, 2021). In the United States, Asians and people of Asian descent have suffered the most as they have been blamed for causing COVID-19 (Choi, 2021; Croucher et al., 2020). For example, a woman in Brooklyn posted a message on Facebook telling New Yorkers to boycott Chinese businesses such as restaurants, shops, and supermarkets (Shahrigian, 2020). As of April 2022, the United States had more than 80 million confirmed cases and almost 1 million deaths from COVID-19.[1] Such actions have not been limited to the United States.

In South and Latin America, different outgroups have been targeted during the pandemic. Argentina and Chile have seen a rise in racism and xenophobia toward Asians, particularly those of Chinese heritage. During the pandemic, racist discourses in media and among politicians have gone largely unchallenged as the pandemic impacted the nations (Chan & Strabucchi, 2021). As of April 2022, Argentina has more than 9 million cases and 128,000+ deaths, and Chile had more than 3.4 million cases and nearly 57,000 deaths. In neighboring Peru, Asians have not been the scapegoat for the spread of COVID-19; instead, individuals who do not follow quarantine regulations have been blamed for the spread of the virus (Zsiga, 2020). The government and social media have largely attributed case numbers to breaking quarantine and partaking in non-essential outings. Such rhetoric portrays rule breakers as uneducated and ignorant, while the government (during a scandal) portrays itself as the protector of the people. As of April 2022, Peru had more than 3.5 million cases and more than 212,000 deaths from COVID-19. In Brazil, Asians have been partially blamed and prejudiced during the COVID-19 pandemic (AFP, 2020). However, Brazil's Afro-Brazilian population has experienced intense prejudice and even been denied health coverage during the pandemic (Caldwell & de Araújo, 2020; Phillips, 2020). As of April 2022, Brazil had more than 30 million cases and more than 660,000 deaths. For many Mexicans, the rising number of U.S. students heading to Mexico for spring break means rising COVID-19 cases. Over the past two years, many cases of COVID-19 have been attributed to spring breakers coming from the United States leading to outrage. However, with the economy dependent on tourism, the government has had no choice but to open the borders. As of April 2022, Mexico had nearly 5.7 million cases and more than 320,000 deaths.

In Europe, like the United States, prejudice toward individuals of Asian heritage increased during the COVID-19 pandemic. In Italy, numerous Chinese-owned stores were vandalized, many Asians reported harassment and assault, and in one case a music conservatory suspended all lessons for Asian students (Casalini, 2020; Giuffrida, 2020; Petrizzelli, 2020). As of April 2021, Italy has had nearly 14.85 million cases and more than 150,000 deaths. In France, Asians have reported higher levels of discrimination, prejudice, and racism, as well as declines in customers to Asian stores and restaurants (Asians in Paris rattled, 2020; Laemle, 2020). In France, news depictions in papers such as *Le Courier Picard* of Asians as the "Yellow Peril" helped a new hashtag trend, "#JeNeSuisPasUnVirus" or "I am not a Virus" (Giuffrida & Willsher, 2020). As of April 2021, France has had nearly 26.2 million cases and more than 140,000 COVID-19–related deaths. In England (and throughout the United Kingdom), Asians reported higher levels of racial abuse, discrimination, and physical assaults, with the Metropolitan Police reporting an increase in race-related crimes in 2020 (Ng, 2021; Whitehead, 2020). Asian-owned businesses also reported declines in revenue (Iqbal, 2020). As of April 2021, the United Kingdom has had nearly 21.4 million cases and more than 166,000 deaths. Spain has also seen rising anti-Asian sentiment since the outbreak of the COVID-19 pandemic (Govan, 2020; Guo et al., 2020). In addition, racially motivated hate speech in right-wing media is surging, particularly via social media (Laudette, 2021). As of April 2021, Spain has had nearly 11.6 million cases and more than 102,000 COVID-19–related deaths.

In Eastern Europe and Western Asia, different outgroups have been prejudiced and blamed for the spread of COVID-19. In Russia, the COVID-19 virus was labeled a biological weapon from China, the United States, and/or caused by foreign migrants (Kleymenov, 2020). However, as the first wave of Chinese nationals tested positive for COVID-19 in Russia in January 2020, prejudice toward individuals of Asian heritage increased (Gerber & He, 2021). As of April 2022, Russia had nearly 17.6 million cases and nearly 363,000 COVID-19–related deaths. In Kyrgyzstan, Asians were not blamed or prejudiced for the spread of COVID-19. Like many other Central Asian republics, COVID-19 arrived late to the region, often arriving with migrant workers returning from neighboring states. As many migrant workers returned with COVID-19, the government was blamed for not taking enough steps to stop returnees, and returning Kyrgyz workers were prejudiced for bringing COVID-19 into the country (Politklinika, 2021; Sputnik, 2020). As of April 2022, Kyrgyzstan had nearly 201,000 cases and almost 3,000 COVID-19-related deaths. In Turkey, like other nations, with rising COVID-19 numbers, prejudice has also increased. The pandemic has revealed deep-seeded prejudice and distrust toward Turkey's Asian, specifically Chinese, population (Gülseven, 2021). As the government response to the pandemic has been criticized for favoring political and economic gains (Gülseven, 2021), Chinese in Turkey have experienced verbal abuse on the streets, and harassment on social media (Tekin, 2020). As of April 2022, Turkey had nearly 15 million cases and just over 98,000 COVID-19–related deaths.

COVID-19 has reportedly been less deadly in Africa, with a relatively lower death and COVID-19 case rate than in other continents. Soy (2020) attributed this to quick action on the part of most governments used to dealing with pandemics, high levels of public adherence to safety measures, a younger population with fewer old-age homes, a more favorable climate, health systems used to responding to pandemics, and possibly lower testing rates that might undermine reporting of cases and deaths. In Kenya, there has been growing unease among Kenya's Asian population after reports of violence and verbal abuse in Nairobi (Solomon, 2020). In addition, a member of Kenya's Parliament posted online that Kenyans had the right to stone and remove Chinese visitors (York, 2020). As of April 2022, Kenya had nearly 324,000 cases and almost 5,700 COVID-19–related deaths. Some Chinese officials have targeted Africans living in Chinese cities for quarantine and for requests to leave China due to fears that they were carriers of the COVID-19 virus (Philling & Wong, 2020). In response to this well-publicized racial profiling, numerous conspiracy theories have emerged in Nigeria of Chinese spreading the virus (Eguegu, 2020). In addition, when a medical team arrived in Lagos in 2020, many Nigerians responded with skepticism and anger, believing the team was there to spread the virus (Eguegu, 2020). In response to the scapegoating of Africans in China, many Nigerians have taken to blaming Chinese (outgroup). As of April 2022, Nigeria had nearly 256,000 cases and over 3,100 COVID-19–related deaths. In South Africa, worsening economic conditions, coupled with the COVID-19 pandemic, have put undocumented foreign nationals at the forefront of the pandemic. As South Africans demand more jobs and economic stability, the presence of undocumented foreign nationals, who have been identified by many as taking away economic resources from native South Africans, is increasingly viewed as negative. In fact, politicians and media increasingly blame undocumented foreign nationals for the spread of COVID-19 to marginalize the community (Fiflani, 2020). As of April 2022, South Africa had more than 3.7 million cases and over 100,000 COVID-19–related deaths.

In India, Muslims have been extensively scapegoated and prejudiced during the COVID-19 pandemic. In response to various Islamic religious gatherings, where COVID-19 positive individuals attended and later returned to their respective regions, Indian newspapers reported on how "Muslims" were spreading the virus (Ghosal et al., 2020). Media depictions and Twitter hashtags such as #coronajihad have contributed to fear and hysteria and fueled Hindu prejudice toward Indian-Muslims (Krishnan, 2020). As of April 2022, India had more than 43 million cases and over 521,000 COVID-19–related deaths. In Singapore, more than two-thirds of Malays and Indians reported that they had experienced racism in their lives, and that this racism had increased during the COVID-19 pandemic (Sen, 2021). There have been numerous cases of Malay and Indian migrants being targets of racial slurs and being physically attacked (Kamil, 2021). Such incidents have been combined with increased negative rhetoric on social media toward Malay and Indian migrants in Singapore. As of April 2022, Singapore had more than 1.1 million cases and 1,283 COVID-19–related deaths. In China, there have been numerous outgroups stigmatized and prejudiced since the outbreak of the pandemic. Foreigners have experienced prejudice throughout China, such as Africans and other Southeast Asians. The Chinese government has denied that discrimination and/or prejudice has taken place in China toward foreigners (Vanderklippe, 2020). One group that has experienced systemic scapegoating and prejudice are Wuhan residents. There have been numerous cases of Wuhan residents being denied entry to events, transport, hotels, verbally abused, and largely blamed for the effects of the pandemic (Gan, 2020). Wuhan residents have essentially become outcasts within their own country. As of April 2022, China has had nearly 1.5 million reported cases and nearly 13,000 COVID-19–related deaths.

Research exploring prejudice and blame during COVID-19 in New Zealand has found New Zealanders tend to not blame or prejudice any outgroup to a great extent (Croucher et al., 2021a; Nguyen et al., 2021; Tan, 2020). In fact, when some incidents of racism or prejudice have occurred, New Zealanders have actively spoken out against them (Collins, 2020). Thus, no one identifiable outgroup has been targeted in New Zealand during the pandemic. As of April 2022, New Zealand has had more than 720,000 cases and nearly 400 COVID-19–related deaths.

All in all, globally, many different groups have been verbally harassed, bullied, and even physically attacked (Lee & Yadav, 2020). Many minority-owned businesses have reported a huge decline in trade amid the pandemic outbreak. Consequently, the COVID-19 pandemic is much more than a public health emergency; it is an economic, social, and human crisis (Guterres, 2020). Research and mass media have demonstrated xenophobia, ethnocentrism, lack of intergroup contact, prejudice, racism, and violence toward outgroups during the COVID-19 pandemic. Thus, the following are put forth to cross-nationally explore prejudice, ethnocentrism, and intergroup contact during the COVID-19 pandemic:

RQ1: To what extent does prejudice toward the outgroup differ among the 20 nations?

RQ2: To what extent does intergroup contact between the ingroup and the outgroup differ among the 20 nations?

In addition, while research has shown correlations between prejudice and intergroup contact, no research has explored these relationships among this many nations nor among some of the nations in this sample. Thus, the third research question is put forth:

RQ3: To what extent are prejudice and intergroup correlated among the 20 nations?

Method and Data Analysis

After receiving ethical approval, date for this study were collected between April 2020 and June 2021 in Argentina ($n = 200$), Brazil ($n = 410$), Chile ($n = 367$), China ($n = 256$), England ($n = 364$), France ($n = 321$), India ($n = 402$), Italy ($n = 311$), Kenya ($n = 226$), Kyrgyzstan ($n = 228$), Mexico ($n = 304$), New Zealand ($n = 650$), Nigeria ($n = 208$), Peru ($n = 251$), Russia ($n = 201$), Singapore ($n = 298$), South Africa ($n = 326$), Spain ($n = 298$), Turkey ($n = 217$), and the United States ($n = 681$). The total sample for this study is 6,539. Data were collected in two ways: via an online survey using Qualtrics or SurveyMonkey, or via paper-based surveys. According to Troia and Graham (2017), online panels and face-to-face paper-based surveys are comparable in composition. It was necessary to use the combination of Qualtrics, SurveyMonkey, and paper-based surveys because participants in each nation could not be reached equally using one particular data collection approach. For example, in Nigeria, Russia, and Kenya, participants were more trusting of paper-based surveys than of online links to surveys. Thus, paper-based surveys were used in these nations. In addition, on-the-ground contacts in Turkey found it easier to use SurveyMonkey, as this is a program participants were familiar with; thus, this method was employed. See Table 10.1 for demographic data for each nation.

All surveys included demographic questions and three previously validated measures: Measure of Intergroup Contact (González et al., 2008), Measure of Symbolic Threat (Stephan et al., 1999), and the Measure of Realistic Threat (Stephan et al., 1999). All measures were translated from English into Spanish ($k = .86$), Portuguese ($k = .83$), Mandarin ($k = .81$), French ($k = .83$), Italian ($k = .85$), Russian ($k = .82$), and Turkish ($k = .87$). All translations were conducted by bilingual speakers who then discussed the translations with additional bilingual speakers to clarify any content and conceptual questions before finalization of translations. With a cross-national study of this nature and with using scales developed in the English language, it was critical to check the linguistic reliability, construct validity, and internal consistency of all measures. As the Measure of Realistic Threat, the Measure of Symbolic Threat, and the Measure of Intergroup Contact measure prejudice, they were analyzed together as "Prejudice." CFA results are presented in Table 10.2. Means, standard deviations, and reliabilities for all measures are presented in Table 10.3.

Measure of Symbolic Threat. Three items from Stephan et al. (1999) assessed symbolic threat. Sample items in English included: "Italian identity is threatened because there are too many Asians today," "Brazilian norms and values are threatened because of the presence of blacks today," and "Asians are a threat to Turkish culture." Responses ranged from (1) *strongly disagree* to (5) *strongly agree*. A higher score indicated a stronger sense of threat. No items were dropped across the 20 nations.

Measure of Realistic Threat. Three items from Stephan et al. (1999) measured realistic threat. These items focused on assessing the effects of the

TABLE 10.1 Participant Demographics by Nation

Nation	Sex (Female/Male)	Age (M; SD)
United States (n = 681)	354 females (52%) and 327 males (48%)	M = 25.18; SD = 6.55
New Zealand (n = 650)	325 females (50%) and 325 males (50%)	M = 28.11; SD = 6.22
Spain (n = 298)	134 females (45%) and 164 males (55%)	M = 28.11; SD = 7.12
Italy (n = 311)	145 females (46.6%) and 166 males (53.4%)	M = 39.17; SD = 9.17
Russia (n = 201)	96 females (47.8%) and 105 males (52.2%)	M = 36.82; SD = 5.72
South Africa (n = 326)	149 females (45.7%) and 177 males (54.3%)	M = 38.16; SD = 9.98
Mexico (n = 304)	156 females (51.3%) and 148 males (48.7%)	M = 37.15; SD = 7.75
India (n = 402)	286 females (71.1%) and 116 males (28.9%)	M = 25.14; SD = 10.29
Singapore (n = 298)	149 females (50%) and 149 males (50%)	M = 26.98; SD = 11.25
Brazil (n = 410)	197 females (48%) and 213 males (52%)	M = 28.97; SD = 8.37
Peru (n = 251)	97 females (38.6%) and 154 males (61.4%)	M = 25.19; SD = 5.01
Chile (n = 367)	173 females (47.1%) and 194 males (52.9%)	M = 36.15; SD = 10.18
Kyrgyzstan (n = 228)	144 females (63.2%) and 84 males (36.8%)	M = 34.79; SD = 9.24
Argentina (n = 220)	95 females (43.2%) and 125 males (56.8%)	M = 32.89; SD = 9.19
Turkey (n = 217)	99 females (43.2%) and 125 males (56.8%)	M = 34.67; SD = 7.89
England (n = 364)	134 females (36.8%) and 230 males (63.2%)	M = 32.45; SD = 6.79
France (n = 321)	160 females (49.8%) and 161 males (50.2%)	M = 30.50; SD = 11.15
Kenya (n = 226)	108 females (47.8%) and 118 males (52.2%)	M = 23.54; SD = 6.78
Nigeria (n = 208)	106 females (51%) and 102 males (49%)	M = 22.98; SD = 9.09
China (n = 256)	134 females (52.3%) and 122 males (47.7%)	M = 30.15; SD = 8.01

outgroup on the economic situation. Sample statements include: "Because of the presence of Asians, New Zealanders have more difficulties finding a job," "Because of the presence of Asians, French have more difficulties finding a house," and "Because of the presence of Muslims, unemployment will increase." Responses ranged from (1) *strongly disagree* to (5) *strongly agree*. A higher score indicated a stronger sense of threat. No items were dropped across the 20 nations.

TABLE 10.2 Validity Results for Measures for Each Nation

Nation	Construct	Validity Results	Dropped Items
United States	Prejudice	$\chi2 = 95.01$, $df = 32$, $p < .0001$. SRMR = .05, GFI = .97, CFI = .99, RMSEA = .05	
New Zealand	Prejudice	$\chi2 = 78.11$, $df = 32$, $p < .0001$. SRMR = .03, GFI = .98, CFI = .99, RMSEA = .05	
Spain	Prejudice	$\chi2 = 81.42$, $df = 32$, $p < .0001$. SRMR = .05, GFI = .95, CFI = .96, RMSEA = .07	
Italy	Prejudice	$\chi2 = 108.21$, $df = 32$, $p < .0001$. SRMR = .05, GFI = .95, CFI = .98, RMSEA = .08	
Russia	Prejudice	$\chi2 = 47.30$, $df = 32$, $p = .003$. SRMR = .05, GFI = .95, CFI = .98, RMSEA = .07	
South Africa	Prejudice	$\chi2 = 84.17$, $df = 32$, $p < .001$. SRMR = .05, GFI = .95, CFI = .97, RMSEA = .07	
Mexico	Prejudice	$\chi2 = 64.91$, $df = 32$, $p < .001$. SRMR = .05, GFI = .96, CFI = .98, RMSEA = .08	
India	Prejudice	$\chi2 = 78.53$, $df = 32$, $p < .001$. SRMR = .05, GFI = .96, CFI = .98, RMSEA = .06	
Singapore	Prejudice	$\chi2 = 108.01$, $df = 32$, $p < .001$. SRMR = .05, GFI = .94, CFI = .97, RMSEA = .08	
Brazil	Prejudice	$\chi2 = 50.93$, $df = 32$, $p = .02$. SRMR = .04, GFI = .98, CFI = .99, RMSEA = .04	
Peru	Prejudice	$\chi2 = 69.19$, $df = 32$, $p < .001$. SRMR = .03, GFI = .95, CFI = .98, RMSEA = .07	
Chile	Prejudice	$\chi2 = 71.66$, $df = 32$, $p < .001$. SRMR = .03, GFI = .96, CFI = .98, RMSEA = .06	

(Continued)

TABLE 10.2 (Continued)

Nation	Construct	Validity Results	Dropped Items
Kyrgyzstan	Prejudice	$\chi 2 = 16.75$, $df = 24$, $p = .12$. SRMR = .02, GFI = .96, CFI = .99, RMSEA = .04	– How many migrant contacts do you have?
Argentina	Prejudice	$\chi 2 = 41.19$, $df = 32$, $p = .13$. SRMR = .03, GFI = .96, CFI = .99, RMSEA = .04	
Turkey	Prejudice	$\chi 2 = 33.40$, $df = 24$, $p = .01$. SRMR = .02, GFI = .97, CFI = .99, RMSEA = .07	– How many Asian contacts do you have?
England	Prejudice	$\chi 2 = 88.03$, $df = 32$, $p < .001$. SRMR = .05, GFI = .96, CFI = .98, RMSEA = .07	
France	Prejudice	$\chi 2 = 83.14$, $df = 32$, $p < .001$. SRMR = .06, GFI = .95, CFI = .97, RMSEA = .07	
Kenya	Prejudice	$\chi 2 = 57.24$, $df = 32$, $p = .004$. SRMR = .07, GFI = .96, CFI = .98, RMSEA = .06	
Nigeria	Prejudice	$\chi 2 = 37.15$, $df = 32$, $p = .10$. SRMR = .02, GFI = .98, CFI = .98, RMSEA = .03	
China	Prejudice	$\chi 2 = 67.82$, $df = 32$, $p < .001$. SRMR = .08, GFI = .95, CFI = .95, RMSEA = .06	

Measure of Intergroup Contact. Four items measured intergroup contact (González et al., 2008). Sample items included: "How many Asians do you know?" "Do you have contact with Muslim friends or co-workers? "Do you have contact with labor migrants in your neighborhood?" and "Do you have contact with Asians somewhere else, such as at a sports club or other organization?" The first item was rated from (1) *none* to (4) *often*. The remaining items were rated from (1) *never* to (4) *often*. A higher score indicated more intergroup contact. The first item was dropped, as it was found to not factor-load properly in two nations.

Results

To answer *RQ1* and *RQ2*, analysis of variance (ANOVA) was conducted. To answer *RQ3*, Pearson correlation analysis was conducted. In answering *RQ1*, an ANOVA showed that the effect of nation was significant for realistic threat, $F(19, 6511) = 32.26$, $p < .001$. Post hoc analyses using the Games-Howell test indicated numerous differences between the nations ($p < .01$); these differences are shown in Table 10.3. Nation also had a significant effect on symbolic threat,

$F(19, 6511) = 37.83$, $p < .001$. Post hoc analyses using the Games-Howell test again indicated numerous differences between the nations ($p < .01$). England ($M = 4.22$), Brazil ($M = 4.03$), and Peru ($M = 4.03$) had the highest scores on realistic threat, with France ($M = 3.28$), Singapore ($M = 3.01$), and India ($M = 2.92$) scoring the lowest. Brazil ($M = 4.36$), England ($M = 4.16$), and Peru ($M = 4.04$) had the highest scores on symbolic threat, with Kyrgyzstan ($M = 3.20$), Singapore ($M = 3.15$), and India ($M = 2.73$) scoring the lowest on symbolic threat.

TABLE 10.3 Means, Standard Deviations, and Reliabilities in Each Nation

Nation	Construct	M; SD	α
United States	Realistic Threat$_{abcdefgh}$	$M = 3.66$; $SD = 1.22$	.94
	Symbolic Threat$_{abcdefg}$	$M = 3.60$; $SD = 1.22$	.92
	Intergroup Contact$_{abcdefgh}$	$M = 2.07$; $SD = .86$	.79
New Zealand	Realistic Threat$_{aijklmnopqrstuv}$	$M = 3.34$; $SD = 1.17$	.91
	Symbolic Threat$_{hijklmn}$	$M = 3.61$; $SD = 1.12$	.94
	Intergroup Contact$_{ahijklmnopqrst}$	$M = 2.53$; $SD = .81$	.71
Spain	Realistic Threat$_{iuvwx}$	$M = 3.79$; $SD = 1.05$	.88
	Symbolic Threat$_{opqrst}$	$M = 3.82$; $SD = 1.08$	.91
	Intergroup Contact$_{bhwxyz}^{abc}$	$M = 2.30$; $SD = .72$	.70
Italy	Realistic Threat$_{jy}^{abcde}$	$M = 3.66$; $SD = .96$	.89
	Symbolic Threat$_{uvwxyz}$	$M = 3.70$; $SD = 1.00$	.93
	Intergroup Contact$_{iw}^{defghij}$	$M = 1.92$; $SD = .70$	.73
Russia	Realistic Threat^{fgh}	$M = 3.64$; $SD = 1.30$	.92
	Symbolic Threat$_{\ldots}^{abcd}$	$M = 3.53$; $SD = 1.26$	.93
	Intergroup Contact$_{c}^{dlmnopqrstuvw}$	$M = 2.54$; $SD = .80$	.76
South Africa	Realistic Threat$_{bkyz}^{ijklmz}$	$M = 3.99$; $SD = .98$	.88
	Symbolic Threat$_{\ldots}^{efghij}$	$M = 3.77$; $SD = 1.08$	.91
	Intergroup Contact$_{j}^{lxy}{}_{ab}$	$M = 2.16$; $SD = .80$	.75
Mexico	Realistic Threat^{inopqrs}	$M = 3.42$; $SD = 1.28$	.91
	Symbolic Threat$_{\ldots}^{klmno}$	$M = 3.51$; $SD = 1.22$	.92
	Intergroup Contact$_{k}^{m}{}_{cdedf}$	$M = 2.15$; $SD = .80$	.72
India	Realistic Threat$_{cluz}^{fntuvwxyz}{}_{abc}$	$M = 2.92$; $SD = 1.16$	.87
	Symbolic Threat$_{ahou}^{aekpqrstuvwxyz}$	$M = 2.73$; $SD = 1.12$	.85
	Intergroup Contact$_{dx}^{ex}{}_{cghijklmnopq}$	$M = 2.61$; $SD = .83$	.79
Singapore	Realistic Threat$_{dmv}^{agjo}{}_{defghijkl}$	$M = 3.01$; $SD = 1.13$	.92
	Symbolic Threat$_{bipv}^{fp}{}_{abcdefgh}$	$M = 3.15$; $SD = 1.13$	.93
	Intergroup Contact$_{l}^{n}{}_{grstu}$	$M = 2.09$; $SD = .76$	.78
Brazil	Realistic Threat$_{en}^{bpt}{}_{dmno}$	$M = 4.03$; $SD = 1.30$	.89
	Symbolic Threat$_{cjqw}^{bglqa}{}_{ijklmnop}$	$M = 4.36$; $SD = 1.25$	.89
	Intergroup Contact$_{m}^{fo}{}_{hvwxy}$	$M = 2.21$; $SD = .82$	.78
Peru	Realistic Threat$_{fo}^{cu}{}_{epqr}$	$M = 4.03$; $SD = .87$	.94
	Symbolic Threat$_{dkx}^{cmr}{}_{bqrstuv}$	$M = 4.04$; $SD = .82$	.90
	Intergroup Contact$_{eny}^{py}{}_{dirvz}$	$M = 1.79$; $SD = .67$	.74

(Continued)

TABLE 10.3 (Continued)

Nation	Construct	M; SD	α
Chile	Realistic Threat$_p{}^{qvf}{}_{stu}$	$M = 3.93; SD = .96$	.89
	Symbolic Threat$_{el}{}^{ns}{}_{ciwxy}$	$M = 3.93; SD = .94$	.90
	Intergroup Contact$_{foz}{}^{qz}{}_{ejsw}{}^{abcdef}$	$M = 1.82; SD = .67$	.70
Kyrgyzstan	Realistic Threat$_q{}^{w}{}_{gvw}$	$M = 3.73; SD = .91$	.85
	Symbolic Threat$_{fmry}{}^{ht}{}_{jqwz}{}^{abcdghijklm}$	$M = 3.20; SD = .85$	.71
	Intergroup Contact$_g{}^{ag}{}_{aftxz}$	$M = 2.59; SD = .82$	.76
Argentina	Realistic Threat$_r{}^{x}{}_{hxy}$	$M = 3.69; SD = .98$	.90
	Symbolic Threat$_{...}{}^{u}{}_{dkrz}{}^{e}$	$M = 3.67; SD = .98$	.90
	Intergroup Contact$_p{}^{br}{}_{k}{}^{gn}$	$M = 1.98; SD = .79$	.77
Turkey	Realistic Threat$_s{}^{ry}{}_{iz}{}^{ab}$	$M = 3.94; SD = .91$	.95
	Symbolic Threat$_{...}{}^{ve}{}_{l}{}^{afg}$	$M = 3.77; SD = 1.03$	.93
	Intergroup Contact$_{hq}{}^{chs}{}_{bfluy}{}^{ahnopqrs}$	$M = 1.34; SD = .55$	.83
England	Realistic Threat$_{gtw}{}^{dhsz}{}_{jsvx}{}^{cdef}{}_f$	$M = 4.22; SD = .88$	.91
	Symbolic Threat$_{gnsz}{}^{diow}{}_{f}{}^{befhijk}$	$M = 4.16; SD = .92$	.92
	Intergroup Contact$_r{}^{t}{}_m{}^{bio}$	$M = 2.10; SD = .74$	.78
France	Realistic Threat$_{hx}{}^{ek}{}_{amptwyz}{}^{c}$	$M = 3.28; SD = 1.24$	.89
	Symbolic Threat$_t{}^{jw}{}_{msx}{}^{gh}$	$M = 3.35; SD = 1.24$	.90
	Intergroup Contact$_s{}^{i}{}_n{}^{cjp}$	$M = 2.23; SD = .77$	.70
Kenya	Realistic Threat$_{...}{}_{ak}{}^{ad}{}_g$	$M = 3.68; SD = 1.10$	.88
	Symbolic Threat$_{...}{}^{x}{}_{gnt}{}^{ci}$	$M = 3.66; SD = 1.10$	.91
	Intergroup Contact$_t{}^{u}{}_o{}^{dkq}$	$M = 2.08; SD = .74$	.70
Nigeria	Realistic Threat$_{...}{}^{l}{}_{bnqu}{}^{be}$	$M = 3.45; SD = 1.27$	.94
	Symbolic Threat$_{...}{}^{y}{}_{ouy}{}^{j}$	$M = 3.45; SD = 1.24$	.93
	Intergroup Contact$_u{}^{jv}{}_{pe}{}^{lr}$	$M = 2.20; SD = .81$	.78
China	Realistic Threat$_{...}{}^{m}{}_{clor}$	$M = 3.58; SD = 1.26$	.93
	Symbolic Threat$_{...}{}^{z}{}_{hpv}{}^{dk}$	$M = 3.64; SD = 1.30$	.93
	Intergroup Contact$_v{}^{kwq}{}_{...}{}^{fms}$	$M = 2.20; SD = .80$	.76

In answering $RQ2$, an ANOVA showed that the effect of nation was significant for intergroup contact, $F(19, 6411) = 44.34$, $p < .001$. Post hoc analyses using the Games-Howell test indicated numerous differences between the nations ($p < .01$); these differences are shown in Table 10.3. India ($M = 2.61$), Kyrgyzstan ($M = 2.59$), and Russia ($M = 2.54$) had the highest scores on intergroup contact, while Chile ($M = 1.82$), Peru ($M = 1.79$), and Turkey ($M = 1.34$) had the lowest scores.

To answer $RQ3$, a Pearson's correlation was conducted. For the entire sample, realistic and symbolic threats are positively correlated ($r = .79$, $p < .001$), realistic threat is positively related to intergroup contact ($r = .06$, $p < .001$), and symbolic threat is also positively related to intergroup contact ($r = .08$, $p < .001$). When considering the results in each nation separately, the correlation between symbolic and realistic threat was positive, but the relationships between threat (realistic and symbolic) and contact varied. In the United States, Russia, Mexico, Peru, Chile, Argentina, England, Kenya, Nigeria, and China,

TABLE 10.4 Correlations in All 20 Nations

United States				New Zealand			
Variable	(1)	(2)	(3)	Variable	(1)	(2)	(3)
Realistic Threat	–			Realistic Threat	–		
Symbolic Threat	.86★★	–		Symbolic Threat	.78★★	–	
Intergroup Contact	.03	.01	–	Intergroup Contact	.23★★	.28★★	–
Spain				Italy			
Variable	(1)	(2)	(3)	Variable	(1)	(2)	(3)
Realistic Threat	–			Realistic Threat	–		
Symbolic Threat	.82★★	–		Symbolic Threat	.78★★	–	
Intergroup Contact	.18★★	.17★★	–	Intergroup Contact	.15★★	.19★★	–
Russia				South Africa			
Variable	(1)	(2)	(3)	Variable	(1)	(2)	(3)
Realistic Threat	–			Realistic Threat	–		
Symbolic Threat	.70★★	–		Symbolic Threat	.55★★	–	
Intergroup Contact	.10	.05	–	Intergroup Contact	.07	.16★★	–
Mexico				India			
Variable	(1)	(2)	(3)	Variable	(1)	(2)	(3)
Realistic Threat	–			Realistic Threat	–		
Symbolic Threat	.82★★	–		Symbolic Threat	.78★★	–	
Intergroup Contact	.10	.10	–	Intergroup Contact	.24★★	.22★★	–
Singapore				Brazil			
Variable	(1)	(2)	(3)	Variable	(1)	(2)	(3)
Realistic Threat	–			Realistic Threat	–		
Symbolic Threat	.80★★	–		Symbolic Threat	.75★★	–	
Intergroup Contact	.10	.11a	–	Intergroup Contact	.14★★	.20★★	–
Peru				Chile			
Variable	(1)	(2)	(3)	Variable	(1)	(2)	(3)
Realistic Threat	–			Realistic Threat	–		
Symbolic Threat	.78★★	–		Symbolic Threat	.80★★	–	
Intergroup Contact	.07	.05	–	Intergroup Contact	.08	.08	–
Kyrgyzstan				Argentina			
Variable	(1)	(2)	(3)	Variable	(1)	(2)	(3)
Realistic Threat	–			Realistic Threat	–		
Symbolic Threat	.75★★	–		Symbolic Threat	.84★★	–	
Intergroup Contact	.40★★	.61★★	–	Intergroup Contact	.10	.08	–

(Continued)

TABLE 10.4 (Continued)

United States				New Zealand			
Turkey				England			
Variable	(1)	(2)	(3)	Variable	(1)	(2)	(3)
Realistic Threat	–			Realistic Threat	–		
Symbolic Threat	.87★★	–		Symbolic Threat	.82★★	–	
Intergroup Contact	.19★★	.24★★	–	Intergroup Contact	.01	.03	–
France				Kenya			
Variable	(1)	(2)	(3)	Variable	(1)	(2)	(3)
Realistic Threat	–			Realistic Threat	–		
Symbolic Threat	.78★★	–		Symbolic Threat	.79★★	–	
Intergroup Contact	.06	.12★	–	Intergroup Contact	.13	.09	–
Nigeria				China			
Variable	(1)	(2)	(3)	Variable	(1)	(2)	(3)
Realistic Threat	–			Realistic Threat	–		
Symbolic Threat	.81★★	–		Symbolic Threat	.85★★	–	
Intergroup Contact	.01	–.03	–	Intergroup Contact	.09	.11	–

Note: ★ $p <.05$, ★★ $p <.001$.

intergroup contact was not correlated with realistic nor symbolic threat. In New Zealand, Spain, Italy, India, Brazil, Kyrgyzstan, and Turkey, intergroup contact was positively correlated with both realistic and symbolic contact. In South Africa, Singapore, and France, intergroup contact and symbolic threat were positively correlated. See Table 10.4 for correlations between the variables in all 20 nations.

Discussion

The purpose of this chapter was to explore prejudice toward outgroups blamed for the spread of the COVID-19 virus in 20 nations. The results showed that in the 20 nations, England, Brazil, and Peru were the highest on realistic and symbolic threats. France, Singapore, and India were the lowest on realistic threat, while Kyrgyzstan, Singapore, and India were the lowest on symbolic threat. India, Kyrgyzstan, and Russia were the highest on intergroup contact, while Chile, Peru, and Turkey were the lowest. In addition, the results revealed that symbolic and realistic threats were positively correlated in the combined sample and in each nation. The relationship between threat and intergroup contact was not as clear. The results of this study illuminate theoretical and methodological implications as we consider prejudice and intergroup contact, particularly during a pandemic.

Theoretical Implications

There are two critical theoretical implications drawn from this study: the connection between historical context and the pandemic on threat perception, and the influence of negative intergroup contact. First, in Brazil, historical relations between the dominant cultural groups and minority group explain the feelings of threat perceived by the dominant group members. For decades the Brazilian government has touted racial democracy while promoting a policy of institutional racism, promoting residential segregation, employment discrimination, lack of health care access, and numerous other forms of discrimination and racism toward its Afro-Brazilian population (Barreto, 2019; Twine, 1997). Thus, when President Jair Bolsonaro diverted funding from Afro-Brazilian areas and blamed them for the spread of the pandemic, it is not surprising many Brazilians perceive Afro-Brazilians as a threat. Inversely, Asians (more specifically Chinese) were blamed for the spread of COVID-19 in France. However, there has not been a long history of systematic racism and discrimination in France toward Asians. Thus, while prejudice and scapegoating of Asians did increase during the pandemic, it did not increase to the same level as it did toward Afro-Brazilians in Brazil. The historical, cultural, economic, and political context in which prejudice occurs must be considered in conjunction with the pandemic situation. Taken collectively, this will explain why in some cases ingroups in some nations will perceive more threat from outgroups than in other nations.

Second, *RQ3* explored the extent to which threat was correlated with intergroup contact. Research is divided on the extent to which intergroup contact influences prejudice. While Allport (1954) hypothesized increased intergroup contact should decrease prejudice, subsequent research has shown that the effect depends on the type of contact (Croucher, 2016; González et al., 2008; Pettigrew & Tropp, 2008). In ten nations, intergroup contact and threat (realistic and symbolic) were not correlated. In seven of the 20 nations examined, intergroup contact was positively correlated with realistic and symbolic threat, and in three nations contact was positively correlated with symbolic threat. In these nations, increased contact is related to increased prejudice. It's essential to explore factors that could further affect this relationship. What influence does the pandemic have on this relationship? Croucher et al. (2021a) argued the influence of the pandemic on intergroup communication is not fully understood. It is highly possible that in the midst of the pandemic ingroups may not only be placing blame on outgroups but may also be experiencing heightened fear of the virus itself. This unconscious or conscious contagion effect or fear of the virus is something that needs to be further explored in relation to how it influences intergroup communication and contact.

Methodological Implications

Two methodological implications emerge from this study: importance of language choice and translation when doing cross-national work, and the timing of data collection when comparing samples. First, when conducting a cross-national study of this kind, it's critical to consider language choice and linguistic equivalence. This study was conducted in eight languages. When approaching each nation, language choice was easy in some and difficult in other nations. In 12 of the nations, the choice of language was simple, as each nation has one dominant language spoken by the dominant cultural group: France (French), New Zealand (English), Italy (Italian), Brazil (Portuguese), Turkey (Turkish), the United States (English), Russia (Russian), Mexico (Spanish), Peru (Spanish), Chile (Spanish), Argentina (Spanish), and England (English). In the remaining eight nations, discussions took place with contacts based in each nation. In Nigeria, India, Singapore, South Africa, and Kenya, contacts within each nation recommended English as the language of data collection. In China, Mandarin was recommended. In Kyrgyzstan, Russian was recommended. Such recommendations from contacts, locally embedded, were integral to developing surveys that were linguistically approachable for participants. The research team also worked with our contacts in each nation on questions of equivalence. The word "presence" was a difficult one in multiple languages. In more than one language, the concept/word could be translated to be physical, emotional, metaphysical, and/or psychological "presence." Based on the measures, we focused on physical "presence." We cannot be sure respondents understood the statements to mean physical "presence." However, this specific issue demonstrates the importance of considering linguistic equivalence when doing cross-linguistic work.

Second, the data for this study were collected between April 2020 and June 2021. The research team tried to collect data in each nation at what was considered a "peak" COVID-19 infection time. However, in some cases, the nations under analysis went through subsequent COVID-19 outbreaks and experienced different strains of the virus. Without collecting data at the exact same time in each nation, it is possible that the study might suffer from sampling and measurement bias (Holmes, 2004). Thus, the results should be interpreted with this in mind.

Future Research

The results of current research offer both theoretical and methodological contributions to the field of integrated threat theory and intergroup communication during the COVID-19 pandemic. In the meanwhile, there are directions for future study.

First, participants of this research were individuals born in these countries. Future studies could include individuals born outside of the surveyed nations as there has been an increasing number immigrants in these countries. Second, future studies should consider to what extent media has framed and distributed messages during a global crisis such as COVID-19. Specifically, how the media frames minority groups and narrates stories could be associated with the perception of realistic threat (Nshom et al., 2022). Moreover, the correlation coefficients of realistic threat and symbolic threat measures in these 20 countries range from .70 to .87, which was relatively high. However, these two variables are among prejudice measure, and Stephan et al. (1999) have argued the high correlation coefficients between two dimensions in the same measure have led to questions to if they measure two different constructs. Therefore, it is crucial to conduct further research on this matter. However, results from different national samples present both similarities and differences on prejudice. Such a cross-cultural study like this is significantly necessary as it sheds new light on providing us better understanding of both theoretical and methodological approaches on related circumstances.

Note

1 All COVID-19 case numbers are from Johns Hopkins Coronavirus Resource Center (updated daily). https://coronavirus.jhu.edu.

References

AFP. (2020, April 6). Brazil minister offends China with racist virus tweet. *AFP Yahoo News*. https://news.yahoo.com/brazil-minister-offends-china-racist-virus-tweet-163351712.html

Allport, G. W. (1954). *The nature of prejudice*. Addison-Wesley.

Ashmore, R. D. (1970). Prejudice: Causes and cures. In B. E. Colling (Ed.), *Social psychology: Social influence, attitude, attitude change, group processes, and prejudice* (pp. 245–339). Addison Wesley.

Asians in Paris rattled. (2020, February 10). *DW News*. https://www.dw.com/en/coronavirus-asians-in-paris-rattled-by-racist-abuse/av-52319444

Atwell, Seate, A., Ma, R., Chien, H.-Y., & Mastro, D. (2018). Cultivating intergroup emotions: An intergroup threat theory approach. *Mass Communication and Society, 21*, 178–197. https://doi.org/10.1080/15205436.2017.1381362

Atwell Seate, A., & Mastro, D. (2016). Media's influence on immigration attitudes: An intergroup threat theory approach. *Communication Monographs, 83*, 194-213. https://doi.org/10.1080/03637751.2015.1068433

Banas, J. A., Bessarabova, E., & Massey, Z. B. (2020). Meta-analysis on mediated contact and prejudice. *Human Communication Research, 46*(2–3), 120–160. https://doi.org/10.1093/hcr/hqaa004

Barreto, R. C. (2019). Brazil's black Christianity and the counter-hegemonic production of knowledge in world Christianity. *Studies in World Christianity, 25*, 71–94.

Berrenberg, J. L., Finlay, K. A., Stephan, W. G., & Stephan, C. (2007). Prejudice toward people with cancer or AIDS: Applying the integrated threat model. *Journal of Applied Biobehavioral Research, 7*, 75–86. https://doi.org/10.1111/j.1751-9861.2002.tb00078.x

Bowles, J. M., Smith, L. R., Verdugo, S. R., Wagner, K. D., & Davidson, P. J. (2020). "Generally, you get 86'ed because you're a liability": An application of Integrated Threat Theory to frequently witnessed overdoses and socially distancing responses. *Social Science & Medicine, 260,* 113190. https://doi.org/10.1016/j.socscimed.2020.113190

Caldwell, K. L., & de Araújo, E. M. (2020, June 11). Covid-19 is deadlier for black Brazilians, a legacy of structural racism that dates back to slavery. *The Conversation.* https://theconversation.com/covid-19-is-deadlier-for-black-brazilians-a-legacy-of-structural-racism-that-dates-back-to-slavery-139430

Casalini, S. (29, January 2020). Roma, psicosi coronavirus. Il Conservatorio di Santa Cecilia impone: "Visita obbligatoria per tutti gli allievi prientali". *La Repubblica.* https://roma.repubblica.it/cronaca/2020/01/29/news/roma_conservatorio_di_santa_cecilia-247107490/

Chan, C., & Strabucchi, M. M. (2021). Many-faced orientalism: Racism and xenophobia in a time of the novel coronavirus in Chile. *Asian Ethnicity, 22*(2), 374–394. https://doi.org/10.1080/14631369.2020.1795618

Choi, S. (2021). "People look at me like I AM the virus": Fear stigma, and discrimination during the COVID-19 pandemic. *Qualitative Social Work, 20,* 233–239. https://doi.org/10.1177/1473325020973333

Clissold, E., Nylander, D., Watson, C., & Ventriglio, A. (2020). Pandemics and prejudice. *International Journal of Social Psychiatry, 66*(5), 421–423. https://doi.org/10.1177/0020764020937873

Collins, S. (26, March 2020). Covid 19 coronavirus: Woman challenges anti-Chinese gesture in Mission Bay. *NZ Herald.* https://www.nzherald.co.nz/nz/covid-19-coronavirus-woman-challenges-anti-chinese-gesture-in-mission-bay/QM5RHKGLTK2OG37IVPXDHTJYUU/.

Covid-19-related discrimination and stigma: A global phenomenon? (2020, May 25). *The United Nations Educational, Scientific and Cultural Organization.* https://en.unesco.org/news/covid-19-related-discrimination-and-stigma-global-phenomenon

Cowan, J. (2021, March 19). Looking at the rise of anti-Asian racism in the pandemic. *New York Times.* https://www.nytimes.com/2021/03/19/us/anti-asian-racism-pandemic.html

Croucher, S. M. (2013). Integrated threat theory and acceptance of immigrant assimilation: An analysis of Muslim immigration in Western Europe. *Communication Monographs, 80,* 46–62. https://doi.org/10.1080/03637751.2012.739704

Croucher, S. M. (2016). Further development of integrated threat theory and intergroup contact: A reply to Aberson (2015). *Communication Monographs, 83,* 269–275. https://doi.org/10.1080/03637751.2015.1119866

Croucher, S. M. (2017). Integrated theory. *Oxford Research Encyclopedia of Communication.* https://doi.org/10.1093/acrefore/9780190228613.013.490

Croucher, S. M., Nguyen, T., Ashwell, D., Spencer, A., Permyakova, T., & Gomez, O. (2022) Prejudice toward Afro-Brazilians. *Journal of Intercultural Communication Research.* https://doi.org/10.1080/17475759.2021.1957702

Croucher, S. M., Nguyen, T., Pearson, E., Murray, N., Feekery, A., Spencer, A., Gomez, O., Girardelli, D., & Kelly, S. (2021a). A comparative analysis of Covid-19 related prejudice: The United States, Spain, Italy, and New Zealand. *Communication Research Reports, 38,* 78–89. https://doi.org/10.1080/08824096.2021.1885371

Croucher, S. M., Nguyen, T., & Rahmani, D. (2020). Prejudice toward Asian-Americans in the Covid-19 Pandemic: The effects of social media use in the United States. *Frontiers in Health Communication.* https://doi.org/10.3389/fcomm.2020.00039

Croucher, S. M., Permyakova, T., & Turdubaeva, E. (2021b). Prejudice toward Asians and migrants during the COVID-19 pandemic in Russia and Kyrgyzstan. *Russian Journal of Communication, 13*(3), 289–301. https://doi.org/10.1080/19409419.2021.1 958697

Eguegu, O. (2020, April 6). Why are so many Nigerian doctors and journalists upset about a Chinese medical team coming to advise on COVID-19? *China Africa Project.* https:// chinaafricaproject.com/analysis/why-nigerian-doctors-journalists-are-so-upset-about-a-chinese-medical-team-coming-to-advise-on-covid-19/

Faulkner, J., Schaller, M., Park, J. H., & Duncan, L. A. (2004). Evolved disease-avoidance mechanisms and contemporary xenophobic attitudes. *Group Processes & Intergroup Relations, 7,* 333–353. https://doi.org/1177/1368430204046142

Fiflani, P. (2020, March 13). Dudula: How South African anger has focused on foreigners. *BBC.* https://www.bbc.com/news/world-africa-60698374

Gan, N. (2020, February 2). Outcasts in their own country, the people of Wuhan are the unwanted faces of China's coronavirus outbreak. *CNN.* https://edition.cnn. com/2020/02/01/asia/coronavirus-wuhan-discrimination-intl-hnk/index.html

Gerber, T. P., & He, Q. (2021). Sinophobia in Russia and Kyrgyzstan. *Journal of Contemporary China.* https://doi.org/10.10180/10670564.2021.1926090

Ghosal, A., Saaliq, S., & Schmall, E. (2020). Indian Muslims face stigma, blame for surge in infections. *Associated Press News.* https://apnews.com/ad2e96f4caa55b817 c3d8656bdb2fcbd

Girardelli, D., Croucher, S. M., & Nguyen, T. (2021). La pandemia COVID-19, la sinofobiae il ruolo dei social media in Italia. *Mondi Migranti,* 85–104. https://doi. org/10.3280/MM2021-001005

Giuffrida, F. (2020, February 26). L'incubo di essere cinesi in Italia con il coronavirus: @Unragazzo preso a bottigliate in Veneto@. *Open.* https://www.open.online/ 2020/02/26/lincubo-di-essere-cinesi-in-italia-con-il-coronavirus-un-ragazzo-preso-a-bottigliate-in-veneto/

Giuffrida, F., & Willsher, K. (2020, January 31). Outbreaks of xenophobia in west as coronavirus spreads. *The Guardian.* https://www.theguardian.com/world/2020/ jan/31/spate-of-anti-chinese-incidents-in-italy-amid-coronavirus-panic

González, K. V., Verkuyten, M., Weesie, J., & Poppe, E. (2008). Prejudice towards Muslims in the Netherlands: Testing integrated threat theory. *British Journal of Social Psychology, 47,* 667–685.

Govan, F. (2020, January 31). Is coronavirus paranoia fuelling racism against the Chinese in Spain. *The Local.* https://www.thelocal.es/20200131/is-the-coronavirus-is-fuelling-racism-against-chinos-in-spain/

Gülseven, E. (2021). Identity, nationalism and the response of Turkey to COVID-19 pandemic. *Chinese Political Science Review, 6,* 40–62. https://doi.org/10.1007/ s41111-020-00166-x

Guo, M., Joanpere, M., Pulido, C., & Cuxart, M. P. (2020). Coping of Chinese citizens living in Spain during the COVID-19 pandemic: Lessons for personal well-being and social cohesion. *Sustainability, 12*(19), 7949. https://doi.org/10.3390/su12197949

Guterres, A. (2020, April 23). We are all in this together: Human rights and Covid-19 response and recovery. *The United Nations.* https://www.un.org/en/un-coronavirus-communications-team/we-are-all-together-human-rights-and-covid-19-re-sponse-and-recovery

Holmes, T. H. (2004). Ten categories of statistical errors: A guide for research in endocrinology and metabolism. *American Journal of Physiology and Endocrinology and Metabolism, 286,* E495–E501. https://doi.org/10.1152/ajpendo.00484.2003

Iqbal, N. (2020, February 1). Coronavirus fears fuel racism and hostility, say British-Chinese. *The Guardian*. https://www.theguardian.com/world/2020/feb/01/coronavirus-weaponised-way-to-be-openly-racist

Johns Hopkins Coronavirus Resource Center. (Updated daily). Coronavirus Resource Center. https://coronavirus.jhu.edu/map.html

Kamil, A. (2021, May 11). Man, 30, arrested for alleged racist attack on woman along Choa Chu Kang Drive. *Today Online*. https://www.todayonline.com/singapore/man-30-arrested-alleged-racist-attack-woman-choa-chu-kang-drive

Kim, B., Cooks, E., & Kim, S.-K. (2021). Exploring incivility and moral foundations toward Asians in English-speaking tweets in hate crime-reporting cities during the COVID-19 pandemic. *Internet Research* (ahead-of-print).

Kleymenov, K. (2020, February 5). Virus_na_voennoy_sluzhbe_proverka_na_prochnost_teorii_zarazivshey_ne_odno_sredstvo_massovoy_informatsii [Virus on military service Resilience check for contagion theory in media]. https://www.1tv.ru/news/2020-02-05/380033-virus_na_voennoy_sluzhbe_proverka_na_prochnost_teorii_zarazivshey_ne_odno_sredstvo_massovoy_informatsii

Krishnan, M. (2020). Indian Muslims face renewed stigma amid COVID-19 crisis. *Made for Minds*. https://www.dw.com/en/indian-muslims-face-renewed-stigma-amid-covid-19-crisis/a-53436462

Laemle, B. (2020, February 7). A Paris, les rues du quartier de Belleville se vident avec la peur du coronavirus. *Le Monde*. https://www.lemonde.fr/societe/article/2020/02/07/a-paris-les-rues-du-quartier-de-belleville-se-vident-avec-la-peur-du-coronavirus_6028851_3224.html

Laudette, C.-L. (2021, January 26). Discrimination worsens in Spain, far-right and fake news largely to blame. *Reuters*. https://www.reuters.com/article/us-spain-rights-discrimination-idUSKBN29U228

Lee, J., & Yadav, M. (2020, May 21). The rise of anti-Asian hate in the wake of Covid-19. *Social Science Research Council*. https://items.ssrc.org/covid-19-and-the-social-sciences/the-rise-of-anti-asian-hate-in-the-wake-of-covid-19/

Lu, J. (2021, March 26). Why pandemics give birth to hate: From bubonic plague to COVID-19. *NPR*. https://www.npr.org/sections/goatsandsoda/2021/03/26/980480882/why-pandemics-give-birth-to-hate-from-black-death-to-covid-19

Mandalaywala, T. M., Gonzalez, G., & Tropp, L. R. (2021). Early perceptions of COVID-19 intensity and anti-Asian prejudice among White Americans. *Group Processes & Intergroup Relations*. https://doi.org/10.1177/13684302211049721

Navarrete, C. D., & Fessler, D. M. T. (2006). Disease avoidance and ethnocentrism: The effects of disease vulnerability and disgust sensitivity on intergroup attitudes. *Evolution and Human Behavior, 27*, 270–282. https://doi.org/10.1016/j.evolhumbehav.2005.12.001

Ng, K. (2021, January 13). How British east and southeast Asians are fighting racism during the pandemic. *Independent*. https://www.independent.co.uk/news/uk/home-news/coronavirus-racism-hate-crime-south-east-asians-b1770177.html

Nguyen, T., Croucher, S. M., Diers-Lawson, A., & Maydell, E. (2021). Who's to blame for the spread of COVID-19 in New Zealand? Applying attribution theory to understand public stigma. *Communication Research and Practice, 7*(1), 379–396. https://doi.org/10.1080/22041451.2021.1958635

Nshom, E., Khalimzoda, I., Sadaf, S., & Shaymardanov, M. (2022). Perceived threat or perceived benefit? Immigrants' perception of how Finns tend to perceive them. *International Journal of Intercultural Relations, 86*, 46–55. https://doi.org/10.1016/j.ijintrel.2021.11.001

Pettigrew, T. F., & Tropp, L. R. (2008). How does intergroup contact reduce prejudice? Meta-analysis of three mediators. *European Journal of Social Psychology, 38*, 922–934. https://doi.org/10.1002/ejsp.504

Petrizzelli, D. (2020, March 8). Incendio doloso al ristorante giapponese: "Ci hanno minacciati dicendoci che portiamo il virus." *Torino Today.* https://www.torinotoday. it/cronaca/incendio-ristorante-king-martiri-rivoli-8-marzo-2020.html

Philling, D., & Wong, S.-L. (2020, April 14). China-Africa relations rocked by alleged racism over COVID-19. *FT.* https://www.ft.com/content/48f199b0-9054-4ab6-aaad-a326163c9285

Phillips, D. (2020). "Enormous disparities": Coronavirus death rates expose Brazil's deep racial inequalities. *The Guardian.* https://www.theguardian.com/ world/2020/jun/09/enormous-disparities-coronavirus-death-rates-expose-brazils-deep-racial-inequalities?emci=94d478d2-52aa-ea11-9b05-00155d039e74&emdi=45829873-54aa-ea11-9b05-00155d039e74&ceid=4606001

Politklinika. (2021). Пандемия маалында саламаттык сактоо министрлиги бахиланы 100 эсе кымбат сатып алган (pk.kg).

Ramsay, J. E., & Pang, J. S. (2017). Anti-immigrant prejudice in rising East Asia: A stereotype content and integrated threat analysis. *Political Psychology, 38*(2), 227–244. https://doi.org/10.1111/pops.12312.

Roberto, K. J., Johnson, A. F., & Rauhaus, B. M. (2020). Stigmatization and prejudice during the COVID-19 pandemic. *Administrative Theory & Praxis, 42*(3), 364–378. https://doi.org/10.1080/10841806.2020.1782128

Rzymski, P., & Nowicki, M. (2020). COVID-19 related prejudice toward Asian medical students: A consequence of SARS-CoV-2 fears in Poland. *Journal of Infection and Public Health, 13*, 873–876.

Schaller, M., & Neuberg, S. L. (2012). Chapter one – Danger, disease, and the nature of prejudice(s). *Advances in Experimental Social Psychology, 46*, 1–54. https://doi. org/10.1016/B978-0-12-394281-4.00001-5

Sen, N. J. (2021, November 21). Today Youth Survey: Majority believe racist episodes rising amid pandemic, further amplified on social media. *Today Online.* https:// www.todayonline.com/singapore/today-youth-survey-majority-believe-racist-episodes-rising-amid-pandemic-further-amplified

Shahrigian, S. (2020, March 2). New York state assembly staffer spreads xenophobic message amid coronavirus fears. *New York Daily News.* https://www.nydailynews. com/news/politics/ny-xenophobia-coronavirus-mathylde-frontus-20200302-inop2dq4bvdxtodsqtjy573vji-story.html

Sorokowski, P., Groyecka, A., Kowal, M., Sorokowska, A., Bialek, M., Lebuda, I., Dobrowolska, M., Zdybek, P., & Karwowski, M. (2020). Can information about pandemics increase negative attitudes toward foreign groups? A case of COVID-19 outbreak. *Sustainability, 12*(12), 4912. https://doi.org/10.3390/su12124912

Solomon, S. (2020, March 4). Coronavirus brings "Sinophobia" to Africa. *VOA News.* https://www.voanews.com/a/science-health_coronavirus-outbreak_coronavirus-brings-sinophobia-africa/6185249.html

Soy, A. (2020, October 8). Coronavirus in Africa: Five reasons why COVID-19 has been less deadly than elsewhere. *BBC.* https://www.bbc.com/news/world-africa-54418613

Sputnik. (2020). "Кытайдагы кыргыз студент: коронавирустан улам айрымдар Бишкекке кетүүгө камынууда" (sputnik.kg).

Stephan, W. G., & Stephan, C. W. (1996). Predicting prejudice. *International Journal of Intercultural Relations, 20*, 409–426.

Stephan, W. G., & Stephan, C. W. (2000). An integrated threat theory of prejudice. In S. Oskamp (Ed.), *Reducing prejudice and discrimination* (pp. 225–246). Lawrence Erlbaum.

Stephan, W. G., Ybarra, O., & Bachman, G. (1999). Prejudice toward immigrants: An integrated threat theory. *Journal of Applied Social Psychology, 29*, 2221–2237.

Stephan, W. G., Ybarra, O., & Rios Morrison, K. (2015). Intergroup threat theory. In T. Nelson (Ed.), *Handbook of prejudice* (pp. 255–278). Lawrence Erlbaum.

Tan, L. (2020, June 24). Covid-19 coronavirus: Prejudice against Asians in NZ lower than elsewhere study finds. *NZ Herald.* https://www.nzherald.co.nz/nz/covid-19-coronavirus-prejudice-against-asians-in-nz-lower-than-elsewhere-study-finds/VDMFZCMJ55JUJVWFEFX62Z63G4/

Tan, X., Lee, R., & Ruppanner, L. (2021). Profiling racial prejudice during COVID-19: Who exhibits anti-Asian sentiment in Australia and the United States? *Australian Journal of Social Issues, 56*(4), 464–484. https://doi.org/10.1002/ajs4.176

Tausch, N., Hewstone, M., & Roy, R. (2008). The relationship between contact, status and prejudice: An integrated threat theory analysis of Hindu-Muslim relations in India. *Journal of Community & Applied Social Psychology, 19*, 83–94. https://doi.org/10.1002/casp.984

Tekin, A. (2020). Türkiye'de yaşayan Çinliler. https://www.gazeteduvar.com.tr/gundem/2020/02/25/turkiyede-yasayan-cinliler-bizi-restoranlara-ve-otellere-almiyorlar

Troia, G. A., & Graham, S. (2017). Use and acceptability of writing adaptations for students with disabilities: Survey of Grade 3–8 teachers. *Learning Disabilities Research & Practice*, 32, 257–269.

Twine, F. W. (1997). *Racism in a racial democracy: The maintenance of White supremacy.* Duke University Press.

Vanderklippe, N. (2020, April 9). "Stay away from here": In China, foreigners have become a target for coronavirus discrimination. *The Globe and Mail.* https://www.theglobeandmail.com/world/article-stay-away-from-here-in-china-foreigners-have-become-a-target-for/

Whitehead, D. (2020, February 12). "You deserve the coronavirus": Chinese people in UK Abused over outbreak. *Sky News Daily.* https://news.sky.com/story/coronavirus-chinese-people-face-abuse-in-the-street-over-outbreak-11931779

York, G. (2020, March 19). Coronavirus triggers xenophobia in some African countries. *The Globe and Mail.* https://www.theglobeandmail.com/world/article-coronavirus-triggers-xenophobia-in-some-african-countries/

Young, J. L., & Cho, M. K. (2021). The invisibility of Asian Americans in COVID-19 data, reporting, and relief. *The American Journal of Bioethics, 21*, 100–102. https://doi.org/10.1080/15265161.2020.1870767

Ziems, C., He, B., Soni, S., & Kumar, S. (2020). Racism is a virus: Anti-Asian hate and counter hate in social media during the COVID-19 crisis. arXiv preprint. arXiv:2005.12423. https://arxiv.org/abs/2005.12423

Zsiga, K. (2020, November 17). Victim-blaming discourse and politics: Media (mis) representation as a political strategy in Peru. *Feminist Perspectives.* https://www.kcl.ac.uk/victim-blaming-discourse-and-politics-media-misrepresentation-as-a-political-strategy-in-peru

11

INSTRUCTIONAL COMMUNICATION DURING PANDEMICS

Stephanie Kelly

In the spring semester of 2020, faculty and students across the world were asked to abruptly transition their classes to online learning to help impede the spread of COVID-19. This shift constituted *emergency remote teaching* in which faculty taught from their homes with limited access to campus technology and limited ability to control their teaching environment that was suddenly shared by family, roommates, and pets (Chen, 2021). Although the circumstances surrounding the emergency remote teaching transition were tragic, the forced pivot to online learning brought about an evolution in online learning perceptions.

Many faculty who had no experience in online learning abruptly found themselves teaching fully online beginning in 2020 (Brown, 2021). Likewise, many classes that had never been offered online before were suddenly being taught fully online, and faculty were finding that not only could these classes be taught well online, but that online technology allowed some to teach more efficiently (Denton, 2021). Faculty found, for example, that they could (Denton, 2021; Foutz, 2021):

1   Ensure greater clarity in their words by recording video lectures that had mistakes edited out and words subtitled
2   Transition quicker between media by teaching from just the computer station rather than having to be present across a large physical space
3   Answer student questions with greater patience when working asynchronously, taking a break after reading a message that prompts frustration, which avoids the accidental grumpiness that sometimes comes across in person

In short, the pandemic taught many faculty who had previously been opposed to online learning to recognize its benefits. Indeed, an editorial from a special issue

DOI: 10.4324/9781003214496-11

of *Frontiers in Communication* on classroom culture and the pandemic concluded that "Perhaps it is time to quit thinking of the face-to-face as the gold standard for teaching and rather think of the gold standard as teaching that has been skillfully adjusted to be effective within its channel" (Claus et al., 2021, p. 4).

Indeed, the COVID-19 pandemic was an eye-opening experience for many educators, equipping them with the experience to realize that online learning, though different from face-to-face learning, was not a lesser type of education if the instructor effectively communicated with students through technology and used the technology strategically for instruction. That does not mean that online learning during COVID-19 was without challenges though. Despite the advances in online education practices and attitudes that came from the COVID-19 emergency remote teaching pivot, faculty and students alike experienced education during this period under an unprecedented confluence of circumstances.

Pandemic Pedagogy

The term "pandemic pedagogy" has been used both colloquially and academically since the COVID-19 outbreak to reference a variety of classroom abnormalities highlighted by the pandemic. This has led to misunderstandings in regard to what the term truly means. Pandemic pedagogy is far more complex a concept than the superficial concept of engaging in online learning during a pandemic; it is an unexpected, forced online education experience in the nexus of abnormal, stressful life circumstances for educators and students of varied preparation and resources. To understand pandemic pedagogy, the unique physical and psychological circumstances affecting education throughout the pandemic must be considered.

Faculty vs. New Technology

In the transition to emergency remote teaching, universities were not just forced online; they were forced online with little to no time for adopting new technologies or for faculty to be trained on how to use those technologies (Floyd, 2020). For faculty new to the virtual learning technology, the transition brought with it a steep learning curve, one that many intended to retire without ever facing. Further, instructors encountered new challenges to distance learning that one would not anticipate from the face-to-face classroom. One such challenge was that many international students across the globe had to return to their home country, making it impossible to have synchronous virtual class at a time that was equitable for all learners across all time zones (Feekery & Condon, 2021). Such challenges meant that in emergency remote teaching conditions, educators could not simply continue to hold class in their standard teaching time, using their standard teaching techniques that required synchronous student engagement. This meant that many needed to learn to teach effectively asynchronously, relying heavily on new technologies (Feekery & Condon, 2021).

A significant amount of discussion in the pandemic pedagogy literature has been focused on instructors' use of technology, especially for those faculty who had distance learning technology and assistive technologies thrust upon them for the first time (Hughes et al., 2020). Largely, this discussion has happened apart from learning goals, focusing on the culture shock that is burgeoned when traditional classroom teaching is forced into an incompatible online platform. Yet, by starting with learning goals, instructors can adapt courses to fit the online learning platform (Costa & Da Silva, 2021; Westerman et al., In Press). While it is true that the same lesson often cannot be taught online with the same method used in the face-to-face classroom, it is possible to meet the same learning goals through skillful use of available technology. This requires instructors to be efficient users of the technology though and to have the time to strategically think through how that technology can best be applied to meet learning goals. For many instructors, the emergency remote teaching pivot happened so swiftly that there was neither time to master the technology nor to consider how the technology best met learning goals (Knight, 2020).

So, though many instructors struggled to learn how to effectively utilize new technology rapidly in the emergency remote teaching transition, the affordances of online learning allowed for greater flexibility in terms of time and location for students. Yet, this flexibility also brought with it a reliance on time management and self-regulation that many students had not been required to build before (Dhawan, 2020). This increased personal responsibility for students brought new stress into the learning process.

Anxiety!!!

The transition to online learning meant learning new technologies for many students as well (Frey, 2021). While some universities planned well ahead for the transition, building time for both students and faculty to receive training before transitioning to distance learning, other universities provided no training at all, transitioning to a fully virtual work environment over a weekend (Knight, 2020). This meant encounters with new technical difficulties and a greater responsibility placed on students to navigate the technology and manage their time to allow time for technological learning curves on top of learning course material...this all caused heightened anxiety (Dhawan, 2020).

Students also struggled with anxieties brought forth through new communication patterns (Prentiss, 2021). Many students who had no anxieties about communicating with peers or instructors in the face-to-face classroom were suddenly riddled with anxieties about working through text-based computer-mediated communication, where their answers were documented for their learning community to continuously review and critique. This anxiety about the permanent documentation of poorly composed messages sent as text-based computer-mediated communication has been studied for decades (c.f., Walther et al., 2015), but it has received very little attention in the classroom context, though it was clearly demonstrated during the COVID-19 pandemic around the world (Prentiss, 2021).

The pandemic laid new anxieties upon students from more sources than just learning through virtual platforms. When the pandemic hit, many on-campus residences were forced to close; fortunate students were able to move back home, while others found themselves with no place to go (Knight, 2020; Schwartzman, 2020). Yet, even the fortunate university students who had a home to return to dealt with new challenges for their work, life, and school balance as they learned to attend school without steady internet connections, a computer of their own, or equipment powerful enough to handle the demands of virtual learning. They also, in many cases, battled for a quiet place to log into class as siblings logged into their own virtual classrooms and parents logged into virtual work meetings (Garland & Violanti, 2021). While college students struggled with the additional stress of learning to attend school from a home that was no longer their home, K-12 students shared with them the stress of not enough bandwidth, not enough computers, and not enough experience summoning the self-discipline to stay on task from home all day without constant supervision.

Beyond the functional difficulties of navigating distance learning technologies and battling for access to classes with limited home resources during COVID-19, students also struggled with psychological burdens. Suddenly college students were thrust home where their parents were in charge of their lives, losing their personal sense of empowerment (Frey & Locker, 2020; Garland & Violanti, 2021; Schwartzman, 2020). As such, college students went home to find themselves having to exert more responsibility for their own learning yet losing autonomy over their own behavior in their parents' home. This dichotomy of responsibility demands was met without the availability of mental health counseling services that are normally available on campuses, as universities struggled to develop ehealth services (Frey & Locker, 2021).

Emergency remote teaching with video conferencing also presented its own unique source of stress beyond accessibility. COVID-19 brought with it "Zoom fatigue" for students, educators, and members of the non-academic virtual workforce alike, who found themselves using video conferencing technology for multiple hours per day (Bailenson, 2021). While many educators thought that all cameras should be turned on when in class through video conferencing software to ensure that students were paying attention, this led to an overload of nonverbal information for students and faculty to process (Westerman et al., In Press). As a result, this overload of visual processing information created undo stress and burnout for all communicators as their senses became overwhelmed trying to process all the nonverbal cues being given equal prominence simultaneously (Bailenson, 2021). The great irony of this forced Zoom fatigue in emergency remote learning was that instructors are not able to focus on all students' nonverbal behaviors inches from their faces when teaching in the face-to-face classroom, meaning that educators were expecting themselves to monitor and process far more communicative cues in the online learning environment than they could possibly process in the traditional face-to-face classroom (Westerman et al., In Press). Additionally, communicators are never forced to observe their own nonverbal communication in a face-to-face setting, which makes synchronous virtual class with cameras on more draining than face-to-face class for both teachers and students (Bailenson, 2021; Westerman et al., In Press).

Additional stress came from life completely removed from learning. Students of all ages were living for the first time during a real pandemic (Arnett, 2020). The realities of illness and death for themselves and those they loved were constantly reiterated. They also faced new realities of limited resources as they themselves, and often their parents, lost jobs during the pandemic (Garland & Violanti, 2021). These stresses outside of the classroom bled over to affect their classroom performance. These feelings were described well by a student in a qualitative study, who shared their feelings by saying,

> I feel like I'm on the Titanic, and the world about me is going down. I'm spending my time reading and talking about ideas with others, and wondering: Is this a good way to spend time before the boat sinks?
>
> *Arnett (2020, p. 9)*

The psychological stress taken on by students during the pandemic became a salient part of their learning experiences.

In short, the pandemic laid stressors upon students at a magnitude many had never experienced. Students felt alone with their struggles and as though they had lost control over their world (Rippé et al., 2021). This sense of lack of control left many students unmotivated to continue working their hardest in the classroom, which in turn placed stress upon faculty who still needed their students to learn (Code et al., 2020).

The Reality of Pandemic Pedagogy

An unfortunate reality of the discussion on pandemic pedagogy is that teaching during the pandemic has been considered a passionate, but less rigorous type of teaching (Rosso, 2021). Because many faculty struggled to adapt to new technologies and students struggled with connectivity and anxiety, pandemic pedagogy has been framed by many as the best education that can be accomplished under less than ideal circumstances (Claus et al., 2021). Yet, university students have always been expected to meet standards during times of grief and loss (Rosso, 2021). Students face tragedy and anxiety every semester, be it personal illness, the loss of an immediate family member, loss of work, or coping with assault. Seasoned educators know from years of working with students as they persevere through personal tragedy, and that it is entirely possible to be compassionate to students while expecting that they rise to the academic rigor required for their degree (Rosso, 2021).

The reality of pandemic pedagogy is not a lesser form of education. No doubt, some students had subpar educational experiences during the early COVID-19 pandemic, which is its own tragedy. This was not necessary though. The advances of online education and communication theory pair to provide effective solutions for teaching online during a pandemic that can make pandemic pedagogy effective pedagogy that focuses on the real needs of students during the pandemic: effective delivery of course material, flexibility to have some control over their lives, and a place to build social connections to help alleviate the burnout and anxiety surrounding their lives.

Key CMC Theories and Models for Teaching Students to Navigate Pandemic Learning

A number of communication theories have focused on explaining how interactions online differ from interactions face-to-face, and how those differences can be beneficial for communicators. These theories offer insight to best practices for managing pivots to virtual learning environments during times of crisis. As such, they provide guidance for how to meet the needs of pandemic pedagogy.

Social Information Processing Theory

Social information processing theory (SIPT) posits that online communicators have the same goals as face-to-face communicators, and that these goals can be accomplished online just as well as face-to-face (Walther, 1992). However, the success of computer-mediated communication is largely dependent upon whether the communicators are willing to put forth the effort necessary to overcome inherent limitations in virtual communication (e.g., not being able to see facial expressions in text-based communication; Walther, 1994). The effort required to successfully communicate through technology relies upon two things (Walther et al., 2005):

1   Thinking through the richness of the medium being used and skillfully adapting a message to accommodate for any limitations of that medium
2   Being actively engaged in the conversation, keeping the other communicator's perception of message timing in mind

Walther and Bunz (2005), in their SIPT-guided work on virtual groups, classify chronemics as one of the most critical pieces of successful computer-mediated communication, especially when working in asynchronous environments. Walther and Bunz point out that in asynchronous work, teammates do not know exactly when other members of the group will be available to engage with the content, and, as such, they should be cognizant of posting their own contributions as expediently as possible so that when their teammates have an opportunity to engage with the content, they are not prevented from making progress because they do not have necessary contributions from their teammates. If all members of a virtual team assume that team success depends on their own expedience, then this greatly limits frustration in working together. Walther and Bunz further explain that making interactions frequent and obvious is an equally important component of virtual group work. Not having frequent interactions can make communicators feel they are all alone, throwing messages out into a void for no one to read, which leads to frustration and loneliness. Therefore, expedient interaction must be prioritized and overt (e.g., acknowledging that messages have been read even if no reply seems warranted).

Although it is a necessary skill for most careers, students are often not trained to work in virtual teams (Kelly, 2021). Yet, to be successful as an online learner (and member of the virtual workforce), most people need this training. Much of the pandemic pedagogy research that focused on preparing students for the transition to emergency remote teaching focused on a lack of training with individual technologies (c.f., Floyd, 2020; Hughes et al., 2020). What received too little attention was teaching students how to communicate effectively to their peers and instructors in the online classroom, which is equally important.

In the online classroom, students often feel the frustration of classmates seeming disengaged or unavailable when their communication is not frequent and overt, but rarely consider how their own timing of asynchronous messages affects their group members (Kelly, 2021). When individuals feel that they are constantly waiting for other virtual group members to be engaged, this leads to frustration with those group members and anxiety about impending project deadlines (Walther & Bunz, 2005). As such, SIPT explains that a critical part of effective pandemic pedagogy is to teach students how to work with others in a virtual environment. This means teaching them the importance of communicating as quickly as possible, and overtly responding to all read messages, keeping in mind that group members cannot physically see their engagement.

Goke and Kelly (2019) also argue that an important, unintuitive skill for working in virtual groups in the classrooms and careers is limiting the channels of communication. In an era in which students have as many informal technologies for communicating with peers (e.g., GroupMe) as they do formal channels (e.g., their learning management system), course messages can be spread throughout a theoretically infinite number of channels. This can become very stressful for students as critical messages and documents become lost across unremembered channels (Kelly, 2021). To minimize this stress, it is critical that students are taught to establish communication plans with classmates that maximize efficiency of their time, agreeing upon only one (preferably), but certainly no more than two, computer-mediated communication channels for group work.

Hyperpersonal Theory

The emphasis on skillfully utilizing the richness of the communication medium in SIPT, particularly in asynchronous environments, has developed into hyperpersonal theory of computer-mediated communication (Walther et al., 2015). Much virtual communication takes place asynchronously. As explained by SIPT, when communicators are not cognizant of the time differences and careful to accommodate the needs of other communicators, this can make computer-mediated communication frustrating. However, hyperpersonal theory posits that the asynchronous nature of computer-mediated communication can be beneficial (Walther et al., 2015).

More specifically, hyperpersonal theory explains that the asynchronous nature of virtual communication is to the sender's advantage if they strategically think about how they can use the time delays. In computer-mediated asynchronous communication, message senders have the power to choose how they wish to portray themselves because they can take as much time as they need to construct the most socially perfect messages (Walther, 2006). This means, for example, that they have time to proofread and consider their written voice to ensure that their message is not laden with negative emotions (Foutz, 2021). More media-rich channels, such as social networks, provide more opportunities for impression management (Walther et al., 2015). For example, rather than choosing the first image of themselves available for a profile photo, communicators have the time to choose their best profile photo option.

One of the greatest benefits of asynchronous learning is that students can access their course material anytime, anywhere, engaging in learning at a time that best suits them (Kelly & Westerman, 2016). Hyperpersonal theory would posit that asynchronous rather than synchronous courses give students the opportunity to perfect the messages and images that they wish to send to other members of the learning environment, providing control of their online presence (Walther et al., 2015). During times of pandemic pedagogy, students need that flexibility more than in normal learning periods because they are operating with limited means from home and often must wait to have access to a computer or adequate bandwidth to join the course. As such, giving students with opportunities to engage in their classrooms hyperpersonally during a pandemic provides a measure of control that students report needing to reclaim (c.f., Garland & Violanti, 2021), in both their time management and self-portrayal.

Community of Inquiry Model

Social presence is the sense of connection communicators have when interacting through technology (Kelly & Westerman, 2016). It is a sense of non-mediation, the degree to which interacting through technology feels like interacting face-to-face (Lombard & Ditton, 1997). Gunawardena and Zittle (1997) explain social presence as the amount of interpersonal interaction two people perceive they have when communicating through technology. Social presence is a critical part of successful distance learning experiences. Meta-analytics review of literature has shown that social presence is strongly connected to students' satisfaction with their learning experience and perceived learning (Richardson et al., 2017).

The community of inquiry model of social presence explains that connections are developed in the virtual classroom by engaging in three types of communication (Garrison et al., 1999, 2010):

1   Affective
2   Cohesive
3   Interactive

Affective communication involves sharing one's personal insight (e.g., feelings, opinions, or self-disclosure). This may range from sharing an emotional reaction to course material to sharing what the weather is like where one is located. Cohesive communication involves the use of inclusive language such as "we," "us," and "our." In the online classroom, this means referring to the class as a unit, as "our class" and what "we" are doing. Interactive communication is a two-part construct. First, it is the active engagement in communication, meaning returning to the channel of communication as frequently as possible to continue the conversation as advised by SIPT. Second, it is inviting further conversation. In the online classroom, this means checking email, discussion boards, and other asynchronous classroom communication channels as often as possible, but then further prompting more communication by inviting questions or asking questions to other communicators. That this need to communicate frequently ties back to SIPT, which implies that part of meeting communicative goals online involves developing social presence.

Courses with high social presence have students with lower anxiety (Angelaki & Mavroidis, 2013) and lower perceived stress (Wang et al., 2021). These are beneficial even during normal teaching conditions; however, during a pandemic which adds its own unique stressors (Garland & Violanti, 2021), developing social presence in the classroom can be more critical than ever. Social presence as a form of connection is also critical during pandemic pedagogy to counteract the loneliness many students feel during lockdown conditions (Rippé et al., 2021).

Although the community of inquiry model of social presence is not directly referenced in many pandemic pedagogy studies, constructs are reflected, as research finds that interactive and affective communication enhanced their learning experiences. A recurring theme throughout the pandemic pedagogy literature is that students felt isolated and lonely once emergency remote teaching began, with students suddenly separated from the presence of their friend groups (c.f., Garland & Violanti, 2021; Rippé et al., 2021). This sense of isolation was assisted when professors engaged in consistent communication with their students, inviting students to interact with the instructor and one another (Rosso, 2021). Constant communication from instructors also helped students who struggled with the transition to remote learning feel that they were likely to achieve the learning goals in their new environment. Students further reported that they appreciated it when instructors put forth an effort to foster communication that gave them a sounding board for their anxieties (Frey & Locker, 2020).

Taking these findings together, it seems that instructors intentionally fostering social presence among their students was a positive step for successful pandemic instructional communication. Teaching students to engage in affective, interactive, and cohesive communication can be incorporated into online classrooms as easily as giving communication guidelines for discussion boards or recommended communication practices in the syllabus (Kelly, 2021). Yet, if this guidance is not provided by instructors, students will struggle to establish social presence with their classmates, missing the positive affective benefits that can be provided through online learning (Richardson et al., 2017).

Further Effective Instructional Pandemic Practices

Research investigating students' experiences with emergency remote teaching has offered additional insight into pandemic instructional communication. Just as hyperpersonal theory posits that students should be given the opportunity to take advantage of asynchronous communication's flexibility, pandemic pedagogy indicates that students need flexibility in all aspects of the classroom. In light of the pandemic, students felt that they had lost a great deal of autonomy in their lives; having flexibility about course deadlines and attendance gave them back a sense of control (Rosso, 2021). In fact, the flexibility was needed for some of them to be successful because many simply could not allot the same amount of time to classwork during the pandemic because of limited resources in their home (Garland & Violanti, 2021; Morgan, 2020). As such, flexibility in deadlines is needed to meet individual student needs. Yet, students need to hear the reinforced message that learning and demonstration of learning are still expected while giving them the flexibility to fit learning into their pandemic schedule (Rosso, 2021).

Again, with respect to students' limited connectivity, pandemic pedagogy also means revitalizing lesson plans for many faculty. Busy work cannot be incorporated into pandemic pedagogy (Garland & Violanti, 2021). Pandemic pedagogy course design needs to begin with assessing the learning goals for the course and designing assignments that will (Costa & Silva, 2021):

1   contribute to students learning or directly assess those learning goals
2   be achievable for students who do not have the bandwidth or computer access to achieve synchronous learning sessions

When assignments and course material are designed with those goals in mind, time spent in the learning management system can be focused not on passively regurgitating course material, but rather on actively engaging with the course material and the learning community (Morgan, 2020).

The transition to emergency remote teaching forced many students into environments that relied on a different type of self-efficacy than their face-to-face classes had, with many suddenly finding themselves more reliant upon their technological self-efficacy than ever before (Goke et al., 2021) or computer-mediated communication efficacy not previously practiced in face-to-face courses (Prentiss, 2021). Goke et al. (2021) found that when students were forced to enroll in online courses during the COVID-19 pandemic, they typically were not as likely to engage in rhetorical dissent (i.e., students asking for clarity and explanations from the instructor, which are critical to their success) as they were in the face-to-face classroom unless instructors put forth an effort to make the course content relevant. This means that communicative practices of the face-to-face classroom are not guaranteed to have the same results in the online classroom. This echoes the findings of work on students' writing anxiety, which found that though instructor clarity and immediate behaviors indirectly lowered student writing apprehension in the face-to-face classroom (Kelly & Gaytan, 2020), these behaviors had no effect on student writing apprehension in the online classroom (Gaytan et al., 2021).

As such, perhaps one of the most important lessons for professors to remember during pandemic instructional communication is that the instructional practices that they have come to rely upon during their normal teaching routine may not be sufficient for pandemic instructional communication. Students will respond to their perception of their professors' communication, not the communication itself (Kelly & Westerman, 2020). The intention that professors have behind their communication is meaningless if students do not perceive it the way it is intended. In pandemic learning conditions, students are learning in uncommon environments with uncommon stressors (Garland & Violanti, 2021), which very well may change the way that they perceive instructor communication. It is recommended that instructors engage in perception checks with their students during normal learning experiences, to ensure that how they intend their communication to be perceived is what is actually perceived (Kelly et al., 2015). These perception checks may be more critical than ever during pandemic learning conditions, when student perceptions are affected by uncommon stressors. This is especially true for instructors who are inexperienced teaching online.

Looking to the Next Pandemic

In reviewing all of the stress that students endured during their pandemic education, it would be naive and incomplete to fail to recognize that faculty were also living through undue stress. Faculty found themselves without a home/work balance – where they ate and slept was suddenly the same place they worked (Schwartzman, 2020). They found it necessary to be online educators, when some had no experience nor training in online education (Frey, 2021). They suddenly needed to teach students distance learning technology on top of their own course material (Garland & Violanti, 2021). Many worked to do this while also dealing with the limited resources that their students struggled with – sharing bandwidth and computers with spouses and children who needed to attend virtual work and school. Undoubtedly, the transition to emergency remote teaching was a stressful period for educators across the world.

There is a critical question to be addressed here. The question is not whether educators dealt with unprecedented stress during the pandemic. The question is whether the full amount of stress endured by some was truly necessary. The question, more specifically, is whether it was reasonable for educators to have had no training with distance learning technology by the year 2020. For many educators, particularly those in K-12 learning, it is probable that much of their online education technology was totally new, with their institutions having never purchased distance learning software packages before as many governments do not support K-12 virtual public education (Kelly & Westerman, 2016). However, it is also probable that many educators, particularly those at higher learning institutions, had many opportunities to receive training in virtual teaching prior to 2020 and chose not to participate, intending to never teach online.

Instructor technology literacy affected students' learning during the COVID-19 pandemic. Instructors who could not effectively navigate their distance learning technology struggled to effectively deliver their course material through it (Frey, 2021; Mok et al., 2021). Students' perceived learning effectiveness during emergency remote teaching was negatively correlated with their instructor's technology literacy (Mok et al., 2021). In short, faculty's lack of technological training negatively affected student learning, and added more stressors and uncertainty to the lives of their students during a tumultuous period of their lives.

Long gone are the days in which faculty can assume that students come into the classroom with technological expertise (Bowman et al., In Press). As Bowman et al. explain, the notion that students are technological experts came from the early days of home computing, in which children had to learn how computers worked to entertain themselves (e.g., learn basic DOS programming to play Oregon Trail in the 1980s). The proliferation of the graphic user interface has resulted in the modern student growing up with no need to understand computers in order to entertain themselves, and teachers can no longer assume any technical knowledge not taught in their course or a prerequisite (Bowman et al., In Press). This means that instructors must assume that they will need to be the individual in the classroom with the highest technical literacy in the classroom.

What's Next?

If COVID-19 taught the field of education nothing else, it demonstrated that educators and educational institutions cannot assume that they will never deliver online courses or never have to use a new distance learning technology. Instructors' lack of familiarity with technology was detrimental to their students' learning experiences when they could not effectively navigate the technology to teach (Frey, 2021; Mok et al., 2021) and when they could not assist the students in navigating the technology to complete learning experiences (Garland & Violanti, 2021). Having some experience teaching online, post-COVID-19 does not mean that faculty are tech-savvy enough to be prepared for the next pandemic. New online technologies release monthly, meaning being prepared to teach effectively online requires constant preparation.

Consider the example of machine teachers. At the time this chapter was written, machine teachers as online teaching aids was becoming a 'hot topic' in education and technology (c.f., Kim et al., 2020, 2021). Machine teachers are artificial intelligence teaching aids that can be embedded into learning management systems to answer basic questions for students and are available to assist 24/7. The intent of machine teachers was to provide a resource available to students any time they are ready to engage in course material that can answer basic questions (e.g., information covered in the syllabus or definitions of concepts). Machine teachers, when instructors utilize them well, can take the burden of answering basic questions via email off of educators and free their time to focus on addressing more complicated questions (Kim et al., 2020, 2021). Machine teachers are a virtual technology that can be used to assist students taking traditional face-to-face courses or online courses across course topics when students need assistance at a time when they cannot interact synchronously with their instructor. As such, machine teachers are an excellent example of a learning technology that educators of all levels should be receiving training on in 2022. Technologies that provide virtual learning enhancement that can be incorporated across face-to-face and online platforms are excellent targets for required educational training, which will help faculty stay current with new technologies regardless of their preferred teaching platform. Machine teachers are not the last technology educators should learn to use though. As new technologies emerge, faculty must have exposure to identify whether these technologies will assist in their classes and have opportunities for training. Therefore, part of being prepared for the next pandemic involves:

1 Schools investing in technology that can help better meet classroom learning goals, particularly those that can affect out-of-class learning
2 Schools must provide training to faculty in these new technologies
3 Faculty must put forth the effort to explore the potential application of new technologies to their classrooms

Yet, schools cannot force technology into the classroom which does not support learning goals. School administrators must trust the expertise of their faculty to make decisions about which technologies are beneficial for their particular classrooms. Technology for technology's sake does not help learners. Van Roy (2019) uses the analogy of chocolate-covered broccoli to describe technology for the sake of technology when applied to learning. It may look appealing on the outside, but learners will soon be demotivated to engage with the tools when they realize once they bite in that it is not what they want.

As such, schools cannot force incompatible technologies into classrooms, but likewise faculty cannot be allowed to stagnate in their pedagogy, assuming that there is no technology that might enhance their teaching or allow their course content to be effectively delivered online. Faculty must receive enough training to know how to use the technology if it will indeed assist in their course learning goals, but then be allowed to make the decision to not incorporate the technology if it does not support their courses. All decisions for adding technology must be based on the learning goals (Costa & Silva, 2021), but faculty need adequate training to understand whether technologies meet those criteria.

Technology and Communication

Faculty should strive to be the most tech-savvy individuals in their classrooms, and institutions need to provide them with the resources to have that technological aptitude. In these technology trainings, it cannot be assumed that just because faculty understand how to use the technologies, they intuitively understand how to communicate effectively through or with those technologies (Frey, 2021). Just as important as knowing the software is training on communicating with students through computer-mediated channels. So often, there is an assumption that because humans communicate through technology every day, they know how to do it. While this is true, they do not necessarily know how to do it well. For optimal educational experiences, both teachers and students need training on how to effectively communicate through technology (Kelly, 2021). They must be taught:

1   How the richness of technology is likely to change perceptions of their messages
2   How to develop social presence
3   How to utilize time responsibly when collaborating through technology

This means that all of the recommended lessons reviewed above for teaching students how to learn and communicate well online must be well understood by online educators. Above all, educators must understand how to take advantage of those differences in face-to-face communication, so that they optimize their learners' experiences.

When emergency remote teaching is discussed colloquially, there is often a discussion of getting back to "normal" (c.f., Claus et al., 2021). Yet, COVID-19 taught many educators ways that technology can make their teaching even more effective. A new normal in which both educators and students are trained to effectively use and communicate through technology should be the goals of distance education. Hopefully, the education field has learned the value of these goals and will consistently strive to meet them so that the next transition to emergency remote teaching will not leave students and instructors feeling stressed from learning to learn and teach through new technology, stressors that do not have to be inevitable, on top of the stress that is truly inevitable, during a pandemic.

References

Angelaki, C., & Mavroidis, I. (2013). Communication and social presence: The impact on adult learners' emotions in distance learning. *European Journal of Open, Distance and e-Learning, 16*(1), 78–93. https://old.eurodl.org/?p=archives&year=2013&halfyear=1&article=563

Arnett, R. C. (2020). Communication pedagogy: The coronavirus pandemic. *Journal of Communication Pedagogy, 3*(1), 5–10. https://doi.org/10.31446/JCP.2018.02

Bailenson, J. N. (2021). Nonverbal overload: A theoretical argument for the causes of Zoom fatigue. *Technology, Mind, and Behavior, 2*(1). https://doi.org/10.1037/tmb0000030

Bowman, N. D., Vareberg, K. R., Rocker, K. T., Kelly, S., & Westerman, D. (In Press). A history of instructional technology. In M. G. Strawser (Ed.), *Instructional communication in professional contexts.* Cognella.

Brown, W. S. (2021). Successful strategies to engage students in a COVID-19 environment. *Frontiers in Communication, 6*, 52. https://doi.org/10.3389/fcomm.2021.641865.

Chen, S. (2021). Interpersonal communication instruction during COVID-19: Challenges and opportunities. *Frontiers in Communication, 6*, 652241. https://doi.org/10.3389/fcomm.2021.652241

Claus, C. J., Girardelli, D., Kelly, S., & Permyakova, T. M. (2021). Editorial: Cultural changes in instructional practices due to Covid-19. *Frontiers in Communication.* https://doi.org/10.3389/fcomm.2021.715180

Code, J., Ralph, R., & Forde, K. (2020). Pandemic designs for the future: perspectives of technology education teachers during COVID-19. *Information and Learning Sciences, 121*(5/6), 419–431. https://doi.org/10.1108/ILS-04-2020-0112

Costa, J., & Da Silva, G. (2021). Presenter becomes facilitator: The instructional design of masspersonal communication. In S. Kelly (Ed.), *Online instructional communication* (pp. 19–32). Cambridge Scholars Publishing.

Dhawan, S. (2020). Online learning: A panacea in the time of COVID-19 crisis. *Journal of Educational Technology Systems, 49*(1), 5–22. https://doi.org/10.1177%2F0047239520934018

Denton, Z. (2021). COVID-19: Expanding the culture of teaching mathematics. *Frontiers in Communication, 6,* 75. https://doi.org/10.3389/fcomm.2021.640181

Feekery, A., & Condon, S. (2021). A response to Covid-19: Recognizing subcultures in the unexpected online student cohort. *Frontiers in Communication, 6,* 642275. https://doi.org/10.3389/fcomm.2021.642275

Floyd, D. L. (2020). The year none of us predicted: COVID-19 and community colleges. *Community College Journal of Research and Practice, 45*(1), 1–7. https://doi.org/10.1080/10668926.2020.1841649

Foutz, B. (2021). Instructor misbehaviors: When professors online are naughty; not nice. In S. Kelly (Ed.), *Online instructional communication* (pp. 97–106). Cambridge Scholars Publishing.

Frey, T. K. (2021). Overcoming technological barriers to instruction: Situating Gen Z students as reverse mentors. *Frontiers in Communication, 6,* 2. https://doi.org/10.3389/fcomm.2021.630899

Frey, L. R., & Loker, E. (2020). Confronting students' personal and interpersonal communication anxieties and needs through constitutive, experiential communication pedagogy. *Journal of Communication Pedagogy, 3*(1), 20–26. https://doi.org/10.31446/JCP.2020.04

Garland, M. E., & Violanti, M. (2021). Rock my world: Rewind to a better transition to remote learning. *Frontiers in Communication, 6,* 23. https://doi.org/10.3389/fcomm.2021.641873

Garrison, D. R., Anderson, T., & Archer, W. (1999). Critical inquiry in a text-based environment: Computer conferencing in higher education. *The Internet and Higher Education, 2*(2–3), 87–105. https://doi.org/10.1016/S1096-7516(00)00016-6

Garrison, D. R., Anderson, T., & Archer, W. (2010). The first decade of the community of inquiry framework: A retrospective. *The Internet and Higher Education, 13*(1–2), 5–9. https://doi.org/10.1016/j.iheduc.2009.10.003

Gaytan, J., Kelly, S., & Brown, W. (2021). Writing apprehension in the online classroom: The limits of instructor behaviors. *Business and Professional Communication Quarterly, Online First.* https://doi.org/10.1177/23294906211041088

Goke, R., Berndt, M., & Rocker, K. (2021). Classroom culture when students are reluctant to learn online: Student dissent behaviors explained by their self-efficacy, control of learning, and intrinsic motivation. *Frontiers in Communication, 6,* 101. https://doi.org/10.3389/fcomm.2021.641956

Goke, R., & Kelly, S. (2019). Developing presence. In S. Kelly (Ed.), *Computer-mediated communication for business: Theory to practice* (pp. 41–48). Cambridge Scholars Publishing.

Gunawardena, C. N., & Zittle, F. J. (1997). Social presence as a predictor of satisfaction within a computer-mediated conferencing environment. *American Journal of Distance Education, 11*(3), 8–26. https://doi.org/10.1080/08923649709526970

Hughes, M. C., Henry, B. W., & Kushnick, M. R. (2020). Teaching during the pandemic? An opportunity to enhance curriculum. *Pedagogy in Health Promotion, 6*(4), 235–238. https://doi.org/10.1177%2F2373379920950179

Kelly, S. (2021). Three presence lessons for all students. In S. Kelly (Ed.), *Online instructional communication* (pp. 2–9). Cambridge Scholars Publishing.

Kelly, S., & Gaytan, J. (2020). The effect of instructors' immediate behaviors and clarity on student writing apprehension. *Business and Professional Communication Quarterly, 83*(1), 96–109. https://doi.org/10.1177/2329490619868822

Kelly, S., Rice, C., Wyatt, B., Ducking, J., & Denton, Z. (2015). Teacher immediacy and decreased student quantitative reasoning anxiety: The mediating effect of perception. *Communication Education, 64*(2), 171–186. https://doi.org/10.1080/0363452 3.2015.1014383

Kelly, S., & Westerman, D. K. (2016). New technologies and distributed learning systems. In P. L. Witt (Ed.), *Handbooks of communication science: Communication and learning* (Vol 16, pp. 455–480). DeGruyter Mouton.

Kim, J., Merrill, K., Xu, K., & Sellnow, D. D. (2020). My teacher is a machine: Understanding students' perceptions of AI teaching assistants in online education. *International Journal of Human–Computer Interaction, 36*(20), 1902–1911. https://doi.org/10.1 080/10447318.2020.1801227

Kim, J., Merrill Jr, K., Xu, K., & Sellnow, D. D. (2021). I like my relational machine teacher: An AI instructor's communication styles and social presence in online education. *International Journal of Human–Computer Interaction, Early Access.* https://doi.org/10.1080/10447318.2021.1908671

Knight, M. (2020). Pandemic communication: A new challenge for higher education. *Business and Professional Communication Quarterly, 83*(2), 131–132. https://doi.org/10.1177%2F2329490620925418

Lombard, M., & Ditton, T. B. (1997). At the heart of it all: The concept of presence. *Journal of Computer-Mediated Communication, 3*(2), 0. https://doi.org/10.1111/j.1083-6101.1997.tb00072.x

Mok, K. H., Xiong, W., & Bin Aedy Rahman, H. N. (2021). COVID-19 pandemic's disruption on university teaching and learning and competence cultivation: Student evaluation of online learning experiences in Hong Kong. *International Journal of Chinese Education, 10*(1), https://doi.org/10.1177%2F22125868211007011

Morgan, H. (2020). Best practices for implementing remote learning during a pandemic. *The Clearing House: A Journal of Educational Strategies, Issues and Ideas, 93*(3), 135–141. https://doi.org/10.1080/00098655.2020.1751480

Prentiss, S. (2021). Speech anxiety in the communication classroom during the COVID-19 pandemic: Supporting student success. *Frontiers in Communication, 6*, 36. https://doi.org/10.3389/fcomm.2021.642109

Rippé, C. B., Weisfeld-Spolter, S., Yurova, Y., & Kemp, A. (2021). Pandemic pedagogy for the new normal: Fostering perceived control during COVID-19. *Journal of Marketing Education, 43*(2) 260–276. https:/doi.org/10.1177/0273475320987287

Richardson, J. C., Maeda, Y., Lv, J., & Caskurlu, S. (2017). Social presence in relation to students' satisfaction and learning in the online environment: A meta-analysis. *Computers in Human Behavior, 71*, 402–417. https://doi.org/10.1016/j.chb.2017.02.001

Rosso, J. D. (2021). How loss teaches: Beyond "pandemic pedagogy". *Humanity & Society, 45*(3), https://doi.org/10.1177%2F0160597620987008

Schwartzman, R. (2020). Performing pandemic pedagogy. *Communication Education, 69*(4), 502–517. https://doi.org/10.1080/03634523.2020.1804602

Van Roy, R. (2019). The office as a playground? The do's and do not's of gamifying work. In S. Kelly (Ed.), *Computer-mediated communication for business: Theory to practice* (pp. 194–204). Cambridge Scholars Publishing.

Walther, J. B. (1992). Interpersonal effects in computer-mediated interaction: A relational perspective. *Communication Research, 19*(10), 52–90. http://doi.org/10.1177/009365092019001003

Walther, J. B. (1994). Anticipated ongoing interaction versus channel effects on relational communication in computer-mediated interaction. *Human Communication Research, 20*(4), 473–501. doi:10.1111/j.1468-2958.1994.tb00332.x

Walther, J. B. (2006). Nonverbal dynamics in computer-mediated communication, or: (and the net: ('s with you,:) and you:) alone. In V. Manusov & M. L. Patterson (Eds.), *Handbook of nonverbal communication* (pp. 461–479). Sage.

Walther, J. B., & Bunz, U. (2005). The rules of virtual groups: Trust, liking, and performance in computer-mediated communication. *Journal of Communication, 55*(4), 828–846. https://doi.org/10.1111/j.1460-2466.2005.tb03025.x

Walther, J. B., Loh, T., & Granka, L. (2005). Let me count the ways: The interchange of verbal and nonverbal cues in computer-mediated and face-to-face affinity. *Journal of Language and Social Psychology, 24*(1), 36–65. https://doi.org/10.1177.0261927X04273036

Walther, J. B., Van Der Heide, B., Ramirez, A., Burgoon, J. K., & Peña, J. (2015). Interpersonal and hyperpersonal dimensions of computer-mediated communication. In S. S. Sundar (Ed.), *The handbook of the psychology of communication technology* (pp. 3–22). John Wiley & Sons, Inc.

Wang, J., Liu, W., Zhang, Y., Xie, S., & Yang, B. (2021). Perceived stress among Chinese medical students engaging in online learning in light of COVID-19. *Psychology Research and Behavior Management, 14*, 549–562. https://doi.org/10.2147%2FPRBM.S308497

Westerman, D. Kelly, S., Vareberg, K. R., Rocker, K. T., & Bowman, N. D. (In Press). Current and future perspectives on instructional technology. In M. G. Strawser (Ed.), *Instructional communication in professional contexts*. Cognella.

12

INTERNATIONAL COMMUNICATION

Anthony Spencer

The COVID-19 pandemic has reached all corners of the world and affected countless lives. We have all seen the images on television and social media of the devastating impacts of the pandemic, which range from illnesses and deaths of family and friends to job losses and serious financial hardships. The pandemic has ravaged our world (Bong et al., 2020; Croucher et al., 2020) in ways that we never could have imagined before 2020. The pandemic changed how we interact within systemic structures in our globalized world, including how we communicate across national borders, particularly through our social media outlets. The pandemic has also revealed the systemic vulnerabilities of marginalized groups (Hotez et al., 2020) and exacerbated and further exposed pre-existing inequalities.

I recognize there are various definitions of international or global communication; however, for the purposes of this chapter, I will use international communication in a way that explores mediated communication within international contexts. Downing (2010) acknowledged that the very definition of international communication is constantly in flux. This is due in part to the fact that the available media and modes of communication are constantly changing. This flux is what makes pandemic communication challenging, yet so interesting to study. The COVID-19 pandemic has placed all of us in more extreme transnational moments than ever before. One thing is certain: the field of international communication has long been overly influenced by the West (Thussu, 2012). To better understand a transmoment and to de-center the heteronormative Western elements of international communication, I turn to Queer Latinx literature to explore how we can understand transmoments and spaces (Moreman, 2020). Transspatial and technological moments have evolved quickly since the onset of the pandemic, which requires scholars to reexamine

DOI: 10.4324/9781003214496-12

these tensions, moments, and fissures across mediated channels and national borders. These spaces have permitted us to live in a truly transnational community while our lives have changed so dramatically. However, this also requires scholars to focus on cross-national research as they examine pandemic-related issues (Diers-Lawson et al., 2021). In a related vein of research, Hepp (2015) argues the notion of transcultural helps us separate from the nation-state concept while transnational keeps us in the mode of national identity. I find this wording very beneficial when we analyze cultural products that are free of the nation-state; however, in this text I employ the term "transnational" because our national identity or passport country predicates many of our interactions in a globalized world, particularly during a pandemic.

We share our stories of the pandemic with one another, post news about the virus on our social media feeds, and watch videos that focus on the damage caused by the illness. COVID-19 or just COVID, as many people refer to it, has become a household term as commonplace as many other words or phrases we use in our daily lives. The name COVID-19 is used around the globe in various regions and in multiple languages. However, the naming of the virus itself has become value-laden. Here I will not use the terms used to blame the virus on peoples or places, though some people have used names that place blame for the pandemic which has led to discrimination and harassment (Besel, 2022). Naming will never be value neutral. However, the very name of the pandemic has been one of the first tasks for global health professionals and scholars.

International interpersonal experiences have been limited by the ability and resources to travel outside of one's own country. International travel became even more difficult as limitations and bans were placed on travel. Many countries require(d) pre-departure COVID testing or in-country pandemic insurance. Island nations such as Australia and New Zealand closed their borders for extended periods of time. Other nations such as the United States and Canada have closed land borders for long periods of time. In Western Europe and North America, irregular migration has complicated border issues while poverty, conflicts, and the effects of the pandemic have pushed migrants to seek a better life in wealthier nations. Martin and Bergmann (2021) note these border closures were not perfect solutions and at times were controversial.

Even though the pandemic has pulled us further apart with forced isolations, it has pushed us closer than ever as we use social media sites to communicate, stream videos together and shop on the same international websites. In many ways we can forge new experiences together while we are still homebound. The pandemic has also given us an incredible opportunity to re-think how we communicate across national boundaries. In this chapter I suggest we consider how we can incorporate other salient issues into the study and practice of international communication in a pandemic world. The mediated interactions we experience do not take place in a vacuum. These experiences are nuanced by the political, economic, and cultural influences that surround us.

In this text I focus on the interconnected concepts of language, migration, and work as they interact with and through social media platforms. These inter-related ideas help us conceptualize transnational communication moments. This is not an exhaustive list of important topics. However, we must start this pandemic discussion with a base of important issues that are salient to people around the world. I merely want to open the dialogue about how we envision and understand international communication through the lens of transnational moments during the COVID-19 pandemic and any other future pandemics we might face.

What does international communication look like in a post-COVID era? How do we want to re-think our globalized connections? These are the guiding questions for this chapter. In today's transglobal world, we are just as much content producers as we are media consumers. The active approach to understanding globalized communication has become increasingly important. Mediated, interpersonal, intercultural, and group communication have in many ways melded early in the 21st century which the pandemic has accelerated.

Background

International communication as a discipline has traditionally been rooted in media research because media content influences transnational issues. As Thussu (2012) explains, media outlets essentially allowed us to share experiences across borders. In our transnational mediascape (Appadurai, 1990), traditional media outlets have allowed us to read the same newspapers, listen to the same songs, and watch the same movies even as we were separated by space and time. Only in the last couple of decades has technology allowed individual media users to share their own content. We now can distribute our own photos, videos, live streams, and other types of content.

As our technology improves, our mass-mediated world continues to become more personalized and synchronous across borders. For the last 20 years, we have seen a change in the way we consume "traditional" media products. TV shows and films are available to stream anytime we want. Long-distance phone calls have become a distant and expensive memory for most people as they use Skype, Zoom, Facetime, WhatsApp, WeChat, and other applications. These applications have allowed us to stay in touch with friends and family anywhere in the world, though while others in the world embrace messaging applications, people in the United States still tend to rely more on text messages (Olvide, 2022). Kraidy (2018) called for us to broaden how we envision international communication and simultaneously think of its specificity in our usage. In this chapter I hope to challenge practitioners and researchers to find new and specific ways to contribute to the conversation(s) related to international communication. We must also find ways to think about the field of international communication, which Thussu (2012) reminds us above has long been far too focused on the West and particularly U.S.-centric without always explaining and exploring the positionality of the researcher and institutions involved (Lee, 2015).

We can argue that newer technologies have created ways to incorporate more diversity of ideas and expressions by focusing on user-generated content, which Castells (2009) called "mass self-communication" (p. 55) in much the same way as citizens' media (Rodriguez, 2001) functioned to create fissures in a pre-social media era, primarily through community media outlets. Even with new technologies we cannot say we do not operate outside of the power structures of traditional media and corporations because we still function within the systems controlled by social media corporations; however, we as media producers/consumers have taken back much of the control and invisible groups and communities are able to participate in the public sphere (Dueze, 2006) in forms previously limited to the elite classes.

Golan et al. (2010) describe how the field of international communication has changed drastically after the Cold War and that subsequent technological advances have continued to reshape the impacts of globalization. However, these changes have not always allowed for voices from the Global South to inhabit the same privileged spaces as Western scholars (Gondwe, 2022). Of course, those technological shifts alone do not guarantee we will de-Westernize the field; however, this does provide opportunities for more access and inclusion.

While the same digital tools are mostly available worldwide there are issues of access in many areas of the world. For example, while a laptop might be common in an elementary school in the Global North, it is not an everyday item in many schools in the Global South (notwithstanding expensive private schools). While computers, tablets, and expensive phones might be out of reach of most people in the developing world, there has been an explosion of less expensive smartphones (Poushter, 2016) which have provided many people an opportunity to both produce and consume media in our transnational pandemic world. Even if we all had the same access to digital devices and high-speed networks (which we don't), not all cultures use technologies in the same way (Spencer et al., 2012).

The pandemic has shown us that international communication is much more than the legacy media we consume or what we produce through user-generated content. At the beginning of 21st century, Comor (2003) explained how political, financial, and technological developments rolled into overlapping interests through the lens of globalization. Only a few very large media corporations controlled the media products we consumed. Baker (2007) explains we must understand the consequences of having too much media power in the hands of such few people. We must re-think how our consumption and production are nuanced by the important global issues of language, migration, and work as nuanced through the lens of social media outlets.

Social Media

While social media outlets are also controlled by just a few companies, these platforms allow users to create their own short posts, blogs, live video feeds, and other formats of content. Most people around the world are familiar with Facebook, Instagram, Twitter, and other platforms. These sites have evolved over time both with the users' blessings and through their objections (Gerlich et al., 2012). Even though most understand and have some knowledge of social media platforms, the outlets vary in popularity by age, geographic location, and personal preferences.

Facebook

A Pew Research study has confirmed that the behemoth Facebook is still the most popular social media site in the United States, but it is not equally popular among all ages and demographics (Gramlich, 2021). Many people consider Facebook to be the default social media outlet because of both its longevity and its incredible number of users around the globe. However, it is not the main social media platform for everyone. Whether due to geography, censorship, age, or even just personal preferences, it is important to acknowledge other social media outlets do influence our international connections during a pandemic.

Twitter

While Facebook is the most well-known media outlet, it also limits us to friend groups and "known" contacts. Twitter provides users the chance to "follow" anyone with a public profile. It is easy to find people from any corner of the world and follow their tweets. Twitter may have had the most influence on our political spectrum across national systems. Twitter has become a platform for politicians to speak to and directly interact with voters (Johnson, 2012, 2021).

You can also interact with people, businesses, or any type of organization that has an account. Pollett and Rivers (2020) note the important role Twitter has played in the dissemination of COVID information to the public. Never have people been able to read scientific updates and even interact with scientists about a major health event. However, due to the speed of dissemination and the abundance of false information on Twitter, it can hurt communities as much as it can help them during a pandemic. However, Twitter is still a preferred source for following credible media outlets. Jurkowitz and Gottried (2022) note that U.S. journalists turn to Twitter as their preferred social media outlet when conducting research.

Instagram

The other of the "Big 3" mainstream social media outlets used worldwide is Instagram. For Instagram the visual is everything. Much like Twitter we can follow and interact with people we do not know. Users seek out one another for the photos and videos they post on the site. Instagram has long been the leading site for imagery (Lee, 2015) in online communication. It has become particularly important for social media influencers (SMIs) who drive trends (Lee et al., 2022). A 2021 post by the Pew Research Center confirms Instagram usage skews young, at least in the United States (Schaeffer, 2021). While Instagram skews younger in demographics than Facebook or Twitter, there are other sites that compete for this younger demographic.

Microcommunities

In the past few years younger social media users often turn away from the larger and more mainstream or legacy social media outlets their parents and grandparents use. While they may have Facebook and Twitter accounts, they are primarily focused on connections and community building, which they (often) find in sites based on online gaming. Wilson (2021) writes that even before the pandemic, Gen Z members, roughly people born after 1997, have been seeking out platforms that serve as microcommunities. Wilson calls these more intimate spaces "digital campfires", which evokes memories of a time before social media usage when young people would literally gather in small groups around a campfire. She explains that these communities have taken off in popularity since the pandemic began. Some of the more popular microcommunities include Discord, Twitch, Fortnite, and, of course, TikTok, which has now become a household name and its content is shared across other platforms.

A non-Western microcommunity not previously mentioned is the Chinese platform WeChat. This social media outlet has gained prominence in usage and in academic research (Sandel and Qiu, 2021; Zhang, 2016, 2022). While most users are in China, there are people in other countries who have WeChat accounts. This is an important social media outlet to mention so we acknowledge there are non-Western platforms in the mediascape which impact the following global issues.

Language

Perhaps one of the most obvious and problematic issues to address across mediated platforms is the dominance of English-language content. English has long been the lingua franca of media, business, and education though it does not come without criticism regarding access to knowledge (Suzina, 2021). The proliferation of English-language media has flourished around the world

(Spencer, 2013). We are even writing this pandemic book in English. For various reasons, there is a clear preference for English in academic research, often to the exclusion of other languages (Liu & Buckingham, 2022). While this may seem a product of convenience or simply a way to reach more people, if we turn to Bourdieu (1991) we are reminded of the symbolic power of language in human interactions and how languages collide and struggle against one another for usage and prestige (Agar, 1996). If we make assumptions that information published in English is more effective or better to reach audiences, we run the risk of excluding populations and limiting other knowledges in the discourse.

English is often envisioned as a value-neutral language or even a solution to problems when other languages contest one another. Jia et al. (2020) note the interesting yet problematic concept of "English-mediated multilingualism" (p. 531) in which English is the imagined solution to intercultural or linguistic interactions in non-English-speaking nations or situations where there is not a common language. Jia et al. provide the example of international students in China who were forced into remote learning with English as the medium when not all students had a high enough level of English for academics, and they anticipated they would be studying in Mandarin. While there may be good intentions with the push for English during the pandemic, we are making assumptions about language competency, access, and possibly limiting the discourse. English is probably not going away as a dominant language in social media; however, it is vital to understand the privileges afforded to English and the potential exclusions by using it.

Rudwick et al. (2021) explain how the pandemic has exacerbated the language inequalities of important COVID information for people who speak non-dominant languages and do not have the same access to information. It is important to note there is a bias for English in international crisis communication (Piller et al., 2020), which is particularly salient during a global pandemic. In many ways English has become a catch-all language for important communiqués to the global community, but we cannot forget that not everyone can or wants to speak English.

Migration

Another salient issue that impacts international communication as it relates to social media usage is migration. While there are varying definitions of who is an immigrant, expat, long-term tourist, refugee, etc., all these designations are value-laden (Koutonin, 2015; Spencer, 2011a). I use the term "migrant" to refer to anyone who lives outside of their birth or passport country. According to the United Nations, a migrant is:

> The UN Migration Agency (IOM) defines a migrant as any person who is moving or has moved across an international border or within a State

away from his/her habitual place of residence, regardless of (1) the person's legal status; (2) whether the movement is voluntary or involuntary; (3) what the causes for the movement are; or (4) what the length of the stay is.

United Nations (p. 4)

Thus, we must consider how the movement of people has impacted our understanding of international communication. While organized international travel was literally impossible for many people during the pandemic, that is changing as even the most restrictive of COVID-19 travel bans are being eased or dropped altogether. Many people have not been allowed to return to their homes or had to put on pause their plans to live, study, or work abroad. COVID-19 border policies have also become stricter in many nations; these policies are thought to most impact vulnerable migrants (Bojorquez-Chapela et al., 2022; González Arias & Araluce, 2021; Maldonado et al., 2020). Through a human security approach (Gómez, 2022), it is possible to explore the vulnerabilities faced by both migrant and host country as their fates are intertwined. Policies that are meant to target one group might have auxiliary ramifications for others. Gamlen (2020) explains how various types of migrants are related through policies, remittances, and other issues. Social media outlets have particularly become important tools for asylum-seeking migrants (Merisalo & Jauhiainen, 2021).

This reflection also provides us the opportunity to re-think how we understand the concept of migration. Historically, the media discourse about migration most exclusively has framed migrants as people fleeing political or, most often, economic problems in their home country and looking for a better life in more developed nations; this outlook often divides the world between Global North and Global South; this split can create erroneous conceptions of migration and reinforces stereotypes about migrants (Blinder, 2015; Cornelius & Rosenblum, 2005; Lutz & Bitschnau, 2022; Moreman, 2008; Santa Ana, 1999).

While migration to the United States and Western Europe has gained the most media attention, people migrate to other countries as well. More and more people from developed nations are moving out of their home countries due to lifestyle preferences, employment opportunities, retirement, other economic benefits, and personal reasons (Croucher, 2018; Hayes, 2014; Liu & Croucher, 2022; Morrissey, 2018; Spencer, 2011a,b; Wilczewski, 2019). In the past decade there has also been an increase in interest for scholars to study migration patterns and impacts within the Global South (Adamson & Tsourapas, 2020; Freier & Pérez, 2021; Ordóñez, & Arcos, 2019; Spencer, 2018), which are important migration trends to understand. We must remember that not every migrant from the developing world travels to the United States or Western Europe.

There are also important issues that influence migration or are in turn impacted by migration. Some of these important topics we must consider during the pandemic include food security (Takenaka et al., 2020), access to quality healthcare (Voorend & Alvarado, 2022), gender issues (Piper, 2005), and the unique challenges faced by LGBTQIA+ migrants (Hadriel et al., 2020) who are often the most vulnerable group with the least protections. Social media platforms are an important pandemic-era tool as migrants travel and navigate a life in a new country.

Work

WhatsApp, Facebook Messenger, Discord, and other social media tools have become commonplace for many people in the workplace. New technologies have also impacted not only how we communicate at work but where and how we can work. The development of platforms like Zoom allows us to interact, study, and even work from home, or wherever we have a stable Internet connection. According to Parker et al. (2022), 60% of the people in the United States who say they can work from home have been doing so either full or part-time. For many people around the world, the pandemic has altered the way we view work and the workplace (Nyberg et al., 2021) and uncovered the inequities involved with labor. For parents and people with family-related obligations, this at-home work movement has created its own challenges (Goldberg et al., 2021).

For many people, working from home is as simple as finding a quiet space and a stable Internet connection. In some countries, the government has begun to regulate remote work. According to a recent *BBC* article on pandemic work, Johanson (2022) explains how some cultures are more resistant than others to remote work. They note businesses and workers in countries like France and Japan are less likely to embrace the work-at-home trend; while in the United States and the United Kingdom, remote work has started to change the way people view labor and the workplace. The Dutch government has considered making remote work a right for employees in the nation (Burton, 2022). Each country is taking a different approach to regulations for at-home work.

Essential workers, migrant laborers, and others did not have the luxury of remote work during the pandemic, nor will they likely be able to do so in the future. We depended on these groups to keep our healthcare systems running, food on our tables, and the products in our stores. The pandemic has uncovered the employment insecurity associated with precarious, at will, or other vulnerable workers (Aloisi & De Stefano, 2021; Ju et al., 2022). This is a transnational phenomenon as all nations have essential, health, and emergency workers who simply cannot perform their jobs remotely.

A few very privileged people can rely on technology to not only work from home but from any remote destination. Many of today's workers literally can live in one country and be employed in another. Digital Nomads or DN is a lifestyle that has become popular for people who can work remotely (Thompson, 2019). As of June 2022, at least 20 countries have set up digital nomad or remote work visas (Jamrisko et al., 2022). The idea is people who already have jobs (in a different country) will come to live and ostensibly spend money in the host country but will not take a job away from a local. Both Digital Nomads and host nations are trying to figure out the logistics of everyday life such as how one opens a bank account, pays taxes, and other seemingly simple tasks (Williams et al., 2019) in this new transnational work environment. It becomes difficult to find out if you have legal permission to work in the host country (usually paid by your home country), how long you can stay as a tourist if there is not a nomad visa, and how you can undertake banking and bill paying if you are not a resident of the new country (Williams et al., 2019).

While the concept of remote work sounds as easy as getting a job and buying a plane ticket to live in your favorite far flung locale, it is much more complicated as we endeavor to live and labor abroad. In the past few years, scholars have begun to examine digital nomads in some of the prime locations for remote-work communities, which include Indonesia (Woldoff & Litchfield, 2021), Thailand (de Loryn, 2022; Jiwasiddi et al., 2022), as well as Spain and Portugal (Almeida & Belezas, 2022). For many remote workers, these communities help develop identity across networks and professions (Litchfield et al., 2021). The digital nomad culture developed before the pandemic started; however, the pandemic and related lockdowns have fueled the imaginations of many people who might want to undertake international remote work.

Discussion

The pandemic has forced us to review not only the definition and structure of international communication but the salient issues that impact how we communicate across both real and imagined borders. We have been in a communication technological shift since the development of social media platforms (Howard & Parks, 2012); however, the pandemic has created an opening for us to examine our communication with purpose and intention. As Ngwainmbi (2022) explains, we now consume multiple cultures through our mediated interactions; we must just critically process those connections in a way that allows us to understand how language, migration, and work have converged in mediated spaces to create these transnational moments. The Internet and digital media products have made this convergence even thicker, more layered, and, most of all, more immediate. New technologies have created a need to better understand digital communication tools more than ever before (Thussu, 2000).

If we more clearly understand how social media platforms merge with these timely issues (Bei & Sandel, 2018), we can more clearly navigate a transnational world. During the pandemic, scholars have begun to focus more on these international connections (Budhwar & Cumming, 2020). The pandemic has revealed systemic racism and discriminatory practices unlike any other communication "event". We have seen the impacts of how prejudice can manifest itself differently in various parts of the world (Croucher et al., 2021a,b). These racial or ethnic prejudices are not new, nor were they created by the pandemic; however, the pandemic has made them more apparent. We now have an opportunity to confront prejudices and systemic inequalities.

The themes of discussion presented here are not meant to be exhaustive or comprehensive. I merely hope to start a discussion about the ways we communicate in a pandemic-nuanced globalized world. If or when we leave this pandemic, we still must understand how it has forever changed our communication processes. As Thussu (2012) reminds us, international communication has been dominated by the West, particularly the United States, and now we have the opportunity to not only re-center global conversations, but we can examine inclusivity, equity, and access to communication through the issues of language, migration, and labor as they intersect in a transglobal community.

References

Adamson, F. B., & Tsourapas, G. (2020). The migration state in the global south: Nationalizing, developmental, and neoliberal models of migration management. *International Migration Review, 54*(3), 853–882. https://doi.org/10.1177/0197918319879057

Agar, M. (1996). *Language shock: Understanding the culture of conversation.* Quill.

Almeida, J., & Belezas, F. (2022). The rise of half-tourists and their impact on the tourism strategies of peripheral territories. In J. Leitão, V. Ratten, & V. Braga (Eds.), *Tourism entrepreneurship in Portugal and Spain.* Tourism, Hospitality & Event Management. Springer. https://doi.org/10.1007/978-3-030-89232-6_9

Aloisi, A., & De Stefano, V. (2021). Essential jobs, remote work and digital surveillance: Addressing the COVID-19 pandemic panopticon. *International Labour Review, 161*(2), 289–314.

Appadurai, A. (1990). Disjuncture and difference in the global cultural economy. *Theory, Culture & Society, 7,* 295–310. https://doi.org/10.1177/026327690007002017

Baker, C. E. (2007). *Media concentration and democracy: Why ownership matters.* Cambridge University Press.

Bei J., & Sandel, T. L. (2018). Who am I? A case study of a foreigner's identity in China as presented via WeChat moments. *China Media Research, 14*(2), 62–74.

Bong, C. L., Brasher, C., Chikumba, E., McDougall, R., Mellin-Olsen, J., & Enright, A. (2020). The COVID-19 pandemic: Effects on low- and middle-income countries. *Anesthesia and Analgesia, 131*(1), 86–92. https://doi.org/10.1213/ANE.0000000000004846

Besel, R. (2022). Global pandemics, ideological conflicts, and racialized denominations: A critical interology perspective. *China Media Research, 18*(2), 1–15.

Blinder, S. (2015). Imagined immigration: The impact of different meanings of 'immigrants' in public opinion and policy debates in Britain. *Political Studies, 63*(1), 80–100. https://doi.org/10.1111/1467-9248.12053

Bojorquez-Chapela, I., Strathdee, S. A., Garfein, R. S., Benson, C. A., Chaillon, A., Ignacio, C., & Sepulveda, J. (2022). The impact of the COVID-19 pandemic among migrants in shelters in Tijuana, Baja California, Mexico. *BMJ Global Health, 7*(3), 1–8. https://doi.org/10.1136/bmjgh-2021-007202

Bourdieu, P. (1991). *Language & symbolic power.* Harvard University Press.

Budhwar, P., & Cumming, D. (2020). New directions in management research and communication: Lessons from the COVID-19 pandemic. *British Journal of Management, 31*, 441–443. https://doi.org/10.1111/1467-8551.12426

Burton, L. (2022, July 6). Dutch to make working from home a legal right – and the rest of Europe could follow: Experts predict a ripple effect across EU once Dutch senate approves new law. *The Telegraph.* https://www.telegraph.co.uk/business/2022/07/06/dutch-make-working-home-legal-right-move-rest-europe-could/

Castells, M. (2009). *Communication power.* OUP Oxford.

Comor, E. (2003). Media corporations in the age of globalization. In B. Mody (Ed.), *International and development communication: A 21st-century perspective* (pp. 19–33). Sage Publications.

Cornelius, W. A., & Rosenblum, M. R. (2005). Immigration and politics. *Annual Review of Political Science, 8*, 99–119. https://doi.org/10.1146/annurev.polisci.8.082103.104854

Croucher, S. (2018). Rooted in relative privilege: US 'expats' in Granada, Nicaragua. *Identities, 25*(4), 436–455. https://doi.org/10.1080/1070289X.2016.1260022

Croucher, S. M., Nguyen, T., Ashwell, D., Spencer, A.T., Permyakova, T., & Gomez, O. J. (2021a). COVID-19 prejudice towards Afro-Brazilians. *Journal of Intercultural Communication Research, 51*(4), 383–399. https://doi.org/10.1080/17475759.2021.1957702

Croucher, S. M., Nguyen, T., Pearson, E., Murray, N., Feekery, A., Spencer, A., Gomez, O., Girardelli, D., & Kelly, S. (2021b). A comparative analysis of Covid-19-related prejudice: The United States, Spain, Italy, and New Zealand. *Communication Research Reports, 38*(2), 79–89. https://doi.org/10.1080/08824096.2021.1885371

Croucher, S. M., Nguyen, T., & Rahmani, D. (2020). Prejudice toward Asian-Americans in the Covid-19 pandemic: The effects of social media use in the United States. *Frontiers in Health Communication.* https://doi.org/10.3389/fcomm.2020.00039

de Loryn, B. (2022). Not necessarily a place: How mobile transnational online workers (digital nomads) construct and experience 'home'. *Global Networks, 22*(1), 103–118. https://doi.org/10.1111/glob.12333

Diers-Lawson, A., Johnson, S., Clayton, T., Kimoto, R., Tran, B. X., Nguyen, L. H., & Park, K. (2021). Pandemic communication: Information seeking, evaluation, and self-protective behaviors in Vietnam and the Republic of Korea. *Frontiers in Communication, 6*, 1–22. https://doi.org/10.3389/fcomm.2021.731979

Dueze, M. (2006). Ethnic media, community media and participatory culture. *Journalism, 7*(3), 262–280. https://doi.org/10.1177/1464884906065512

Downing, J. D. H. (2010). International communication. In W. Donsbach (Ed.), *The International Encyclopedia of Communication.* https://doi-org.ezproxy.gvsu.edu/10.1002/9781405186407.wbieci061

Freier, L. F., & Pérez, L. M. (2021). Nationality-based criminalisation of south-south migration: The experience of Venezuelan forced migrants in Peru. *European Journal on Criminal Policy and Research, 27*(1), 113–133. https://doi.org/10.1007/s10610-020-09475-y

Gamlen, A. (2020). Migration and mobility after the 2020 pandemic: The end of an age. *IOM's Migration Research High Level Advisers*, 2–14. Retrieved 11/9/2022 from https://publications.iom.int/system/files/pdf/migration-%20and-mobility.pdf.

Gerlich, R., Drumheller, K., Rasco, K., & Spencer, A. (2012). Marketing to laggards: Organizational change and diffusion of innovation in the adoption of Facebook timeline. *Journal of the Academy of Business & Economics, 12*(3), 91–101.

Golan, G. J., Johnson, T. J., & Wanta, W. (2010). *International media communication in a global age*. Routledge.

Goldberg, A. E., McCormick, N., & Virginia, H. (2021). Parenting in a pandemic: Work–family arrangements, well-being, and intimate relationships among adoptive parents. *Family Relations, 70*(1), 7–25. https://doi.org/10.1111/fare.12528

Gómez, O. A. (2022). International migration and human security under the COVID-19 pandemic. In R. Shaw, & A. Gurtoo (Eds.), *Global pandemic and human security*. Springer. https://doi.org/10.1007/978-981-16-5074-1_9

Gondwe, G. (2022). Can African scholars speak? Situating African voices in International Communication scholarship. *Media, Culture & Society, 44*(4), 848–859 https://doi.org/10.1177/01634437211071056

González Arias, A., & Araluce, O. A. (2021). The impact of the Covid-19 pandemic on human mobility among vulnerable groups: Global and regional trends. *Journal of Poverty, 25*(7), 567–581. https://doi.org/10.1080/10875549.2021.1985867

Gramlich, J. (2021, June 1). 10 facts about Americans and Facebook. *Pew Research Center.* https://www.pewresearch.org/fact-tank/2021/06/01/facts-about-americans-and-facebook/

Hadriel, T., Cogo, D., & Huertas Bailén, A. (2020). Dinámicas de (in)visibilidad en la migración LGBTQ+: Una cuestión communicacional. *REMHU Revista Interdisciplinar da Mobilidade Humana, 28*(59), 113–131. http://dx.doi.org/10.1590/1980-85852503880005908H

Hayes, M. (2014). 'We gained a lot over what we would have had': The geographic arbitrage of North American lifestyle migrants to Cuenca, Ecuador. *Journal of Ethnic and Migration Studies, 40*(12), 1953–1971. https://doi.org/10.1080/1369183X.2014.880335

Hepp, A. (2015). *Transcultural communication* [electronic resource]. Wiley Blackwell.

Hotez, P. J., Huete-Perez, J. A., Bottazzi, M. E. (2020). COVID-19 in the Americas and the erosion of human rights for the poor. *PLoS Neglected Tropical Diseases, 14*(12). https://doi.org/10.1371/journal.pntd.0008954

Howard, P. N., & Parks, M. R. (2012). Social media and political change: Capacity, constraint, and consequence. *Journal of Communication, 62*(2), 359–362. https://doi.org/10.1111/j.1460-2466.2012.01626.x

Jamrisko, M., Yuvejwattana, S., & Jiao, C. (2022, June 29). Working from a tropical island is the new working from home business: Leisure travelers are a growing breed, and tourist hotspots want their trade. *Bloomberg.* https://www.bloomberg.com/news/articles/2022-06-30/travel-2022-tropical-island-remote-working-is-the-new-work-from-home-trend

Jurkowitz, M. & Gottfried, J. (2022). *Twitter is the go-to social media site for U.S. journalists, but not for the public*, Pew Research Center. United States of America. Retrieved from https://policycommons.net/artifacts/2480855/twitter-is-the-go-to-social-media-site-for-us/3503030/ on 09 Nov 2022. CID: 20.500.12592/kqn22m.

Jia, L., Ping, X., Bin, A., & Lisheng L. (2020). Multilingual communication experiences of international students during the COVID-19 pandemic. *Multilingua, 39*(5), 529–539. https://doi.org/10.1515/multi-2020-0116

Jiwasiddi, A., Schlagwein, D., & Leong, C. (2022). Assessing the impacts of digital nomadism on local communities: The case of Chiang Mai, Thailand. *Proceedings from the Pacific Asia Conference on Information Systems (PACIS)*, 1–9.

Johanson, M. (2022, May 17). The countries resisting remote work. *BBC*. https://www.bbc.com/worklife/article/20220511-the-countries-resisting-remote-work

Johnson, J. (2012). Twitter bites and Romney: Examining the rhetorical situation of the 2012 presidential election in 140 characters. *Journal of Contemporary Rhetoric, 2*(3/4), 54–64.

Johnson, J. (2021). *Political rhetoric, social media, and American presidential campaigns*. Lexington Books.

Ju, Chikaire and Ajaero, J. O. and Atoma, C. N., (2022). Socio-Economic Effects of COVID-19 Pandemic on Rural Farm Families' Well-Being and Food Systems in Imo State, Nigeria. *Journal of Sustainability and Environmental Management, 1*(1)2022, 18–21. https://doi.org/10.5281/zenodo.6206234

Koutonin, M. R. (2015). Why are white people expats when the rest of us are immigrants? *The Guardian, 13*(5), 2013.

Kraidy, M. M. (2018). Global media studies: A critical agenda. *Journal of Communication, 68*(2), 337–346. https://doi-org.ezproxy.gvsu.edu/10.1093/joc/jqx024.

Lee, C. C. (2015). International communication research: Critical reflections and a new point of departure. In C. C. Lee (Ed.), *Internationalizing "International communication"* (pp. 1–28). University of Michigan Press. https://doi.org/10.2307/j.ctv65sxh2.3

Lee, J. A., Sudarshan, S., Sussman, K. L., Bright, L. F., & Eastin, M. S. (2022). Why are consumers following social media influencers on Instagram? Exploration of consumers' motives for following influencers and the role of materialism. *International Journal of Advertising, 41*(1), 78–100. https://doi.org/10.1080/02650487.2021.1964226

Litchfield, R. C., Hirst, G., & van Knippenberg, D. (2021). Professional network identification: Searching for stability in transient knowledge work. *Academy of Management Review, 46*(2), 320–340. https://doi-org.ezproxy.gvsu.edu/10.5465/amr.2017.0388

Liu, Y., & Buckingham, L. (2022). Language choice and academic publishing: A social-ecological perspective on languages other than English. *Journal of Multilingual and Multicultural Development*, 1–15. https://doi.org/10.1080/01434632.2022.2080834

Liu, Y., & Croucher, S. M. (2022). Becoming privileged yet marginalized other: American migrants' narratives of stereotyping-triggered displacement in China. *Asian Journal of Social Science, 50*, 7–15. https//doi.org.10.1016/j.ajss.2021.06.006

Lutz, P., & Bitschnau, M. (2022). Misperceptions about immigration: Reviewing their nature, motivations and determinants. *British Journal of Political Science*, 1–16. https://doi.org/10.1017/S0007123422000084

Maldonado, B. M. N., Collins, J., Blundell, H. J., & Singh, L. (2020). Engaging the vulnerable: A rapid review of public health communication aimed at migrants during the COVID-19 pandemic in Europe. *Journal of Migration and Health, 1*. https://doi.org/10.1016/j.jmh.2020.100004

Martin, S., & Bergmann, J. (2021). (Im)mobility in the age of COVID-19. *International Migration Review, 55*(3), 660–687. https://doi.org/10.1177/0197918320984104

Merisalo, M., & Jauhiainen, J. S. (2021). Asylum-related migrants' social-media use, mobility decisions, and resilience. *Journal of Immigrant & Refugee Studies, 19*(2), 184–198. https://doi.org/10.1080/15562948.2020.1781991

Moreman, S. T. (2008). Hybrid performativity, South and North of the border: Entre la teoría y la materialidad de hibridación. In A. N. Valdivia (Ed.), *Latina/o communication studies today* (pp. 91–111). Peter Lang.

Moreman, S. T. (2020). Narrative embodiment of Latinx queer futurity: Pause for dramatic affect. Gender futurity, intersectional autoethnography: Embodied theorizing from the margins. In A. L. Johnson & B. LeMaster (Eds.), *Gender Futurity, Intersectional Autoethnography* (pp. 223–236). Routledge.

Morrissey, M. (2018). Imaginaries of North American lifestyle migrants in Costa Rica. *Population, Space and Place, 24*(8), 1–9. https://doi-org.ezproxy.gvsu.edu/10.1002/psp.2168

Ngwainmbi, E. K. (2022). A revisit to networked communities and human identity. In E. K. Ngwainmbi (Ed.), *Dismantling cultural borders through social media and digital communications*. Palgrave Macmillan. https://doi.org/10.1007/978-3-030-92212-2_14

Nyberg, A. J., Shaw, J. D., & Zhu, J. (2021). The people still make the (remote work-) place: Lessons from a pandemic. *Journal of Management, 47*(8), 1967–1976.

Olvide, S. (2022, February 6). Americans can't quit SMS. *New York Times.* https://www.nytimes.com/2022/02/02/technology/sms-whatsapp.html

Ordóñez, J. T., & Arcos, H. E. R. (2019). At the crossroads of uncertainty: Venezuelan migration to Colombia. *Journal of Latin American Geography, 18*(2), 158–164. https:-doi.org/10.1353/lag.2019.0020

Parker, K., Horowitz, J. M., & Minkin, R. (2022). COVID-19 Pandemic continues to reshape work in America. *Pew Research Center.* https://www.pewresearch.org/social-trends/2022/02/16/covid-19-pandemic-continues-to-reshape-work-in-america/

Piller, I., Zhang, J., & Li, J. (2020). Linguistics diversity in a time of crisis: Language challenges of the Covid-19 pandemic. *Multiligua, 39*(5), 505–515. https://doi.org/10.1515/multi-2020-0136

Piper, N. (2005). Gender and migration. *Policy analysis and research programme of the Global Commission on International Migration, 40*(1), 133–164.

Pollett, S., & Rivers, C. (2020). Social media and the new world of scientific communication during the COVID-19 pandemic. *Clinical Infectious Diseases, 71*(16), 2184–2186. https://doi.org/10.1093/cid/ciaa553

Poushter, J. (2016). Smartphone ownership and internet usage continues to climb in emerging economies. Pew Research Center. https://www.pewresearch.org/social-trends/2022/02/16/covid-19-pandemic-continues-to-reshape-work-in-america/

Rodriguez, C. (2001). *Fissures in the mediascape.* Hampton Press.

Rudwick, S., Sijadu, Z. & Turner, I. (2021) Politics of language in COVID-19: Multilingual perspectives from South Africa, *Politikon, 48*(2), 242–259. https:doi.org//10.1080/02589346.2021.1917206

Santa Ana, O. (1999). "Like an animal I was treated": Anti-immigrant metaphor in US public discourse. *Discourse & Society, 10*, 191–224. https://doi.org/10.1177/0957926599010002004

Sandel, T., & Qiu, P. (2021). Code switching and language games in contemporary China; or, Convergence and identity construction on WeChat. In P. S. W. Dodge (Ed.), *Communication convergence in contemporary China* (pp. 175–205). Michigan State University Press.

Schaeffer, K. (2021). 7 facts about Americans and Instagram. Pew Research Center. https://www.pewresearch.org/fact-tank/2021/10/07/7-facts-about-americans-and-instagram/

Spencer, A. T. (2011a). Americans create hybrid spaces in Costa Rica: A framework for exploring cultural and linguistic integration, *Language & Intercultural Communication, 11*(1), 59–74. https:doi.org//10.1080/14708477.2010.517847

Spencer, A. T. (2011b). Through the linguistic looking glass: An examination of a newspaper as negotiator of hybrid cultural and linguistic spaces. *Speaker & Gavel, 48*. Retrieved from http://cornerstone.lib. mnsu.edu/speaker-gavel/vol48/iss1/5/?utm_source=cornerstone.lib.mnsu.edu%2Fspeaker-gavel%2Fvol48%2Fiss1%2F5&utm_medium=PDF&utm_campaign=PDFCoverPages

Spencer, A. T. (2013). High-end immigrants create an imagined community in Costa Rica: Examining the evolving discourse in ethnic-minority media. *Human Communication, 16*, 13–30.

Spencer, A. T. (2018). Nicaraguan immigration to Costa Rica: Understanding power and race through language. In S. M. Croucher, J. Caetano, & E. A. Campbell (Eds.), *Companion to migration, communication, and politics* (pp. 266–281). Routledge.

Spencer, A. T., Croucher, S. M., & Hoelscher, C. (2012). Uses and gratifications meets the Internet: A cross-cultural comparison of U.S. & Nicaraguan new media usage. *Human Communication, 15*(4), 229–240.

Suzina, A. C. (2021). English as lingua franca. Or the sterilisation of scientific work. *Media, Culture & Society, 43*(1), 171–179. https://doi.org/10.1177/0163443720957906

Takenaka, A. K., Gaspar, R., Villafuerte, J., & Narayanan, B. (2020). *COVID-19 impact on International migration, remittances, and recipient households in developing Asia*. Asian Development Bank. http://hdl.handle.net/11540/12258

Thompson, B. Y. (2019). The digital nomad lifestyle: (Remote) work/leisure balance, privilege, and constructed community. *International Journal of the Sociology of Leisure, 2*(1), 27–42. https://doi.org/10.1007/s41978-018-00030-y

Thussu, D. K. (2000). *International communication: Continuity and change*. Bloomsbury Publishing.

Thussu, D. K. (2012). *International communication*. (Vols. 1–4). SAGE Publications Ltd, https://dx.doi.org/10.4135/9781446262085

Voorend, K., & Alvarado, D. (2022). Barriers to healthcare access for immigrants in Costa Rica and Uruguay. *Journal of International Migration and Integration*, 1–25. https://doi.org/10.1007/s12134-022-00972-z

United Nations. Last accessed: June, 28, 2022. https://www.un.org/en/global-issues/migration.

Williams, A. C., Mark, G., Milland, K., Lank, E., & Law, E. (2019). The perpetual work life of crowdworkers: How tooling practices increase fragmentation in crowdwork. *Proceedings of the ACM on Human-Computer Interaction, 3*(CSCW), 1–28.

Wilson, S. (2021). Where brands are reaching Gen Z. *Harvard Business Review*. https://hbr.org/2021/03/where-brands-are-reaching-gen-z

Wilczewski, M. (2019). *Intercultural experience in narrative: Expatriate stories from a multicultural workplace*. John Benjamins Publishing Company.

Woldoff, R. A., & Litchfield, R. C. (2021). *Digital nomads: In search of freedom, community, and meaningful work in the new economy*. Oxford University Press.

Zhang, M. (2016). A rhetorical analysis of Chinese WeChat messages among midlife adults. *China Media Research, 12*(3), 7–16.

Zhang, M. (2022). Using WeChat to communicate with Chinese exchange students. *China Media Research, 18*(1), 84–100.

13

PANDEMIC RHETORIC

Orla Vigsø

Rhetoric is inherently contextual. No matter if the term is used to teach people to address a public, or to discuss the communicative performance of a rhetor, it is always about a specific communicator addressing a specific audience at a certain time and place to influence their ways of making meaning of a certain aspect of life. In classic rhetoric, this is often seen as quite straightforward: John F. Kennedy saying "Ich bin ein Berliner" in West Berlin in 1963, or Mark Antony speaking to the citizens of Rome on the Forum, claiming that he has come to bury Ceasar, not to praise him, at least as narrated by William Shakespeare in *Julius Cæsar*. But how do we go about when the situation is much more complex, as is the case with a pandemic? Does it make sense to talk about communication in the time of a pandemic as if it were a situation like any other, with a well-defined speaker, audience, time, place, and purpose? Or do we need to develop new approaches to analyze this kind of rhetoric?

The Rhetorical Situation – And Beyond

Classic rhetoric was concerned with the means a speaker could use to persuade a given public on a specific occasion, or rather, an occasion belonging to a specific category. Each category of occasion had its specific characteristics, but in each case the speaker should consider what constituted the audience, and even how they looked upon the speaker. This combination of a question, that is, that which the speaker wants to influence the audience on, a specific speaker, and a specific audience, was the very core of rhetoric for a very long time. But it was not until 1966 that Lloyd F. Bitzer asked the question, "What characterized the situations in which rhetorical discourse was produced?" Not all situations result in rhetorical discourse, Bitzer claimed, so what is it that decides

DOI: 10.4324/9781003214496-13

which situations give birth to rhetoric? It is not all situations that call rhetorical discourse into existence, but rather specific "rhetorical situations":

> Let us regard rhetorical situation as a natural context of persons, events, objects, relations, and an exigence which strongly invites utterance; this invited utterance participates naturally in the situation, is in many instances necessary to the completion of situational activity, and by means of its participation with situation obtains its meaning and its rhetorical character.
>
> *Bitzer (1968, p. 5)*

Rhetoric is a response to a situation in the same way that an answer is the response to a question; the situation calls for an "answer", and the "exigence" of the situation must be solvable through rhetoric. Bitzer's text has had an immense impact on rhetorical criticism, but it has also attracted a lot of criticism due to the way he narrows down the scope of rhetoric, excluding situations where speakers (individuals or organizations) clearly are trying to influence the public, but where neither the question nor the audience can be described in direct terms. Furthermore, there is very little in Bitzer's definition that points to the dynamics of an actual situation, with a plurality of speakers using a variety of media to influence the general opinion on several questions related to each other. In the case of a pandemic, it is clear to all that a specific kind of rhetorical discourse evolves. It is a discourse where rhetors try and influence others on questions related to the pandemic, but it is very hard to subsume all of this under one "exigence", and dismissing the major part of the discourse as "not rhetorical" seems very unsatisfying. So how can we describe the situation in an inclusive manner, without pre-established notions of which parts to consider?

The most realistic model for describing what happens rhetorically during a pandemic is, in my opinion, the Rhetorical Arena Theory developed by Frandsen and Johansen (2017). The theory was developed to analyze communication in a crisis, something which a pandemic surely must be seen as, but it can actually be understood as a general model for understanding the communicative actions taking place in any question unfolding in the public sphere. In the case of a pandemic, I suggest that the Rhetorical Arena Theory (RAT) is a way to grasp the rhetorical complexity of a situation where a multiplicity of voices communicate about issues relating to the pandemic but address a variety of questions in connection with this situation. Frandsen and Johansen define crisis communication in this way:

> Crisis communication is a complex and dynamic configuration of communicative processes which develop before, during, and after an event or a situation that is interpreted as a crisis by an organization and/or by other voices in the arena. Crisis communication also includes how

various actors, contexts, and discourses (manifested in specific genres and specific texts) relate to each other.

(p. 148)

The RAT has, as is evident from the quote above, been developed within an organizational context, with the organization subjected to a crisis as the point of departure. However, in its form it is not organization-centered. The arena is without a center; the organization is not a privileged voice. One could say that its structure is like a rhizome, the organically growing, unpredictable root system of certain plants, made into a theoretical term by Deleuze and Guattari (1980). So, instead of a privileged center, the network of communicative connections determines which voice gets the most attention. Furthermore, the extension of the arena is not possible to establish beforehand, as it may grow in all directions depending on which voices join the arena as the crisis progresses.

What is important to take into consideration is the fact that media play a crucial role in the RAT. Not only are some media organizations voices, but most of the voices heard are encountered through media of some form. In other words, the voices act through and in relation to media; this is where they are heard, this is where they build relations to other voices. Without media, there is no rhetorical arena, and as today's media landscape has changed, this includes both legacy media and social media, all of which are now mainly consumed in digital form. The network of relations in the figure thus moves through a variety of media, with some voices favoring particular media.

The Pandemic as a Multivocal and Multifocal Rhetorical Arena

It is evident to anybody who has lived through this pandemic that it is a situation where scores of voices are trying to make themselves heard. As the COVID-19 case showed, a pandemic is characterized by its scope, meaning that no organization in society is unaffected. Every organization is entangled in several questions relating to the pandemic, as all stakeholders are in some way influenced by the spreading of the disease. All organizations must take a stand as to whether or not they want to impose specific measures for their employees, in the contact with persons from the external world, etc. So even if an organization decides not to impose any restrictions, it will have to communicate this, and most probably even defend it against those accusing it of not understanding the severity of the situation. In other words, a pandemic is inescapable as a fact, triggering expectations on any organization's behavior as well as imposing a variety of restrictions from government, administrative departments, and even other private organizations (e.g., in order to continue business). All of this requires communication of some kind or other, and it has to be more or less public in order to make a position known. So, there is no doubt that the multivocality aspect of RAT is a fitting description of what happens during a pandemic.

But what also becomes clear in a pandemic is the linking together of different topics of the communication. Even within the general frame of the pandemic, numerous sub-topics evolve. In the case of the "swine flu", naming the pandemic became one very important topic (Vigsø, 2010). In some countries, the name assigned blame to a specific religious group within the country. In other countries, the name was seen as an unfair accusation against a country, and pork producers in several countries were adamant that the name of the pandemic should not in any way put into question the safety of pork products. The topic of naming thus became linked to religion, nationalism, and economy. Each of these sub-topics was, in its turn, connected to other topics. One example was the linking of pork production to the more general question of animal welfare and its negative influence on the world's climate, calling for a significant decrease of meat consumption. The pandemic thus becomes a possibility to link together positions and questions which existed before the pandemic, but now can gain an increased urgency (see Figure 13.1).

In the case of COVID-19, the world has experienced the linking of many topics, from the beginning in March 2020 until 2022 where hopefully we are in the last stages of the pandemic. In the following, I describe some of these points of focus during a pandemic and how they have developed specific rhetorical traits. But what is interesting is also the way in which these areas have been linked to each other and to the general area of the pandemic. What I propose is an extension of the RAT to include several specific arenas subsumed under the pandemic arena. One might imagine it as a series of panes of glass positioned as floors of a building and with connecting flights of stairs leading from one floor to another – maybe the next, maybe the one after that, but all framed within the general structure of the building (see Figure 13.2). Each of these floors has the structure of the Rhetorical Arena, but with arrows connecting voices with other voices on other floors.

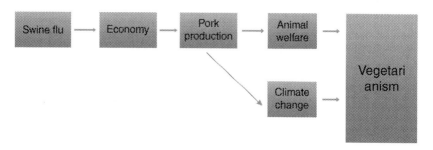

FIGURE 13.1 How Topics Can Become Linked.

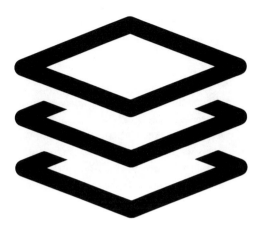

FIGURE 13.2 Multilayer Structure (http://www.onlinewebfonts.com).

Using the metaphor of a house, we will however soon find ourselves within the realm of a science fiction novel: as we discussed above, the extent of each arena is not possible to describe beforehand, or in other words, we do not know how big each floor is. And in a parallel to this, we do not know the number of floors either as it develops throughout the pandemic. A rather strange house, one has to admit…

But this indeterminate nature and the fluidity is the very reason why I believe this is the most realistic way to describe the rhetoric developing during a pandemic. Seeing the pandemic as a single rhetorical situation will only lead to a few restrictions on what to include and it will necessitate a focus on a specific rhetor for whom the pandemic is an exigence. One might be tempted to opt for the metaphor of a battlefield instead, as many of the voices being heard in a pandemic are without doubt in a relation of conflict to each other. But even this is a reductive and simplistic way of excluding other voices not directed against other parties, and it will even distort the picture of the "goals" of the voices' rhetoric, leaving us with the impression that a "win" for one part necessarily will imply a "loss" for another part.

Topics Discussed during Pandemics

A pandemic is a crisis which potentially affects all aspects of life, both personal and societal. Just as RAT shows that there is no limit to the number of voices appearing on the arena, the extension proposed above indicates that there are no "natural" limits to the number of topics involved in the multifocal arena. The topics mentioned below are some of those that to me seem most likely to pop up, judging from the work I have done on pandemic crisis communication during the last decade or so. Some may seem more culturally limited, that is appearing only in some countries, but my claim is that the ones mentioned here will in some way appear in most societies, at least countries without censorship of the media. If they can be considered global, I hesitate to say.

Origin

The question of origin is one topic which manifests itself very early on in a pandemic. One reason, of course, is the medical interest in this, as pinpointing the origin can be an important part of determining the path and strength of the virus. It can also provide clues about which vaccines might be effective, so there is a scientific and neutral rhetoric developing in relation to this. But, at the same time, another aspect is related to this topic, namely that of *blaming*. The attribution of responsibility for the pandemic plays a huge role, as I have documented in a study of the swine flu (Vigsø, 2010), and a large part of the discourses evolving around this are far from neutral. No country, region, or city wants to have its name associated with a deadly pandemic, and even if the connection might be factually correct (the virus was first found in this location), the association is far from harmless. The origin of a pandemic is often linked with the *cause* of the pandemic, meaning that highlighting a geographical location will be interpreted as pointing out the people in this location as responsible.

In some cases, this attribution of responsibility is mere "collateral damage" and not intended by the ones using the name, but in other cases the naming is clearly part of an attempt to smear another country, either because there are some historical and political issues with that country, or because it is a means to an end: blaming another country will ease the criticism against one's own country. The blame game is thus a way to "get off the hook" and direct the attention toward another country, but always a country which is not a close ally. "You don't accuse your friends", to put it bluntly.

The geographical origin of a virus is of course not the only origin of interest. The past decades have given us the avian flu (A H5N1) as well as the swine flu (A/H1N1pdm09), and even the mad cow's disease (Bovine spongiform encephalopathy, BSE) which, although not a virus, caused much concern and drastic measures. The BSE scare lead to a significant amount of bad publicity for the meat industry, as did the avian flu for the poultry industry. But while these two cases were neutral, in the sense that no particular groups were attacked for their engagement with cows and birds, it was a completely different story with the swine flu. Pigs play a very different role in different societies, as the animal is considered unclean in several religions. Naming the pandemic *swine flu* is a way of implicitly putting the blame on pork producers, which in the case of a country as Egypt with a Muslim majority was equal to putting the blame on Christians, as they were the only ones farming pigs. Thus, the naming of the pandemic leads to an association with Christians through their pork production, which in its turn leads to acts of violence from Muslims against Christians.

So, the naming of the virus behind a pandemic might be related to internal differences between majorities and minorities within a country, and it might also have to do with animosity against certain countries. This was at least the accusation from Mexico against the US when *the swine flu* was first named *the Mexican flu* in the US. One could even claim that the prevalence of Asian place names in the Western descriptions of various strains of flu throughout the post-WWII period has played a role in the general prejudices about Asian countries. In the case of COVID-19, "some politicians, conservative journalists and others persisted in calling the COVID-19 virus the 'Chinese virus,' or some variant of this term, such as the 'China virus,' 'Wuhan virus' (after the Chinese city that first reported the virus), 'Chinese flu' and 'Kung flu'" (Bushman 2022). This happens in spite of the WHO strongly advising against it, which proves that there are other factors at play here than the mere naming. Politics and prejudices mingle with language to create a framing which has an impact on citizens. Bushman writes:

> The way media frame, depict and describe events can have a profound influence on the public's perception of those events. Researchers have found that audiences are prone to interpret media stories in the context of their biases, especially in relation to racial groups. My colleagues Lanier Frush Holt, Sophie Kjærvik and I found that simply reading one media article calling the coronavirus the "Chinese virus" made people more likely to blame China for the pandemic.
>
> *Bushman (2022)*

In other words, naming a virus should exclude all references which can be used for political purposes by any party.

Danger and Risk

A pandemic means that there is a risk for the general population of becoming sick and even dying. According to the WHO, a pandemic is "the worldwide spread of a new disease" (Shannon, 2020), but even though everybody can agree that neither disease nor death is a good thing, the risk of being infected and the danger it entails are very much subjects of discussion. Not only is the empirical evidence lacking, as it is per definition a new disease, which means that the level of risk must be determined on the basis of other outbreaks, it is also a question which looks different when considered from a societal point of view than when it is seen in relation to an individual. As the assessment of danger and risk is the basis for a lot of decisions regarding a pandemic, the choices made in the assessment will have far-reaching consequences. First and foremost, the assessment of the level of danger and risk will work as a warrant for the different claims (Toulmin, 2003) regarding which measures should be taken and whether restrictions on the daily life in a country should be in the form of recommendations or laws. In short, the higher the level of danger and/ or risk as it is communicated by the authorities, the easier it will be to argue for strict measures.

Danger in a pandemic is often assessed by the fatality or serious illness it causes in those infected, which is something that is becoming evident first as the pandemic evolves. As the number of fatalities rises, the discussion will to a large degree focus on the scientific arguments for or against possible future continuations of the curves. The rhetoric here is often very technical, while at the same time very visually accessible to non-experts: what is the relation between the number of infected individuals and the number of fatalities? And who are dying from the pandemic, is it evenly distributed across all variables, or are the victims people who were already either suffering from health conditions or elderly people, or, as is often the case, both? In short: how deadly is the pandemic to people infected?

Even the rhetoric regarding the risk of becoming infected is to a large extent governed by a technical rhetoric. As the ways of infection may be unclear from the beginning, as well as the number of infected, the argument about how big the risk is for citizens in various situations is a projection of many uncertain variables. But at the same time, this projection has very physical consequences when it comes to the authorities' decisions regarding policy decisions like the number of people allowed to be in a specific place at the same time, the distance required between people, etc. In both the rhetoric about danger and the one about risk, there is a tendency to split into two opposing camps: the "better safe than sorry" camp or the "no need for alarmism" camp. The first argues that lack of evidence should lead to a pre-paredness for the worst, meaning measures as soon as possible and as strict as possible to avoid a potential disaster. The other camp argues that the societal and human cost of strict measures should lead to authorities applying the minimum necessary when it comes to restrictions.

Time

The topic of time is one which pops up as soon as a pandemic is declared, simply because everybody is wondering how long this is going to last. When can we expect the rate of infected people to drop, when will the first wave end and when will the second wave hit, how long until an effective vaccine has been produced, how long before everybody has been inoculated, etc. From the moment a pandemic is declared, everything is seen in relation to the future, or rather to different futures. But, as the Danish humorist Robert Storm Petersen said, "it's hard to predict anything, particularly about the future". The uncertainty about the future does, however, not hold back people from making predictions. Of course, these predictions vary, and this often results in not so much a discussion about the solidity of the predictions but rather a division between two groups. The group with the most positive outlook is labeled *optimists* by the other group, the one painting a darker picture, and these people are in their turn labeled *pessimists* or *apocalyptics* by the others, with a term borrowed from Umberto Eco. This distinction can be seen as a variant of the one described earlier regarding danger and risk, and it is as a matter of fact a recurring theme in the pandemic rhetorical arena, as many aspects of the pandemic depend on the interpretation of an unclear situation and how it shall develop over time.

Measures

There are a few people who argue that a pandemic is a natural phenomenon and should be allowed to run its course, but there seem to be extremely few of them and they are generally not granted much media attention. So, there is a consensus that the government should play an active role of some sort, but apart from this there is much debate about exactly how the government should react to a pandemic, and what sort of measures should be introduced and when. The arguments regarding the measures span from the listing of possible measures, the efficacy of each measure in helping society through the pandemic, the benefits in relation to the economic, social, and psychological cost of the measure, and the duration of the measure.

During earlier pandemics we have been faced with the culling of animals deemed responsible for the spreading of the disease – be it sheep, cows, pigs, chickens, or mink. In each of these cases, the possible benefit in terms of reduced spread of the virus is weighed against the economic cost, but also against the psychological impact of this intervention on the people farming these animals. A central point here is the question whether the action of mass culling is an efficient anti-pandemic measure or rather an intervention directed at making people feel that the government is doing something to help the situation. Critics often point to such measures as "showcase politics" rather than necessary precautions; in order to strengthen its credibility by showing agency and determination, it is more important that the government decides on apparently drastic measures rather than being able to support their efficacy through research or previous results. As all measures taken to alleviate the effects of a pandemic are parts of an epidemiological, economic, and political arena, it is impossible to avoid clashes between voices as they interpret the measures as either too little or too much, inefficient or overkill. The arena of measures can without doubt be considered the most conflict-laden of all topics brought into play by a pandemic – not necessarily due to the incompetency of governments, but rather as a fundamental characteristic.

In the aftermath of the COVID pandemic (and even during it), probably all countries have been affected by the discussion of the nature and efficacy of measures taken. Statistics are being compared between countries with different measures, trying to establish which measures were indeed effective – and thus necessary – and which were not, that is were more of a showcase nature. In Denmark, the mass culling of mink is currently a subject of interrogation: was it necessary, did it prevent further spreading of the disease, and was it in fact in accordance with the laws of the country? But what must be remembered in all cases, no matter where, the governments were under severe time pressure. Decisions had to be made quickly, and the leaders faced the impossible task of choosing between not implementing a measure and risking lives, not to mention a political crisis afterward, or implementing a measure and risking expenditures and a political crisis due to unnecessary costs and accusations of "overreacting". It is only afterward that his verdict can be made, and there is a high risk for politicians of being "damned if you do and damned if you don't".

Nation and Nationalism

While a pandemic can awaken latent negative feelings against other nations when it comes to attributing responsibility, there are other ways in which nation and nationalism turn up in the pandemic rhetoric. All the topics mentioned above may include comparisons with other nations as part of the arguments, and specifically as support for the argument that our way of doing things is the right and efficient way. The topics of danger/risk and measures are intertwined with comparisons of what other nations are doing, either to strengthen the argument that this is the right way to do things, or as bad examples of what happens if a country does not do as we are doing. During the first months of the COVID-19 crisis, the three Scandinavian countries, which to outsiders are almost indistinguishable, made comparisons with the other two – a main part of their justification for implementing highly different policies. And even within the European Union, strong restrictions on travels between countries were explained as a result of other countries' lack of control over the pandemic, while in other cases other countries' stronger restrictions were criticized for being unnecessary overreactions.

A pandemic is, of course, a national problem and the COVID-19 crisis showed clearly that European countries which had for decades fought for more mobility across borders suddenly adopted what can only be described as a more nationalist approach. Borders were closed, travelers were subjected to restrictions and control, and containment became the answer to a threat from outside of the nation. In the media, other countries' lack of control or "zealousness" was discursively connected to "national characteristics", all in a sort of free-for-all blame game. Certain politicians and certain popular media could thus use this situation to favor their own ideological goals, which may or may not have influenced the decisions of the governments.

The Economy

A pandemic is a threat to people's health, but it is also immediately talked about in terms of an economic threat, and this aspect is probably the most pervasive of all. A pandemic is a stress factor on the economy in a number of different ways: sick people cost money – they require medical staff resources, medicine, and often physical interventions in hospitals and with medical equipment – but there is also the cost inflicted across sectors like industry and transport through workers' absence, the cost of parents having to stay home to take care of their children when schools are closed, the slowing down of the economy due to lockdowns, etc. Both the pandemic and the measures to combat it are expensive to society as a whole. During the COVID-19 pandemic, states and the EU have administered large subsidies to businesses which have been struck by either the pandemic or the imposed measures to prevent further spreading of the virus. Voices were raised from both politicians and small and big businesses about the cost to society for imposing limitations on opening hours, numbers of customers allowed at any time, lockdowns, etc., from the very beginning. The economy is the prime example of a rhetorical arena which is in principle unlimited, as the economy is of concern to everybody, and the consequences are complex. The care of the sick and elderly is necessary to avoid death, but how shall the rising costs be financed? And what about support for businesses, recompense for unemployment or forced leave, and the testing and vaccination of the population? In short, the question of costs is inseparable from a pandemic.

The arguments put forth regarding costs are, of course, related to the question of political views, in particular relating to the view on public spending and private enterprise.

Personal Freedom of Movement, Surveillance, and Control

An aspect of pandemic rhetoric which has gained a more prominent position with the development of electronic surveillance and the computerization of information is that of an opposition between the state's measures to combat the spreading of the disease and the individual's freedom of movement. In pre-modern times, cities could close their walls to stop strangers from entering the area and bringing the virus inside the city. But since World War II, we have grown used to increasing degrees of freedom, not only inside the country but even between countries and continents. Meanwhile, the state apparatus has instituted more and more ways of surveilling the inhabitants, as everything is stored as digital data. When the state reinstates limitations on movement, either through closed borders, restricted opening hours, or limits to the number of people allowed to gather in one place, and combines this with different sorts of digital "passports", the rhetorical arena is extended by the topic of individual freedom from state interference. During the COVID-19 crisis, this opposition to the state was in many cases, but not solely, associated with a general distrust of the state as found in often right-wing and populist movements. The opposition targeted lockdowns, shorter opening hours, limitations on assemblies, but especially attempts at compulsory vaccination. Conspiracy theories are a part of this rhetoric, but even concern about the right to choose, as well as previous examples of serious side effects from vaccines.

Many of the protest movements against restrictions imposed by the government on the lives of the citizens (either in the form of demanding vaccination in order for people to do certain things, or in the restrictions of assemblies) very quickly created a heated atmosphere. One particularly strong reaction was in the case of the protests by Canadian truckers (Horowitz, 2022), which lead to the prime minister declaring Canada's first national public order emergency in half a century. Even in other countries with less violent confrontations, a clear schism emerged between those putting the freedom of the individual above all and those putting the consideration of others above all, as it was pointed out that lack of vaccination in those who could become vaccinated posed a threat to citizens who for health reasons could not take the shot. This conflict between the individual and the collective is unsolvable, which once again poses a conundrum for any government, as any choice will lead to protest from some.

The Interaction of Topics in the Multivocal, Multifocal Rhetorical Arena

The above-mentioned topics are some of the more prominent, but as stated in the beginning, an important trait of the pandemic situation is that there is no limit to how many topics ("layers") might appear in the rhetorical arena. What complicates the situation even more is the fact that these topics are linked by several unforeseeable lines. Some topics are tightly intertwined with others, while some connections appear out of the blue and lead to unforeseen consequences. A rhetorical arena is an arena of conflict and cooperation, and when the multifocal approach is introduced, this can become both a helping hand and an obstacle to action, for example, the state's attempts at limiting the consequences of a pandemic. The introduction of one topic into the discussions on another topic often takes the form of support for a claim, meaning that argumentation is strengthened through this operation, but this argument can be either positive or negative in relation to official policies.

In other words, all agents within a topical rhetorical arena might use other topical arenas for their argumentation, and often in a way where one topic is supposed to "trump" arguments from other topics. One such topic is *human rights*, as the individual's right to, e.g., move freely is argued to be above the right to be protected from diseases, or vice versa, that the right to be protected overrules other rights to freedom. What is at stake here is the right of the sovereign state to declare a state of emergency, which puts normal rights on a hiatus – a right which may be contested on a general level or on a particular level. Some voices consider the measures not fitting for the present situation, while others strongly protest any kind of limitations by the state.

Analyzing the interrelatedness of topics in the arena is a laborious task, but generally one will find that there are many underlying ideological positions which determine both the stance of the voice on a particular topic, and the way topics are linked to each other. A pandemic rhetorical arena is probably one of the strongest examples of the strength of ideological positions on argumentation in several topical fields. For example, as the aftermath of the COVID pandemic has shown us, managing this situation has proved a difficult task for many governments. In the UK, the unwillingness of the Tory government and PM to follow the rules imposed on everybody (else) has lead to a prolonged and severe crisis for the government, and in other countries dissatisfaction in the public with restrictions, level of preparedness, economic compensation, and a general lack of planning has lead to serious disruptions in the political landscape. As in other serious crises, the ability of the organizations (that is, governments and health agencies) to actually learn from this situation will be a central feature of political debates in the years to come.

Topics, Metaphors, and Tropes

Tropes and figures of speech have been of specific interest to rhetorical studies for a long time, and even if the scope of rhetoric has changed considerably during the last decades, the study of the expressions used still plays an important role. And what happens during a pandemic is not just that the topics of discourse change; the tone also changes, and specific metaphors and tropes take over. Jonathan Charteris-Black (2021) has devoted a whole book to the study of metaphors during COVID-19.

One metaphor which is very common during a pandemic is that of *war*, which constitutes a frame not only for understanding the situation but also for the measures taken. The virus is seen as an enemy, which in some cases comes from foreign areas and in other cases is already among us, but which needs to be fought, controlled, and preferably terminated. The extent to which the war metaphor gives rise to an extended vocabulary of war depends on the cultural and historical background of the country in question, in particular its experiences with war. As Charteris-Black (2021) points out, the government discourse in the UK during COVID was heavily laden with words associated with war: casualties, strategy, tactics, field hospitals, an army of health workers, fight, frontline, weapons, etc. Charteris-Black quotes Musolff (2021) on the function of this metaphor:

> [...] uses of the PANDEMIC-AS-WAR metaphor fulfil different rhetorical and argumentative functions: a) to rally support, b) to frame a

narrative that explains developments in public health management and c) to justify specific policies. In view of such multi-functionality of metaphorical scenarios, some of the 'blanket criticism' of all occurrences of WAR and FIGHTING terminology appears to be unjustified.

Musolff (2021, p. 1)

The war metaphor is well rooted in our languages even when there is no pandemic going on, just browse through the sports news or news about election campaigns. Winners, losers, fights, attacks, weapons – apparently, we find it hard to understand any confrontation between opposing groups striving to achieve a goal which excludes the other part without framing it as war. So, there is nothing inherently wrong about the war metaphor, but when applied to a pandemic situation, there are some problematic consequences.

Alongside the war metaphor, we have adopted a language that not long ago would have seemed strange, idiosyncratic, or foreign. Scientific notions like "social distancing" or terms like "effective reproduction number" have infiltrated our daily jargon, as we collaborate to "flatten the curve". In rhetoric we could consider this the use of ethos – convincing the audience by referring to the authority or credibility of the persuader (Aaslund 2021, p. 168). People adopted the words used by the experts interviewed in the news, even if they probably did not use them in the way the experts did. The reason for this rise in technical terms from epidemiology, medicine, and microbiology was, as Aaslund (2021) points out, to supply the arguments with support. Using technical terms is a way of trying to increase one's ethos and thus the force of one's arguments, and it is a technique used by us all from time to time – just think of the terms used in debates about global warming. The proliferation of this terminology is self-amplifying; the more others use these terms, the more people feel obliged to use them to be taken seriously.

Ethos and the Role of Experts

During a pandemic, experts are given a central position in questions pertaining to the disease, its spreading, and the policies to counter it. The description of the situation is left to experts as is the recommendations to both governments and citizens, as Chapter 3 on Science Communication in this book discusses at length. Within the COVID-19 context, as Charteris-Black (2021) suggests:

… with the arrival of COVID-19 governments everywhere relied on the authority of experts in molecular evolution, epidemiology, clinical science and practice, modelling infectious diseases, behavioural science, statistics, virology, microbiology, social science, social psychology, economics and other disciplines. The list was so long that in statements of policy the government justified decisions with the simple claim that they were based on 'what science has advised'. Quite swiftly appeals to the desires and wishes of the 'people' were replaced by those based on the authority of 'science' which now formed the main argument for the legitimacy of their decisions.

(pp. 13–14)

Not only governments but almost every voice in the pandemic rhetorical arena bases their arguments on other voices, belonging to what is, as Charteris-Black mentioned, labeled as "science". This is a strong support for the claims made, but it also plays a significant role as a support for the ethos of the one making the claim. By referring to "science", the rhetor becomes a trustworthy, reasonable person who, in this dire situation, is not led astray by emotions. "Science" is a backing which trumps all other forms of backing, or at least it is supposed to do so. As discussed above, there might be ideological standpoints which are immune to the notion of "science" as a counter-argument, e.g., when *freedom* is understood as more important. But in general, the public is supposed to (and most often do) accept "science" as *the* definitive voice in all arguments related to the pandemic.

The problem here is, of course, that "science" is not a unified voice in the rhetorical arena. This was demonstrated during the COVID crisis, but also during other epidemics like the Swine flu, where scientists were involved in constant argumentation with each other about the validity of data and the interpretation of results, not to mention the projection of developments on the basis of what has happened so far. This is the very core of science, the continuous discussion to produce the best possible interpretations and prognoses, but this logic is often on a collision course with the logic of the media. The use of expertise in public discussions and policy making follows a different logic, where the production of reliable results is subservient to supporting one's own position (see also Hartelius, 2011). In some countries, this leads to heated discussions about *which* science to believe, while in other countries, divergent voices within the scientific community are finding it hard to make their voice heard in the arena. In other words, some national arenas are rooms for discussions about scientific matters between researchers while others only present the voices which are supporting the official interpretation. During the beginning of the COVID crisis, this difference could be observed between Denmark, where scientists were attacking each other in public, and Sweden, where voices critical of the Public Health Agency were rarely allowed to comment in mainstream media.

What a pandemic thus makes evident is the political use of science and expertise, with the contextual factor of the need to make swift decisions based on imperfect data, and this will also have repercussions for the topic of measures. It has also become evident that governments must be better at explaining that science is not one thing, but that the continuous discussion between sciences and scientists is what makes science as such progress. In other words, being transparent about which scientist the government chooses to follow, and why, is the only way to gain some control of the multifocal and multivocal rhetorical arena and to hope for cooperation from the media, rather than them promoting voices which have little support in the scientific community.

The Narratives of a Pandemic

A pandemic is, as has been argued throughout this text and as we all have experienced during the COVID-19 period, a complex and dramatic situation. It is no surprise that narratives play a great part in the way the pandemic is depicted, analyzed, and interpreted, as narratives are fundamental for our understanding of the world and our own role in it. Furthermore, narratives are crucial in argumentation as a means of persuasion, and it is central in the way the media relate news, so we should be expecting narratives in all aspects of a pandemic.

On the individual level, the narratives of a pandemic are related to sickness, recovery, death, psychological and economic hardship, isolation, physical distance from loved ones, etc. – all of which must be said to be perfect material for media on the lookout for emotionally charged personal stories. The "personal interest" stories play different roles in the argumentation during the pandemic, as the protagonists – and the media – may draw conclusions relating to policy decisions. But these narratives are also used as *exemplars* by politicians when arguing for or against measures, adding pathos to the argumentation while providing proof which cannot be dismissed: "The language of the pandemic is also the language of pathos – convincing the audience by creating an emotional response to an impassioned plea or convincing story" (Aaslund 2021, p. 168). Nobody can argue against the feelings of people whose parents, spouses, or close friends have been taken away by the pandemic, making the narrative a strong support for one's claims.

The pandemic itself develops over time, and thus a larger narrative is formed, one which is in some cases almost personalized as the virus and its travels from country to country take the form of a travel account. The struggle between the virus and the countries affected easily becomes an account of a struggle (cf the war metaphor), as does the tale of the virus' mutations to survive the deployment of vaccines. The "master narrative" may be described as the struggle between man and nature (i.e., the virus), and when linked to other topics in the rhetorical arena, the accomplices of the virus may be human stupidity, lack of international cooperation, lack of funding for research, economics, religion, or political incompetence. The narrative takes the form of the classic fairytale, as described by Propp (1968), with heroes, villains, and a goal which in this case is the survival of the population. This, of course, can have the effect of engaging the public in the "fight", but as mentioned earlier, there are also consequences for how a pandemic is understood.

Concluding Remarks

This chapter is an attempt to try and take two steps back and reflect on what is going on rhetorically during a pandemic. It is of course highly influenced by the fact that I am now writing during a pandemic, but I have tried to find ways to describe what has been seen during other pandemics in modern times. The important part is to find ways to grasp the complexity of the rhetoric used, as there are so many voices making themselves heard in so many different media, and on such a large number of topics. What I have suggested here is to use the rhetorical arena theory as a general frame of understanding, but to extend it by seeing it as not only multivocal but also multifocal. A pandemic opens a space with several rhetorical arenas, devoted to specific topics, but interrelated through the presence of the voices in several arenas, and using arguments from one topical arena in others. I likened this to several planes of glass positioned as the stories in a multi-story house, but with the additional twist that each arena is dynamic in shape and may extend in all directions. The structure can be said to be rhizomatic, as there is no center in any of the arenas linked together by the voices, but it is still layered as topical discussions are to a large extent kept apart.

During a pandemic, several discourses are revived, produced, or transformed, in relation to the rhetorical arenas establishing themselves. The rhetoric of a pandemic is therefore not to be seen as a singular unit, but rather as a plethora of different narratives, metaphors, and other means of expression, developing to suit the argumentation in the different arenas from different voices. But what may at first sound like a cacophony can be understood as the result of the multivocal and multifocal rhetorical arena of today's media environment during a time of crisis.

References

Aaslund, H. (2021). Ethos of science, pathos of war: Social work and pandemic rhetoric. *Qualitative Social Work, 20*(1–2), 168–170.

Bitzer, L. F. (1968). The rhetorical situation. *Philosophy & Rhetoric, 1*(1), 1–14. http://www.jstor.org/stable/40236733?origin=JSTOR-pdf

Bushman, B. (2022). Calling the coronavirus the 'Chinese virus' matters – research connects the label with racist bias. *The Conversation*, Published: February 18, 2022. https://theconversation.com/calling-the-coronavirus-the-chinese-virus-matters-research-connects-the-label-with-racist-bias-176437

Charteris-Black, J. (2021). *Metaphors of Coronavirus. Invisible enemy or zombie apocalypse?* Palgrave Macmillan.

Constable, M. (2020). In the midst of... Words inside-out: Pandemic rhetorics. *Philosophy and Rhetoric, 53*(3), 261–266.

Deleuze, G. & Guattari, F. (1980). *Mille plateaux.* Editions de Minuit.

Frandsen, F. & Johansen, W. (2017). *Organizational crisis communication: A multivocal approach.* Sage.

Hartelius, E. J. (2011). *The rhetoric of expertise.* Lanham.

Horowitz, J. (2022). Trucker protests in Canada: What you need to know. *The New York Times*, Feb. 20, 2022. https://www.nytimes.com/article/canada-trucker-protests.html.

Musolff, A. (2021). War against COVID-19: Is the pandemic as war metaphor helpful or hurtful. *Pandemic and Crisis Discourse: Communicating COVID-19 and Public Health Strategy*. London: Bloomsbury (2021). Pre-publication version, academia.edu

Propp, V. (1968). *Morphology of the folk tale* (2nd revised ed.). University of Texas Press.

Shannon, J. (2020). Coronavirus has been declared a pandemic: What does that mean, and what took so long? *USA Today*, https://eu.usatoday.com/story/news/nation/2020/03/11/coronavirus-pandemic-world-health-organization/5011903002/

Toulmin, S. (2003). *The uses of argument*. Cambridge University Press.

Vigsø, O. (2010). Naming is framing: Swine Flu, New Flu, and A(H1N1). *Observatorio (OBS★)*, *4*(3), 229–241.

14

LANGUAGE AND PANDEMIC COMMUNICATION

Tatiana M. Permyakova, Elena A. Smolianina, and Irina S. Morozova

Introduction

People respond to disasters in culturally constructed ways of speaking and writing. These can take many forms before, during, and after the event (Bromhead, 2021). It is important to study not only these cultural constructs but also the words for extreme phenomena, in this case, the COVID-19 pandemic. Even naming the pandemic itself by the World Health Organization (WHO) took a few months since the start of the outbreak. Therefore, linguistic inquiry into the pandemic is of theoretical interest and a matter of social action. Unlike other crises and disasters, the COVID-19 pandemic is of global concern, and cannot be geographically, historically, or culturally anchored. As a result, it cannot be studied as one event among many within the linguaculture (Alyeksyeyeva et al., 2020). Moreover, studies in language change help to answer pressing questions in cognitive sciences, including the social construction of cognition and mechanisms underlying socio-cultural change in general (Hruschka et al., 2009). The evolving pandemic provides rare advances in an emergent framework for the study of language change through multilingual corpora and data-driven models to infer change and compare competing linguistic variants to dis/prove claims about social and cognitive influences of the pandemic.

Therefore, to explore language, social change, and pandemic communication, this chapter is outlined as follows. First, it presents a general introduction of linguistic research issues and pandemic communication through the lens of sociolinguistics regarding language and social change. Second, it dwells on lexical studies focusing on new words and terms, i.e., neologisms. Next, it describes metaphor studies, which explore the cognitive strategies in relation

DOI: 10.4324/9781003214496-14

to a new pandemic. The chapter concludes with a summary of new features of linguistic investigations of the COVID-19 pandemic.

Language and Social Change

Linguistics examines a global event that changes the society through a set of approaches. Following the classifications in sociolinguistics (Agha, 2006; Krauss & Chiu, 1998; Philips, 2004; Robinson & Giles, 2001; Romaine, 2000), Table 14.1 describes linguistic sub-fields, research issues, and a sample of publications regarding COVID-19.

Studies of linguistics during the pandemic examine to what extent social changes (and subsequential political, technological, spatial changes) caused by the virus have impacted everyday linguistic interactions and have contributed to language shifts. They argue that several factors (domains, power, policies, new behavior) interact to accelerate shifts to stress risk and safety features and coin terms that particularly serve communicative purposes.

History shows pandemics are not new: the Spanish flu, the Zika virus, the swine flu, the avian flu, or the SARS-CoV-2 pandemic (Sismat, 2021). What makes the COVID-19 pandemic different is that we are witnessing change in the very fabric of speech acts in real time. Both the linguistic (or the verbal) and the extra-linguistic (or the nonverbal) are now facing tremendous pressure from people living in isolation and from restrictions imposed by authorities, which have resulted in extensive changes in context and in the entire process of communication. Hence, comparing previous pandemics with the COVID-19 pandemic, we notice a shift from cultural inter-texts to everybody inter-texting as the only means of communicating (Șorcaru, 2020).

One of the methods to observe such a shift is linguistic technologies, i.e., generated texts on the web and machine-learning tools to extract, process, and analyze textual data. These technologies have become 'text-based epidemic intelligence' to detect outbreaks using formal medical records and informal sources such as user texts and queries on the web (Joshi et al., 2019; Madani et al., 2021). For instance, text analytics techniques were used to extract the important concepts of the Zika virus from social media, which may serve as multilingual platforms for epidemic tracking services (Abouzahra & Tan, 2021). Another line of research is analyzing written messages and directives in university and educational communication during the transition from face-to-face to distance teaching (Jansen, 2021). Through the LWIC (Linguistic Inquiry and Word Count) investigation of the language of university-based communications, the models of crisis communication and epidemic management can be built. The use of certain words helps create resilience and achieve organizational goals.

The COVID-19 pandemic highlights the role of internet technology as the only way to solve educational problems. The language of online classroom interaction has changed in lexical and grammatical forms (Qodriani &

TABLE 14.1 Summary of Intersection of Linguistics and Pandemic Communication

Linguistic Fields	Research Issues	Publications
Territorial division	• Territorial spread, e.g., of the virus • Speech domains, e.g., the language of health and education for different social groups of varying communicative competence • Language, society, and reality – different worlds and different words	Sismat, M. A. H. (2021). The language of pandemic and its significance in effective communication. *Journal of Humanities and Social Sciences Studies*, *3*(4), 54–60. Jansem, A. (2021). The feasibility of foreign language online instruction during the COVID-19 pandemic: A qualitative case study of instructors' and students' reflections. *International Education Studies*, *14*(4), 93–102.
Language choice	• Multilingualism • Languages on different continents and in countries • Language shift, code-switching	Piller, I., Zhang, J., & Li, J. (2020). Linguistic diversity in a time of crisis: Language challenges of the COVID-19 pandemic. *Multilingua*, *39*(5), 503–515. Shen, Q. (2020). Commentary: Directions in language planning from the COVID-19 pandemic. *Multilingua*, *39*(5), 625–629. Olimat, S. N. (2020). COVID-19 pandemic: Euphemism and dysphemism in Jordanian Arabic. *GEMA Online® Journal of Language Studies*, *20*(3).
Sociolinguistic patterns	• Social stratification • Social networks • Standardization	Szabó, R. (2020). No going back: The impact of the COVID-19 pandemic on corporate language and communication training Robert Szabó. *Horizon*, *2*, 23–30. Adami, E., Al Zidjaly, N., Canale, G., Djonov, E., Ghiasian, M. S., Gualberto, C.,... & Zhang, Y. (2020). PanMeMic Manifesto: Making meaning in the Covid-19 pandemic and the future of social interaction. *Working Papers in Urban Language and Literacies no 273*. Dada, S., Ashworth, H. C., Bewa, M. J., & Dhatt, R. (2021). Words matter: Political and gender analysis of speeches made by heads of government during the COVID-19 pandemic. *BMJ global health*, *6*(1), e003910.

(Continued)

TABLE 14.1 (Continued)

Linguistic Fields	Research Issues	Publications
Language change in social perspective	• Variation and change • Social ideology	Piekkari, R., Tietze, S., Angouri, J., Meyer, R., & Vaara, E. (2021). Can you speak Covid-19? Languages and social inequality in management studies. *Journal of Management Studies, 58*(2), 587–591. Mohlman, J., & Basch, C. (2020). The language of university communications during the COVID-19 pandemic. *Journal of American College Health,* 1–4.
Linguistic problems as social problems	• Social action, e.g., education failures	Charney, S. A., Camarata, S. M., & Chern, A. (2021). Potential impact of the COVID-19 pandemic on communication and language skills in children. *Otolaryngology–Head and Neck Surgery,* 0194599820978247.

Wijana, 2020). For example, instead of conventional face-to-face greetings in the classroom, online greetings use imperative verbs such as 'Drop your hello in a chat box!', which adapts communication contextually in a new situation. It is exactly this investigation into the change of lexicon and grammar used in online learning and communication that we need to understand to improve online teaching-learning activities.

Multilingual techniques are employed in online media research to measure the effects of framing (López & Naranjo, 2021). The significant contribution of these studies is not only clarifying translation strategies in crisis situations for different language groups, but also understanding target group perception and recommendations for online media in how to mitigate evaluative language in different kinds of texts, not to increase anxiety levels among readers (Sismat, 2021). For instance, politeness theory is used to analyze slogans in China's health campaigns against COVID-19 and the public's conflicting comments on campaigns' messages across time and space. Again, once establishing the language that conveys threats of death and disease, insults or negative evaluation, and harsh demands, the stigmatizing language, we yield the results of the factors that contribute to the change of judgments over the campaign communication and, therefore, more public safety (Han, 2021; McGinty et al., 2019). The value of linguistic studies is in its practice positioning not only in discourse, genres, and institutions, but also in social, cultural, and political contexts, e.g., rural areas, territorial emergencies, and forthcoming political elections.

Language Innovations: Neologisms, Terms, and Semantic Change

Many new words, neologisms, have entered people's vocabulary when talking about the COVID-19 pandemic. There are three main aspects in analyzing lexical units coined during the pandemic. The first is the analysis of lexical units in different languages: English (Al-Azzawi & Haleem, 2021; Al-Salman & Haider, 2021; Alyeksyeyeva et al., 2020; Asif et al., 2020; Bonta & Galiţa, 2020; Chaiuk, 2020; Ibrahim et al., 2020), Russian (Butseva & Zelenin, 2020; Gekkina & Kozhevnikov, 2021; Golovanova & Madzhaeva, 2020; Severskaya, 2020), Chinese (Lei et al., 2021; Wang & Huang, 2021), Serbian (Nikolić et al., 2021), French (Belkina, 2021), Spanish (Zholobova, 2021), Arabic (Hamawi et al., 2020), Jordan Arabic (Olimat, 2020), Filipino (Cahapay, 2020), and Indonesian (Foster & Welsh, 2021), and the comparative analysis of neologisms in two languages: English and Russian (Karachina, 2020), English and Ukrainian (Goltsova & Chybis, 2021), Russian and Czech (Samylicheva & Gazda, 2020), Greek and German (Katsaounis, 2020), and French and Moroccan (Ilham & Hassan, 2020).

The second is the analysis of categorization of domains neologisms denote. Scholars analyze English neologisms presented in dictionaries, online mass media, social media, and linguistic studies (Bonta & Galiţa, 2020), British governmental websites and pandemic-related publications in online British and American media (Alyeksyeyeva et al., 2020), Russian neologisms used in mass media (Golovanova & Madzhaeva, 2020), Filipino neologisms on Twitter (Cahapay, 2020), Arabic neologisms on Twitter (Hamawi et al., 2020), Chinese neologisms from the Baidu Index, the COVID-19 official website of China's CDC (Chinese Center for Disease Control and Prevention) (Lei et al., 2021), and South Korean neologisms in online mass media (Mozol, 2021).

The third is the analysis of productive neologism-building models in English online articles (Akut, 2020), English platforms (Al-Salman & Haider, 2021; Ibrahim et al., 2020), online British and American media (Alyeksyeyeva et al., 2020), Russian pandemic dictionaries and corpora (Gekkina & Kozhevnikov, 2021; Karachina, 2020), spoken and written Polish mass media discourse (Cierpich-Kozieł, 2020), and German online neologisms dictionary *Stichwortlisteder Neologismen der Zehnerjah* (Rys & Pasyk, 2020).

Pandemic Neologisms in Languages

During a pandemic, neologisms reflect the transition of information from a new knowledge domain to an old one by words combining new and existing meanings. This two-component model of neologisms makes communication and, thus, understanding and adjustment to changing social conditions possible. Communication based on neologisms allows the pursuit of effective strategies to administer society, as was the case in China at the start of the pandemic (Lei et al., 2021). Even though the source of COVID-19 is thought to be Wuhan, China, the source of most neologisms is English medicine.

Many English medical terms have entered the English language: *symptomatic, asymptomatic, zoonotic, flatten the curve*, etc. Between January and April 2020, on internet platforms, the most frequent medical terms were *pandemic* and **sanitizer** (Asif et al., 2020) and the most frequent hashtags in social networks were #clinicaltrials, #contacttracing, #contagious, #epidemic, #herdimmunity, #pandemic, #quarantine, #self-isolation, #socialdistancing, and #vaccine (Al-Azzawi & Haleem, 2021; Ibrahim et al., 2020). The British press framed the pandemic in lexical units related to fear: *the fatality rate, nightmare of pandemics, a deadly epidemic, deadly coronavirus outbreak, inevitable onslaught of the virus*, etc., heightening the anticipation of danger (Chaiuk, 2020). Numerous neologisms have been created as 'a result of the fear people experience and of their desperate effort to survive in unprecedented times' (Bonta & Galiţa, 2020, p. 145). One of the ways to cope with pandemic fear was to use slang. Some slang neologisms for the pandemic were rather cynical, for instance, a *boomer remover* was used to emphasize the high death rate caused by the virus among baby boomers, or a *herd thinner* denoted the morbidity rate among patients (Alyeksyeyeva et al., 2020). Humorous slang expressions included *Miley Cyrus, Miss Rona, Rona, Lady Rona, Roni, Rone, Sanny* (Australian), and *Iso* (Australian) (Al-Salman & Haider, 2021).

In Russian such medical neologisms as *pandemic* with the meaning COVID-19 pandemic and *disinfector* with the meaning *sanitizer* appeared as well as emotion-based neologisms like *vaccinewilding, covidsceptic*, and *COVID is harsh but it is COVID* (by analogy with the Latin saying *Dura lex, sed lex!*) (Severskaya, 2020). Many English words entered the Russian language: *lockdown, doomscrolling, coronial*, etc. A number of Russian words were built with the word covid: *covid-pneumonia, covid mortality, covid lethal, covid-positive, covid-negative*, etc.; *quarantine: quarantine hour, quarantine holidays, quarantine summer, quarantine creativity, quarantine walk, quarantine regime, quarantine courses*, etc.; and *zoom: zoom interview, zoom lesson, zoom consultation, zoom discussion*, etc. (Gekkina & Kozhevnikov, 2021). Some words were used with humorous implications as well, especially in proverbs and sayings. The Russian saying '*Have your business where you were born*' was transformed into '*Observe your quarantine where you were born*', '*He who will reap must sow*' was changed into '*He who will reap must wear a mask*', and '*Promises are like piecrust*' was replaced with '*Vaccines are like piecrusts*' (Golovanova & Madzhaeva, 2020). There are more than 600 lexical units in the contemporary COVID lexicon as part of the Contemporary Russian Language Dictionary. There are 160 lexical units expected to enter the dictionary if they meet the criteria of key units in the sphere of illness, high frequency of usage in mass media discourse, typical of COVID units' word formation, and variants of words spelling (Butseva & Zelenin, 2020).

The Chinese used the strategy of categorization aimed at assigning a new name to an existing category; therefore, COVID-19 fell under the broad categories of the epidemic situation, pneumonia-like epidemic, and the highest profiled virus. They also adopted the strategy of lexical avoidance because of cultural taboos. For example, the use of the number 4 in Chinese culture is associated with death; thus, it is avoided in discourse. Chinese people pursued the strategy of synthesis manifested in combination of facts about the pandemic and authorities' efforts. The latter was presented by euphemisms (Lei et al., 2021). In the Chinese language, the neologism contact prevention was mainly used in Guangzhou, while the neologism social distancing was competing with the 'contact prevention' term in Hong Kong. The latter exhibited a diversified style of a complex pattern of social interaction based on advice, whereas the former presented the collectivist culture based on prohibition (Wang & Huang, 2021).

In the Serbian language, the most frequent neologisms during the pandemic were COVID, post-COVID, and crown, while less frequent words – occasionalisms – words created for a single concept to name it in a particular situation, were COVID spread, and a man who had COVID (Nikolić et al., 2021). The French language borrowed several English words: *contact tracing, superspreader, barrier gestures, social distancing,* and *physical distancing.* It also borrowed medical terms: *patient zero, asymptomatic course of the disease, plateau, oximeter,* etc. Many French joking neologisms appeared during the pandemic: *lundimanche* (an endless monotonous week in self-isolation), *confinemanche* (confinement at home on Sunday), and *immobésité* (excess weight that appears) (Belkina, 2021). In Spanish a few 'pure' neologisms formed (*COVID, to quarantine, confine,* and *de-confine*); many words were coined before the pandemic (*video chat, video call,* and *de-escalate*) but became widespread during it; others developed new meanings and, thus, are considered semantic (a mask) (Zholobova, 2021).

Arabic Jordanians used various euphemisms, acceptable expressions used instead of offensive ones, to discuss fear-based taboos caused by Coronavirus pandemic. Instead of Coronavirus disease, they used the *novel virus, problem, disease, virus, cloud* (as something invisible), *adversity, a test of God, challenge, worry, concern,* etc. Jordanians used dysphemisms, offensive words used instead of acceptable ones, to express their apprehension of COVID-19's negative features. Coronavirus was called *crisis, calamity, plague, wrath of God, a warning from God,* etc. (Olimat, 2020). In the Arabic language, the most frequent unigrams (one-word patterns) were *corona, epidemic,* and *Wuhan*; the most frequent bigrams (two-word patterns) were *virus corona, home quarantine, curfew, corona epidemic, virus spread,* etc.; the most frequent trigrams (three-word patterns) were *new corona virus, corona virus spread, virus corona outbreak, facing virus corona,* etc. (Hamoui et al., 2020).

In the Filipino language, the most popular neologisms during the pandemic were abbreviations No CON connected with St. Valentines' Day: *No Chocolates on Valentines, No Crush on Valentines, No Companion on Valentines, No Chance on Valentines*, and *No Contact on Valentines* (Cahapay, 2020). In the Indonesian language, many English words formed word bases for Indonesian neologisms; for example, the English noun militarization was transformed into the Indonesian verb *memiliterasi* that had not been in the Indonesian language before (Foster & Welsh, 2021).

The words common for both English and Russian were coronavirus and COVID-19, whereas culturally different words were *rona, self-isolation, quarantine, self-quarantine, shelter-in-place, shelter-at-home*, and *cocooning* in English and *a small crown, corona dissident, coronaskeptics, corona cat,* and *panic monger* in Russian (Karachina, 2020). The words shared by English and Ukrainian were *coronials, covidivorce, quarantine challenge,* and *infodemic* while culturally specific words were *the Rona, to magpie,* and *lockdown* in the United States and Australian variants of English and *coronabandit, corona absurd,* and *coronadissident* in Ukrainian (Goltsova & Chybis, 2021). Both Russian and Czech languages borrowed the English word *covidiot* for which Russian and Czech users created synonyms using the morphemes of their languages: *koronaidiot, coronapofigist,* and *covigist*. Both languages produced similar neologisms expressing psychological state: *coronapanic, coronaneurosis, coronadepression,* and *coronafrustration*. Some neologisms had an ironic meaning, for example, *coronacircus, coronacarnival,* and *maskintruder* (Samylicheva & Gazda, 2020). The comparative analysis of Greek and German revealed people speaking about the future of the pandemic use words with the meaning *to decrease (the pandemic), to weaken (the virus),* and *to control (the pandemic)*. In French and Moroccan, common words were borrowed from English. The words *confinement* and *déconfinement* acquired a new meaning of physical distancing during the pandemic in both languages. Such dysphemisms as *covidiot* and *super-propagateur* were too offensive for Moroccan, but frequently used in French (Ilham & Hassan 2020).

All the languages under question borrowed English medical terms. Among the most frequent in all the languages are *COVID, pandemic, quarantine, sanitizer, zoom,* and *social distancing*. In most languages, people used fear-inducing words, humorous expressions, slang, euphemisms, and dysphemisms in accordance with their national cultures.

Pandemic Neologisms Categorization

Categorization, naming a new object by assigning it a category, is a cognitive process based on thinking and speech production. English neologisms offered by dictionaries, online mass media, social media, and authorized voices in the field of linguistics were categorized in the following domains: not taking the threat seriously (*coronageddon, coronapocalypse, infodemic,* etc.), giving particular identity to people around (*corona worriers, lockdowners, quarantimates, quaranteam,* etc.), trying to stay healthy/safe (*an elbump, observe the Corona corridor, coronacation, homecation,* etc.), trying to cope with changes in habits (*a Covideo-party, drinking a quarantini, ronavation, covidivorce,* etc.), continuing the ordinary activities (*Coronaviva, a spendemic, a locktail hour,* etc.), and coping with emotions (*cornteen, shelter,* etc.) (Bonta & Galiţa, 2020).

Neologisms from British governmental websites and pandemic-related publications in online British and American media were divided into several categories: social groups based on such criteria as health, profession, or attitude toward the pandemic and socially responsible behavior (e.g., *clinically vulnerable people, key workers, covadults*); development of new or modification of old cultural practices that embrace lifestyle (*coronacooing, WFH, drivecation*), appearance (*corona hair, coronabesity*), patterns of online and offline communication (*homeference, video party, coronadating, Wuhan shake*); reconceptualization of pre-pandemic concepts (*home*); and, finally, the emergence of new types of interpersonal relations (*coronarelationship, corona boyfriend*) (Alyeksyeyeva et al., 2020).

Analysis of Russian mass media content shows that during the pandemic, speakers grouped new words into the following categories: disease, administrative measures, and people's attitude toward pandemic. The category disease comprised names of the disease (virus) and its infective agents (*COVID-19, covid, SARS-CoV-2, Coronavirus,* etc.), kinds of patients and contact people (asymptomatic patients, affected people, contactee, etc.), names of health facilities and their parts (*observation facility, covid hospital, mobile hospital, red zone, green zone,* etc.), names of methods for COVID identification, its treatment and control (*oxygen saturation, computed tomography scanning, artificial lung ventilation,* etc.), names of stages, zones, and characteristics of COVID-19 spread (*outbreak hot zone, peak, plateau, second wave,* etc.), names of professions and specialists (*virologist, epidemiologist, immunologist,* etc.), and names of epidemiological measures (*immunization, immunoprophylactic vaccine, epidemic control,* etc.). The category administrative measures included names of administrative measures aimed to stop the spread of COVID-19 (*social distancing, gloves requirement, mask requirement,* etc.), names of personal protection equipment (*mask, respirator, sanitizer,* etc.), control devices (*thermovision camera, pyrometer, no-contact thermometer*), and administrative measures (*evacuation flight, self-isolation,* etc.). The category, people's attitude toward COVID-19, consisted of the following subcategories: people labeling (*covidiot, covid-dissident, coronasceptic,* etc.), social attitudes (*coronaphobia, coronapanic, coronacrisis,* etc.), names of processes and actions connected with the COVID epoch (*to corona hang out, to zoom, big quarantine cleaning up,* etc.), names of states and moods (*remote work, distance teaching, distance learning,* etc.), names of items and places (*covidcorridor, coronathing,* etc.), and social practices (*quarantine pics, coronatines* (by analogy to valentines), *quarantini* (quarantine and Martini), etc.) (Golovanova & Madzhaeva, 2020).

There are three ways neologism categorization is related to COVID-19, known at that time as NCOVID-19, on Twitter in the Philippines. The first dealt with St. Valentine's Day in February, the start of the overseas spread of COVID-19. The second was the use of COVID-19 as part of a baby's name:

Covid Marie, Covid Bryant, and *Covid Rose.* The third was use of a politician's proper name as part of the term COVID. Senator Aquilino 'Koko' Pimentel violated COVID-19 regulations and was called *KokoVID, KokoPimentel,* and *COVID19PH* (Cahapay, 2020). On Arabic Tweeter various tweets covered the following 11 domains: prevention, quarantine, coronavirus epidemic, China, curfew, coronavirus in Egypt, the latest news, Ramadan, corona outbreaks, and healthcare organizations (Hamawi et al., 2020).

In the Chinese language the neologisms collected from the Baidu Index covered five categories: under-specifications consisting of subcategories situation of the epidemic, pneumonia, and virus; pre-official names, consisting of pneumonia of unknown sources, viral pneumonia, novel type virus, novel type pneumonia, and corona virus; stigmatizing names, comprising Wuhan pneumonia, Wuhan viral pneumonia, Chinese virus, Wuhan novel type pneumonia, and Wuhan virus; official names, covering novel type crown-shape virus pneumonia, novel corona pneumonia, novel corona pandemic, novel corona virus, and novel corona; and English abbreviations including COVID-19, 2019-nCov, Coronavirus, SARS-CoV-2 Chinese (Lei et al., 2021).

In the Korean language neologisms frequently used in South Korean mass media (Chosun Ilbo, Chosun Biz, Ilyo Sinmun, Donga Ilbo, Mail Ilbo, news agencies YTN, SBS, blogs Naver и Daum) fell under three categories of nomination: health care, social activities and trends, and economy. In the healthcare domain there were the names of the disease (*Wuhan corona, Wuhan pneumonia, corona-beer virus* (by analogy with the beer brand), *corona fraud,* etc.), Coronavirus characteristics (*'golden' mask, hand-made mask, mask-bitcoin, Homo maskus, mask on the chin,* etc.), and measures against coronavirus (*social distancing, self-isolation control, group control, electronic pass,* etc.). In the domain of social activities and trends, there were the following topics: leisure (*online attraction park, online concert, online playground,* etc.), study (*online lesson, online education,* etc.), food (*homemade food, talkan* (made of flour) *food, endless home cooking*), outdoor activities (*mountains first-timer, golf first-timer, camping first-timer,* etc.), and social activity (*one-off payment, social workers team, social allowances,* etc.). The economic domain included words connected with the economy during the pandemic (*coronaeconomy, starving time during the pandemic, potato grant-in-aid, calmari grant-in-aid,* etc.) (Mozol, 2021).

In the Polish language 11 categories of neologisms were identified: social reality (*coronation*), time of social isolation (*coronavacations*), social meetings (*coronaparty*), people (*crownteam*), education (*coronamature*), politics (*coronavirus elections*), economy (*corona bonds*), services (*coronabot*), religion (*koronaczas – coronahour*), emotions (*coronadepression*), and works (*crown-song*) (Cierpich-Kozieł, 2020). The categories presented in most languages are disease, everyday activities, habits, emotions, health, and people. Less frequent categories are threat, administration, economy, education, humor, religion, and politics. This categorization puts more emphasis on private life than on public life.

The analysis of pandemic neologisms' categorization shows that in American and European cultures, users were lexically productive in the domains of health condition, disease naming, new habits, lifestyle, communication, and social interaction. Americans and Europeans are worried about the influence of COVID-19 on their personal everyday activities. In Asian and Arabic cultures, the categorization covered such domains as quarantine, epidemic, politics, and economy. Arabs and Asians expressed their concerns about the impact of changes, caused by the virus, on their common cultural practices, for example, public holiday celebrations. The unifying feature of neologisms for all the cultures is a strategy to name the virus, identify the pandemic conditions, and adjust to them by integrating new meanings into language practice.

Pandemic Neologism-Building

Many neologism patterns were borrowed from English. However, languages are different from English in their morphological structure. What are the linguistic ways to build new words? In English online articles, pandemic neologisms were created by means of compounding (*doomscrolling, contact tracing, social distancing*), blending (*covexit, covideo, covidiot*), affixation (*coronnials, self-quarantine, superspreader*), conversion (*contact tracing, social distancing*), abbreviation (*COVID-19, nCov*), acronym (*PUI – person under investigation*), clipping (*rona*), and onomatopoeia (*quaranteens, quaranteams*) (Akut, 2020). On the English platforms (Facebook, Twitter, and YouTube), single word-formation patterns were coinages (*COVID-19*), affixation (*maskless, masklessness*), compounding (*coronacome, coronaviva*), blending (*Loxit, coronials*), clipping (*pandy, rona*), backformation (*vaccination*), borrowing (*unlockdown*), abbreviation (*BC – before Corona*), acronyms (*WHO – World Health Organization*), and folk-etymology (*pando* (Australian) – coronavirus pandemic). Among dual word-formation patterns, there were compounding and affixation (lockdowners), blending and affixation (*covidpreneurs*), and clipping and compounding (*ronadobbing* (Australian) for informing on those contravening crisis-related restrictions) (Al-Salman & Haider, 2021). Specifically, on Twitter such clipped compounds as *coronacation, covexit, morona, pandumic*, etc. were widely used as well as lexical deviations *cornteens, corona cuts, Kung Flu, doom scrolling*, etc. (Ibrahim et al., 2020). In English texts from British governmental websites and pandemic-related publications in online British and American media, the most frequent neologism-building pattern was blending, which denotes new properties of an existing object under specific circumstances. The first component of the blending names the circumstances in which the object exists, for example, *corona-* or *covid-*, while the second component denotes the concept itself (*activity, hoarder*, or *dating*). As a result, there is a blending: *coronadating* or *corona-dating* that reflects a speaker's perception of the phenomenon named (Alyekseyeva et al., 2020).

Analysis of Russian pandemic dictionaries and corpora reveals most neologisms were formed due to derivation. There were two types of derivatives: the first was derivation with the root morpheme (for example, *covidiot*) and the second was derivation based on composition (*zoomlesson*), abbreviation (*CVI – coronavirus infection*), contamination (*zoominar – zoom and seminar*), and conversion (*to zoom*). The most frequent parts of speech involved in derivation were the noun, adjective, and verb (Gekkina & Kozhevnikov, 2021). The comparative analysis of neologism-building in Russian and English shows speakers adjusted medical terms to everyday communication by using clipping. For instance, instead of coronavirus, the English used corona and the Russians used the diminutive suffix 'ка' (коронарка – a small crown). A similar pattern is observed when speaking about distance learning in English and дистанционка (the diminutive suffix 'ка') in Russian. The English words quarantine, self-quarantine, and shelter-in-place tend to be nouns and verbs in English following the verbalization principle, while in Russian they are primarily nouns. A striking feature is also that the English used the euphemistic acronym c-word for coronavirus whereas in Russian this acronym is considered a vulgarism evoking negative associations and, thus, inappropriate (Karachina, 2020).

In the Polish language, the keyword for linguistic analysis was the Anglicism *koronawirus*. The frequently occurred part of speech and neologism-building pattern was the compound noun with the productive stem *korona-*. The Polish adjective *koronawirusowy* was often used as a constituent of the noun phrase, following the English sentence structure (Cierpich-Kozieł 2020). Analysis of the German language shows the transition of professional terminology from the field of epidemiology and medicine to the common vocabulary. The main types of morphological word formation of new lexical units were composition (*Distanzrege – distance regulation*), affixation (*Coronismus – measures against the pandemic*), and blending (*Panikdemie panic during the pandemic*). The most frequent were the neologisms represented by composites to express an idea in one word. Other derived lexical units were represented by derivatives, mainly suffix formations, and abbreviations (Rys & Pasyk, 2020).

The most frequent neologism-building patterns in all the analyzed languages are compounding, blending, affixation, abbreviation, clipping, acronym, composition, and conversion. Less frequent are borrowing, folk-etymology, backformation, contamination, and onomatopoetic patterns. The analysis of pandemic neologisms shows most languages borrowed English medical terms to provide effective communication during the pandemic. The most frequently loaned words in all the languages are *COVID, pandemic, quarantine, sanitizer, zoom,* and *social distancing* and words denoting fear, and humorous attitude to the pandemic. People also used cultural euphemisms and dysphemisms either to conceal fear or to show it. Neologisms are categorized in the domains connected with private life: disease, everyday activities, habits, emotions, health, and people. Categorization in the languages analyzed follows such neologism-building patterns as compounding, blending, affixation, abbreviation, clipping, acronym, composition, and conversion. These patterns express several ideas in one lexical unit. These findings are in line with studies on special medical language that interpret medical terms during a pandemic (Badziński, 2020). They also find medical language development based on English borrowings, abbreviations, and WHO proposed terms (Maroto & de Goedele, 2021) deepened research on the neologism COVID in cardiology (Upadhyayula & Kasliwal, 2020), the key pandemic term Coronavirus disease (COVID-19) (Upadhyay & Maroof, 2020), and filiation (Türev & Halil, 2020).

Metaphors: Categorization and Cognition

Metaphor is defined as an explanation of a mental scheme by reflecting it on another mental schema and by establishing a relationship between those two schemas (Lakoff & Johnson, 1980). Metaphors are crucial tools for communication and thinking and are accepted as an important way to reveal and connect abstract ideas, attitudes, feeling or beliefs, which are indirect and often difficult to express. Being a rhetorical device that helps meet the need to make the unknown familiar, since they associate the new with an image of the familiar, metaphors can provide easy-to-understand and powerful explanations for threatening or unexpected events, including pandemics, and can guide human behavior. To affect massive social change in a population within a short period of time, governments need various strategies, with coercion, persuasion, and the inducing of intense, directed emotional responses being among them. While legislative measures clearly implement coercion, metaphor can work alongside such measures to help persuade and induce widespread emotional responses in the population – perhaps most significantly fear – but also solidarity and empathy (Gillis, 2020). Thus, metaphors have been commonly used in medicine because having an awareness of how health and metaphors interact can lead to an increased understanding of how individuals can or should act as healthcare recipients.

The importance of metaphors in medical practice was discussed by Charon (2001), who wrote metaphors help readers 'identify... governing image[s] in a work and this often helps to orient the reader toward its [the work's] figural or even figurative meaning' (p. 119). Sontag (1989) also focused on the relationship between illness and metaphor and showed the latter plays a strong role in the public understanding of illness. Metaphors are found particularly useful in public health communication as they influence how people interpret health concerns and have influenced the public for decades, most recently with the AIDS and cancer epidemics, as well as SARS, avian and swine flu, and the current COVID-19 pandemic. Since metaphors enable individuals to conceive and make sense of their experiences (Redden et al., 2013), pointing to the ways the phenomenon is unfolding or existing for them (Tracy et al., 2006), the study of individuals' use of COVID-19 metaphors can present mental models, which reflect individuals' perception and responses to the global pandemic as well as help find paths toward collective healing and resilience.

Past research has demonstrated that in an epidemic, war metaphors are quite common as they evoke images with positive connotations like resistance and heroism. Sontag (1989) showed the abundance of military metaphors in AIDS discourses. Horne (2009) also demonstrated that the AIDS pandemic is frequently conceptualized through the metaphor of war. The HI-virus is commonly represented in the media as an enemy which '*invades*', '*attacks*', and '*destroys*' the human body. In her analysis, Horne also points out that the 'military' metaphorical model has been well established in relation to cancer, especially in expressions such as someone dying '*after a long battle*'. Many countries have used war metaphors when referring to SARS (Wallis & Nerlich, 2005) and swine flu. H1N1 was referred to as a '*terrorist*' waging war on the human population. The battle language was also frequently used in discussion of H1N1, characterizing it as a '*battle*' with cities and public officials '*fighting*' to '*control*' the '*rising*' cases. Another war model emerging in language surrounding swine flu was that of a victimizer, as war has causalities and those who are innocent and harmed by the war are often seen as victims.

Not surprisingly, the arrival of the COVID-19 pandemic has triggered the use of war metaphors. The similarities established between war and the COVID-19 pandemic are not accidental, and they generate subjective conceptual frames that outline certain components (Semino, 2008), for instance, the opposition between the enemy (the virus) and those fighting against it (society or essential workers); the means (cleanliness and physical distance) to participate in the battle and lack of those, etc. Society is conceptualized as soldiers with greater emphasis placed on health workers (or foreground) who are seen as the army fighting the virus. By way of example, Donald Trump was considered America's '*wartime President*'. He delivered his briefings, surrounded by a '*task force*' that included his '*Surgeon General*', and Americans themselves are also referred to as a nation still at war with the virus. 'Covidian' military metaphors also manifest themselves in President Trump's description of '*front-line workers*', who vary from sanitation and restaurant laborers to the gig employees and medical workers, as '*warriors*' willing to risk their lives (Megerian, 2020). Other country's leaders also declared their nations '*are at war*' with the battle cry of '*retreat*' inside one's home (Erlanger, 2020).

However, the use of the war metaphor appears problematic and inadvisable because it also dredges up other images denoting conflict and confrontation, and it leads to breakdowns in both social behavior and the democratic system. On the one hand, war metaphors conventionally evoke the images of suffering, shortages, etc., and increase negative emotions, sometimes giving way to prosocial behavior or selfish, irrational thoughts of 'every man for himself'. On the other hand, the metaphor of war clashes with the core democratic values, affecting the political system and causing criticism of the leaders (Sabucedo et al., 2020). Many authors focus on alternative metaphors used in relation to COVID-19 instead of war terminology. Filardo-Llamas (2021) presented a review of the COVID-19 metaphors used in English and Spanish cartoons, describing several of the most creative uses of alternative metaphors, which are often humorous response to current events. The study showed frequent use of metaphors in cartoons consisted of showing the virus as a person, an animal, a force of nature, or even a monster or an alien. For example, the virus is conceptualized as a bird of prey ready to eat some worms as soon as they leave the house. Examples also include the visual depiction of the virus as an animal in a slaughterhouse, where two butchers physically resembling two Spanish leaders are preparing to butcher the animal to 'make good use of everything'. Also, the coronavirus is often visualized as a round, spiked entity.

Another metaphorical description of the pandemic found in cartoons is a game of chess, in which the health workers and essential workers are the pawns, sacrificed so the rest of the pieces (politicians, the army, and the European Union) could survive. In cartoons, healthcare workers are also shown arm wrestling or boxing the coronavirus, once again anthropomorphizing the virus. In some examples there was a depiction of healthcare workers as angels or superheroes.

As for the forces of nature, the analogy between the coronavirus and a volcano was found in a cartoon. In addition, the author showed that references to waves and tsunamis are especially common to describe Trump's political activity. The 'wave' metaphor is one kind of movement metaphor, frequently used to refer to the temporal stages of a disease. Sontag (1989) showed AIDS and cancer discourses widely used the movement metaphor, and Wallis and Nerlich (2005) wrote about the movement of SARS. Although the movement metaphor is not new in the COVID-19 context, another kind of movement is used for it. In contrast to the movement from HIV to full-blown AIDS, 'diffuse' or 'spread' of cancer from one organ to another, and roller coaster-like movement of the SARS pandemic, COVID-19 moves in the form of 'waves'. The metaphor of the pandemic as a series of waves suggests changes in the number of infections are due to the virus itself, rather than the result of actions taken to slow its spread. In addition, precisely because waves follow one another uncontrollably, this metaphor presents new increases in infection as inevitable.

Based on the analysis of two different datasets, Semino (2021) suggested a more apt and versatile metaphor of COVID-19 than that of a wave – a *fire*, specifically a *forest fire*. The author points out that forest fire metaphors for COVID-19 have been used since the start of the pandemic for multiple purposes, including to convey danger and urgency. Semino also notes that despite being dangerous and hard to control, forest fires can be controlled with prompt and appropriate action. They can even be prevented by looking after the land properly, protecting the environment, and educating citizens to behave responsibly.

Interestingly, disaster metaphors were also used instead of war metaphors by the UK's media in the avian flu pandemic, implying scientists and social policy makers had no control over the pandemic. The virus was compared to a storm, a flood, and an earthquake (Nerlich & Halliday, 2007). Like the metaphors that surrounded avian flu, H1N1 was referred to as a natural disaster (Angeli, 2012). The disaster metaphors described the flu as a *'surge'* that was *'peaking'*, *'rising'* and *'declining'* like waves. So, the term referring to movements of waves emerged in the swine flu discourse. However, unlike COVID-19, only one article explicitly referred to H1N1 as being in its *'third wave'* (Nerlich & Halliday, 2007).

More recently, Stanley et al. (2021) carried out a metaphor analysis of COVID-19 and found four convergent mental models for framing the pandemic. The models include those of uncertainty, danger, grotesque, and misery and reveal the primary implicit emotions of grief, disgust, anger, and fear. This perception of the pandemic as well as a perceived lack of control over the virus manifests in participants' choosing insect metaphors such as wasps, gnats, bedbugs, and cockroaches that *'come out of nowhere'*, *'sting you for no reason'*, invade personal space and freedom, and are ultimately difficult to kill. The pandemic is also commonly compared to reptiles, for example a snake or a lizard, which marks the virus as shifty and cunning, infringing upon peoples' agency and control. Comparing the pandemic with predators or scavengers is also quite common.

Gök and Kara (2021) also investigated the perceptions of individuals living in Turkey during the COVID-19 pandemic through metaphor analysis. Seven metaphor categories were obtained based on common features: being restricted, restlessness, uncertainty/obscurity, deadly/dangerous, struggling, faith/destiny, and supernatural. The categories were further subsumed under three themes (anxiety/concern, risk, and faith) based on similarities in meaning. A striking detail is participants compared the COVID-19 pandemic with a sign of the apocalypse. Interestingly, the apocalyptic model was often linked to AIDS ('AIDS is death').

Taylor and Kidgell (2021) tracked metaphor usage across four time periods from the 1890s to the 2000s and found there is considerable continuity in the metaphors used to frame flu-like pandemics over the time with all early metaphor groups appearing in the latest time. As with previous pandemics, the war metaphors consistently account for a large proportion of the metaphorical framings. However, they appear to be in decline in the four time periods investigated by the authors. The natural disaster language and the water metaphor have also been common. In the current pandemic, the water metaphor is lexicalized through *wave*, which remove agency from the virus and may suggest inevitability with a potential effect of reducing accountability of the government. Unlike previous pandemics, for instance AIDS or H1N1 (Angeli, 2012; Sontag, 1989), in the context of COVID-19 no plague metaphors are widely used, and only the COVID-19 discourse includes the metaphors of social distancing.

Conclusion

Unfolding in real time, the emergent studies into the language of the COVID-19 pandemic provided a unique chance to advance the linguistics of social change through wide access to mediated language sources, building multilingual and comparative databases, and developing analytical tools to assess the social and cognitive impacts of the pandemic. The story of research into language and communication during the pandemic reflects the course of the pandemic itself. It goes from the idea of a natural disaster with the efforts to confine it in time and space, inescapable fear and anxiety caused by isolation and separation, to the idea transcending boundaries of political frameworks, to the emergency of translating science into other areas and shaping a healthy new normal. Findings of studies into new words, categorization, and metaphors signify critical tensions in languages: science terms vs. slang, private vs. public, the language of division vs. humor. In future, sociolinguistics, cognitive linguistics, discourse analysis, and applied linguistics are set to address the relevant knowledge gaps.

The major sociolinguistic theories are found to be universally applicable in this global epidemic because of the biological nature of the virus: language diversity, multilingualism, standardization, and variation. These theories are well fit to address urgent problems in various political, geographical, and technological contexts. The theories that produce culturally diverging results and worth further exploration include language ideology, language as social action, and pragmatics.

Methodologically, we study the language of the pandemic through novel methods, especially with regard to data access, open digital texts, social media messages, and machine-learning analytical instruments. The advantage of these methods is not only big data but making the best of distributed knowledge found in the many differentiated traditions and involving the broader public in science (Adami et al., 2020, see also https://publicinterest.org.uk/part-4-metaphors/). Forming a new transmedia, collective, bottom-up culture of inquiry, observing, recording, sharing, and reflecting on the changes to communication and interaction caused by the COVID-19 crisis and its enduring effects is expected to yield significant results. The future of the pandemic communication research lies at the intersection of disciplines, channels, and knowledge domains: metaphors and political discourse, language and teaching, health costs and public policing behavior, and many more.

References

Abouzahra, M., & Tan, J. (2021). Twitter vs. Zika—The role of social media in epidemic outbreaks surveillance. *Health Policy and Technology*, 10(1), 174–181.

Adami, E., Al Zidjaly, N., Canale, G., Djonov, E., Ghiasian, M. S., Gualberto, C., … Zhang, Y. (2020). PanMeMic Manifesto: Making meaning in the Covid-19 pandemic and the future of social interaction. *Working Papers in Urban Language and Literacies No 273, 273*.

Agha, A. (2006). *Language and social relations* (Vol. 24). Cambridge University Press.

Akut, B. K. (2020). Morphological analysis of the neologisms during the COVID-19 pandemic. *International Journal of English Language Studies (IJELS), 2*(3), 1–7.

Al-Azzawi, Q. O., & Haleem, H. A. (2021). "Do you speak Corona?": Hashtags and neologisms since the COVID-19 pandemic outbreak. *International Journal of Linguistics, Literature and Translation, 4*(4), 113–122.

Al-Salman, S., & Haider, A. S. (2021). COVID-19 trending neologisms and word formation processes in English. *Russian Journal of Linguistics, 25*(1), 24–42.

Alyeksyeyeva, I. O., Chaiuk, T. A., & Galitska, E. A. (2020). Coronaspeak as key to Coronaculture: Studying new cultural practices through neologisms. *International Journal of English Linguistics, 10*(6). https://doi.org/10.5539/ijel.v10n6p202

Angeli, E. (2012). Metaphors in the rhetoric of pandemic flu: Electronic media coverage of H1N1 and swine flu. *Technical Writing and Communication, 42*(3), 203–222.

Asif, M., Zhiyong, D., Iram, A., & Nisarl, M. (2020). Linguistic analysis of neologism related to Coronavirus (COVID-19). *Social Sciences and Humanities.* https://doi.org/10.2139/ssrn.3608585

Badziński, A. (2020). COVID-19: Ocena aktualnej sytuacji, zalecenia, wyzwania i wytyczne w zakresie postępowania dla tłumaczy ustnych medycznych w czasie pandemii SARS-CoV-2. *Beyond Philology, 17*(4), 147–164.

Belkina, E. O. (2021). The language of the pandemic (based on the French language materials). *SSRN.* https://doi.org/10.2139/ssrn.3861176

Bonta, E., & Galiţa, R. (2020). Scrolling the Internet: Fear in disguise. A corpus-based analysis of the new langdemic. *Interstudia, 27*, 145–160.

Bromhead, H. (2021). Disaster linguistics, climate change semantics and public discourse studies: A semantically-enhanced discourse study of 2011 Queensland floods. *Language Sciences, 85*, 101381.

Butseva, T. N., & Zelenin, A. V. (2020). Lexicography in the situation of neology extreme (based on the new coronavirus lexicon). *Bulletin of the Cherepovets State University, 6*(99), 86–105.

Cahapay, B. M. (2020). Trending phrases, names, and hashtags related to covid-19 in the Philippines: The language of social crisis. *Muallim Journal of Social Science and Humanities Online, 4*(4), 1–9.

Chaiuk, T. (2020). Fear culture in media: An examination on Coronavirus discourse. *Journal of History Culture an Art Research, 9*(2), 184–194.

Charney, S. A., Camarata, S. M., & Chern, A. (2021). Potential impact of the COVID-19 pandemic on communication and language skills in children. *Otolaryngology–Head and Neck Surgery, 165*(1), 1–2. https://doi.org/10.1177/0194599820978247

Charon, R. (2001). Narrative medicine: Form function, and ethics. *Annals of Internal Medicine, 134*(1), 83–87.

Cierpich-Kozieł, A. (2020). Koronarzeczywistość – o nowych złożeniach z członem korona- w dobie pandemii. *Język Polski, 100*(4), 102–117. (In Polish).

Craig, D. (2020). Pandemic and its metaphors: Sontag revisited in the COVID-19 era. *European Journal of Cultural Studies, 23*(6), 1025–1032.

Dada, S., Ashworth, H. C., Bewa, M. J., & Dhatt, R. (2021). Words matter: Political and gender analysis of speeches made by heads of government during the COVID-19 pandemic. *BMJ Global Health, 6*(1), e003910.

Erlanger, S. (2020, March 16). Macron declares France 'at war' with virus, as E.U. proposes 30-day travel ban. *The New York Times*, 16 March. https://www.nytimes.com/2020/03/16/world/europe/coronavirus-france-macron-travel-ban.html?searchResultPosition=3

Filardo-Llamas, L. (2021). Tsunami, waves, quixotes, and ko-vid: Metaphors about the pandemic as seen in cartoons. *Mètode Science Studies Journal, 11*, 14–20.

Foster, M., & Welsh, A. (2021). A 'new normal' of code-switching: Covid-19, the Indonesian media and language change. *Indonesian Journal of Applied Linguistics, 11*(1), 200–210.

Gekkina, E. N., & Kozhevnikov, A. Y. (2021). Lexical updating trends in the reflection of "Coronavirus" words. *Cherepovets State University Bulletin, 3*(102), 95–108. (In Russian).

Gillis, M. (2020). Ventilators, missiles, doctors, troops ... the justification of legislative responses to COVID-19 through military metaphors. *Law and Humanities, 14*(2), 135–159.

Gök, A., & Kara, A. (2021). Individuals' conceptions of COVID-19 pandemic through metaphor analysis. *Current Psychology.* https://doi.org/10.1007/s12144-021-01506-z

Golovanova, E. I., & Madzhaeva, S. I. (2020). On the vocabulary of the Coronavirus pandemic epoch. Bulletin of Chelyabinsk State University. No. 7 (441). *Philology Sciences, 121*, 48–55. (In Russian).

Goltsova, M. G., & Chybis L. V. (2021). Coronavirus neologisms in the English and Ukrainian languages. *International Journal of Philology, 12*(1), 45–48.

Hamawi, B., Alashaikh, A., & Alanazi, E. (2020). What are covid-19 Arabic tweeters talking about? https://www.researchgate.net/publication/342803140_What_Are_COVID-19_Arabic_Tweeters_Talking_About

Horne, F. (2009). What does AIDS mean? *Scrutiny2 Issues in English Studies in Southern Africa, 14*, 31–48.

Hruschka, D. J., Christiansen, M. H., Blythe, R. A., Croft, W., Heggarty, P., Mufwene, S. S.,... Poplack, S. (2009). Building social cognitive models of language change. *Trends in Cognitive Sciences, 13*(11), 464–469.

Ibrahim, E. R., Kadhim, S. A.-h., Mayuuf, H. H., & Haleem, H. A. (2020). A sociolinguistic approach to linguistic changes since the COVID-19 pandemic outbreak. *Multicultural Education, 6*(4), 122–128.

Ilham, E., & Hassan, B. (2020). La crise sanitaire due 'Au Coronavirus' et le nouveau lexique. *Interstudia, 28*, 50–58. (In French).

Jansem, A. (2021). The feasibility of foreign language online instruction during the COVID-19 pandemic: A qualitative case study of instructors' and students' reflections. *International Education Studies, 14*(4), 93–102.

Joshi, A., Karimi, S., Sparks, R., Paris, C., & MacIntyre, C. R. (2019). Survey of text-based epidemic intelligence: A computational linguistics perspective. *ACM Computing Surveys (CSUR), 52*(6), 1–19.

Karachina, O. E. (2020). Language of pandemic: Linguists and cultural aspects. *Russian Linguistic Bulletin, 2*(22), 45–48.

Katsaounis, N. (2020). Language and the pandemic: The construction of semantic frames in Greek-German comparison. *Training, Language and Culture, 4*(3), 55–65.

Krauss, R. M., & Chiu, C.-Y. (1998). Language and social behavior. In D. T. Gilbert, S. T. Fiske, & G. Lindzey (Eds.), *The handbook of social psychology* (pp. 41–88). McGraw-Hill.

Lakoff, G., & Johnson, M. (1980). *Metaphors we live by.* Chicago University Press.

Lei, S., Yang, R., & Huang, C.-R. (2021). Emergent neologism: A study of an emerging meaning with competing forms based on the first six months of COVID-19. *Lingua, 258*, 103095. https://www.sciencedirect.com/science/article/pii/S002438412100067X

López, A. M. R., & Naranjo, B. (2021). Translating in times of crisis: A study about the emotional effects of the COVID19 pandemic on the translation of evaluative language. *Journal of Pragmatics, 176*, 29–40.

Madani, Y., Erritali, M., & Bouikhalene, B. (2021). Using artificial intelligence techniques for detecting Covid-19 epidemic fake news in Moroccan tweets. *Results in Physics, 25*, 104266.

Maroto, N. G. P., & de Goedele, M. S. (2021). Prueba de solvencia a la neología terminológica en Español en tiempos de pandemia: Los repertorios terminológicos. *Bulletin of Hispanic Studies, 98*(5), 433–451. (In Spanish).

McGinty, E. E., Stone, E. M., Kennedy-Hendricks, A., & Barry, C. L. (2019). Stigmatizing language in news media coverage of the opioid epidemic: Implications for public health. *Preventive Medicine, 124*, 110–114.

Megerian, C. (2020, May 6). Trump calls Americans 'warriors' in fight to open economy. *Los Angeles Times*. https://www.latimes.com/politics/story/2020-05-06/trump-americans-warriors-fight-to-open-economy

Mohlman, J., & Basch, C. (2020). The language of university communications during the COVID-19 pandemic. *Journal of American College Health, 35*(14), 1–4. https://doi.org/10.1080/07448481.2020.1856116

Mozol, T. S. (2021). Language creativity in the era of the Coronavirus (focusing on Korean language neologisms). *Vestnik of Moscow State Linguistic University. Humanities, 4*(846), 154–163. (In Russian).

Naming the coronavirus disease. https://www.who.int/emergencies/diseases/novel-coronavirus-2019/technical-guidance/naming-the-coronavirus-disease-(covid-2019)-and-the-virus-that-causes-it

Nerlich, B., & Halliday, C. (2007). Avian flu: The creation of expectations in the interplay between science and media. *Sociology of Health & Illness, 29*(1), 46–65.

Nikolić, M. M., Slijepčević-Bjelivuk, S. M., & Novokmet, S. B. (2021). Nove reči u srpskom javnom diskursu kao posledica pandemije kovida 19. *Zbornik radova Filozofskog fakulteta u Prištini, 51*(1), 365–390. (In Serbian).

Olimat, S. N. (2020). "COVID-19 Pandemic: Euphemism and Dysphemism", in Jordanian Arabic, GEMA Online®. *Journal of Language Studies, 20*(3), 268–290. http://doi.org/10.17576/gema-2020-2003-16

Philips, S. U. (2004). Language and social inequality. In A. Duranti (Ed.), *A Companion to Linguistic Anthropology*, (pp. 474–495). Blackwell.

Piekkari, R., Tietze, S., Angouri, J., Meyer, R., & Vaara, E. (2021). Can you speak Covid-19? Languages and social inequality in management studies. *Journal of Management Studies, 58*(2), 587–591.

Piller, I., Zhang, J., & Li, J. (2020). Linguistic diversity in a time of crisis: Language challenges of the COVID-19 pandemic. *Multilingua, 39*(5), 503–515.

Qodriani, L. U., & Wijana, I. D. P. (2020, December). Language Change in 'New-Normal' Classroom. In *4th International Conference on Language, Literature, Culture, and Education (ICOLLITE 2020)* (pp. 385–389). Atlantis Press.

Redden, M., Tracy, S. J., & Shafer, M. S. (2013). A metaphor analysis of recovering substance abusers' sense-making of medication-assisted treatment. *Qualitative Health Research, 23*(7), 951–962.

Robinson, W. P., & Giles, H. (2001). *Handbook of language and social psychology*. Wiley.

Romaine, S. (2000). *Language in society: An introduction to sociolinguistics*. Oxford University Press.

Rys, L., & Pasyk, L. (2020). Neologisms of the German language in the corona crisis period. *Kremenetski komparatyvni studii, X*, 289–299.

Sabucedo, J. M., Alzate, M., & Gómez-Román, C. (2020). Extremismos e secessionismo em contextos de crise. O movimiento independentista na Catalunha/Espanha. In D. U. Hur & J. M. Sabucedo (Eds.), *Psicología dos extremismos políticos* (pp. 16–41). Editora Vozes.

Samylicheva, N., & Gazda, J. (2020). Derivative neologisms as sociocultural dominants in the Russian and Czech languages of the modern period. SHS Web of Conferences 88, 01022. https://doi.org/10.1051/shsconf/20208801022

Semino, E. (2021). Not soldiers but fire-fighters – metaphors and Covid-19. *Health Communication, 36*(1), 50–58.

Severskaya O. I. (2020). Covidiots on Coronacation: Coronaviral lexicon as a diagnostic field for actual discursive practices. *Communication Studies, 7*(4), 887–906. (In Russian).

Shen, Q. (2020). Commentary: Directions in language planning from the COVID-19 pandemic. *Multilingua, 39*(5), 625–629.

Sismat, M. A. H. (2021). The language of pandemic and its significance in effective communication. *Journal of Humanities and Social Sciences Studies, 3*(4), 54–60.

Sontag, S. (1989). *Illness as metaphor and AIDS and its metaphors.* St. Martin's Press.

Şorcaru, D. (2020). Inter-texting cultures during pandemic(s): A pragmatic approach and beyond. *Cultural Intertexts, 10*(10), 96–106.

Stanley, B. L., Zanin, A. C., Avalos, B. L., Tracy, S. J., & Town, S. (2021). Collective emotion during collective trauma: A metaphor analysis of the COVID-19 pandemic. *Qualitative Health Research, 31*(10), 1890–1903.

Szabó, R. (2020). No going back: The impact of the COVID-19 pandemic on corporate language and communication training Robert Szabó. *Horizon, 2,* 23–30.

Taylor, C., & Kidgell, J. (2021). Flu-like pandemics and metaphor pre-covid: A corpus investigation. *Discourse, Context & Media, 41*(2), 100503.

Tracy, S. J., Lutgen-Sandvik, P. & Alberts, J. K. (2006). Nightmares, demons and slaves: Exploring the painful metaphors of workplace bullying. *Management Communication Quarterly, 20*(2), 148–185.

Türev, D., & Halil, T. (2020). Etymlogical analysis of the medical term filiation connected with COVID-19. *Erciyes Medical Journal/Erciyes Tip Dergisi, 42*(3), 354–358.

Upadhyay, M. K., & Maroof, Kh. A. (2020). Understanding the emerging and reemerging terminologies amid the COVID-19 pandemic. *Journal of Family Medicine and Primary Care, 9*(12), 5881–5887.

Upadhyayula, S., & Kasliwal, R. R. (2020). Covid cardiology: A neologism for an evolving subspecialty. *Journal of Clinical and Preventive Cardiology* [serial online]. https://www.jcpconline.org/text.asp?2020/9/2/40/291227

Wallis, P. & Nerlich, B. (2005). Disease metaphors in new epidemics: The UK media framing of the 2003 SARS epidemic. *Social Science & Medicine, 60,* 2629–2639.

Wang, X., & Huang, Ch-R. (2021). From contact prevention to social distancing: The co-evolution of bilingual neologisms and public health campaigns in two cities in the time of COVID-19. *Sage Open, 11*(3). https://doaj.org/article/6337a7e8d49d4add9bc99d2747315276

Zholobova, A. (2021). Linguistic innovation during the COVID-19 pandemic: The Spanish language case. *XLinguae, 14*(2), 331–349.

15

POLITICAL COMMUNICATION AND PANDEMICS

Benjamin R. Bates and Jason A. Edwards

The National Communication Association Political Communication Division (2010, n.p.) defines political communication as the study of how "citizens, public officials, and media organizations argue about and represent electoral and institutional politics in campaigns, deliberations, mediated images, speeches, and more." More broadly, the joint International Communication Association Political Communication Division and the American Political Science Association Political Communication Section (2011, n.p.) state that the agenda of political communication "interrogates questions about communication, power and governance in domestic and international settings." Functionally, however, political communication scholarship has tended to assume that political communication is the study of *public* messages delivered by *national leaders* that are delivered either *at in-person events* or through *mass media* on topics of *public affairs* at the *national* level. In addition, the models for political dialogue, political deliberation, and political voice have tend to be drawn from Anglo-American and continental European assumptions.

Political communication in the COVID-19 pandemic requires us to question these assumptions, both because the practice of political communication in the COVID-19 pandemic has deviated from these conventions and because opening these traditions may allow us to better respond to future pandemics by offering insight and advice for political communicators.

In this chapter we begin by showing how pandemic communication turns health and medical topics into public affairs to be studied in political communication. Beyond challenging the assumption of what topics are political topics for communication, we then illustrate how pandemic communication requires us to challenge assumptions about how political messages and political campaigns are made public, to challenge assumptions about which speakers are

DOI: 10.4324/9781003214496-15

important to study in political communication, to challenge assumptions that political communication occurs primarily at the national level, and, finally, to challenge the norms of political communication that are premised on the patterns of the Global North.

Expanding the Scope of What Counts as Political Communication

Perhaps the most basic impact that the study of pandemic communication has on political communication is that it expands the scope of what counts as political communication. In his foundational definition, Chaffee (1975) asserted that political communication is "the role of communication in the political process," a definition that would seem to be quite broad (p. 15). However, as it has been operationalized in the study of political communication, the "political process" is primarily about how politicians, the media, and the public interact in electoral and campaign processes. In his outline of key areas of study for political communication, Soukup (2014) argues that agenda setting, rhetoric, persuasion, framing, and priming are the core processes of political communication. Although these five topics are applicable to multiple sub-fields in communication, almost every example offered by Soukup is about electoral, pressure group, or party processes or toward the socialization of individuals to engage with politics through electoral, pressure group, or party processes. Reviews of political communication from Semetko and Price (1994), Sampedro (2011), and Boulianne (2019) indicate that this focus on participation in electoral, pressure group, and party processes by politicians, media houses, and (potential) voters is longstanding.

This focus may be attributable to an historic division in political communication between topics that belong in the public sphere, and are therefore subject to political communication analysis, and those that belong in the technical and personal spheres. Goodnight (2012) argues that issues that "extend the stakes of argument beyond private needs and the needs of special communities to the interests of the entire community" are those that are properly within the public sphere (p. 202). Issues of health and well-being, because they are either seen as within the domain of individual decision-making, and thus part of the personal sphere, or "created in such a way as to narrow the range of permissible subject matter while requiring more specialized forms of reasoning," and thus within the realm of the technical, would not be subject to political communication (p. 198).

With very few exceptions, issues of health and well-being are seldom discussed in political communication. Although there are discussions of rhetoric and health (see Chapter 13 that pandemic communication has for rhetoric and public address), the emergence of health topics as going beyond private needs to becoming a public question that affects the interest of the whole community is rare, with very limited discussions of how the emergence of illicit drug use (Levinson, 2008), school attendance by children living with HIV/ AIDS (Gonzenbach & Stevenson, 1994), and regulation of electronic cigarettes (Sangalang, 2015) became political issues. Generally, policymaking and regulation have remained in the technical sphere where specialized reasoning was applied using the rules of scientific and medical discourse rather than political discourse.

The COVID-19 pandemic, however, disrupted the assumption that there was a separation between this health issue and other issues that have long been considered political. Although science and health had long been considered technical topics with technical disputes by political communications scholars, everything it seemed, especially from an American perspective, about addressing COVID-19 became political. The very existence of the disease became a political topic; agenda setting in the face of COVID was widespread. Acts of rhetoric to assign blame, for example to China, to the World Health Organization, or to others in an international political system, were common. Attempts at persuasion in electoral politics throughout the world in 2020 and 2021 used response (or failure to respond) to COVID-19 as an issue on which voters were asked to judge candidates. Competing frames between social lockdowns as health measures or as attacks on national economics emerged. In these frames, closure of businesses, schools, and public accommodations engaged as issues of the economy, education, and participation in public life. Vaccine and testing mandates created conflicts between personal autonomy and collective goods. Restrictions on movement and closure of borders implicated politics of immigration, migration, and mobility. Fundamental questions of morbidity and mortality from COVID-19, its etiology, diagnosis, and prognosis, and the accuracy of COVID tests and efficacy of COVID vaccines moved from being considered questions with scientific answers that should be discovered through scientific processes to political topics on which there would be multiple answers competing for legitimacy confirmed through political processes.

Because the pandemic forces us to consider seriously how health and medicine are inherently connected to political systems, it offers the opportunity to resist the segregation of topics into the personal, the technical, and the public sphere. The pandemic also allows us to bring ideas and methods from political communication to understand how issues of health and well-being are communicated and made relevant to audiences. Additionally, the pandemic allows us to bring ideas from rhetoric of health and medicine and from health communication to offer additional strategies that might be used in political communication to engage individuals with electoral, pressure group, and party processes. In sum, if the lived body and its health and the body politic and its health are seen as intersecting bodies, pandemic communication can allow us to engage health and well-being on the personal, technical, and public levels together through political communication.

Presidential Campaigning in a Pandemic:
The US 2020 Front-Porch Campaign

Although pandemic communication has forced us to change and expand the way we talk about political communication, traditional topics within political communication continue to be relevant within the pandemic. Although there is a longstanding focus on political campaigns and their messages in political communication, the pandemic has also forced a rethinking of how these traditional forms of political communication are done. To show how the pandemic has demanded rethinking how politicians and the public interact with one another during the pandemic, we look at campaigning in the United States as an example of how the pandemic requires us to revisit well-known contexts in political communication. Political campaign communication has generated a large portion of political communication scholarship (Boulianne, 2019; Sampedro, 2011; Semetko & Price, 1994). The pandemic changed the way campaigning was done in the United States and throughout the world. In the 2020 US presidential campaign, we assert the pandemic forced President Donald Trump and former Vice President Biden to return to a 19th century form of political campaigning known as the "front-porch campaign."

Most American political campaigns in the 19th century were done through surrogates, and not by the candidate holding a large in-person rally themselves (Denton, et al., 2019). Presidential campaigns would instead use prominent individuals and political party structures to hold rallies, generate public interest, and deliver public messages on behalf of the candidate. Moreover, newspapers—often sponsored by political parties—were an extremely important way to get campaign messages out to the public (Laracey, 2003; Sheppard, 2007). It was not until the 1840 presidential election where presidential candidates delivered election addresses and that was an extremely limited fashion. In the post-Civil War era, presidential candidates began to speak more often, but did so from their front porch. Other campaigners, as the 20th century approached, began to use the barnstorming technique, where they would travel to their audiences and hold mass rallies.

Front porch campaigns are a low-key campaign, where the political candidate stays close to home. Rather than the candidate going to the voters, audiences are often brought to the candidate. Candidates adapt their stump speech to the audience that was in front of them. Campaign events are more intimate and there is considerably less stage management than in a typical 20th century campaign rally. Successful front porch presidential campaigns were run in the 1880, 1888, and 1920 presidential campaigns. Perhaps the most famous clash between the front porch campaign and the barnstorming campaign was the 1896 presidential election between Republican William McKinley and Democrat William Jennings Bryan. The 1896 presidential campaign is the most famous because it is seen as a turning point in American political campaigns.

William McKinley gave dozens of speeches to supporters who made the journey to his home, which was not far from the local train station in Canton, Ohio. The press would then cover these and report on these events for national press coverage (Harpine, 2006). By contrast, the Democratic candidate, William Jennings Bryan, barnstormed the United States via train. Bryan gave over 600 speeches to audiences across much of the Midwest and Western part of the United States. He used populist appeals to generate support among voters who were disaffected by traditional party politics. Bryan's style of campaigning—holding rallies and giving speeches across the United States—became the norm of presidential candidates, until the 2020 presidential election. During the pandemic, President Trump employed techniques more akin to barnstorming while former Vice President Joe Biden rekindled echoes of past front porch campaigns.

President Trump attempted to conduct a normal campaign in the 2020 presidential election. While Trump built a massive virtual presence that Brad Parscale, his campaign manager, likened to the Death Star in the movie *Star Wars,* Trump attempted at every turn to engage in a traditional campaign. Trump's campaign knocked on doors, held in-person fundraising events, and committed to as many huge rallies as he could. The pandemic thwarted some of these efforts in the late spring and summer of 2020, but as the campaign wore on, Trump crisscrossed the United States, holding events that flouted public health rules concerning the gatherings of large audiences. White House Press Secretary Kayleigh McEnany argued that "if people want to show up and express their political views, that's their choice to do so" (Miller & Jaffe, 2020, n.p.). At these events, Trump spoke, using populist appeals that carried him to victory in 2016. His audience was primarily made up of his base of loyal supporters, among whom he attempted to generate as much enthusiasm and support as possible, something he thought would translate to the ballot box. At the same time, the Trump campaign consistently criticized Biden's method of campaigning. Trump and his surrogates accused Biden of hiding in his basement (Khalid & Keith, 2020). For example, Minnesota Republican Senate Candidate Jason Lewis argued his opponent, Tina Smith, was "stuck in the basement with Joe Biden right now" (Condon, 2020, n.p.). *The Atlantic*'s Andrew Ferguson (2020) called Biden's campaign a "disaster." As Ferguson asked, "what is a presidential candidate without cheer crowds, balloon drops, overbearing music, a stage choked with grinning sycophants?" (n.p., see also Milligan, 2020). Pre-pandemic norms of political communication led many commentators to expect a barnstorming campaign, failing to account that the pandemic could, and perhaps should, change the way political campaign communication is performed.

Despite these criticisms and some early setbacks, the Biden team continued with its virtual front-porch campaign because the public health demands of the pandemic required, for his team, a change in the ways that political communicators campaign. One of the ways that Biden's front porch campaign was like the past was that it centered on low-key events. Eschewing large open-air campaign rallies that Donald Trump thrived upon, Biden conducted virtual events from his home. And when Biden did travel it was typically to a specific place, for a very short time, and with a small audience, aligning with public health recommendations and the norms of front porch campaign. In doing so, however, Biden's campaign events were about stitching together as broad of a campaign coalition as possible. Inspired by his victory in the Democrat primary, Biden sought to build:

> the biggest coalition possible and you don't necessarily build it through the buzziest of politics or flashiest moments. The campaign doesn't want Biden to go viral as much as it wants him to connect with the most people in the broadest possible sense.
>
> *Hatmaker (2020, n.p.)*

To that end, he held virtual exchanges, gave virtual speeches, and answered questions with members of groups like the American Federation of Teachers or the Service Employees International Union on videoconference computer technology (Jansen, 2020). In battleground states, Biden would speak via Zoom with supporters in different locales throughout the day. His fundraisers were primarily virtual. Considering Joe Biden, by his own admission, is at his political best when he meets people and talks to them in-person, getting a sense of their trials and tribulations so that he can speak to them personally, these campaign events were a radical change. Thus, to create a greater sense of "normal" politicking, Biden insisted that he took time out of his schedule each day to talk to a handful of voters or volunteers just to make sure he was keeping in touch with people (Burns et al., 2020). These smaller events online and personal connections allowed Joe Biden to directly appeal to interest groups and take some questions (Jansen, 2020). It was attempting to re-create normal out of what was not a normal time. These virtual events, while open to most people, were much targeted and intimate, like the audiences who would hear McKinley speak at his home.

During these virtual campaign stops, fundraisers, and discussions with voters, Biden continually criticized Donald Trump's handing of the pandemic, as one would expect. But he did so with an emphasis on empathy, compassion, consistency, and character. Biden's reactions to the pandemic were cautious, measured, and were a result of information he received from the best minds in the medical field. That messaging, as Biden's Deputy National Press Secretary Matt Hill noted, was meant for "Joe Biden's values to shine through…it's also decency, empathy, and hope, and everything that is just the polar opposite of Donald Trump" (Hatmaker, 2020, n.p.). Biden campaign's digital director Rob Flaherty similarly argued that the smaller events but consistent messaging were done to "sort of fill the void of leadership that we're seeing in Washington right now where the VP is empathetic and competent leader in a time where people are craving both empathy and competence" (Khalid & Keith, 2020, n.p.; see also Strauss, 2020). In short, Biden's messaging was more presidential. It was more of a "normal" politicking that Americans were/are used to but reframed through strategies drawn from front porch campaign norms.

The other historical echo in Biden's campaign was of Warren G. Harding's 1920 front porch presidential campaign during the second year of the Spanish flu pandemic. Harding made his campaign theme a "return to normal" where he would eschew foreign entanglements that got the United States involved in World War I and would focus on economic recovery from the Spanish flu (Pietrusza, 2008). Similarly, Joe Biden's campaign messaging offered a return to "normalcy," and also made economic recovery in the face of a pandemic a central strategy. As Jonah Goldberg (2019), who advocated that Biden run a front-porch campaign even before the pandemic hit, maintained, "most voters are sick of all the drama, and they're turned off by calls for socialism and the like" (n.p.). After four years of Donald Trump's rhetoric, exacerbated further by his inconsistent handling of the pandemic, Biden's messaging was a return to a more normal campaign messaging. The front porch campaign may lack the spectacle of barnstorming, but after five years of Donald Trump's campaign and presidential rhetoric, that "boring" rhetoric was an elevated discourse that many voters wanted and craved.

Biden's successful front porch campaign may have implications for the performance of political communication in an age of pandemic and digital technology, but it may not mean that pandemic communication has fundamentally changed campaigns going forward. Are political candidates going to suddenly stop doing campaign rallies when the pandemic abates? Will the traditions of the modern campaign suddenly fade away? The answer is clearly no. Political leaders will not give up the adoring crowds, the mass rallies, and the ability to drive the news cycle when they come to a community near you. It is a given that virtual campaigning will only grow as part of political campaigns in the future. In the United States, the digital infrastructure for voter outreach had begun long before the pandemic hit the world.

Rather than asking an either/or question of whether campaigns will barnstorm or use the front porch, campaigns will likely do both as the pandemic has shown clearly how digital infrastructure can be used to recreate the front porch. Biden's campaign was successful, in part, because voters crave some sense of connection with the candidate. Connection can certainly be felt at a traditional political rally, but the Biden campaign proved that connection can be created with voters through a digital infrastructure. While these events might not garner the press coverage of a campaign rally in a community, combined with barnstorming forms of campaigning, events done via Zoom, YouTube, and Facebook Live may be more low-key but also have a lower barrier of entry for people digitally. Through these events, campaigns can reach even more people than can in-person rallies and can harness a grassroots energy that one might not get in a normal campaign event (Harris, 2020).

These phenomena are not limited to the United Sates. Political candidates across the world attempted to increase personal connections through digital campaign events. In South Korea, for instance, candidates hosted YouTube talk shows, uploaded speeches online, and offered QR codes for people to download materials. In Singapore, candidates held e-rallies and livestreamed question and answer sessions (Lange, 2020). As one political candidate in Canada's province of Saskatchewan noted,

> Facebook Live town halls were useful as a replacement for in-person events to raise awareness on what we considered to be important issues in the election. In fact, the number of people that watched our Facebook town halls was much larger than the number of people who would normally show up at traditional town hall held in-person.
>
> *(McGrane, 2020, n.p.)*

The traditional norm of modern campaigning met with the virtues of a virtual front-porch style may be the future for a plethora of political candidates, particularly those that do not thrive in arena-style politics.

Challenging Assumptions of Who Speaks in Political Communication

Although potential changes to campaigns may focus us on the candidates for public office, pandemic communication also requires us to challenge assumptions about which political communicators are significant for analysis. Generally, political communication has been concerned with the communicative acts of executive heads of government, such as presidents and prime ministers, or the communicative acts of political parties. From World War II to the turn of the century, Blumler and Kavanagh (1999) argued that the increasing professionalization of both politicians and the media that cover them has centered heads of government – and those who desire to be heads of government – in conversations about political communication. In parliamentary systems, such as the United Kingdom, political communication analysis often "magnifies the modern prime minister, placing him or her center stage in key political processes" through a focus on the prime minister's personal actions and the speeches they make (Heffernan, 2006, p. 582). Presidential systems, like the United States, often credit the president with commanding a "bully pulpit" that shapes which topics are significant enough to be discussed and how those topics should be understood (Zarefksy, 2004). Jordan et al. (2019) claim this trend is cross-national, likely to accelerate, and to lead other national leaders to emulate the personal stylings of the US president as defining political leadership and political communication style globally, at least among anglophone countries.

At the same time, as there is an increasing focus on presidents and prime ministers, these leaders encounter a media system that "must loom like a hydra-headed beast, the many mouths of which are continually clamoring to be fed" with commentary and information to be satisfied (Blumler & Kavanagh, 1999, p. 213). As a counterweight, and as the COVID-19 pandemic has shown, however, the media system also encounters an array of political communicators beyond the national executive. In cooperation with one another and in competition with one another, the communicators seek to feed that hydra. Political communication as pandemic communication challenges the assumption the presidents and prime ministers are always the most significant political communicators in a political system.

Pandemic communication reminds us, first, that there are a series of significant political actors within national governments who offer political communication that is significant and impactful for publics. Pandemic communication reminds us, second, that all political communication can be localized, often with influence and impact that is at least as important as communication that takes place at the national level.

Additional Significant Political Actors

The COVID-19 pandemic has revealed that there are significant political actors in communication systems that are not the president or the prime minister. Because pandemic communication is both a political topic and a health and medical topic, political communication in a pandemic is marked by shifts away from the unitary executive in authority to speak and in what marks the expertise to speak.

The authority to speak in a pandemic becomes a shared responsibility. In their analysis of speeches made by 20 heads of government to address the COVID-19,[1] Dada et al. (2021) found that national leaders attempt to exert authority to frame the pandemic to allow particular approaches to managing the nation's response. Simultaneously, Dada et al. (2021) acknowledged that these leaders often spoke alongside or with ministers and secretaries of significant departments who took on the authority to speak within specific contextual domains. For example, in examining Aotearoa New Zealand's response to the COVID-19 pandemic, Gilray (2021) argued that the Attorney General's interpretation of the legality of border closure and the Minister of Tourism's command of information over the flow of people across the border invested them with unique authority to speak. Alternatively, Fujita et al. (2020) claimed that the lack of public involvement by the Minister of Health, Labor, and Welfare in Japan undermined the government's "stay at home" orders because the Minister's specific authority over housing and economic conditions that would sustain such an order was not activated. The series of 30 case studies, drawn from throughout the globe, represented in Lilleker et al.'s (2021) collection offers additional examples of how ministry heads can play an important role in supporting or challenging the Chief Executive's national response.

Perhaps the best-known example of interactions between the executive's political authority and a second political actor's other authority is the tension between former US President Donald Trump and the National Institute of Allergy and Infectious Diseases Director who served under him, Anthony Fauci. Relatively few members of the public knew of Fauci before the COVID-19 pandemic, but the pandemic and Fauci's co-presence with Trump on the national stage invited Fauci to participate more broadly in framing the US national response to the pandemic (Rutledge, 2020). Fauci's participation in press conferences and news media was, in part, enabled by Trump's political authority and Trump's elevation of Fauci to the position of Chief Medical Advisor to President Trump. Meanwhile, appearing alongside, Fauci invested Trump's early political communication with a sense of scientific authority (Ceccarelli, 2020). Although this relationship soured into competing positions, one with political authority and the other with scientific authority, it reveals the significance of examining alternative actors within national governments as sources of influential messages for a national public or segments of that national public.

Pandemic communication, then, asks political communication scholars to take seriously communication activities taken throughout all levels of national governments to influence actions by members of the public. Pandemics are not the kind of national crisis presidents and prime ministers are used to addressing; the military vocabularies that unitary executives tend to deploy are not appropriate responses because the political communication they enable draws on an improper authority for speaking (Bates, 2020; Panzeri, et al., 2021). Yes, a pandemic is a crisis that can be securitized and call for a war footing. A pandemic is a communication problem of national security. However, a pandemic is also a problem of health, economics, housing, food access, social belonging, and more.

To understand a national response, how that response is communicated, and how that communication is understood should require political communication scholars to access the communication offered by national authorities on these topics, not just the condensation point who is the president or prime minister. Because pandemics are also health issues, evaluating communication from health agencies and their agents is necessary to understand how health is being framed and encouraged by health authorities. However, this makes it clearly both a health issue and a part of the political communication offered by state actors. But it is also political because it is economic. Therefore, engaging with communication from government economics agencies begins to demonstrate the difficult balance of health with topics of economic growth, development, employment, and purchasing as these topics emerge over the course of a pandemic. The pandemic further complicates political communication because the runs on food and other basic household supplies demonstrated the importance of considering agriculture and commerce government agencies because they provide insights for understanding how access to safe and sustainable food and other consumables is preserved and that access is communicated throughout the pandemic. Because pandemics are multi-faceted political problems, the political communication that emerges from the political actors who engage those facets must be studied if we are to improve the state's communication on these topics to the multiple audiences within the nation.

Additional Levels of Political Action

The COVID-19 pandemic has also revealed that pandemic communication requires understanding local political communication in addition to national political communication. Because political systems are made up of nations, but also of states and provinces, and within those states and provinces localities of all types, many political actors in communication systems operate at more local levels. Because pandemic communication occurs at the state and provincial, as well as the local level, political communication scholars may wish to remember United States Speaker of the House Tip O'Neill's maxim that "all politics is local."

States, Provinces, Counties, and Regions

Although there is substantial variation among nations in their responses to COVID-19 (Hale et al., 2020), there is also substantial variation within nations. These differences within nations indicate a significant opportunity to expand the scope of sectors that we consider when we examine political communication. For example, in the United States, Watkins and Clevenger (2021) found that the governors of different states clashed with President Trump's political conclusions and employed different political communication styles when disagreeing with Trump (and each other) over personal protective equipment, the reporting of COVID-19 cases, what counted as essential businesses, and who had authority over the opening and closing of schools, businesses, and other establishments. There were also divisions within states over responses to COVID-19, leading to political clashes, and accompanying competitive political communication, between different parts of the state government. In Florida, for example, political conflict between Governor Ron DeSantis and communication emerging from the Florida Department of Public Health allegedly led to the firing and arrest of Rebekah Jones, a now-former employee of the Department (Blaskey, 2021). In other places, different state leaders complemented one another's political communication and the accompanying policies. In the US state of Ohio, the joint appearances by Governor Mike DeWine and then-Ohio Department of Health Director Amy Acton, and the mutually reinforcing political communication when they spoke separately, created a cohesive and coherent political response to the pandemic (Balduf, 2020).

Similarly, in Canada, Fafard et al. (2020) found several tensions between normative expectations that provincial health authorities be independent actors planning for provincial health and the national government's demand for a consistent and coordinated response across the nation. In particular, the Province of Quebec, which desired culturally and linguistically appropriate materials for its French-speaking population, found itself in tension with the anglophone-dominated national government, a challenge that exacerbated ongoing political tensions between Montreal and Ottawa. The history of federalism in the United States and Canada (among other nations), in which some political actions are undertaken at the state or provincial level, some at the national level, and some by both levels, creates different political sovereignties such that the citizens of different states or provinces may be exposed to different political decisions and their accompanying political communication.

In other nations, histories that prompt skepticism of national governments may make provincial and state efforts at communication essential. In their study of receptiveness to communication about COVID-19 in Nigeria, for instance, Ilesanmi et al. (2021) argued that many Nigerians find the national government's COVID-19 risk communication messages unreliable and that they would prefer messages from state or local leaders. Because there are historical splits between Muslim-majority northern Nigeria and Christian-majority southern Nigeria, neither grouping of states fully trusts the national government's messages and, therefore, state ministers of health may be more influential communicators. As part of an adaptation to this political reality, Nigeria's national response has taken the role of state-level political actors seriously and sought to channel messages through them rather than imposing a nation-wide message (*Risk Communication and Community Engagement Strategy: COVID-19 Prevention and Control in Nigeria*, 2021). These adaptations to political systems provide yet another opportunity to examine different levels at which political communication takes place.

Municipalities

Although governors and premiers have sought to adapt messages to the political realities of their state and provincial responses, the COVID-19 pandemic also encourages us to take seriously the political communication that emerges at the municipal level. In the United States, just as governors found their responses to the pandemic to conflict with President Trump's response, mayors and other municipal leaders also found themselves navigating between the needs of their cities and towns and the demands imposed on them by governors. The robust communicative and practical responses from mayors led Foster (2020) to argue that "the COVID-19 crisis has shown dramatically why local government, where mayors and health officials are on the frontlines of responding to global health threats like pandemics, is increasingly where effective governance happens in America" (n.p.).

In other places, the failure to authorize local leaders to respond to COVID-19 may have been harmful, both politically and to the nation's health. In Ecuador, for example, Torres and López-Cevallos (2021) found that the National Emergency Operations Committee demanded that national response strategies involve local community leaders, as mayors were more informed of local constituents' needs and desires and were prominent figures in the community who could connect people to resources. At the same time, however, anti-corruption measures implemented in the healthcare system have concentrated resource allocation in the national Ministry of Public Health and undermined local control. This tension meant that local political leaders needed to navigate a complex set of demands from above (to impose national mandates) and below (to preserve civil society), created views of the public as unruly and in need of control by the military and law enforcement, and undermined public confidence in national, provincial, and local politicians.

As with the variation that emerges among states and provinces, the differences among cities and between cities and larger components of the political system allow for unique political communication strategies to emerge based on the needs of a municipality, its demographic constituents, and the relationships between municipal leaders, state and provincial leaders, and national leaders. Because ambulance and law enforcement services, hospitals, health departments, vaccine clinics, and other essential components of pandemic response are often managed at the municipal level, understanding the ways that local politicians advocate for their use, seek funding, and negotiate their fit into state and provincial and into national response strategies is a significant topic to explore in pandemic communication. As a counterpart to Kim and Kreps's (2020) claim that local, national, and international governmental agencies should learn from communication theory ways to avoid public communication errors in responding to the pandemic, we argue that an examination of the political communication that emerges at the local, state, provincial, national, and international level can offer insight into successful strategies and inform communication theory that seeks to address future pandemics.

Going Beyond the Global North and Taking New Directions

The final set of assumptions in political communication that pandemic communication requires us to question is the rootedness of political communication in Anglo-American and European political theory and political practice. The examination of political communication is far more common in Global Northern contexts than in Global Southern contexts. For example, the 62-chapter *Oxford Handbook of Political Communication* has no chapters devoted to contexts outside the United States and Europe (Kenski & Jamieson,

2017), while the *Handbook of Political Communication Research* contains one chapter on "Political Communication in Asia" with the remaining 18 chapters from European and North American perspectives (Kaid, 2004). The 41-chapter *SAGE Handbook of Political Communication* contains more representation with chapters devoted to political communication in South Korea, China, Latin America (taken as a whole), India, South Africa, and the television network al-Jazeera (Semetko & Scammell, 2012). The approach taken to the inclusion of these chapters in each handbook, however, is one of comparative political communication; that is, when a chapter is devoted to a context outside of the Global North, the chapter begins by assuming that the Global North is the reference point, and the Global Southern context is the thing being compared to that reference point. In the other more general chapters in these handbooks, the mention of Global Southern contexts is always within a larger pattern established by the Global North.

Indeed, this chapter likely falls into the same set of assumptions. Our outline of what has traditionally "counted" as political communication and our use of concepts from Goodnight (2012) of public, private, and technical spheres reflect an orientation drawn from European and Anglo-American commitments to public dialogue and deliberation as parts of politics. Similarly, our examples of how political communication in campaigns has been impacted by the pandemic draw primarily on examples from the United States. Our identification of presidents and prime ministers as the key communicative agents in traditional political communication draws clearly on Anglo-American and European political structures as reference points, even as it seeks to expand the range of significant communicative agents. Moreover, our argument that additional levels of political action include states and provinces, as well as municipalities, relies on a concept of government that is strongly guided by the European and Anglo-American ideas of the nation-state and of federalism and confederalism.

Pandemic communication may require us to question whether this reference point is always appropriate. Responses in other contexts may question these assumptions. For example, the non-state actor Hezbollah, and its Islamic Health Organization, originally sought to work with the Lebanese state to respond to COVID but has since emerged as a political actor competing with the state in the health sector (Barak, 2020). Whereas Hezbollah's actions were in competition with state actors, actions undertaken by First Nations people in the United States and Canada were undertaken in a vacuum of state action on their territories. Drawing on indigenous principles for community organizing and native epistemologies that inform First Nations politics broadly, First Nations people created collective resilience in the face of limited governmental action from the national governments of the United States and Canada (Romero-Briones et al., 2020). It is likely that other non-state and unrecognized sovereign nations had similar responses elsewhere. Their actions indicate that the assumption that the nation-state and its governmental apparatus are needed in pandemic response and pandemic communication may be questioned.

In a different way, the political coordination in strong regional alliances where regional political interests are communicated ahead of national ones shows that intergovernmental response can make pandemic political communication different than pre-pandemic communication. For example, the strong regionalism in the Pacific Alliance among Chile, Colombia, Mexico, and Peru intends to set aside competitive interests for information and commercial integration to respond to COVID-19 (Alianza del Pacifico, 2021), even as the weak regionalism of the Andean Community among Bolivia, Colombia, Ecuador, and Peru found the competitive political interests among these countries more significant than cooperative goals in responding (Rios Sierra, 2020). As shown by Colombia's and Peru's memberships in both the Pacific Alliance and the Andean Community, national political communication can change as it enters different regional conversations. Examining political communication among regional groupings, such as the African Union, the Gulf Cooperation Council, and other international organizations that emerged to provide political counterweights to US-, European-, or Russian-led influence in the 1970s, may provide alternative ways of understanding political organizing and their influence on pandemic response.

Overall, questioning the relevance of the nation-state as an actor may also require us to delve into other fundamental assumptions of political communication that emerge from Anglo-American and European political theory. We might also ask what kind of voices can be heard when different political assumptions are made, as well as how those voices can express themselves within different social and cultural contexts that are not founded on Anglo-American and European norms. Given the surge in different voices speaking to address the pandemic – as individuals, as organizations, and as collectives of all sorts – we will want to attend to recognizing, hearing, and taking seriously these voices. Although this chapter has recognized some other voices, it does not comprehend the full range of those who speak meaningfully as political actors in a pandemic.

As the pandemic also begins to undermine assumptions about the stability of Anglo-American and European-based economic and health systems and structures, political communication in the pandemic may also cause us to question the structures of government, policy, and democratic participation that have long gone unquestioned in contemporary political communication. Whether these structures are contained within nation-states, integrate nation-states, or operate beyond the nation-state, their stability, and sometimes relevance, is no longer assured. Although this chapter has identified other levels and kinds of structures that may be becoming more important in politics during pandemic communication, there are more to be identified and then questioned or strengthened to allow a better response to global public health threats.

Note

1 The Presidents, Prime Ministers, or National Executives of Bangladesh, Belgium, Bolivia, Brazil, Dominican Republic, Finland, France, Germany, India, Indonesia, New Zealand, Niger, Norway, Russia, South Africa, Scotland, Sint Maarten, United Kingdom, United States, and Taiwan.

References

Alianza del Pacifico. (2021). Plan de trabajo frente al COVI-19. *Alianza del Pacifico.* Retrieved from https://alianzapacifico.net/wp-content/uploads/PLAN_TRA-BAJO_COVID_19.pdf

Balduf, J. (2020). Amy Acton leaves DeWine adviser role for new job. *Dayton Daily News.* Retrieved from https://www.daytondailynews.com/local/amy-acton-leaves-dewine-adviser-role-for-new-job/DY2VUB45TFCM7CHWRIIFEVECCU/

Barak, M. (2020). Hezbollah and the global corona crisis. *ICT Herzliya.* Retrieved from https://www.ict.org.il/images/Hezbollah%20Corona.pdf

Bates, B. R. (2020). The (in)appropriateness of the war metaphor in response to SARS-CoV-2: A rapid analysis of Donald J. Trump's rhetoric. *Frontiers in Communication, 5*(50). https://doi.org/10.3389/fcomm.2020.00050

Blaskey, S. (2021). Records in Rebekah Jones case give peek at Florida COVID-19 response. *Tampa Bay Times.* Retrieved from https://www.tampabay.com/news/health/2021/06/04/florida-whistleblower-rebekah-jones-gives-a-look-behind-the-scenes/

Blumler, J. G., & Kavanagh, D. (1999). The third age of political communication. *Political Communication, 16*, 209–230.

Boulianne, S. (2019). US dominance of research on political communication: A meta-view. *Political Communication, 36*(4), 660–665. https://doi.org/10.1080/10584609.2019.1670899

Burns, A., Goldmacher, S. & Glueck, K. (2020, April 25). A candidate in isolation: Inside Joe Biden's cloistered campaign. *The New York Times.* Retrieved from https://www.nytimes.com/2020/04/25/us/politics/joe-biden-coronavirus-quarantine.html

Ceccarelli, L. (2020). The polysemic facepalm: Fauci as rhetorically savvy scientist citizen. *Philosophy & Rhetoric, 53*(3), 239–245. https://doi.org/10.5325/philrhet.53.3.0239

Chaffee, S. (1975). *Political communication: Issues and strategies for research.* Sage.

Condon, P. (2020, August 17). Biden campaign goes virtual in Minnesota, while Trump campaign continues in person. *Star Tribune.* Retrieved from https://www.startribune.com/biden-campaign-goes-virtual-in-minnesota-while-trump-campaign-continues-in-person/572127642/

Dada, S., Ashworth, H. C., Bewa, M. J., & Dhatt, R. (2021). Words matter: Political and gender analysis of speeches made by heads of government during the COVID-19 pandemic. *BMJ Global Health, 6*(1), e003910. https://doi.org/10.1136/bmjgh-2020-003910

Denton, R.E., Trent, J.S. & Friedenberg, R.V. (2019). *Political campaign communication: Principles and practices* (9th ed.), Rowman & Littlefield.

Fafard, P., Wilson, L. A., Cassola, A., & Hoffman, S. J. (2020). Communication about COVID-19 from Canadian provincial chief medical officers of health: A qualitative study. *CMAJ Open, 8*(3), E560–E567. https://doi.org/10.9778/cmajo.20200110.

Ferguson, A. (2020, May 15). Biden's virtual campaign is a disaster. *The Atlantic*. Retrieved from https://www.theatlantic.com/ideas/archive/2020/05/bidens-virtual-campaign-disaster/611698/

Foster, S. R. (2020). As COVID-19 Proliferates mayors take response lead, sometimes in conflicts with their governors. *The Georgetown Project on State and Local Government Policy and Law (SALPAL)*. Retrieved from https://www.law.georgetown.edu/salpal/as-covid-19-proliferates-mayors-take-response-lead-sometimes-in-conflicts-with-their-governors/

Fujita, M., Matsuoka, S., Kiyohara, H., Kumakura, Y., Takeda, Y., Goishi, N., & Fujita, N. (2020). "Staying at home" to tackle COVID-19 pandemic: Rhetoric or reality? Cross-cutting analysis of nine population groups vulnerable to homelessness in Japan. *Tropical Medicine and Health, 48*(1), 92. https://doi.org/10.1186/s41182-020-00281-0

Gilray, C. (2021). Performative control and rhetoric in Aotearoa New Zealand's response to COVID-19. *Frontiers in Political Science, 3*(86). https://doi.org/10.3389/fpos.2021.662245

Goldberg, J. (2019, September 2). Joe Biden should run a front porch campaign for the digital age. *The Baltimore Sun*. Retrieved from https://www.baltimoresun.com/opinion/op-ed/bs-ed-op-goldberg-biden-campaign-20190902-n3vh2pje4baaz-plqs6u7ax3enq-story.html

Gonzenbach, W. J., & Stevenson, R. L. (1994). Children with AIDS attending public school: An analysis of the spiral of silence. *Political Communication, 11*(1), 3–18. https://doi.org/10.1080/10584609.1994.9963007

Goodnight, G. T. (2012). The personal, technical, and public spheres of argument: A speculative inquiry into the art of public deliberation. *Argumentation and Advocacy, 48*(4), 198–210. https://doi.org/10.1080/00028533.2012.11821771

Hale, T., Angrist, N., Cameron-Blake, E., Hallas, L., Kira, B., Majumdar, S., & Webster, S. (2020). Variation in government responses to COVID-19. *Blavatnik School of Government, University of Oxford*. Retrieved from: https://www.bsg.ox.ac.uk/sites/default/files/2020-09/BSG-WP-2020-032-v7.0.pdf

Harpine, W. (2006). *From the front porch to the front page: McKinley and Bryan in the 1896 presidential campaign*. Texas A&M University Press.

Harris, R. (2020, August 21). How the pandemic reshaped election campaigns—maybe forever. *Wired*. Retrieved from https://www.wired.com/story/pandemic-reshaped-2020-election-campaigns-democrats-republicans/.

Hatmaker, T. (2020, May 15). Biden campaign releases a flurry of digital DIY projects and virtual banners. *TechCrunch*. Retrieved from https//techcrunch.com/202/05/15/biden-campaign-zoom-digital-strategy/.

Heffernan, R. (2006). The Prime Minister and the news media: Political communication as a leadership resource. *Parliamentary Affairs, 59*(4), 582–598.

Ilesanmi, O. S., Akosile, P. O., Afolabi, A. A., & Ukwenya, V. O. (2021). Handling distrust on risk communication in Nigeria: A strategy to atrengthening the COVID-19 outbreak response. *Disaster Medicine and Public Health Preparedness*, 1–6. https://doi.org/10.1017/dmp.2021.245

International Communication Association Political Communication Section & American Political Science Association. (2011, February). *Welcome*. Retrieved from http://politicalcommunication.org/apsa-section/

Jansen, B. (2020, August 10). There is no playbook: How Trump and Biden are trying to run virtual campaigns during coronavirus. *USA Today*. Retrieved from https://www.usatoday.com/story/news/politics/2020/08/10/donald-trump-joe-biden-running-virtual-campaigns-amid-coronavirus/3288147001/

Joe Biden's cloistered campaign. *The New York Times*. Retrieved from https://www.nytimes.com/2020/04/25/us/politics/joe-biden-coronavirus-quarantine.html

Jordan, K. N., Sterling, J., Pennebaker, J. W., & Boyd, R. L. (2019). Examining long-term trends in politics and culture through language of political leaders and cultural institutions. *Proceedings of the National Academy of Sciences, 116*(9), 3476–3481. https://doi.org/10.1073/pnas.1811987116

Kaid, L. L. (Ed.) (2004). *Handbook of political communication research*. Lawrence Erlbaum Associates.

Kenski, K., & Jamieson, K. H. (Eds.). (2017). *The Oxford handbook of political communication*. Oxford University Press.

Khalid, A. & Keith, T. (2020, May 21). Trump and Biden wage an uneven virtual campaign. *NPR*. Retrieved from https://www.npr.org/2020/05/21/859932268/trump-and-biden-wage-an-uneven-virtual-campaign

Kim, D. K. D., & Kreps, G. L. (2020). An analysis of government communication in the United States during the COVID-19 pandemic: Recommendations for effective government health risk communication. *World Medical & Health Policy*. https://doi.org/10.1002/wmh1003.1363

Lange, C. (2020, November 26). Pandemic politics: Targeted influence in the age of COVID-19. *Heinrich Boll Stiftung*. Retrieved from https://www.boell.de/en/2020/11/26/pandemic-politics-targetted-influence-age-covid-19

Laracey, M. C. (2003). *Presidents and the people: The partisan story of going public*. Texas A&M University Press.

Levinson, M. H. (2008). Examining five "over/under- defined" terms used in American political discourse. *ETC: A Review of General Semantics, 65*(2), 134–140.

Lilleker, D. G., Coman, I., Milos, G., & Novelli, E. (Eds.). (2021). *Political communication and COVID-19: Governance and rhetoric in times of crisis*. Routledge.

McGrane, D. (2020, December 28). Campaigning in Canada during a pandemic. *Policy Options*. Retrieved from https://policyoptions.irpp.org/magazines/december-2020/campaigning-in-canada-during-a-pandemic/

Miller, Z. & Jaffe, A. (2020, September 9). Trump and Biden run vastly different pandemic campaigns. *The Associated Press*. Retrieved from https://apnews.com/article/winston-salem-health-north-carolina-joe-biden-campaigns-146dacef-4667f78152897c0d9d164083

Milligan, S. (2020, May 21). Not quite there: Joe Biden's struggling virtual campaign. *U.S. News and World Report*. Retrieved from https://www.usnews.com/news/elections/articles/2020-05-21/joe-biden-struggles-to-campaign-virtually.

National Communication Association Political Communication Division. (2010). *Welcome*. Retrieved from http://politicalcommunication.org/websites/ncapcd/index.html

Panzeri, F., Di Paola, S., & Domaneschi, F. (2021). Does the COVID-19 war metaphor influence reasoning? *PLoS One, 16*(4), e0250651. https://doi.org/10.1371/journal.pone.0250651

Pietrusza, D. (2008). *1920: The year of the six presidents*. Basic Books.

Rios Sierra, J. (2020). El endeble regionalismo de América Latina frente al coronavirus. *Esglobal*. Retrieved from https://www.esglobal.org/el-endeble-regionalismo-de-america-latina-frente-al-coronavirus/

Risk communication and community engagement strategy: COVID-19 prevention and control in Nigeria. (2021). Lagos: Nigeria Centre for Disease Control, Presidential Task Force on COVID-19. Retrieved from https://covid19.ncdc.gov.ng/media/files/UPDATED_RCCE_Strategy_web_version.pdf

Romero-Briones, A.-d., Biscera Dilley, S., & Renick, H. (2020). *COVID-19 in Indian country*. First Nations Development Institute.

Rutledge, P. E. (2020). Trump, COVID-19, and the war on expertise. *The American Review of Public Administration, 50*(6–7), 505–511. https://doi.org/10.1177/0275074020941683.

Sampedro, V. (2011). Introduction: New trends and challenges in political communication. *International Journal of Press/Politics, 16*(4), 431–439. https://doi.org/10.1177/1940161211418291

Sangalang, A. (2015). The need for communication research in regulatory science: Electronic cigarettes as a case study. *International Journal of Communication, 9*(19328036), 3485–3493.

Semetko, H. A., & Price, V. E. (1994). Guest editors' introduction: Setting the scene. *Political Communication, 11*(4), 323–329. https://doi.org/10.1080/10584609.1994.9963043

Semetko, H. A., & Scammell, M. (Eds.). (2012). *The SAGE handbook of political communication*. SAGE.

Sheppard, S. (2007). *The partisan press: A history of media bias in the United States*. McFarland Press.

Soukup, P. A. (2014). Political communication. *Communication Research Trends, 33*(2), 3–43.

Strauss, D. (2020, June 4). Trump hankers for the roar of the crowd while Biden takes campaign virtual. *The Guardian*. Retrieved from https://www.theguardian.com/us-news/2020/jun/04/trump-biden-campaign-virtual-rallies-targetted-influence-age-covid-19

Torres, I., & López-Cevallos, D. (2021). In the name of COVID-19: legitimizing the exclusion of community participation in Ecuador's health policy. *Health Promotion International, 36*(5), 1324–1333. https://doi.org/10.1093/heapro/daaa139

Watkins, D. V., & Clevenger, A. D. (2021). US political leadership and crisis communication during COVID-19. *Cogent Social Sciences, 7*(1), 1901365. https://doi.org/10.1080/23311886.2021.1901365

Zarefksy, D. (2004). Presidential rhetoric and the power of definition. *Presidential Studies Quarterly, 34*, 607–619. https://www.jstor.org/stable/27552615

16

REFLECTING ON THEORY AND RESEARCH IN PANDEMIC COMMUNICATION

Audra Diers-Lawson

The COVID-19 pandemic has been very different from previous pandemics in recent history (e.g., HIV/AIDS, the Zika virus, Ebola, H1N1, or MERS) because of the magnitude and duration of its effects on global health, politics, business, and people's daily lives. Unsurprisingly, the pandemic has inspired unprecedented levels of academic research across all fields. For example, in the first ten months of the pandemic, more than 125,000 COVID-19 scientific articles were published (Fraser et al., 2021). Communication research has explored, for example, attitudes and self-protective behaviors (Papageorge et al., 2021; Rui et al., 2021; Yildirim & Akgül, 2021), fake news and disinformation (Love et al., 2020; Salvi et al., 2021; Sun et al., 2021), prejudice and blame attribution (Croucher et al., 2021; Nguyen et al., 2021), and evaluation and critique of different approaches to communication strategy and pandemic response (Maak et al., 2021; Stolow et al., 2020). By this stage in the book, readers will have seen a diverse collection of perspectives, theories, methods, and arguments about pandemic communication and its implications across the broad field of communication. In putting the book together, we wanted to try to reflect the diversity of approaches to the field of communication while we were also addressing the issue of pandemic communication across our field because we are trying to capture a moment of transition in people's lives and what that means for a multi-disciplinary, multi-perspective field like communication.

With the hundreds of thousands of academic articles related to COVID-19 that are already or soon to be published (Fraser et al., 2021), we have also begun to see the evolution of publication practices with an increasing number of academic journals focusing on rapid review and consistent early online access. Therefore, also emerging with the tsunami of research is an ongoing debate about the implications of the proliferation and quality of 'knowledge'

DOI: 10.4324/9781003214496-16

being produced with the rapid publication of research related to the pandemic (Dinis-Oliveira, 2020; King, 2020; Steinberg, 2020). Part of the challenge of both the volume of research and the evolving socio-cultural and political factors connected to the pandemic is that good theory-building and rigorous research methodology take time to develop, and as we all know, the academic publication machine often moves slowly. The adaptations for academic publications to catch up may have important implications on practice because, as lessons learned from pandemics and crises teach us, getting the message wrong can literally cost lives (Diers-Lawson, 2020). Therefore, this chapter's purpose is to discuss the state of theory and research within the context of pandemic communication across the field of communication. In so doing, I will make arguments about: (1) the importance of internationalization; (2) engaging with existing research in risk, crisis, and/or pandemic communication; and (3) theory building and re-building in the pandemic and crisis context.

Amplifying the Importance of Internationalization in Communication Studies

In this editorial for the *Journal of Applied Communication*, Dutta (2022) argues that as a field of study, the field of communication has been guilty of reifying colonialist mindsets and capitalism through its largely U.S.-based scholarship, which 'severely limits how we come to understand and respond to problems emergent from and rooted in racism' (p. 227). In risk and crisis communication, the problem of U.S.-centric analysis is something we have acknowledged (de Fatima Oliveira, 2013; Diers-Lawson, 2017; Diers-Lawson & Meissner, 2021; Zhao, 2014) and, through a community-wide endeavor, have begun to address this issue. For example, my review of the field's research from 1953 to 2015 found the field was too U.S.-centric and too corporate-focused (Diers-Lawson, 2017, 2020). Yet, scholars studying crisis contexts outside of the U.S. still share that they get reviews from major journals in the field of communication that critique the lack of a U.S.-based sample as a reason for rejection. More than just being a problem of access to the top tier journals in the field of communication, this is a fundamental problem for conceptual development as well. For example, within the pandemic context, the disproportionately U.S.-centric research means that topics like 'fake news', political polarization, and public rejection of public health recommendations are overly addressed while theoretical and applied lessons that can be learned from other parts of the world are not as well-developed (Diers-Lawson et al., 2021).

However, one of the positive aspects to emerge with the global pandemic has been increasing internationalization of research related to the pandemic, notably with publications in the field of risk and crisis communication reflecting a meaningful growth in internationalization. For example, the *Journal of International Crisis and Risk Communication Research* – the field's first and only dedicated journal to the subject – published a special issue on COVID-19 with a diverse group of authors and topics from Africa, Asia, Europe, and North America (Jin et al., 2021). The diverse representation in the issue was not an accident – the editorial team discussed and agreed that it was important that we try to ensure the broadest coverage possible, and we were particularly proud of the issue and its representation of different voices and pandemic communication experiences. While COVID-19 communication research still has a U.S. bias in terms of volume, the breadth of the research has provided vital global information with both single-nation and cross-national comparisons of COVID-19 experiences from Asia (Azadeh et al., 2020; Dai et al., 2020; Jin et al., 2020; Nguyen et al., 2020), to Europe (Betsch et al., 2020; Breakwell et al., 2021; Meier et al., 2020), and to the Americas (Bruine de Bruin et al., 2020; Croucher et al., 2022; Glenn et al., 2020).

The groundwork for internationalization in risk and crisis communication has been years in the making, but with growing conference and editorial support and books like *Culture and Crisis Communication: Transboundary Cases from Nonwestern Perspectives* (George & Kwansah-Aidoo, 2017) and *The Handbook of International Crisis Communication Research* (Schwarz et al., 2016), there is demonstrable evidence that the field of risk and crisis communication sets a good example in our discipline for beginning to address hegemonic perspectives in communication research. Our field is not alone in this respect; rhetoric, intercultural communication, and health communication notably have been working for years to broaden the perspectives and voices heard. Also, as I have argued before (Diers-Lawson, 2017, 2020), I do not believe this is a result of overt discriminatory practices but rather the result of the U.S.'s size and power of its institutional funding. Therefore, building on the example and work we have begun in the field of risk and crisis communication, there are tangible ways to support internationalization on the part of conference organizers, researchers, editors, and reviewers.

Building on the Virtual Experience of the Pandemic to Improve Research Inclusiveness

We can all probably acknowledge there is both value and limitation in full conferences being online. In a post-pandemic context, many of the large international organizations have retained some element of virtual conferencing for those who cannot attend conferences in person. Of course, this opens the accessibility of the conferences to those who could not ordinarily attend. However, this is not sufficient to support diverse voices from diverse places. One of the innovations during the pandemic was smaller and typically free or low-cost events like workshops or single session panel presentations and discussions. For example, as the management team for crisis communication section of the European Communication Research and Education Association (ECREA), we decided that instead of hosting long events daylong or multi-day events, we would put together a six-month series of panels, inviting colleagues to submit panel ideas or individual presentations. These were not onerous nor costly to produce or promote and we had both presenters and audience members from around the world at each of the sessions. In a post-pandemic context, some of these have persisted, but to ensure this kind of open-access research and best practice exchanges continue, there needs to be institutional support (e.g., from organizations like ECREA, the International Communication Association) and realistic infrastructure for these practices to continue.

Researching and Supporting Research in Diverse Contexts

The U.S.-centric and Western/Northern dominance of published research in the field of communication is simply a fact (Diers-Lawson, 2017, 2020; Dutta, 2022; Zhao, 2014). As researchers, but most especially for reviewers and editors, there are opportunities to reduce these biases in the peer-review process. As researchers, we should look for projects that create opportunities for collaboration across borders. Of course, there are increasingly multinational funding opportunities that provide excellent opportunities for internationalization; however, building collaborative multinational projects does not need large grants. For example, this book's co-editor Professor Stephen Croucher put together a more than 20-nation study of COVID-related prejudice by designing a questionnaire and reaching out to people in his personal network from around the world to contribute and collaborate on the project. This study, which is reported – in part – in this book, has provided important insights about the impact of prejudice in pandemics, resulting in several publications and media appearances. Yet, each of the participating collaborators simply needed to translate the questionnaire (if necessary) into their own language and then recruit 200–500 participants from their country. Because of the central coordination, this project was a low-cost way to support researchers around the world on an important challenge that manifests differently in different countries. It provides an accessible model to build research and support international networks of collaborating researchers.

The examples of low-cost workshops or panel presentations and international collaborations are just two examples of ways we can build participation and invite diverse voices in our field. However, if that research is never published then it is not as likely to contribute to the broad body of knowledge in our field. There is a need for reviewers and editors to be more mindful of the assumptions they make about whose voices matter. Good academic research should not be ethnocentric. As a starting point, minimizing ethnocentrism in research means that as researchers, reviewers, and editors we should minimally expect the following: (1) reading beyond traditional sources and theories in the field of communication – we are an interdisciplinary field and our research is published in many different outlets (see

Diers-Lawson, 2017, 2020) to ensure diverse voices developed in the literature reviews (Dutta, 2022); (2) viewing the review process as a developmental process, so that even if we reject a piece of research we provide feedback that is reasonable and useful – we should be mindful not to be the proverbial 'reviewer 2'; (3) avoiding dogmatism about theory, ontology, and methodology; and (4) bluntly, any reviewer or editor who questions the usefulness of the research simply because its sample or context for study is outside the U.S. or from a small country(ies) or different region(s) needs to have a hard look at themselves. Ultimately, it is editors' responsibilities to be good stewards of inclusiveness, but from research questions to reviews, internationalization needs to be better valued and materially supported in the field of communication.

The Importance of Due Diligence in Desk Research on Risk and Crisis Communication

The proliferation of research related to the pandemic can also make it seem like everyone has become risk and/or crisis communication researchers, but that is not the case. As an editor and reviewer in the field of risk and crisis communication, one of the primary reasons I have rejected articles in the last two years is their lack of engagement with the previous literature related to the field of risk and crisis communication on pandemic-related pieces of research submitted. The pandemic is more than a context, like a particular organization that researchers can just describe; it profoundly influences the communication environment (Breakwell & Jaspal, 2020; Rickard et al., 2013; Saliou, 1994; Stephens et al., 2020). Therefore, research – both at the conceptualization and operationalization stages – must reflect knowledge and appreciation of the issue management, risk, and/or crisis research that has been published. From both the conceptual and operational standpoints, this means doing more than citing one or two of the more common crisis-related theories – regardless of whether they apply to the context of study or cramming in one or two crisis-related publications. Due diligence in writing about the pandemic context means putting issue, risk, and crisis-related research and theory alongside the sub-field of interest. This is not a particularly tall order because over the last half century, crisis research has (see Table 16.1):

- Developed its own theories including risk-related theories, message-centered crisis communication theories, and theories about crises and crisis management.
- Applied communication theories from across the field including public relations, communication, persuasion, rhetoric, media, and mediated communication.
- Applied theories from other disciplines like psychology, organizational studies, marketing and advertising, management and leadership, and cultural studies (Diers-Lawson, 2020).

ment, risk communication,6ic,\n   contingency theory, expectancy violation\n   theory, excellence theory, theory\n   of publics, public diplomacy model,\n   narrative |\n| | Persuasion | Elaboration Likelihood Model (ELM),\n   Extended Parallel Process Model\n   (EPPM), inoculation theory,\n   cognitive functional model,\n   credibility, self-presentation\n   theory |\n| | Rhetoric | Burkean rhetoric, deliberative rhetoric,\n   rhetorical arena theory |\n| | Media | Agenda setting, framing, media\n   richness, media dependence, theory\n   of channel complementarity, third-\n   person effect, mass, material, access, and\n   motivation model, uses and gratifications\n   theory |\n| | Technology-Related | Digital convergence theory, information\n   exchange theory, network theory |

Complementary fields of study	Psychology and learning	Conflict management, behavioral resistance, attribution theory, cognitive appraisal, congruence theory, Theory of Planned Behavior (TPB), Social Cognitive Theory (SCT), emotional dimensionality theory, adult learning theory, identity theory, self-discrepancy theory, self-determination theory, social approval theory
	Organizational	Stakeholder, decision-making, institutional, social capital theory, organizational change, ownership theory, organizational learning, general failure type model, organizational perception management theory, groupthink, neoinstitutional
	Marketing and advertising	Brand commitment
	Management and leadership	Human resource development, systems theory, leadership performance, integrated strategic management model, leader member exchange theory, situational leadership theory
	Cultural	Critical theory, hofstede's dimensions of culture, sensemaking, symbolic interaction, gender-related theories, cultural trauma theory, theory of cultural competence, uncertainty avoidance

Adapted from Diers-Lawson (2020).

Thus, it is fair to characterize the extant body of research in risk and crisis communication as one that embraces all ontological perspectives and applies all research methodologies or approaches. While there is yet much conceptual development still needed in risk and crisis communication, for any researcher exploring the pandemic context, it is simply poor academic practice not to engage with the extant body of research in the field.

Theory Building and Re-Building in the Pandemic Context

As Table 16.1 suggests, there is a rich tapestry of theories that have been developed and applied in research related to crisis communication. While at this stage in research on pandemic communication, I suggest good academic practice actively incorporates relevant risk, issues, and crisis communication research, I do not equate the pandemic context with traditional risk and crisis communication. For example, in an analysis of information-seeking and self-protection behavior in Vietnam and the Republic of Korea, my colleagues and I argued that because the COVID pandemic has: (1) been very different from other pandemics because of the magnitude of its effects on global health, politics, business, and daily lives; (2) the centrality of good communication practice to improve health outcomes; and (3) the need to update thinking about crises as 'untimely but predictable *events*' '…analyses of COVID-19 should begin with the assumption that pandemic communication is unlikely traditional health and crisis communication…' (Diers-Lawson et al., 2021, p. 2). We pointed out many of the theories used in the field of communication often have overlapping concepts. For example, efficacy is a stable predictor of attitudes and behaviors related to health crises with theories like the IDEA model (Sellnow et al., 2019), risk information-seeking and processing model (Ahn & Noh, 2020; Gutteling & Vries, 2017), risk perception attitude framework (Denga & Liu, 2017; Grasso & Bell, 2015), extended parallel process model (Zheng et al., 2021), situational public engagement model (Lim et al., 2016), protection motivation theory (Liu & Jiao, 2018), and planned risk information-seeking model (Willoughby & Myrick, 2016) all applying it within their models or theories. Certainly, efficacy was not the only concept with broad recent application across health crises, including pandemics (see Table 16.2).

In a systematic literature review of recent peer-reviewed research related to information-seeking and self-protective behaviors, we found 11 predictive factors with significant overlap between many theories (see Table 16.2). Therefore, considering the uniqueness of the pandemic context (Saliou, 1994), we suggested that to evaluate, create, and adapt existing theory to the global COVID-19 context, adopting a contingency approach to test valid and reliable factors could provide a useful approach to theory building in a pandemic context. Though an unconventional approach to theoretically based analyses, given the importance of including multiple voices and international perspectives that I have already discussed, this approach can also help to mitigate the 'colonial' bias in theorizing in a global context as well without abandoning decades of research that provides a starting point for research questions and hypothesis building in pandemic communication research.

It can also be tempting in the early stages of a new field or new 'problem' to research to focus on descriptive and case-study–based research. Certainly, in the field of crisis communication, there were significantly more studies earlier in the field's development that were atheoretical (Diers-Lawson, 2017, 2020). This also seems to be the case in many of the early publications regarding COVID-19; however, while this pandemic is unique in its scope and impact, there is significant research on pandemics, risk, and crisis in

TABLE 16.2 Overlapping Factors Predicting Information-Seeking and Self-Protective Behavior

Factor	Description	Example Theory(ies)
Demographics	Personal identity factors found to influence information processing like gender, language, age, and political views.	BCT, IDEA
Efficacy	Belief in both the ability to perform an action and/or by performing the action there will be a positive response.	RISP, RPA, EPPM, SPEM, PMT, PRISM
Negative affect	Emotions including anxiety, fear, uncertainty, and/or anger toward the risk issue.	RISP, TPE, Appraisal, SMCC, BCT, PRISM, EPPM
Perceived risk (threat appraisal)	Combination of problem recognition, susceptibility, and severity in judging behaviors or issues as personally risky.	RPA, EPPM, RISP, SPEM, PMT, BCT, IDEA, PRISM
Social support	Exchange of resources through social ties. This includes emotion, esteem, and appraisal support.	RPA, CCT, TPE
Institutional trust	Trust in agencies responsible for making decisions to protect the public and thus managing threat from risks.	RISP, Game, SPEM, BCT, EPPM
Subjective knowledge	What people think or believe that they know related to a risk/threat.	PMT BCT, IDEA, PRISM
Cognitive elaboration	Extent to which people think about a message depends on association with prior knowledge about the crisis and emotional arousal (aka uncertainty discrepancy).	TPE, SPEM, SMCC, CCT, PRISM, EPPM
Source accessibility	Information-seekers can easily access information when they want it.	MRM, SMCC, BCT, CCT
Information insufficiency	Perception that the individual lacks information about a risk issue that they think is important.	RISP, CIP, SMCC, BCT, CCT, IDEA, PRISM
Information equivocality	Degree to which people may reasonably draw multiple conclusions from information presented.	MRM, BCT

Adapted from Diers-Lawson et al. (2021).
Theories or frameworks identified included: belief in conspiracy theory (BCT), IDEA, risk information-seeking and process model (RISP), risk perception attitude framework (RPA), extended parallel process model (EPPM), protection motivation theory (PMT), planned risk information-seeking model (PRISM), third-person effect (TPE), appraisal theory, social-mediated crisis communication model (SMCC), situational public engagement model (SPEM), channel complementarity theory (CCT), game theory, and media richness model (MRM).

addition to the communication subfields (e.g., organizational, intercultural, applied) in which research is being conducted. The implication of this is that, as a field, we should expect better theory-building research objectives. The chapters in this volume provide excellent illustrations of tackling the application, adaptation, and development of theory in the study of pandemic communication across our field. More than simply describing the pandemic, these chapters provide conceptual, critique, and empirical analyses of the pandemic context.

Conclusions about Research for Pandemic Communication

As we were considering our objectives for this book and discussing it with our authors, one of the questions we were considering is whether pandemic communication is a new concept or just another context in the field of communication. Across the chapters in this volume and emerging pandemic research, it seems clear that while pandemic communication affords communication scholars the opportunity to apply existing theories and methodologies, it also requires adaptation of assumptions and theories to design more predictive research. Because it is a societal-level crisis (Wang et al., 2020; Williams, 2021), it is hard to say which of the societal, work, political, economic, cultural, and interpersonal changes will remain and how they will continue to evolve; yet, it is clear the COVID-19 pandemic will have enduring impact on society and certainly on the field of communication.

Does this mean the field will simply change to incorporate the new communication needs? Probably. For example, the global nature of the pandemic has already begun encouraging international collaboration and more attention to underrepresented voices and perspectives. However, as we have witnessed with the technology age, while issues connected to technology changes have permeated research across the field, studying technology and communication has also evolved into a new subfield. Thus, based on the convergence of theory and research we are seeing today – in the early stages of societal-level crisis communication research – we are also beginning to see the need for and emergence of a new field of study in communication that is distinctive from any others. Pandemic communication has more in common with what is often termed 'wicked problems' or those enduring long-term challenges that are necessarily multi-national, difficult to solve, and have far-reaching consequences. In the coming decades, the global community will face many societal-level crises with future pandemics, global inflation/poverty, climate change, mass migration, political conflict, and sustainability. I believe the hundreds of thousands of journal articles and book chapters produced on the COVID-19 pandemic will converge into a new field of study that focuses directly on societal-level crises and tries to help people, organizations, and governments prepare and respond to these wicked problems.

References

Ahn, J., & Noh, G.-Y. (2020). Determinants of environmental risk information seeking: An emphasis on institutional trust and personal control. *Health, Risk & Society, 22*(3), 214–230. https://doi.org/10.1080/13698575.2020.1813261

Azadeh, M., Ramezani, T., & Taheri-Kharameh, Z. (2020). Factors affecting workplace protective behaviours against Covid-19 disease in employees of crowded public offices: Application of protection motivation theory. *Iran Occupational Health,* 17(Covid-19).

Betsch, C., Korn, L., Sprengholz, P., Felgendreff, L., Eitze, S., Schmid, P., & Bohm, R. (2020). Social and behavioral consequences of mask policies during the COVID-19 pandemic. *Proceedings of the National Academy of Sciences, 117*(36), 21851–21853. https://doi.org/10.1073/pnas.2011674117

Breakwell, G. M., Fino, E., & Jaspal, R. (2021). The COVID-19 preventive behaviors index: Development and validation in two samples from the United Kingdom. *Evaluation and the Health Professions, 44*(1), 77–86. https://doi.org/10.1177/0163278720983416

Breakwell, G. M., & Jaspal, R. (2020). Identity change, uncertainty and mistrust in relation to fear and risk of COVID-19. *Journal of Risk Research, 24*(3/4), 1–17. https://doi.org/10.1080/13669877.2020.1864011

Bruine de Bruin, W., Saw, H. W., & Goldman, D. P. (2020). Political polarization in US residents' COVID-19 risk perceptions, policy preferences, and protective behaviors. *Journal of Risk and Uncertainty, 61,* 177–194. https://doi.org/10.1007/s11166-020-09336-3

Croucher, S., Nguyen, T., Ashwell, D., Spencer, A., Permyakova, T., & Gomez, O. (2022). COVID-19 prejudice towards Afro-Brazilians. *Journal of Intercultural Communication Research, 51*(4), 383–399. https://doi.org/10.1080/17475759.2021.1957702

Croucher, S. M., Nguyen, T., Pearson, E., Murray, N., Feekery, A., Spencer, A., Gomez, O., Girardelli, D., & Kelly, S. (2021). A comparative analysis of Covid-19-related prejudice: The United States, Spain, Italy, and New Zealand. *Communication Research Reports, 38*(2), 79–89. https://doi.org/10.1080/08824096.2021.1885371

Dai, B., Fu, D., Meng, G., Liu, B., Li, Q., & Liu, X. (2020). The effects of governmental and individual predictors on COVID-19 protective behaviors in China: A path analysis model. *Public Administrative Review.* https://doi.org/10.1111/puar.13236

de Fatima Oliveira, M. (2013). Multicultural environments and their challenges to crisis communication. *Journal of Business Communication,* 0021943613487070. https://doi.org/10.1177/0021943613487070

Denga, Z., & Liu, S. (2017). Understanding consumer health information-seeking behavior from the perspective of the risk perception attitude framework and social support in mobile social media websites. *International Journal of Medical Informatics, 105,* 98–109. https://doi.org/10.1016/j.ijmedinf.2017.05.014

Diers-Lawson, A. (2017). A state of emergency in crisis communication an intercultural crisis communication research agenda. *Journal of Intercultural Communication Research, 46*(1), 1–54.

Diers-Lawson, A. (2020). *Crisis communication: Managing stakeholder relationships.* Routledge.

Diers-Lawson, A., Johnson, S., Clayton, T., Kimoto, R., Tran, B. X., Nguyen, L. H., & Park, K. (2021). Pandemic communication: Information seeking, evaluation, and self-protective behaviors in Vietnam and the Republic of Korea. *Frontiers in Communication, 6*(731979), 160. https://doi.org/10.3389/fcomm.2021.731979

Diers-Lawson, A., & Meissner, F. (2021). Editor's essay: Moving beyond western corporate perspectives: On the need to increase the diversity of risk and crisis communication research. *Journal of International Crisis and Risk Communication Research*, 4(1), 165–176. https://doi.org/10.30658/jicrcr.4.1.6

Dinis-Oliveira, R. J. (2020). COVID-19 research: Pandemic versus "paperdemic", integrity, values and risks of the "speed science". *Forensic Sciences Research*, 5(2), 174–187. https://doi.org/10.1080/20961790.2020.1767754

Dutta, M. J. (2022). Communication as raced practice. *Journal of Applied Communication Research*, 50(3), 227–228.

Fraser, N., Brierley, L., Dey, G., Polka, J. K., Pálfy, M., Nanni, F., & Coates, J. A. (2021). The evolving role of preprints in the dissemination of COVID-19 research and their impact on the science communication landscape. *PLoS Biology*, 19(4), e3000959. https://doi.org/10.1371/journal.pbio.3000959

George, A. M., & Kwansah-Aidoo, K. (2017). *Culture and crisis communication: Transboundary cases from nonwestern perspectives*. John Wiley & Sons.

Glenn, J., Chaumont, C., & Dintrans, P. V. (2020). Public health leadership in the times of COVID-19: A comparative case study of three countries. *International Journal of Public Leadership*, 17(1), 81–94. https://doi.org/10.1108/IJPL-08-2020-0082

Grasso, K. L., & Bell, R. A. (2015). Understanding health information seeking: A test of the risk perception attitude framework. *Health Communication*, 20(12), 1406–1414. https://doi.org/10.1080/10810730.2015.1018634

Gutteling, J. M., & Vries, P. W. d. (2017). Determinants of seeking and avoiding risk-related information in times of crisis. *Risk Analysis*, 37(1), 27–39. https://doi.org/10.1111/risa.12632

Jin, Y., Choi, S. I., & Diers-Lawson, A. (2021). Special issue editor's essay: Advancing public health crisis and risk theory and practice via innovative and inclusive research on COVID-19 communication. *Journal of International Crisis and Risk Communication Research*, 4(2), 1. https://doi.org/10.30658/jicrcr.4.2.0

Jin, Z., Zhao, K.-b., Xia, Y.-y., Chen, R.-j., Yu, H., Tamutana, T. T., Yuan, Z., Shi, Y.-M., Adamseged, H. Y., Kogay, M., & Park, G. Y. (2020). Relationship between psychological responses and the appraisal of risk communication during the early phase of the COVID-19 pandemic: A two-wave study of community residents in China. *Frontiers in Public Health*, 8. https://doi.org/10.3389/fpubh.2020.550220

King, A. (2020). Fast news or fake news? The advantages and the pitfalls of rapid publication through pre-print servers during a pandemic. *EMBO Reports*, 21(6), e50817. https://doi.org/10.15252/embr.202050817

Lim, J. S., Greenwood, C. A., & Jiang, H. (2016). The situational public engagement model in a municipal watershed protection program: Information seeking, information sharing, and the use of organizational and social media. *Journal of Public Affairs*, 16(3), 231–244. https://doi.org/10.1002/pa.1583

Liu, T., & Jiao, H. (2018). How does information affect fire risk reduction behaviors? Mediating effects of cognitive processes and subjective knowledge. *Natural Hazards*, 90, 1461–1483. https://doi.org/10.1007/s11069-017-3111-0

Love, J. S., Blumenberg, A., & Horowitz, Z. (2020). The parallel pandemic: Medical misinformation and COVID-19. *Society of General Internal Medicine*, 35(8), 2435–2436. https://doi.org/10.1007/s11606-020-05897-w

Meier, K., Glatz, T., Guijt, M. C., Piccininni, M., van der Meulen, M., Atmar, K., Jolink, A. C., Kurth, T., Rohmann, J. L., Zamanipoor Najafabadi, A. H., & Group, C.-S. S. (2020). Public perspectives on protective measures during the COVID-19 pandemic in the Netherlands, Germany and Italy: A survey study. *PLoS One*, *15*(8), e0236917. https://doi.org/10.1371/journal.pone.0236917

Maak, T., Pless, N. M., & Wohlgezogen, F. (2021). The fault lines of leadership: Lessons from the global Covid-19 crisis. *Journal of Change Management*, *21*(1), 66–86. https://doi.org/10.1080/14697017.2021.1861724

Nguyen, N. P. T., Hoang, T. D., Tran, V. T., Vu, C. T., Siewe Fodjo, J. N., Colebunders, R., Dunne, M. P., & Vo, T. V. (2020). Preventive behavior of Vietnamese people in response to the COVID-19 pandemic. *PLoS One*, *15*(9), e0238830. https://doi.org/10.1371/journal.pone.0238830

Nguyen, T., Croucher, S. M., Diers-Lawson, A., & Maydell, E. (2021). Who's to blame for the spread of COVID-19 in New Zealand? Applying attribution theory to understand public stigma. *Communication Research and Practice*, *7*(4), 379–396. https://doi.org/10.1080/22041451.2021.1958635

Papageorge, N. W., Zahn, M. V., Belot, M., van den Broek-Altenburg, E., Choi, S., Jamison, J. C., & Tripodi, E. (2021). Socio-demographic factors associated with self-protecting behavior during the Covid-19 pandemic. *Journal of Population Economics*, *34*, 691–738. https://doi.org/10.1007/s00148-020-00818-x

Rickard, L. N., McComas, K. A., Clarke, C. E., Stedman, R. C., & Decker, D. J. (2013). Exploring risk attenuation and crisis communication after a plague death in Grand Canyon. *Journal of Risk Research*, *16*(2), 145–167. https://doi.org/10.1080/13669877.2012.725673

Rui, J. R., Yang, K., & Chen, J. (2021). Information sources, risk perception, and efficacy appraisal's prediction of engagement in protective behaviors against COVID-19 in China: Repeated cross-sectional survey. *Human Factors*, *8*(1), e23232. https://doi.org/10.2196/23232

Saliou, P. (1994). Crisis communication in the event of a flu pandemic. *European Journal of Epidemiology*, *10*(4), 515–517. https://doi.org/10.1007/BF01719693

Salvi, C., Iannello, P., Cancer, A., McClay, M., Rago, S., Dunsmoor, J. E., & Antonietti, A. (2021). Going viral: How fear, socio-cognitive polarization and problem-solving influence fake news detection and proliferation during COVID-19 pandemic. *Frontiers in Communication*, *5*, 562588. https://doi.org/10.3389/fcomm.2020.562588

Schwarz, A., Seeger, M. W., & Auer, C. (2016). *The handbook of international crisis communication research*. John Wiley & Sons.

Sellnow, D. D., Johansson, B., Sellnow, T. L., & Lane, D. R. (2019). Toward a global understanding of the effects of the IDEA model for designing instructional risk and crisis messages: A food contamination experiment in Sweden. *Journal of Contingencies and Crisis Management*, *27*(2), 102–115. https://doi.org/10.1111/1468-5973.12234

Steinberg, I. (2020). Coronavirus research done too fast is testing publishing safeguards, bad science is getting through. *The Conversation*, *9*, 2020.

Stephens, K. K., Jahn, J. L., Fox, S., Charoensap-Kelly, P., Mitra, R., Sutton, J., Waters, E. D., Xie, B., & Meisenbach, R. J. (2020). Collective sensemaking around COVID-19: Experiences, concerns, and agendas for our rapidly changing organizational lives. *Management Communication Quarterly*, *34*(3), 426–457. https://doi.org/10.1177/0893318920934890

Stolow, J. A., Moses, L. M., Lederer, A. M., & Carter, R. (2020). How fear appeal approaches in Covid-19 health communication may be harming the global community. *Health Education and Behaviour*, *47*(4), 531–535. https://doi.org/10.1177/1090198120935073

Sun, Y., Oktavianus, J., Wang, S., & Lu, F. (2021). The role of influence of presumed influence and anticipated guilt in evoking social correction of COVID-19 misinformation. *Health Communication.* https://doi.org/10.1080/10410236.2021.1888452

Wang, Y., Xu, R., Schwartz, M., Ghosh, D., & Chen, X. (2020). COVID-19 and retail grocery management: Insights from a broad-based consumer survey. *IEEE Engineering Management Review, 48*(3), 202–211. https://doi.org/10.1109/EMR.2020.3011054

Williams, C. (2021). The future of work. *The Economist.* Retrieved 29 June, 2022, from https://www.economist.com/special-report/2021-04-10?utm_source=google&utm_medium=cpc&utm_campaign=a_21futurework&utm_content=work&gclid=CjwKCAiAhreNBhAYEiwAFGGKPGsvl6UrTQWn8nNDEuSIm8UiJOVZ73UjcHBOEbja3ovjkEesvA0SsxoCGb4QAvD_BwE&gclsrc=aw.ds

Willoughby, J. F., & Myrick, J. G. (2016). Does context matter? Examining PRISM as a guiding framework for context-specific health risk information seeking among young adults. *Journal of Health Communication, 21*(6), 696–704. https://doi.org/10.1080/10810730.2016.1153764

Yildirim, M. G., E., & Akgül, Ö. (2021). The impacts of vulnerability perceived risk and fear on preventive behaviours against COVID 19. *Psychology Health and Medicine, 26*(1), 35–43. https://doi.org/10.1080/13548506.ci2020.1776891

Zhao, Y. (2014). Communication, crisis, & global power shifts: An introduction. *International Journal of Communication, 8*, 26.

Zheng, D., Luo, Q., & Ritchie, B. W. (2021). Afraid to travel after COVID-19? Self-protection, coping and resilience against pandemic 'travel fear'. *Tourism Management, 83*, 104261. https://doi.org/10.1016/j.tourman.2020.104261

INDEX

Note: **Bold** page numbers refer to tables; *italic* page numbers refer to figures.

Printed in the United States
by Baker & Taylor Publisher Services